2/95

An Introduction to
Computer
Simulation
Methods
Applications to Physical Systems

PART 2

HARVEY GOULD

Department of Physics, Clark University

JAN TOBOCHNIK

Department of Physics, Kalamazoo College

An Introduction to
Computer Simulation Methods
Applications to Physical Systems
PART 2

Addison-Wesley Publishing Company

Reading, Massachusetts•Menlo Park, California•New York
Don Mills, Ontario•Wokingham, England•Amsterdam•Bonn•Sydney
Singapore•Tokyo•Madrid•San Juan

This book is in the Addison-Wesley Series in Physics

Library of Congress Cataloging-in-Publication Data

Gould, Harvey, 1938-
    An introduction to computer simulation methods.

    Includes bibliographies and indexes.
    1. Physics—Mathematical models. 2. Physics—Data
processing. 3. Stochastic processes—Mathematical
models. 4. Stochastic processes—Data processing.
5. BASIC (Computer program language) I. Tobochnik,
Jan, 1953-   . II. Title.
QC21.2.G67   1987   530'.072'4   86–28825
ISBN 1-201-16503-1 (v. 1)
ISBN 1-201-16504-X (v. 2)

Reprinted with corrections, June 1988.

7 8 9 10-CRS-98979695

To the memory of
Sheng-keng Ma

ACKNOWLEDGMENTS

Many colleagues and students have generously commented on preliminary drafts of chapters of the manuscript and have given general encouragement and advice. We particularly wish to thank Harold Abelson, Daniel Ben-Avraham, John Davies, Hugh DeWitt, Lisa Dundon, Fereydoon Family, Jim Given, Jim Gunton, Marilyn Jimenez, Gabor Kalman, Tom Keyes, Robert Kilmoyer, Bill Klein, Roger Kohin, Christopher Landee, François Leyvraz, Jon Machta, Gene Mazenko, Bill Michalson, Robert Pelcovits, Joseph Priest, Stan Rajnak, Sidney Redner, Peter Reynolds, Qun Ru, David Stork, Oriol Valls, Gerard Vichniac, George Weiss, Pieter Visscher, and Ju-xing Yang. Needless to say, all errors, omissions and unclear passages are our responsibility.

The course on which this book is based could not have been developed without an initial donation of personal computers from IBM to Clark University and a small grant for course development from the National Science Foundation. One of us also wishes to thank the Mellon Committee of Clark University for support of curriculum development and the Digital Equipment Corporation for support of a related project involving the incorporation of computers into the undergraduate curriculum. We would also like to acknowledge the hospitality of the Department of Physics at Boston University where parts of the book were written.

Special thanks go to Stacey Bressler, Sherry Howlett, and Greg Smedsrud of the Apple Computer Corporation for their interest in our project. It would be difficult to imagine writing this book without the use of a Macintosh computer and an Apple LaserWriter, both donated to us by the Apple Computer Corporation. Many thanks are due to Bruce Spatz, former science editor at Addison-Wesley, for his support, interest, and patience, Sharon Van Gundy for finding some of our grammatical errors and to Mona Zeftel for producing the manuscript in camera-ready form. The text was produced using TEXtures and MacWrite; the figures were drawn by the authors using MacPaint, MacDraw, and Cricket Graph.

We are grateful to our wives, Patti Gould and Andrea Moll Tobochnik, and to the Gould children, Joshua, Emily and Evan, for their encouragement and understanding during the course of this work.

CONTENTS

PART II Simulations with Random Processes

PREFACE

Computer simulation is now an integral part of contemporary basic and applied science and is approaching a role equal in importance to the traditional experimental and theoretical approaches. Hence, the ability "to compute" is part of the essential repertoire of research scientists and educators.

The philosophy of this book is expressed well by the Chinese proverb (source unknown to us):

"I hear and I forget. I see and I remember. I do and I understand."

We ask not how can the computer be used to teach physics, but how can students be trained to teach the computer. Our primary goal is to create an environment in which the reader teaches the computer to simulate physical systems. Our experience is that an active involvement with computer simulations leads to a greater intuitive understanding of physical concepts. Other goals of the book are to introduce molecular dynamics and Monte Carlo methods, to integrate simple but realistic research-type problems into the undergraduate curriculum, and to teach by example structured programming techniques.

Much of the material in this text has been used in a one semester course entitled "Computer Simulation Laboratory" offered at Clark University. Prerequisites for the course are one semester each of physics and calculus. A background in computer programming is not necessary. The interests of the undergraduate and graduate students in the course have included physics, chemistry, biology, mathematics, computer science, geography and electrical engineering. The physics and programming background of these students has ranged from minimal to extensive. We have found that many computer simulations are accessible to those with a limited background in physics and that students with a stronger background can gain additional insight into material that they have already studied. The course is organized in the same way as other laboratory courses at Clark with two weekly lectures in which the subject matter is presented and student progress is reviewed. Programming methods are introduced in the context of a regularly scheduled laboratory. The course is project oriented and allows students the freedom to work at their own pace and to pursue problems consistent with their own interests and backgrounds.

We believe that computer simulation has become sufficiently important for courses of this kind to be taught at other institutions. However, other uses of this book might work equally well. For example, this book could be used as a supplement to an introductory physics course for honors students and in intermediate level courses on classical mechanics, waves, electricity and magnetism, statistical and thermal physics, quantum mechanics, and physical chemistry. The text can also form the basis of a numerical methods course. Although the book begins with basic concepts in physics and calculus, we believe that in general the most successful use of the book will be at the intermediate level.

The programming language used in the body of the text is True BASIC. Translations of several of the programs into Pascal and FORTRAN 77 are listed in the appendices to each part of the book. True BASIC is our language of choice because it is easy to learn and use, has "true" subroutines, excellent graphics capabilities, and is identical on the IBM PC and compatible computers and the Apple Macintosh computer. Readers familiar with "street" BASIC should have few problems adapting the programs in the text as long as they clearly distinguish local and global variables. In our view, the similarities of BASIC, FORTRAN and Pascal are much greater than their differences.

We believe you can learn programming the same way we did—in the context of a discipline. Although the book is as independent as possible of any particular brand of computer, we strongly recommend that readers with little programming experience should write their programs on a personal computer. Personal computers are easier to use than mainframe computers and also offer readily available graphics capabilities. The problems in the text should be done with a programming manual and a physics text as handy references.

Each chapter contains a brief discussion of the important physical concepts, followed by program listings, problems, and relevant questions. The discussion, programs and problems are interrelated and the discussions will be more readily understood after the problems are completed. We regard the program listings as text for the reader rather than source code for the computer. Our programs are designed to be simple and easy to read, rather than elegant or efficient. To do most of the problems, the reader must understand the logic of the programs and hence the logic of the underlying physical system. Most of the problems require at least some modification of the programs. We believe that typing in the programs line-by-line will help you learn programming more easily. Most of the programs are short and you are encouraged to change the programs. The problems are organized so that the earlier ones in a chapter provide the basis for the later problems in the same chapter and in following chapters. Problems denoted by an asterisk are either more advanced or require significantly more time than the average problem and are not a prerequisite for work in succeeding chapters. The recommended readings at the end of each chapter have been selected for their pedagogical value rather than for completeness or for historical accuracy. We apologize to our colleagues whose work has been inadvertently omitted and we would appreciate suggestions for new and additional references.

We emphasize classical physics in Part I and statistical physics in Part II. These areas reflect our own research interests but also are areas in which the methods of computer simulation can be introduced most easily. We also discuss waves, optical phenomena, electricity and magnetism, and quantum mechanics. Each part of the book contains enough material for a semester course on computer simulation. Part I of the text emphasizes the simulation of deterministic systems. Chapter 1 discusses the uses of the computer in physics and the nature of several popular computer languages. Chapter 2 introduces the Euler method for the numerical integration of first order differential equations. Since many readers are familiar with the Euler method, the main purpose of the chapter is to introduce the core syntax of True BASIC. Although this introduction might cover too much material for those without programming experience, remarkably little additional syntax is used in the remainder of the text. Chapters 3–5 use a modified form of the Euler method to simulate falling objects, planetary motion, and oscillatory motion. Chapter 5 also includes a section on electrical circuits and an appendix on other numerical methods for the solution of Newton's equation of motion. Chapter 6 introduces the method of molecular dynamics. Unless the reader has access to large scale computing (or the next generation of microcomputers), only a qualitative picture of thermal phenomena can be obtained from the simulations. However this method is important in physics and chemical physics and the ideas underlying it are straightforward extensions of the previous chapters. Chapter 7 introduces non-linear dynamical systems and the use of the computer to "discover" new knowledge. Chapters 8 and 9 mainly contain traditional material on oscillations and waves, and electrostatics and magnetostatics. Much of the material in these two chapters is oriented toward visual demonstrations.

Each chapter in Part II of the text applies a random sampling technique, known generally as "Monte Carlo" methods, to problems in statistical physics and quantum mechanics. Chapter 10 introduces Monte Carlo methods in the context of numerical integration. Although this chapter does not directly discuss physical phenomena, it allows us to survey the various methods in a well known context. Chapter 11 is devoted to random walks and their application to physical phenomena. Chapters 12 and 13 treat current research areas which are becoming important in many fields of science. In these chapters we discuss percolation, simple ideas of phase transitions and the renormalization group, fractals, local growth laws, and cellular automata. Many of the applications are not difficult to formulate but yield complex behavior which is visually interesting. Chapter 14 discusses an example of the approach to equilibrium and methods for computing the entropy. Chapter 15 uses a relatively new method to simulate the microcanonical ensemble and to "discover" the canonical Boltzmann distribution. Chapter 16 introduces Monte Carlo methods for simulating thermal systems. In Chapter 17 we discuss Monte Carlo and more traditional numerical methods for treating quantum systems. Chapter 18 briefly discusses how the same methods can solve many apparently unrelated problems.

The availability of personal computers and the demands from industry for meaningful computer literacy is putting pressure on all disciplines to incorporate computer related material into the basic curriculum. Thus far, most physics departments have used computers as a tool for data analysis and for demonstrations. Some physics departments now offer courses in computational physics and in measurement and control processes. However, the impact on the curriculum as measured by greater student understanding, increased numbers of physics students, or changes in textual material has been negligible. We realize that the nontrivial use of computers in physics education will take many years to accomplish. We hope that this book makes a contribution to that end, and we welcome your comments, suggestions and encouragement.

We have taken care to check our programs for errors and typos. It is our experience however that few programs remain error free forever, and we make no guarantee that the programs in this text are totally free of error. Instructors who adopt this book for a course may request a program disk (IBM PC or Macintosh format) at no charge from Addison-Wesley.

NUMERICAL INTEGRATION

10

Simple classical and Monte Carlo methods are illustrated in the context of the numerical evaluation of definite integrals.

10.1 SIMPLE NUMERICAL INTEGRATION METHODS IN ONE DIMENSION

The main purpose of this chapter is to introduce Monte Carlo methods in the context of the numerical evaluation of definite integrals. However, in order to place the Monte Carlo method of integration in perspective, it is useful to first discuss the common "classical" methods of *numerical integration*. We will see that these methods, although usually preferable in low dimensions, are not practical for multi-dimensional integrals and that Monte Carlo methods are most suitable for the evaluation of the latter.

Consider a one-dimensional definite integral of the form

$$F = \int_a^b dx\, f(x) \quad . \tag{10.1}$$

For certain choices of the integrand $f(x)$, the integration in (10.1) can be done analytically, found in reference books, or evaluated as an asymptotic series. However there are many common functions whose integrals are intractable and which must be evaluated numerically.

The classical methods of numerical integration are based on the geometrical interpretation of the integral (10.1) as the area under the curve of the function $f(x)$ from $x = a$ to $x = b$ (see Fig. 10.1.)

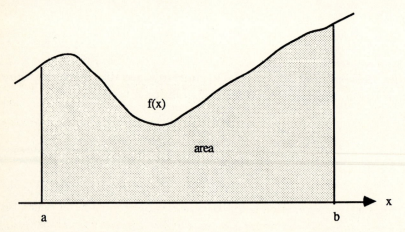

Fig. 10.1 The integral F equals the area under the curve $f(x)$.

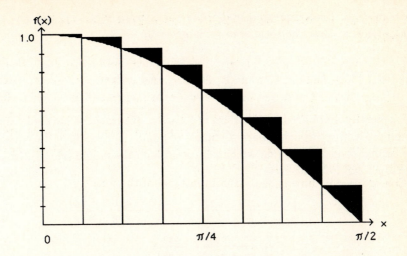

Fig. 10.2 The rectangular approximation for $f(x) = \cos x$ for $0 \le x \le \pi/2$. The error in the rectangular approximation is shaded. The numerical value of the estimate with $n = 8$ is given in Table 10.1.

The x-axis is divided into n equal intervals of width Δx, where Δx is given by

$$\Delta x = \frac{b-a}{n} \tag{10.2a}$$

and

$$x_n = x_0 + n\Delta x \quad . \tag{10.2b}$$

In the above $x_0 = a$ and $x_n = b$.

The simplest estimate of the area under the curve $f(x)$ is the sum of rectangles shown in Fig. 10.2. In the usual *rectangular* approximation, $f(x)$ is evaluated at the *beginning* of the interval and the estimate F_n of the integral is given by

$$F_n = \sum_{i=0}^{n-1} f(x_i)\Delta x \quad . \tag{10.3}$$

Another approximation is the *trapezoidal* approximation for which the integral is estimated by computing the area under a trapezoid with one side equal to $f(x)$ at the beginning of the interval and the other side equal to $f(x)$ at the end of the interval. This approximation is equivalent to replacing the function by a straight line connecting the values of $f(x)$ at the beginning and the end of each interval. Since the area under the curve from x_i to x_{i+1} is given by $\frac{1}{2}[f(x_{i+1}) + f(x_i)]\Delta x$, the total area F_n is given by

$$F_n = [\frac{1}{2}f(x_0) + \sum_{i=1}^{n-1} f(x_i) + \frac{1}{2}f(x_n)]\Delta x \quad . \tag{10.4}$$

A generally more accurate method is to use a quadratic or parabolic interpolation procedure through adjacent triplets of points. For example the equation of the second-order polynomial which passes through the points (x_0, y_0), (x_1, y_1) and (x_2, y_2) can be written as

$$y(x) = y_0 \frac{(x - x_1)(x - x_2)}{(x_0 - x_1)(x_0 - x_2)} + y_1 \frac{(x - x_0)(x - x_2)}{(x_1 - x_0)(x_1 - x_2)}$$
$$+ y_2 \frac{(x - x_0)(x - x_1)}{(x_2 - x_0)(x_2 - x_1)} \quad . \tag{10.5}$$

What is the value of $y(x)$ for $x = x_1$? The area under the parabola $y(x)$ between x_0 and x_2 can be found by simple integration and is given by

$$F_0 = \frac{1}{3}(y_0 + 4y_1 + y_2)\Delta x \quad . \tag{10.6}$$

where $\Delta x = x_1 - x_0 = x_2 - x_1$. The total area under all the parabolic segments yields *Simpson's rule* estimate for the total area:

$$F_n = \frac{1}{3}[f(x_0) + 4f(x_1) + 2f(x_2) + 4f(x_3) + \ldots$$
$$+ 2f(x_{n-2}) + 4f(x_{n-1}) + f(x_n)]\Delta x \quad . \tag{10.7}$$

Note that Simpson's rule requires that n be even.

10.2 NUMERICAL EXAMPLE

In practice Simpson's rule is adequate for functions $f(x)$ which are reasonably well-behaved, i.e. which can be adequately represented by a polynomial. If $f(x)$ is such a "smooth" function, we can evaluate the area for a given number of intervals n and then double the number of intervals and evaluate the area again. If the two evaluations are sufficiently close, we stop. Otherwise we can double n again until we achieve the desired accuracy. Of course this strategy will fail if $f(x)$ is not well behaved.

Can we know in advance whether the trapezoidal or Simpson's rule will be adequate? One way is to assume that the $f(x)$ can be adequately represented by a polynomial; in this case the error can be estimated (see Appendix 10A). However we emphasize that the magnitude of the error depends strongly on the nature of $f(x)$ and its behavior at the limits of integration and consequently no numerical method can be applied with universal success.

An example of a program which implements the rectangular approximation for the integral of $f(x)$ is given below.

```
PROGRAM integ
! compute integral of f(x) from x = a to x = b
CALL initial(a,b,h,n)
CALL rectangle(a,b,h,n,area)
CALL output(area)
END

SUB initial(a,b,h,n)
    LET a = 0                        ! lower limit
    LET b = 0.5*pi                   ! upper limit
    INPUT prompt "number of intervals = ": n
    LET h = (b - a)/n                ! mesh size
END SUB

SUB rectangle(a,b,h,n,area)
    DECLARE DEF f
    LET x = a
    FOR i = 0 to n - 1
       LET sum = sum + f(x)
       LET x = x + h
    NEXT i
    LET area = sum*h
END SUB

SUB output(area)
    PRINT using "####.#######": area
END SUB

DEF f(x) = cos(x)
```

An implementation of Simpson's rule which demonstrates its relation to the trapezoidal approximation is given in the following subroutine which replaces **SUB rectangle** in **Program integ**.

```
SUB Simpson(a,b,h,n,area)
   ! Simpson's approximation
   DECLARE DEF f
   LET sumall = f(a) + f(b)
   LET sumall = 0.5*sumall              ! contribution from end-points
   LET sumeven = sumall                 ! contribution from even terms only
   LET x = a
   FOR i = 1 to n - 1
      LET x = x + h
      LET integrand = f(x)
      LET sumall = sumall + integrand    ! even and odd terms
      LET parity = mod(i,2)              ! 0 even number, 1 odd number
      IF parity = 0 then LET sumeven = sumeven + integrand
   NEXT i
   LET sum = 4*sumall - 2*sumeven
   LET area = h*sum/3                    ! numerical estimate
END SUB
```

In lieu of a derivation of the error estimates associated with the various classical formulae discussed in Sec. 10.1, we consider the accuracy of the rectangular approximation for the integral of $f(x) = \cos x$ from $x = 0$ to $x = \pi/2$. In Table 10.1 the numerical results of **Program integ** are given for increasing values of n. Inspection of the n-dependence of the discrepancy betweeen the numerical estimate F_n and the exact result of unity indicates that the error decreases as n^{-1}. This observed n-dependence of the error is consistent with the general result obtained in Appendix 10A.

PROBLEM 10.1 The rectangular approximation

a. Modify **Program integ** so that the area under the curve $y = f(x)$ and the area of the rectangles can be visualized (see Fig. 10.2.)

b. Use the rectangular approximation to determine numerical estimates for the definite integrals of $f(x) = 2x + 3x^2 + 4x^3$ and $f(x) = e^{-x}$ for $0 \le x \le 1$. What is the approximate n-dependence of the error in each case?

TABLE 10.1 Rectangular approximation estimates of the integral of $\cos x$ from $x = 0$ to $x = \pi/2$ as a function of n, the number of intervals. The error Δ_n is the difference between the rectangular approximation and the exact result of unity. Inspection of the n-dependence of Δ_n indicates that Δ_n decreases approximately as n^{-1}.

n	F_n	Δ_n
2	1.34076	0.34076
4	1.18346	0.18346
8	1.09496	0.09496
16	1.04828	0.04828
32	1.02434	0.02434
64	1.01222	0.01222
128	1.00612	0.00612
256	1.00306	0.00306
512	1.00153	0.00153
1024	1.00077	0.00077

PROBLEM 10.2 The mid-point approximation

a. One common modification of the rectangular approximation is to evaluate $f(x)$ at the *mid-point* of each interval. Make the necessary modifications of **Program integ** and estimate the integral of $\cos x$. How does the magnitude of the error compare with the results shown in Table 10.1? What is the approximate dependence of the error on n?

b. Use the mid-point approximation to estimate the definite integrals of $f(x) = 2x+3x^2+4x^3$ and $f(x) = e^{-x}$ for $0 \le x \le 1$. What is the approximate n-dependence of the error in each case?

PROBLEM 10.3 The trapezoidal approximation and Simpson's rule

a. How can **SUB Simpson** be modified to obtain simultaneously the trapezoidal approximation and Simpson's rule estimate for the integral of $f(x)$?

b. Use both approximations to estimate the integrals of $f(x) = 2x + 3x^2 + 4x^3$ and $f(x) = e^{-x}$ for $0 \le x \le 1$. What is the approximate n-dependence of the error in each case? Which approximation yields the best results for the same computation time?

c. Use Simpson's rule to estimate the integral of $f(x) = (2\pi)^{-1/2}e^{-x^2}$ for $-1 \le x \le 1$, $-2 \le x \le 2$ and $-3 \le x \le 3$.

d. Use both approximations to estimate the definite integral of $f(x) = (1 + x^2)^{-1}$ for $0 \leq x \leq 1$ and $0 \leq x \leq 2$. Which approximation yields the best results? Remember that a higher order method does not always imply higher accuracy.

e. We have already described a strategy for estimating one-dimensional definite integrals, i.e. choose one of the classical integration formulae and compute F_n and F_{2n} for a reasonable choice of n. If the difference $|F_{2n} - F_n|$ is too large, then double n again until the desired accuracy is reached. Does the sequence F_n, F_{2n}, ... converge to the true integral F and if so, is there a way of extrapolating to the limit? Let us explore this idea for the trapezoidal rule. Since we have found that the error in this rule decreases as approximately n^{-2}, we can write $F = F_n + Cn^{-2}$. Plot the estimate F_n as a function of n^{-2} and obtain the extrapolated result F. What assumptions are necessary for this extrapolation procedure to be successful? Apply this procedure to the integrals considered in the above problems and compare its results to those of the trapezoidal and Simpson's rule alone. A more sophisticated application of this idea is *Romberg* integration (cf Press et al).

10.3 NUMERICAL INTEGRATION OF MULTI-DIMENSIONAL INTEGRALS

Many problems in physics involve averaging over many variables. For example, suppose we know the position and velocity dependence of the total energy of ten interacting particles. Since in three dimensions each particle has three velocity components and three components of position, the total energy is a function of 60 variables. Hence a calculation of the average energy per particle involves computing an $N = 60$ dimensional integral. If we divide each coordinate into p intervals, there will be p^{60} points to sum in this example. Clearly we cannot apply the usual numerical techniques for large N; however for N in the range 2–5, the standard methods are still useful.

An additional complication associated with N-dimensional integrals is that the $(N - 1)$-limits of integration can be difficult to determine. In contrast the boundary of a one-dimensional integral consists of two numbers, the lower and upper limits.

A straightforward method for evaluating multi-dimensional integrals is to reduce the integrals to a product of one-dimensional integrals. This method will be effective if the boundary is simple and the function to be integrated is well behaved. We illustrate the method for a two-dimensional integral of the form

$$F = \int_{x_1}^{x_2} \int_{y_1(x)}^{y_2(x)} dx \, dy f(x, y) \quad . \tag{10.8}$$

The region of integration is determined by the lower and upper limits of y at a given value of x, denoted by $y_1(x)$ and $y_2(x)$ respectively, and by the lower and upper limits of x, denoted by x_1 and x_2. We define the function $g(x)$ as the inner y-integral:

$$g(x) = \int_{y_1(x)}^{y_2(x)} dy f(x, y) \tag{10.9}$$

and write

$$F = \int_{x_1}^{x_2} dx \, g(x) \quad . \tag{10.10}$$

A program for two-dimensional integration has the following structure. Note that, for simplicity, the rectangular approximation has been used.

```
PROGRAM integ2                    ! compute two-dimensional integral of f(x,y)
CALL initial(x1,x2,h,n)
CALL integx(x1,x2,h,n,area)
CALL output(area)
END

SUB initial(x1,x2,h,n)
    LET x1 =-1                    ! lower x-limit
    LET x2 = 1                    ! upper x-limit
    INPUT prompt "number of intervals = ": n
    LET h = (x2 - x1)/n
END SUB

SUB integx(x1,x2,h,n,area)
    LET x = x1
    FOR i = 0 to n - 1
        CALL integy(x,n,g)
        LET sum = sum + g
        LET x = x + h
    NEXT i
    LET area = sum*h
END SUB
```

```
SUB integy(x,n,g)
   DECLARE DEF y1
   DECLARE DEF y2
   DECLARE DEF f
   LET h = (y2(x) - y1(x))/n
   LET y = y1(x)
   LET g = 0
   FOR i = 0 to n - 1
      LET g = g + f(x,y)
      LET y = y + h
   NEXT i
   LET g = g*h                        ! estimate of y-integration for given x
END SUB

SUB output(area)
   PRINT using "####.#######": area
END SUB

DEF y1(x) = -sqr(1 - x*x)

DEF y2(x) = sqr(1 - x*x)

DEF f(x,y) = x*x + 6*x*y + y*y
```

PROBLEM 10.4 Two-dimensional numerical integration

a. Integrate the function $f(x, y) = x^2 + 6xy + y^2$ over the region defined by the condition $x^2 + y^2 \leq 1$. Use the rectangular approximation as in **Program integ2** and choose $n = 2^p$ intervals for each integration. Use values of p in the range $p = 2$–7.

b. Modify **Program integ2** so that each integration is done using Simpson's rule and repeat the evaluation done in part (a).

c. Estimate the n-dependence of the error in parts (a) and (b) by considering various values of p.

A discussion of the n-dependence of the error associated with the numerical approximation of a d-dimensional integral is given in Appendix 10A. It is shown that if an approximation yields an error which decreases as n^{-a} for $d = 1$, then the error decreases as $n^{-a/d}$ in d dimensions.

10.4 SIMPLE MONTE CARLO EVALUATION OF INTEGRALS

How can we use a pile of stones to measure the area of a pond? Suppose the pond is in the middle of a field of known area A. Throw the stones at random such that they land at random within the boundary of the field and count the splashes when a stone lands in a pond. The area of the pond is approximately the area of the field times the fraction of stones which make a splash. This simple procedure is an example of a *Monte Carlo* method.

More explicitly, imagine a rectangle of height H and width $(b - a)$ such that $f(x)$ is within its boundaries (see Fig. 10.3). Compute n pairs of random numbers x_i and y_i such that $a \leq x_i \leq b$ and $0 \leq y_i \leq H$. The fraction of points x_i, y_i which satisfy the condition $y_i \leq f(x_i)$ is an estimate of the ratio of the integral of $f(x)$ to the area of the rectangle. Hence the estimate F_n in the "hit or miss" method is given by

$$F_n = A \frac{n_s}{n} \tag{10.11}$$

where n_s is the number of "splashes" or points below the curve, n is the total of points, and A is the area of the rectangle. Note that n in (10.11) should not to be confused with the number of intervals used in the numerical methods discussed earlier.

Another Monte Carlo procedure is based on a theorem of calculus which states that the integral (10.1) is determined by the average value of the integrand $f(x)$ in the range $a \leq x \leq b$. In order to determine this average, we choose the x_i

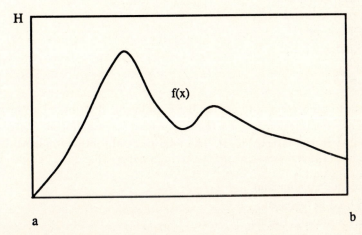

Fig. 10.3 The function $f(x)$ is in the domain determined by the rectangle of height H and width $(b - a)$.

at random instead of at regular intervals and *sample* the value of $f(x)$. For the one-dimensional integral (10.1), the estimate F_n of the integral in the "sample mean" method is given by

$$F_n = (b-a) <f> = (b-a)\frac{1}{n}\sum_{i=1}^{n} f(x_i) \qquad (10.12)$$

where the x_i are random numbers distributed uniformly in the interval $a \le x_i \le b$, and n is the number of *trials*. Note that the form of (10.3) and (10.12) are identical except that the n points are chosen with equal spacing in (10.3), and with random spacing in (10.12). We will find that for low dimensional integrals (10.3) is more accurate, but for higher dimensional integrals (10.12) does better.

It might seem strange that we can use a deterministic computer to generate sequences of "random" numbers. For the present we will be content to use the "pseudorandom" sequences supplied with various languages. The following program illustrates the use of the **rnd** and **randomize** functions in True BASIC to generate random numbers uniformly distributed in the interval $[0, 1]$. A discussion of the nature of these functions is given in Chapter 11.

```
PROGRAM random
RANDOMIZE                          ! generate different sequence each time
LET nrandom = 10                   ! number of random numbers
CALL random1(nrandom)
END

SUB random1(nrandom)
   FOR i = 1 to nrandom
      LET x = rnd
      PRINT x
   NEXT i
END SUB
```

If we wish to generate a random number x uniformly distributed in the interval $[a, b]$, we use the relation $x = a + (b-a)r$, where r is a uniformly distributed random number in the interval $[0, 1]$. The following subroutine implements this relation.

```
SUB random2(a,b,nrandom)
   FOR i = 1 to nrandom
      LET x = a + (b - a)*rnd
      PRINT x
   NEXT i
END SUB
```

The following subroutine generates random integers in the interval $[1, N]$.

```
SUB random_integers(nrandom)
   LET N = 10
   FOR i = 1 to nrandom
      LET x = int(N*rnd + 1)
      PRINT x
   NEXT i
END SUB
```

PROBLEM 10.5 Monte Carlo integration in one dimension

a. Write a program which implements the hit or miss Monte Carlo procedure summarized by (10.11). Find the estimate F_n for the integral of $f(x) = 4\sqrt{1 - x^2}$ as a function of n, the number of trials. Choose $a = 0, b = 1, H = 1$, and sample the function $\sqrt{1 - x^2}$. Multiply the estimate by 4. Calculate the difference between F_n and the exact result of π. This difference is a measure of the error associated with the Monte Carlo estimate. Make a log-log plot of the error as a function of n. What is the approximate functional dependence of the error on n for large n?

b. Estimate the integral of $f(x)$ using the sample mean Monte Carlo method of (10.12) and compute the error as a function of the number of trials n for n up to $10,000$. Determine the approximate functional dependence of the error on n for large n. How many trials are needed to determine F_n to two decimal places?

c. Determine the computational time per trial using the two Monte Carlo methods. Which method is to be preferred in this case?

10.5 MULTI-DIMENSIONAL MONTE CARLO INTEGRATION

The Monte Carlo method of integration is most suitable for the evaluation of multiple integrals for which conventional numerical methods are not generally useful. As an example of the Monte Carlo evaluation of multiple integrals, we consider the center of mass and moment of inertia of rigid bodies. We assume that the mass is distributed continuously with a known mass density $\rho(x, y)$. For simplicity we consider two-dimensional objects. The mass of a small area element $dxdy$ is given by

$$dm = \rho(x, y)dxdy \tag{10.13}$$

and the total mass of the object is

$$M = \int\int \rho(x,y)\,dx\,dy \quad .$$
(10.14)

The limits of integration depend on the geometry of the object. In the same way we can write the components X, Y of the center of mass as

$$X = \frac{1}{M} \int\int x\,\rho(x,y)\,dx\,dy$$
(10.15a)

and

$$Y = \frac{1}{M} \int\int y\,\rho(x,y)\,dx\,dy \quad .$$
(10.15b)

If the object rotates about the z-axis, its moment of inertia is given by

$$I_z = \int\int (x^2 + y^2)\,\rho(x,y)\,dx\,dy \quad .$$
(10.16)

The evaluation of M, R, and I using the mean sample method is straightforward. For example, the generalization of the sample mean method for the evaluation of the moment of inertia is

$$I_{z,n} = (x_2 - x_1)(y_2 - y_1)\frac{1}{n}\sum_{i=1}^{n}(x_i{}^2 + y_i{}^2)\rho(x_i, y_i)$$
(10.17)

where $I_{z,n}$ is the estimate of I_z for n trials, and x_i and y_i are independent random numbers in the intervals $x_1 \le x \le x_2$ and $y_1 \le y \le y_2$.

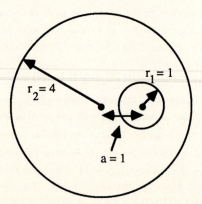

Fig. 10.4 The shape of the rigid disk considered in Problem 10.6.

PROBLEM 10.6 Properties of a rigid disk

   a. Use Monte Carlo methods to evaluate the total mass, the center of mass, and the moment of inertia of the disk shown in Fig. 10.4. The disk has an outer radius $r_2 = 4$ and an inner circular cavity of radius $r_1 = 1$. The cavity is centered a distance $a = 1$ from the center of the larger disk. Otherwise the disk has a uniform density $\rho = 1$.

   b. Repeat the calculations in part (a) with $\rho(x, y) = 1 + \frac{1}{2}(x^2 + y^2)$, where x and y are measured from the center of the larger disk.

   *c. Calculate the above quantities using Simpson's rule. Which method is easier to apply in this case? Which method makes more efficient use of computer time?

10.6 MONTE CARLO ERROR ANALYSIS

Both the Monte Carlo method and the classical numerical integration methods yield approximate answers. The accuracy depends on the number of trials in the Monte Carlo method, and on the number of intervals in the classical methods. In Problem 10.5 we used our knowledge of the exact value of the integrals to determine that the error in the Monte Carlo method approaches zero as approximately $n^{-1/2}$ for large n. In the following we will estimate the error when the exact answer is unknown. Our main result is that this n-dependence of the error is independent of the nature of the integrand and, most importantly, independent of the number of dimensions. Since we found in Problem 10.3 that the error using Simpson's rule for a one-dimensional integral was proportional to n^{-4}, we conclude that for low dimensions the conventional numerical methods such as Simpson's rule are usually preferable to Monte Carlo methods unless the domain of integration is very complicated. However, since the error in the conventional numerical methods increases with dimension (see Appendix 10A), Monte Carlo methods are essential for higher dimensional integrals.

   Because the appropriate measure of the error in Monte Carlo calculations is a subtle one, we find the error for an explicit example. Consider the Monte Carlo evaluation of the integral of $f(x) = 4\sqrt{1 - x^2}$ in the interval $[0, 1]$. Our calculated result for a particular sequence of $n = 10,000$ random numbers using the sample mean method is $F_n = 3.1489$. By comparing this estimate to the exact result of $F = \pi \approx 3.1416$, we find that the error associated with $n = 10,000$ trials is approximately 0.0073. How does our result for F_n compare with your result found in Problem 10.5 for the same value of n? We know that unless the integrand is a constant, F_n will not be equal in general to F. How can we know if $n = 10,000$ trials is sufficient to achieve a desired accuracy? How close can we expect F_n to be to F for a given value of n? Of course we cannot answer these questions definitively since if the actual error in F_n were known, we could correct F_n by the required amount and obtain F. The best we can do is to calculate the *probability* that the true value F is within a certain range centered on F_n.

One possible measure of the error which might be familiar to you is the *variance* σ^2 defined by

$$\sigma^2 = <f^2> - <f>^2 \tag{10.18}$$

where

$$<f> = \frac{1}{n} \sum_{i=1}^{n} f(x_i) \tag{10.19a}$$

and

$$<f^2> = \frac{1}{n} \sum_{i=1}^{n} f(x_i)^2 \quad . \tag{10.19b}$$

The *standard deviation* is σ. We know that if f were independent of x, σ would be zero. For our example and the same sequence of random numbers used to obtain F_n, we obtain $\sigma = 0.8850$. Since we know that the actual error is much smaller than σ, we conclude that σ cannot be a direct measure of the error.

One criterion for a measure of the error is that it should decrease with n. Do you think that σ as defined in (10.18) decreases with n? One way to obtain an estimate for the error is to make additional runs of n trials each. Each run of n trials yields a mean value or *measurement* which we denote as M_α. These measurements will not be equal in general since each measurement uses a different sequence of random numbers. Qualitatively, the magnitude of the differences between the measurements is a measure of the error associated with a single measurement. Suppose we have a set of m measurements $\{M_\alpha\}$ each consisting of the same number of trials. A convenient measure of the differences of these measurements is the *standard deviation of the means* σ_m which we define as

$$\sigma_m^2 = <M^2> - <M>^2 \tag{10.20}$$

where

$$<M> = \frac{1}{m} \sum_{\alpha=1}^{m} M_\alpha \tag{10.21a}$$

and

$$<M^2> = \frac{1}{m} \sum_{\alpha=1}^{m} M_\alpha^2 \quad . \tag{10.21b}$$

TABLE 10.2 Monte Carlo measurements of the mean value of $f(x) = 4\sqrt{1-x^2}$ in the interval $[0, 1]$. A total of 10 measurements (runs) of $n = 10,000$ trials each were made. The mean value M and the standard deviation σ associated with a single measurement are shown.

run α	M	σ
1	3.14892	0.88501
2	3.13255	0.89865
3	3.14042	0.88924
4	3.14600	0.88525
5	3.15257	0.88757
6	3.13972	0.89698
7	3.13107	0.89700
8	3.13585	0.89406
9	3.13442	0.89746
10	3.14047	0.89213

In order to aid our understanding of σ_m, we *estimate* σ_m by making $m = 10$ measurements. Each measurement is for $n = 10,000$ trials and yields its own mean M and σ. The values of M and σ for each measurement are shown in Table 10.2.

An inspection of Table 10.2 shows that the measurements M vary in different runs. From the values of M in Table 10.2 and the relation (10.20), we obtain the estimate for σ_m:

$$\sigma_m = 0.0068 \quad . \tag{10.22}$$

This value of σ_m is consistent with our known result for the error which is 0.0073. Hence we conclude that σ_m, the standard deviation of the means, is a measure of the error for a single measurement. The more precise interpretation of σ_m is that $F_n(M_\alpha)$ has a 68% chance of being within σ_m of the "true" mean. Hence the probable error associated with our first measurement of F_n with $n = 10,000$ is 3.149 ± 0.007.

Although σ_m gives us an estimate of the probable error, our method of obtaining σ_m, namely the necessity of making additional measurements, is not useful. In Appendix 10B we give an analytical derivation of the relation

$$\sigma_m \approx \sigma/\sqrt{n} \quad . \tag{10.23}$$

The relation (10.23) between σ_m and σ becomes exact in the limit of a very large number of measurements. Note that (10.23) implies that the probable error decreases with the square root of the number of trials. For our example

TABLE 10.3 The average values f_s of $f(x) = 4\sqrt{1 - x^2}$ for $0 \leq x \leq 1$ is shown for 10 subsets of $1,000$ trials each. The average value of $f(x)$ over the 10 subsets is 3.14892, in agreement with the result for F_n shown for the first measurement in Table 10.2.

subset s	f_s
1	3.14326
2	3.15633
3	3.10940
4	3.15337
5	3.15352
6	3.11506
7	3.17989
8	3.12398
9	3.17565
10	3.17878

we find that the probable error of our initial measurement is approximately $0.8850/100 \approx 0.009$, an estimate consistent with the known error of 0.007 and with our estimated value of $\sigma_m \approx 0.007$.

One way to verify the relation (10.23) is to divide the initial measurement of n trials into s subsets rather than to make additional measurements. We denote the mean value of $f(x_i)$ in each of the s subsets as f_s and analyze the differences F_s of each subset. As an example, we divide the $10,000$ trials of the first measurement into $s = 10$ subsets of $n/s = 1,000$ trials each. The results for f_s are shown in Table 10.3.

Note that as expected, the mean values of $f(x)$ for each subset are not equal. A reasonable candidate for a measure of the error is the standard deviation of the means of each subset. We denote this quantity as σ_s where

$$\sigma_s{}^2 = <f_s{}^2> - <f_s>^2 \tag{10.24}$$

where the averages are over the subsets. From Table 10.3 we obtain $\sigma_s = 0.025$. Although σ_s is a candidate for the probable error, we see that the magnitude of σ_s is almost three times larger than the estimate 0.009 given by (10.22). Moreover, we need to obtain an error estimate which is independent of how we subdivide the data. This quantity is not σ_s but the ratio $\sigma_s/\sqrt{s}$, which for our example is approximately $0.025/3.16 \approx 0.008$. This value is consistent with both σ_m and the ratio $\sigma/\sqrt{n}$. We conclude that we can interpret the n trials either as a single measurement or as a collection of s measurements. In the former interpretation, the probable error is given by the standard deviation of the n trials divided by the square root of the number of trials. In the same spirit, the latter interpretation implies that the probable error is given by the standard deviation of the s measurements of f_s divided by the square root of the number of measurements.

Note that we can make the error as small as we wish by either increasing the number of trials or by increasing the "efficiency" of the trials and thereby reducing the standard deviation σ. Several *reduction of variance* methods are introduced in Secs. 10.8–10.9.

PROBLEM 10.7 Estimate of the Monte Carlo error

a. Estimate the integral of $f(x) = e^{-x}$ in the interval $0 \leq x \leq 1$. Use the sample mean Monte Carlo method with $n = 3,600$ trials. Compute the standard deviation σ as defined by (10.18). Does your estimate of σ change significantly if more trials are generated? Since the exact answer can be obtained analytically, determine the error. How does the error compare with the error estimate obtained from the relation (10.23)?

b. Generate nineteen additional measurements of the integral; each measurement has $n = 3,600$ trials. What is σ_m, the standard deviation of the twenty measurements? Is the magnitude of σ_m consistent with your estimate of the error obtained in part (a)? Will your estimate of σ_m change significantly if more measurements are made?

c. Divide your first measurement into $s = 20$ subsets of 180 trials each. Compute the standard deviation of the subsets σ_s. Is the magnitude $\sigma_s/s^{1/2}$ consistent with your previous error estimates?

d. Divide your first measurement into $s = 10$ subsets of 360 trials each and again compute the standard deviation of the subsets. What is the value of $\sigma_s/s^{1/2}$ in this case? How do the standard deviation of the subsets compare using the two different divisions of the data?

e. Estimate the integral

$$\int_0^1 dx\, e^{-x^2} \tag{10.25}$$

to two decimal places using $\sigma_n/\sqrt{n}$ as an estimate of the probable error.

*PROBLEM 10.8 Importance of randomness

We will learn in Chapter 11 that the random number generator included with many programming languages is based on the "power residue" method. In this method each term in the sequence can be found from the preceding one by the relation

$$x_{n+1} = ax_n + c \bmod m \tag{10.26}$$

where x_0 is the "seed," and a, c and m are nonnegative integers. The random numbers on the unit interval $[0, 1]$ are given by $r_n = x_n/m$. The notation $y = x \bmod m$ means that if x exceeds m, then the *modulus m* is subtracted from x as many times as necessary until $0 \leq y \leq m$. Eventually, this sequence of numbers will repeat itself, thus defining a *period* for the random number generator. In order to examine the effect of a poor random number generator, we choose values of x_0, m, a, c such that (10.26) has poor statistical properties, e.g. a short period. What is the period for $x_0 = 1$, $a = 5$, $c = 0$, and $m = 32$? Estimate the integral in Problem 10.7a by making a single measurement of $n = 3,600$ trials using the "random number" generator (10.26) with the above values of x_0, a, c, and m. Analyze your measurement in the same way as before, i.e. calculate the mean, the mean of each of the twenty subsets, and the standard deviation of the means. Then divide your data into ten subsets and calculate the same quantities. Are the standard deviations of the subsets related as before? If not, why?

10.7   NON-UNIFORM PROBABILITY DISTRIBUTIONS

In the previous two sections we learned how uniformly distributed random numbers can be used to estimate definite integrals. However in general, it is desirable to sample the integrand $f(x)$ more often in regions of x where $|f(x)|$ is large or rapidly varying. Since such "importance sampling" methods require nonuniform probability distributions, we consider here the "inverse transform" method for generating random numbers which are not distributed uniformly.

It is necessary to introduce the *probability density* $p(x)$, where $p(x)dx$ is the probability that the random number x is in the interval $[x, x + dx]$. The probability density $p(x)$ is normalized such that

$$\int_{-\infty}^{+\infty} dx\, p(x) = 1 \quad . \tag{10.27}$$

We adopt the notation that r is a uniform random number in the unit interval $[0, 1]$ with the probability density function

$$p_u(r) = \begin{cases} 1, & \text{if } 0 \leq r \leq 1 \\ 0, & \text{otherwise} \end{cases} \quad . \qquad (10.28)$$

A variable which satisfies the probability distribution (10.28) is known as a *uniform deviate*. Our goal is to find a relation between x and r such that if r is distributed according to (10.28), x will be distributed according to $p(x)$. In order to obtain this relation, we first compute the integral

$$P(x) = \int_{-\infty}^{x} dx'\, p(x') \quad . \qquad (10.29)$$

The interpretation of $P(x)$ is that $P(x)$ is the *cumulative distribution function*, the probability of obtaining a random number less than or equal to x. The geometrical interpretation of $P(x)$ is that $P(x)$ is the fractional area under the probability curve $p(x)$ to the left of x. The desired relation for the value of x corresponding to the value of r is easier to state than to derive. We indicate in the following that the inverse of the relation

$$P(x) = r \qquad (10.30)$$

leads to the desired relation

$$x = P^{-1}(r) \quad . \qquad (10.31)$$

In order to understand the relations (10.30) and (10.31), we note that since r is uniformly distributed on the unit interval, the function $P(x)$ which is related to r by (10.30) is also distributed uniformly. The probability that $P(x)$ is in the range $[P(x), P(x) + dP(x)]$ is $dP(x)$ which according to (10.30) equals dr. The relation between $dP(x)$ and dx can be found by differentiating (10.29):

$$\frac{dP(x)}{dx} = p(x) \quad . \qquad (10.32)$$

Hence we have using (10.28) and for $0 \leq r \leq 1$

$$dP(x) = p(x)dx = p_u(r)dr \quad . \qquad (10.33)$$

From (10.33) we see that x is distributed according to the desired probability density $p(x)$.

The sequence of steps associated with the inverse transform method is to generate a random number r and solve (10.31) for the corresponding value of

x. As an example, we use (10.31) to generate random numbers according to the uniform probability distribution on the interval $[a, b]$. The desired probability density $p(x)$ is

$$p(x) = \begin{cases} 1/(b-a), & a \le x \le b \\ 0, & \text{otherwise} \end{cases} \tag{10.34}$$

The cumulative probability distribution function $P(x)$ for $a \le x \le b$ can be found by substituting (10.34) into (10.29) and performing the integral. The result is

$$P(x) = \frac{x-a}{b-a} \quad . \tag{10.35}$$

If we substitute the form (10.35) for $P(x)$ in (10.30), we find the desired relation

$$x = P^{-1}(r) = a + (b-a)r \quad . \tag{10.36}$$

The variable x given by (10.36) is distributed according to the probability distribution $p(x)$ given by (10.34). The relation (10.36) has been used in **SUB random2** in Sec. 10.4.

We now give an example of the inverse transform method applied to the distribution function

$$p(x) = \begin{cases} ae^{-ax}, & \text{if } 0 \le x \le \infty \\ 0, & x < 0 \end{cases} \quad . \tag{10.37}$$

If we substitute (10.37) into (10.29) and perform the integration, we find $P(x) = 1 - e^{-ax}$. In this case the solution of the relation (10.30) yields $x = -a^{-1} \ln(1-r)$. Since $1 - r$ is distributed in the same way as r, we can write

$$x = P^{-1}(r) = -a^{-1} \ln r \quad . \tag{10.38}$$

The variable x found from (10.38) is distributed according to the probability distribution $p(x)$ given by (10.37). Note that on most computers the computation of the natural logarithm in (10.38) involves a power series expansion for each value of r. Thus the inverse transform method might not necessarily be the most efficient method to use.

To apply the inverse transform method, two conditions must be satisfied. The form of $P(x)$ must allow the integral in (10.29) to be performed analytically or numerically and it must be feasible to invert the relation $P(x) = r$ for x. Unfortunately the Gaussian or normal distribution

$$p(x) = \sigma^{-1}(2\pi)^{-1/2} e^{-x^2/2\sigma^2} \tag{10.39}$$

is an example of a distribution for which $P(x)$ cannot be obtained analytically. However we can generate the two-dimensional Gaussian probability $p(x,y)dxdy$

$$p(x,y)dxdy = \sigma^{-2}(2\pi)^{-1}e^{-(x^2+y^2)/2\sigma^2}dxdy \qquad (10.40)$$

using the *Box-Muller* method. Make a change of variables to polar coordinates

$$r = (x^2 + y^2)^{1/2} \qquad \theta = arctan\, y/x \qquad (10.41)$$

let $\rho = r^2/2$, and write the probability as

$$p(\rho,\theta)d\rho d\theta = (2\pi)^{-1}e^{-\rho}d\rho d\theta \quad . \qquad (10.42)$$

An inspection of (10.42) shows that if we generate ρ according to the exponential distribution (10.37) and generate θ uniformly in the interval $[0, 2\pi]$, then the variables

$$x = (2\rho)^{1/2}\cos\theta \qquad y = (2\rho)^{1/2}\sin\theta \qquad (10.43)$$

will be generated according to (10.39) with zero mean and $\sigma = 1$. We discuss other procedures for generating the Gaussian distribution in Problem 11.12 and Appendix 10C.

PROBLEM 10.9 Non-uniform probability densities

a. Write a program to verify that the sequence of random numbers $\{x_i\}$ generated by (10.38) is distributed according to the exponential distribution (10.37).

b. Generate random variables according to the probability density function

$$p(x) = \begin{cases} 2(1-x), & \text{if } 0 \le x \le 1; \\ 0, & \text{otherwise} \end{cases} . \qquad (10.44)$$

c. Verify that the variables x and y in (10.43) are distributed according to the Gaussian distribution. What is the mean value and standard deviation of x and y?

*d. How can you use the relations (10.43) to generate a Gaussian distribution with arbitrary mean and standard deviation?

10.8 IMPORTANCE SAMPLING

Since the analysis of Sec. 10.6 showed that the error estimate associated with a Monte Carlo calculation is proportional to σ, we wish to introduce "importance sampling" techniques which reduce σ and improve the efficiency of each trial. As an example of this technique, we introduce a positive function $p(x)$ such that

$$\int_a^b dx\, p(x) = 1 \quad . \tag{10.45}$$

Then we can rewrite the integral (10.1) as

$$F = \int_a^b dx \left[\frac{f(x)}{p(x)} \right] p(x) \quad . \tag{10.46}$$

We can evaluate the integral (10.46) by sampling according to the "probability distribution" $p(x)$ and constructing the sum

$$F_n = \frac{1}{n} \sum_{i=1}^{n} \frac{f(x_i)}{p(x_i)} \quad . \tag{10.47}$$

Note that for the uniform case, $p(x) = 1/(b-a)$, and (10.47) reduces to (10.12).

We wish to choose a form for $p(x)$ which minimizes the variance of the integrand $f(x)/p(x)$. Since we cannot evaluate σ analytically in general, we determine σ a posteriori and choose a form of $p(x)$ which mimics $f(x)$ where $f(x)$ is large. If we are able to determine an appropriate $p(x)$, the integrand $f(x)/p(x)$ will be slowly varying and hence the variance will be reduced. As an example we again consider the integral (see Problem 10.7)

$$F = \int_0^1 dx\, e^{-x^2} \quad . \tag{10.48}$$

The estimate of F with $p(x) = 1$ for $0 \le x \le 1$ is shown in the first column of Table 10.4. A reasonable choice of a weight function is $p(x) = Ae^{-x}$, where A is chosen such that $p(x)$ is normalized on the unit interval. Note that our choice of $p(x)$ is positive definite and is qualitatively similar to $f(x)$. The results are shown in the second column of Table 10.4. We see that even though the computation time per trial for the nonuniform case is larger, the smaller value of σ makes the use of the nonuniform probability distribution more efficient.

TABLE 10.4 Monte Carlo estimates of the integral (10.48) using the uniform probability density $p(x) = 1$ and non-uniform probability density $p(x) = Ae^{-x}$. The normalization constant A is chosen such that $p(x)$ is normalized on the unit interval. The exact value of the integral is approximately 0.7468. The estimates F_n, standard deviation σ, and the probable error $\sigma/n^{1/2}$ are shown. The CPU time (seconds) is shown for comparison only and was found on a Macintosh computer running True BASIC.

	$p(x) = 1$	$p(x) = Ae^{-x}$
n (trials)	20000	1000
F_n	0.7452	0.7482
σ	0.2009	0.0544
$\sigma/n^{1/2}$	0.0016	0.0017
CPU time per trial (sec)	0.0077	0.0280
Total CPU time (secs)	154	28

PROBLEM 10.10 Importance sampling

a. Choose the importance function $p(x) = e^{-x}$ and evaluate the integral:

$$\int_0^\infty dx\, x^{3/2}\, e^{-x} \quad . \tag{10.49}$$

b. Choose $p(x) = e^{-ax}$ and estimate the integral

$$\int_0^\pi dx\, \frac{1}{x^2 + \cos^2 x} \quad . \tag{10.50}$$

Determine the value of a which minimizes the variance of the integral.

10.9 RANDOM WALK METHODS

One general way to produce an arbitrary nonuniform probability distribution was introduced by Metropolis, Rosenbluth, Rosenbluth, Teller and Teller in 1953. The *Metropolis* method is a special case of an importance sampling procedure in which certain possible sampling attempts are rejected (see Appendix 10C). It will be used in Chapter 16 to generate the Boltzmann probability distribution in statistical mechanics.

For simplicity, we introduce the Metropolis method in one dimension. Suppose we wish to generate random variables according to an arbitrary probability density $p(x)$. The Metropolis method produces a "random walk" of points $\{x_i\}$ whose asymptotic probability distribution approaches $p(x)$ after a large number of steps. The random walk is defined by specifying a *transition probability* $w(x_i \rightarrow x_j)$ from one value x_i to another value x_j in order that the distribution of points x_0, x_1, x_2, ... converges to $p(x)$. It can be shown that it is sufficient (but not necessary) to satisfy the "detailed balance" condition

$$p(x_i)w(x_i \rightarrow x_j) = p(x_j)w(x_j \rightarrow x_i) \quad . \tag{10.51}$$

The relation (10.51) does not specify $w(x_i \rightarrow x_j)$ uniquely. A simple choice of $w(x_i \rightarrow x_j)$ which is consistent with (10.51) is

$$w(x_i \rightarrow x_j) = min\left[1, \frac{p(x_j)}{p(x_i)}\right] \quad . \tag{10.52}$$

This choice of $w(x_i \rightarrow x_j)$ can be described by the following steps. Suppose that the "walker" is at position x_n. To generate x_{n+1}, we

1. choose a trial position $x_t = x_n + \delta_n$, where δ_n is a random number in the interval $[-\delta, \delta]$.
2. Calculate $w = p(x_t)/p(x_n)$.
3. If $w \geq 1$, accept the change and let $x_{n+1} = x_t$.
4. If $w < 1$, generate a random number r.
5. If $r \leq w$, accept the change and let $x_{n+1} = x_t$.
6. If the trial change is not accepted, then let $x_{n+1} = x_n$.

It is necessary to sample a number of points of the random walk before the asymptotic probability distributed $p(x)$ is attained. How do we choose the maximum "step size" δ? If δ is too large, a small percentage of trial steps will be accepted and the sampling of $p(x)$ will be inefficient. On the other hand if δ is too small, a large percentage of trial steps will be accepted but again the sampling of $p(x)$ will be inefficient. A rough criterion for the magnitude of δ is that approximately one-third to one-half of the trial steps should be accepted. We also wish to choose the value of x_0 such that the distribution of x_i will attain the asymptotic distribution as quickly as possible. An obvious choice is to begin the random walk at a value of x at which $p(x)$ is a maximum.

A subroutine which implements the Metropolis algorithm is given below.

```
SUB Metropolis(x,delta,naccept)
   DECLARE DEF p
   LET xtrial = x + delta*(2*rnd - 1)
   LET w = p(xtrial)/p(x)
   IF rnd <= w then
      LET x = xtrial
      LET naccept = naccept + 1          ! number of acceptances
   END IF
END SUB
```

PROBLEM 10.11 The Gaussian distribution

a. Develop a program using **SUB Metropolis** to generate the Gaussian distribution $p(x) = A\,exp(-x^2/2\sigma^2)$. Is the numerical value of the normalization constant A relevant? Determine the qualitative dependence of the acceptance ratio and the equilibration time on the maximum step size δ. One possible criterion for "equilibrium" is that $<x^2> \approx \sigma^2$. For $\sigma = 1$, what is a reasonable choice for δ? How many trials are needed to reach equilibrium for your choice of δ? (Choose $x_0 = 0$.)

b. Modify your program so that it plots the asymptotic probability distribution generated by the Metropolis algorithm.

*c. Calculate the auto-correlation function C(j) defined by

$$C(j) = \frac{<x_{i+j}x_i> - <x_i>^2}{<x_ix_i> - <x_i>^2} \qquad (10.53)$$

where $<\ldots>$ indicates an average over the random walk. What is the value of $C(j = 0)$? What would be the value of $C(j \neq 0)$ if x_i were completely random? Calculate $C(j)$ for different values of j and determine the value of j for which $C(j)$ is essentially zero.

PROBLEM 10.12 Application of the importance sampling method

a. Although the Metropolis method is not the most efficient in this case, use it to estimate the integral

$$\int_0^4 dx\, x^2 e^{-x} \qquad (10.54)$$

with $p(x) = x^2 e^{-x}$ for $0 \leq x \leq 4$. Plot the number of times the walker is at the points x_0, x_1, x_2, ... Is the integrand sampled uniformly? If not, what is the approximate region of x where the integrand is sampled more often?

b. Evaluate the integral

$$\int_0^1 dx \, x^2 e^{-x^2} \qquad (10.55)$$

using an efficient importance sampling method.

REFERENCES AND SUGGESTIONS FOR ADDITIONAL READING

F. S. Acton, *Numerical Methods That Work*, Harper and Row (1970). A delightful book on numerical methods.

S. E. Koonin, *Computational Physics*, Benjamin/Cummings (1986). Chapter 8 covers much of the same material on Monte Carlo methods as discussed in this chapter.

Malvin H. Kalos and Paula A. Whitlock, *Monte Carlo Methods, Vol. 1: Basics*, John Wiley & Sons (1986). The authors are well known experts on Monte Carlo methods.

W. H. Press, B. P. Flannery, S. A. Teukolsky and W. T. Vetterling, *Numerical Recipes*, Cambridge University Press (1986). A *tour de force* on the art of scientific computing. A valuable reference book.

Reuven Y. Rubinstein, *Simulation and the Monte Carlo Method*, John Wiley & Sons (1981). An advanced but clearly written treatment of Monte Carlo methods.

G. L. Squires, *Practical Physics*, 3rd ed. Cambridge University Press (1985). An introduction to the practical problems associated with error analysis.

John R. Taylor, *An Introduction to Error Analysis*, University Science Books, Oxford University Press (1982).

Hugh D. Young, *Statistical Treatment of Experimental Data*, McGraw-Hill (1962).

APPENDIX 10A ERROR ESTIMATES FOR NUMERICAL INTEGRATION

We derive the dependence on the number of intervals of the truncation error estimates of the numerical integration methods considered in Secs. 10.1 and 10.3. These estimates are based on the assumed adequacy of the Taylor series expansion of the integrand $f(x)$

$$f(x) = f(x_i) + f'(x_i)(x - x_i) + \frac{1}{2}f''(x_i)(x - x_i)^2 + \ldots \tag{10.56}$$

and the integration of (10.1) in the interval $x_i \leq x \leq x_{i+1}$:

$$\int_{x_i}^{x_{i+1}} dx f(x) = f(x_i)\Delta x + \frac{1}{2}f'(x_i)(\Delta x)^2 + \frac{1}{6}f''(x_i)(\Delta x)^3 + \ldots \tag{10.57}$$

We first estimate the error associated with the rectangular approximation with $f(x)$ evaluated at the left side of each interval. The error Δ_i in the interval $[x_i, x_{i+1}]$ is the difference between (10.57) and the estimate $f(x_i)\Delta x$ is

$$\Delta_i = \left[\int_{x_i}^{x_{i+1}} dx f(x)\right] - f(x_i)\Delta x \approx \frac{1}{2}f'(x_i)(\Delta x)^2 \quad . \tag{10.58}$$

We see that to leading order in Δx, the error in each interval is order $(\Delta x)^2$, or symbolically $O\big((\Delta x)^2\big)$. Since there are a total of n intervals and $\Delta x = (b-a)/n$, the total error associated with the rectangular approximation is order $n\Delta_i \approx n(\Delta x)^2$ or $O(n^{-1})$.

The estimated error associated with the trapezoidal rule can be found in the same way. The error in the interval $[x_i, x_{i+1}]$ is the difference between the exact integral and the estimate $[f(x_i) + f(x_{i+1})]\Delta x/2$

$$\Delta_i = \left[\int_{x_i}^{x_{i+1}} dx f(x)\right] - \frac{1}{2}[f(x_i) + f(x_{i+1})]\Delta x \quad . \tag{10.59}$$

If we use (10.57) to estimate the integral and (10.56) to estimate $f(x_{i+1})$ in (10.59), we find that the term proportional to f' cancels and that the error associated with one interval is $O\big((\Delta x)^3\big)$. Hence the total error in the interval $[a, b]$ associated with the trapezoidal rule is $O(n^{-2})$.

Since Simpson's rule is based on fitting $f(x)$ in the interval $[x_{i-1}, x_{i+1}]$ to a parabola, error terms proportional to f'' cancel. We might expect that error terms of order $f'''(x_i)(\Delta x)^4$ contribute, but these terms cancel by virtue of their symmetry. Hence the $(\Delta x)^4$ term of the Taylor expansion of $f(x)$ is adequately represented by Simpson's rule. If we retain the $(\Delta x)^4$ term in the Taylor series of $f(x)$, we find that the error in the interval $[x_i, x_{i+1}]$ is of order $f''''(x_i)(\Delta x)^5$

and that the total error in the interval $[a, b]$ associated with Simpson's rule is $O(n^{-4})$.

We now extend the error estimates to two dimensions. The two-dimensional integral of $f(x, y)$ is the volume under the surface determined by $f(x, y)$. In the "rectangular" approximation, the integral is written as a sum of the volumes of parallelograms with cross sectional area $\Delta x \Delta y$ and a height determined by $f(x, y)$ at one corner. To determine the error we expand $f(x, y)$ in a Taylor series

$$f(x, y) = f(x_i, y_i) + f'_x(x_i, y_i)(x - x_i) + f'_y(x_i, y_i)(y - y_i) + \cdots \qquad (10.60)$$

where f'_x and f'_y represents the partial derivatives of $f(x, y)$ with respect to x and y respectively. We write the error as

$$\Delta_i = \left[\int\int f(x, y) dx dy \right] - f(x_i, y_i) \Delta x \Delta y \quad . \qquad (10.61)$$

We substitute (10.60) into (10.61) and integrate each term. We find that the term proportional to f cancels and the integral of $(x - x_i) dx$ yields $(\Delta x)^2/2$. The integral of this term with respect to dy gives another factor of Δy. The integral of the term proportional to $(y - y_i)$ yields a similar contribution. Since Δy is also $O(\Delta x)$, the error associated with the intervals $[x_i, x_{i+1}]$ and $[y_i, y_{i+1}]$ is to leading order in Δx:

$$\Delta_i \approx \frac{1}{2}[f'_x(x_i, y_i) + f'_y(x_i, y_i)](\Delta x)^3 \quad . \qquad (10.62)$$

We see that the error associated with one parallelogram is $O\big((\Delta x)^3\big)$. Since there are n parallelograms, the total error is order $n(\Delta x)^3$. However in two dimensions, $n = A/(\Delta x)^2$ and hence the total error is $O(n^{-1/2})$. In contrast the total error in one dimension is $O(n^{-1})$

The corresponding error estimates for the two-dimensional generalizations of the trapezoidal approximation and Simpson's rule are $O(n^{-1})$ and $O(n^{-2})$ respectively. In general if the error goes as $O(n^{-a})$ in one dimension, then the error in d dimensions goes as $O(n^{-a/d})$. In contrast, Monte Carlo errors vary as $O(n^{-1/2})$ independent of d. Thus for large enough d, Monte Carlo integration will lead to smaller errors for the same choice of n.

APPENDIX 10B ANALYTICAL DERIVATION OF THE STANDARD DEVIATION OF THE MEAN

In Sec. 10.6 we gave empirical reasons for the claim that the error associated with a single measurement consisting of n trials equals $\sigma/\sqrt{n}$, where σ is the standard deviation in a single measurement. We now present an analytical derivation of this relation. The quantity of experimental interest is denoted as x. Consider m sets of measurements each with n trials for a total of mn trials. We use the index α to denote a particular measurement and the index i to designate the ith trial within a measurement. We denote $x_{\alpha,i}$ as measurement i in the set α. The value of a measurement is given by

$$M_\alpha = \frac{1}{n} \sum_{i=1}^n x_{\alpha,i} \quad . \tag{10.63}$$

The mean $\overline{M}$ of the *total mn* individual trials is given by

$$\overline{M} = \frac{1}{m} \sum_{\alpha=1}^m M_\alpha = \frac{1}{nm} \sum_{\alpha=1}^m \sum_{i=1}^n x_{\alpha,i} \quad . \tag{10.64}$$

The difference between measurement α and the mean of all the measurements is given by

$$e_\alpha = M_\alpha - \overline{M} \quad . \tag{10.65}$$

Hence we can write the variance of the means as

$$\sigma_m{}^2 = \frac{1}{m} \sum_{\alpha=1}^m e_\alpha{}^2 \quad . \tag{10.66}$$

We now wish to relate σ_m to the variance of the individual trials. The discrepancy $d_{\alpha,i}$ between an individual trial and the mean is given by

$$d_{\alpha,i} = x_{\alpha,i} - \overline{M} \quad . \tag{10.67}$$

Hence the variance σ^2 of the nm individual trials is

$$\sigma^2 = \frac{1}{mn} \sum_{\alpha=1}^m \sum_{i=1}^n d_{\alpha,i}{}^2 \quad . \tag{10.68}$$

We write

$$e_\alpha = M_\alpha - \overline{M} = \frac{1}{n} \sum_{i=1}^n x_{\alpha,i} - \overline{M}$$

$$= \frac{1}{n} \sum_{i=1}^n (x_{\alpha,i} - \overline{M}) = \frac{1}{n} \sum_{i=1}^n d_{\alpha,i} \quad . \tag{10.69}$$

If we insert (10.69) into (10.66), we find

$$\sigma_m{}^2 = \frac{1}{m} \sum_{\alpha=1}^{n} \left(\frac{1}{n} \sum_{i=1}^{n} d_{\alpha,i}\right)\left(\frac{1}{n} \sum_{j=1}^{n} d_{\alpha,j}\right) \quad . \tag{10.70}$$

The sum in (10.70) over trials i and j in set α contains two kinds of terms—those with $i = j$ and those with $i \neq j$. We expect that $d_{\alpha,i}$ and $d_{\alpha,j}$ are independent and equally positive or negative on the average. Hence in the limit of a very large number of measurements, we expect that only the terms with $i = j$ in (10.70) will survive. Thus we write

$$\sigma_m{}^2 = \frac{1}{mn^2} \sum_{\alpha=1}^{n} \sum_{i=1}^{n} d_{\alpha,i}{}^2 \quad . \tag{10.71}$$

If we combine (10.71) with (10.68), we arrive at the desired result

$$\sigma_m{}^2 = \frac{\sigma^2}{n} \quad . \tag{10.72}$$

APPENDIX 10C THE ACCEPTANCE-REJECTION METHOD

Although the inverse transform method discussed in Sec. 10.7 can in principle be used to generate any desired probability distribution, in practice the method is limited to functions for which the inverse transform function $P^{-1}(r)$ can be found analytically or by simple numerical approximation. Another method for generating non-uniform probability distributions is the *acceptance-rejection* method due to von Neumann. This technique is based on a generalization of the simple geometrical argument used in the hit or miss estimation of definite integrals discussed in Sec. 10.4.

Suppose that $p(x)$ is a (normalized) probability distribution function which we wish to generate. For simplicity we assume $p(x)$ is nonzero in the unit interval. Consider a positive definite *comparison function* $w(x)$ such that $w(x) > p(x)$ in the entire range of interest. A simple although not generally optimum choice of w is a constant greater than the maximum value of $p(x)$. Since the area under the curve $p(x)$ in the range x to $x + \Delta x$ is the probability of generating x in that range, we can follow a procedure similar to that used in the hit or miss method. Generate two random numbers which define the location of a random point in two dimensions which is distributed uniformly in the area under the comparison function $w(x)$. If this point is outside the area under $p(x)$, the point is rejected; if it lies inside the area, we accept it. This procedure implies that the accepted points are uniform in the area under the curve $p(x)$ and that their x values are distributed according to $p(x)$.

One procedure for generating a uniform random point (x, y) under the comparison function $w(x)$ is as follows.

1. Choose a form of $w(x)$. One choice would be to choose $w(x)$ such that the values of x distributed according to $w(x)$ can be generated by the inverse transform method. Let the total area under the curve $w(x)$ be equal to A.
2. Generate a uniform random number in the interval $[0, A]$ and use it to obtain a corresponding value of x distributed according to $w(x)$.
3. For the value of x generated in step (2), obtain a uniform random number y in the interval $[0, w(x)]$. The point (x, y) is uniformly distributed in the area under the comparison function $w(x)$. If $y \leq p(x)$, then accept x as a random number distributed according to $p(x)$.

Of course steps (2) and (3) must be repeated many times.

Note that the acceptance-rejection method is efficient only if the comparison functon $w(x)$ is close to $p(x)$ over the entire range of interest.

RANDOM WALKS

11

We introduce concepts of probability and random processes in the context of model physical systems.

11.1 BACKGROUND

The original statement of the "random walk" problem was posed by Pearson in 1906. If a drunkard begins at a lamppost and takes N steps of equal length in random directions, how far will the drunkard be from the lamp post? Since this formulation of a random walk, random walk models have attained a high degree of utility in the physical, biological and social sciences. Familiar textbook applications are to the diffusion of a molecule in a gas and to the Brownian motion of colloidal suspensions in a fluid. Another important application is the characterization of long polymer chains, discussed in Sec. 11.4. In Sec. 10.9 we learned that definite integrals can be estimated using random walk methods. In fact many problems, such as the solution to Schrödinger's equation, can be reformulated in terms of a random walk (see Chapter 17). However in order to appreciate these applications, it is first necessary to understand random walk models in a simple context.

11.2 A ONE-DIMENSIONAL RANDOM WALK

Although the main concern of physics is not with drunkards, we first consider an idealized one-dimensional example of a drunk (a walker) who begins at a lamppost located at $x = 0$ (see Fig. 11.1). Each step is of equal length l. The direction of each step is independent of the preceding one. At each interval of time, the walker has a probability p of a step to the right and a probability $q = 1 - p$ of a step to the left. Let $n_\rightarrow$ be the number of steps to the right and let $n_\leftarrow$ be the number of steps to the left. The total number of steps N is given by $N = n_\rightarrow + n_\leftarrow$. Then the net displacement of the walker from the origin after N steps is $x = (n_\rightarrow - n_\leftarrow)l$, where $-Nl \leq x \leq Nl$. The main quantity of interest is the probability $P_N(x)$ that after N steps, the walker has undergone a net displacement x. We can compute the mean net displacement $<x_N>$ and the variance $<\Delta x_N^2>$ of the walker from the relations

$$<x_N> = \sum_{x=-Nl}^{Nl} x P_N(x) \tag{11.1}$$

and

$$<\Delta x_N^2> = <x_N^2> - <x_N>^2 \tag{11.2}$$

where

$$<x_N^2> = \sum_{x=-Nl}^{Nl} x^2 P_N(x) \quad . \tag{11.3}$$

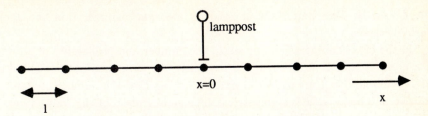

Fig. 11.1 The random walk of a drunkard in one dimension.

The averages are over all possible walks of N steps.

The analysis of the random walk problem posed above can be obtained analytically using probability theory (cf Reif). The analytical results for $<x_N>$ and $<\Delta x_N^2>$ are

$$<x_N> = (p - q)Nl \qquad (11.4)$$

and

$$<\Delta x_N^2> = 4pqNl^2 \quad . \qquad (11.5)$$

Note that according to (11.4), $<x_N> = 0$ for the symmetrical case $p = q = 1/2$.

We now reformulate our example of a random walk in terms of the diffusion of a molecule in a dilute gas. Suppose that a given molecule travels a distance ℓ between collisions with other molecules. If we assume that successive displacements suffered by the molecule betwen collisions are statistically independent, then the motion of the molecule is identical to the motion of the drunk. Since the motion of such a molecule can also be described by a diffusion process, we briefly describe the relation between the random walk and diffusion. We will find in Sec. 11.6 that diffusion is characterized in part by the linear relation

$$<\Delta R(t)^2> = 2dDt \qquad (11.6)$$

between the time t and the net mean square displacement $<R(t)^2>$ of a molecule from its position at $t = 0$. The proportionality constant D in (11.6) is known as the *self-diffusion constant* of the molecule, and d is the dimensionality of space. In order to compare (11.5) and (11.6), we take the time between steps to be τ so that $N = t/\tau$ and identify the step lengths l and ℓ. Then we can rewrite (11.5) in the form

$$<\Delta x^2> = 4pq\,\ell^2(t/\tau) \quad . \qquad (11.7)$$

From a comparison of (11.6) and (11.7), we conclude that the diffusion constant of a random walker in one dimension is given by $D = \ell^2/2\tau$ for $p = 1/2$.

Although the relations (11.4) and (11.5) can be derived using simple analytical methods, we need to develop techniques for walks which cannot be solved exactly. Two important approaches are exact enumeration and Monte Carlo methods.

In the exact enumeration approach, the number and probability of all walks of a given N and x are determined explicitly. As an example, the eight walks for $N = 3$ and $d = 1$ are shown in Fig. 11.2. Note that the number of walks for positive and negative x is symmetrical. The enumeration of the walks allows us to calculate $P_3(x)$ (see Fig. 11.2) and we obtain

$$\begin{aligned}
<x_3> = \sum x P_3(x) &= -3q^3 - 3pq^2 + 3p^2q + 3p^3 \\
&= 3(p^2 - q^2)(p + q) \\
&= 3(p + q)(p - q) = 3(p - q)
\end{aligned} \tag{11.8a}$$

$$\begin{aligned}
<x_3^2> = \sum x^2 P_3(x) &= 9q^3 + 3pq^2 + 3p^2q + 9p^3 \\
&= 12pq + [3(p - q)]^2 \quad .
\end{aligned} \tag{11.8b}$$

We have used the relation $p + q = 1$ in (11.8). From (11.8) we find that the net mean square displacement is given by $<\Delta x^2> = <x_3^2> - <x_3>^2 = 12pq$, a result consistent with (11.5). In the enumeration approach, the computer is used as a "bookkeeper" to generate the possible walks and ultimately the exact expressions for the quantities of interest. Since the total number of possible N-step walks in one dimension is 2^N, exact enumeration is in general limited to small N. (Of course this limitation can be overcome if the model can be solved analytically.) We will use exact enumeration results as a check on our Monte Carlo simulations.

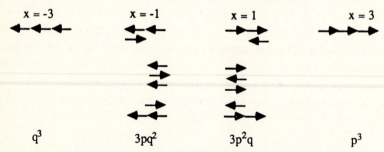

Fig. 11.2 The eight random walks in $d = 1$ with $N = 3$ and net displacement x. For clarity the individual steps are displaced vertically. The probability $P_3(x)$ is also shown where p is the probability of a step to the right, and $q = 1 - p$ is the probability of a step to the left.

PROBLEM 11.1 Exact enumeration of random walks in one dimension

a. For $N = 3$, there are three walks with $x = 1$ and three walks with $x = -1$ (see Fig. 11.2). How many $N = 4$ walks are there with $x = 0$? How is this number related to the number of walks with $x = \pm 1$ and $N = 3$? How is the number of 4-step walks with $x = 2$ related to the number of 3-step walks with $x = 1$ and $x = 3$? Obtain an exact relation between the number of N-step walks with displacement x and the number of $(N - 1)$-step walks with displacement $x \pm 1$. Use this derived relation to determine the number of possible walks of a given value of x for $N = 4$ and $N = 5$ and the exact results for $P_N(x)$, $<x_N>$, and $<\Delta x_N^2>$ for $N = 4$ and $N = 5$.

b. Use the relation obtained in part (a) to write a program which enumerates the number of possible walks of a given N and x. Calculate $P_N(x)$, $<x_N>$, and $<\Delta x_N^2>$ exactly for $N = 1$ to 8. Use your exact enumeration results to show that $P_N(x)$ can be written in the form

$$P_N(x) = \frac{N!}{(\frac{N}{2} + \frac{x}{2})!\,(\frac{N}{2} - \frac{x}{2})!}\, p^{(\frac{N}{2} + \frac{x}{2})}\, q^{(\frac{N}{2} - \frac{x}{2})} \tag{11.9}$$

where $(N + \frac{1}{2}x)$ and $(N - \frac{1}{2}x)$ are the number of steps to the right and to the left respectively.

In contrast to the exact enumeration of all walks of N steps for small N, the Monte Carlo method samples walks of many steps, e.g. $N \sim 100$ to $10,000$. We generate a large number of random walks with the correct probabilities to ensure that the sampled walks are representative of the total population of possible walks. Clearly the more walks we use, the closer we will come to the exact result. In practice, we obtain the desired accuracy by comparing our results for an increasing number of trials until the results do not appear to vary within our desired accuracy.

An example of a Monte Carlo program for a one-dimensional random walk is given below; **SUB walk** corresponds to the random walk algorithm.

```
PROGRAM random_walk          ! Monte Carlo simulation of random walk in d = 1
DIM prob(-64 to 64)
CALL initial(p,N,ntrial)
FOR itrial = 1 to ntrial
   CALL walk(x,p,N)
   CALL data(x,xcum,x2cum,prob)          ! collect data after N steps
NEXT itrial
CALL average(N,ntrial,xcum,x2cum,prob)
END

SUB initial(p,N,ntrial)
   RANDOMIZE
   LET ntrial = 100                          ! number of trials
   LET p = 0.5                               ! probability of step to the right
   INPUT prompt "number of steps = ": N
END SUB

SUB walk(x,p,N)
   LET x = 0                                 ! initial position for each trial
   FOR istep = 1 to N
      IF rnd <= p then
         LET x = x + 1
      ELSE
         LET x = x - 1
      END IF
   NEXT istep
END SUB

SUB data(x,xcum,x2cum,prob())
   LET xcum = xcum + x
   LET x2cum = x2cum + x*x
   LET prob(x) = prob(x) + 1
END SUB
```

```
SUB average(N,ntrial,xcum,x2cum,prob())        ! average values for N-step walk
    LET norm = 1/ntrial
    LET xbar = xcum*norm
    LET x2bar = x2cum*norm
    FOR x = -N to N
        LET prob(x) = prob(x)*norm
        IF prob(x) > 0 then print x,prob(x)
    NEXT x
    LET variance = x2bar - xbar*xbar
    LET sigma = sqr(variance)
    PRINT "mean displacement = "; xbar
    PRINT "sigma = "; sigma
END SUB
```

In order to determine the probability distribution $P_N(x)$, we need to consider many trials and record the fraction of times that the walker is at position x after N steps. It is not necessary to calculate $<x_N>$ and $<\Delta x_N^2>$ separately in the program, since these quantities can be obtained from $P_N(x)$. However in many applications, $<x_N>$ and $<\Delta x_N^2>$ yield sufficient information and the calculation of $P_N(x)$, a memory intensive array, is not necessary.

PROBLEM 11.2 Monte Carlo simulation of random walks in one dimension

a. Modify **Program random_walk** so that the path of each random walker is shown and $P_N(x)$ is plotted after every 100 trials. Use your modified program with $p = 0.5$, $N = 64$ and $ntrial = 1,000$. Does the path of each walker appear "random" to the eye? How does the qualitative form of $P_N(x)$ change with the number of trials?

b. Use **Program random_walk** with $p = 0.5$ to determine $P_N(x)$, $<x_N>$ and $<\Delta x_N^2>$ for $N = 8$, 16, 32 and 64. Compare your results for $<x_N>$ and $<\Delta x_N^2>$ to the exact answers (11.4) and (11.5) respectively. If you wish to calculate $<\Delta x_N^2>$ to the same relative degree of accuracy for $N = 8$ and $N = 64$, do you need more or less trials for the larger value of N?

c. Plot $P_N(x)$ versus x for the above values of N. Is x a continuous function? What is the value of $P_N(x)$ at its maximum for each value of N? What is the approximate "width" of $P_N(x)$ in each case?

d. Show from your plot of $P_N(x)$ that for sufficiently large N, the computed distribution $P_N(x)$ can be approximated by the Gaussian distribution

$$P(x) = \sigma^{-1}(2\pi)^{-1/2} exp[-(x- <x>)^2/2\sigma^2] \qquad (11.10)$$

where $\sigma^2 =<\Delta x^2>$. Use as input in (11.10) the calculated values of $<x>$ and $<\Delta x^2>$. Does the form (11.10) fit the calculated distribution equally well for all x?

e. Use the error analysis discussed in Sec. 10.6 to estimate the number of trials necessary to obtain $<\Delta x_N^2>$ for $N = 8$ and $N = 64$ to 5% accuracy. A discussion of this analysis is given in Appendix 11A. What is the standard deviation of $<\Delta x_N^2>$?

f. Suppose that $p = 0.7$. Compute $<x_N>$ and $<x_N^2>$ for the same values of N as considered in part (b). What is the interpretation of $<x_N>$ in this case?

Many applications of random walk models make use of asymptotic results for large N. For example in many random walk models, $<\Delta x_N^2>$ satisfies a power law for sufficiently large N, e.g.

$$<\Delta x_N^2> \sim N^{2\nu} \qquad (N \gg 1) \quad . \qquad (11.11)$$

The relation (11.11) is an example of an asymptotic *scaling law.*. That is, if the number of steps is doubled, the net mean square displacement of the walk is increased by a factor of 2^ν. For one-dimensional random walks, we find from (11.5) that $\nu = 1/2$. In many of the problems we will consider in this chapter, we will determine if power law behavior exists and if the exponent ν depends on the structure and dimension of the lattice as well as on the nature of the walk.

PROBLEM 11.3 Asymptotic properties of random walks in one dimension

a. Make a log-log plot of $<\Delta x_N^2>$ versus N and estimate the exponent ν defined by (11.11). A least-square analysis of the estimate for ν is given in Appendix 11A.

b. Another interesting property of random walks is the mean number $<S_N>$ of *distinct* lattice sites visited during the course of an N-step walk. Do a Monte Carlo simulation of $<S_N>$ and determine the asymptotic N-dependence of $<S_N>$.

11.3 EXTENSIONS OF RANDOM WALKS

Random walk models are not restricted to one dimension nor are the applications limited to the wanderings of inebriates or molecules. In the following problems, we survey some of the more general and popular random walk models and indicate some of the applications. Other applications are given in the references.

The statistical nature of the random walk problem implies that we either consider a large number of successive walks as in Problems 11.2 and 11.3 or a large number of similar walkers moving at the same time. In the following problem we consider the motion of many walkers all moving at random and independently of one another.

PROBLEM 11.4 A simple random walk problem in two dimensions

Consider a collection of M "bees" which are initially localized in a circle of unit radius centered about the origin. At each time step, each bee moves at random with equal probability to one of four possible directions, north, south, east, or west. The following program implements this algorithm and shows the positions of the bees as points on the screen.

```
PROGRAM random_walk2                    ! random walk in two dimensions
DIM x(200),y(200)
CALL initial(N,M,x,y)
CALL move(N,M,x,y)
END

SUB initial(N,M,x(),y())
    RANDOMIZE
    INPUT prompt "total number of steps = ": N
    INPUT prompt "number of particles = ": M
    LET aspect_ratio = 1.5
    LET ymax = 0.5*N
    LET xmax = aspect_ratio*ymax
    SET window -xmax,xmax,-ymax,ymax
```

```
    ! place particles at random in circle of radius 1
    FOR i = 1 to M
        LET r = 2*rnd - 1
        LET theta = 2*pi*rnd
        LET x(i) = r*cos(theta)
        LET y(i) = r*sin(theta)
        PLOT POINTS: x(i),y(i)
    NEXT i
END SUB

SUB move(N,M,x(),y())
    FOR istep = 1 to N
        FOR i = 1 to M
            CALL choice(i,x,y)
        NEXT i
        CLEAR
        FOR i = 1 to M
            PLOT POINTS: x(i),y(i)
        NEXT i
    NEXT istep
END SUB

SUB choice(i,x(),y())              ! two-dimensional random walk algorithm
    LET prob = rnd
    IF prob <= 0.25 then
        LET x(i) = x(i) + 1
    ELSEIF prob <=0.5 then
        LET x(i) = x(i) - 1
    ELSEIF prob <=0.75 then
        LET y(i) = y(i) - 1
    ELSE
        LET y(i) = y(i) + 1
    END IF
END SUB
```

a. Run **Program random_walk2** and describe the qualitative nature of
the motion of the swarm of bees.

b. Suppose that each bee is placed at random within a circle of unit radius
and is given a random initial velocity in one of the four possible directions.
At each time interval, each bee takes a step of magnitude unity in the same

direction as its original velocity. Is the motion of the swarm of bees changed from the motion of the swarm in part (a)?

c. Use the original random walk formulation and compute $<x_N>$, $<y_N>$, $<\Delta x_N^2>$, and $<\Delta y_N^2>$ as a function of the number of steps N. The average is over all M bees. Also compute the net mean square displacement $<R_N^2>$ defined as

$$<\Delta R_N^2> = <x_N^2> + <y_N^2> - <x_N><x_N> - <y_N><y_N> \qquad . \qquad (11.12)$$

What is the qualitative dependence of these quantities on the number of steps? Compute the N-dependence of R_{max}^2, where R_{max}^2 is the maximum displacement of the bees at step N. Is the N-dependence of R_{max}^2 qualitatively different than the N-dependence of $<\Delta R_N^2>$ for all N?

d. Repeat the calculations of part (c) using the random velocity rather than the random walk formulation. Is there a qualitative difference in the average motion of the bees? If there is, explain the nature and cause of the difference.

In Problem 11.4 we assumed that each step was of equal length and in one of four directions. Hence we implicitly assumed that each walk occurred on a *square* lattice as shown in Fig. 11.3a. The *coordination number z*, the number of nearest neighbor sites, is four for the square lattice. Another useful two-dimensional lattice is the *triangular* lattice (see Fig. 11.3b) for which $z = 6$. As discussed in Chapter 6, two-dimensional solids usually form triangular lattices rather than square lattices. We choose the lattice spacing to be unity unless otherwise stated.

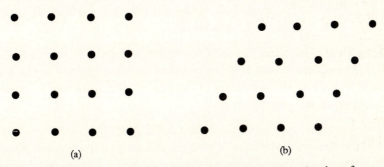

(a)   (b)

Fig. 11.3 (a) Example of a square lattice; each lattice site has four nearest neighbors. (b) Example of a triangular lattice; each lattice site has six nearest neighbors. The vertical distance between rows is $(1/2)\sqrt{3}$. Each row is displaced horizontally by $(1/2)$ from its neighboring rows. The lattice spacing is unity.

Since we will often consider the large N behavior of the net mean square displacement $<\Delta R_N^2>$ (see (11.12)), it is convenient to adopt the notation:

$$R_N \equiv \sqrt{<\Delta R_N^2>} \quad . \tag{11.13}$$

The quantity R_N is known as the *root mean square (rms) displacement* and should not be confused with the absolute value of the vector R_N. The exponent ν is defined by the asymptotic (large N) relation

$$R_N \sim aN^\nu \tag{11.14}$$

where a in (11.14) is a constant of the order of unity.

PROBLEM 11.5 Random walks on two and three-dimensional lattices

a. Enumerate all random walks on a square lattice for $N = 4$ and obtain exact results for $<x_N>$, $<y_N>$ and $<\Delta R_N^2>$. Write a Monte Carlo program to determine $<x_N>$, $<y_N>$ and $<\Delta R_N^2>$ and verify your program by comparing your Monte Carlo and exact enumeration results. Consider the case where all four directions are equally probable.

b. Do a Monte Carlo simulation of R_N for $N = 8$, 16, 32, and 64 and a reasonable number of trials for each value of N. Note that in general the estimated mean values $<x_N>$ and $<y_N>$ will not be identically zero and best results are obtained by calculating R_N directly from its definition (11.12) and (11.13). Estimate the exponent ν from a log-log plot of R_N versus N. If $\nu \approx 1/2$, estimate the magnitude of the self-diffusion constant D as defined by (11.6) with the "time" t replaced by N.

*c. Do a Monte Carlo simulation of R_N on the triangular lattice and estimate ν. Can you conclude that ν is independent of the symmetry of the lattice? Does D depend on the symmetry of the lattice? If it does, give a qualitative explanation of this dependence.

*d. What are the appropriate generalizations of $<R_N^2>$, $<\Delta R_N^2>$, and R_N for a three-dimensional lattice? Calculate R_N for a simple three-dimensional cubic lattice ($z = 6$) and estimate ν. Does ν depend on the spatial dimension?

*e. Consider a random walker on a square lattice which starts at a site a distance h above a horizontal line (see Fig. 11.4). Assume that the probability $p_\downarrow$ of a step "down" is greater than the probability $p_\uparrow$ of a step "up". Since $p_\downarrow > p_\uparrow$, we expect that after a certain number of steps, the walker will be

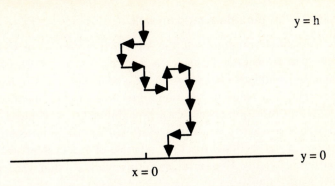

Fig. 11.4 Example of the random "fall" of a raindrop from a height h to the ground.

"absorbed" at a site on the horizontal line. Reasonable values for the jump probabilities are $p_\downarrow = 0.5$, $p_\uparrow = 0.1$ and $p_\rightarrow = p_\leftarrow = 0.2$. Do a Monte Carlo simulation to determine the mean time τ for the walker to reach a site on the horizontal line and determine the functional dependence of τ on h. Is it possible to define a velocity for motion in the vertical direction? Since the walker does not always move vertically, it suffers a net displacement x in the horizontal direction. How does $<\Delta x^2>$ depend on h and τ? This random walk might be thought of as an idealized model of a rain drop in the presence of a random swirling breeze.

PROBLEM 11.6 Random walk on a continuum

One of the first continuum models of a random walk is due to Rayleigh (1919). In the Rayleigh model the length a of each step is a random variable with probability density $p(a)$ and the direction of each step is random. For simplicity consider two dimensions and choose $p(a)$ so that each step has unit length. Hence at each step the walker takes a step of unit length at a random angle. Write a Monte Carlo program to compute $P_N(r)dr$, the probability that the walker is in the range r to $r + dr$, where r is the distance from the origin after N steps. Show that for sufficiently large N, your computed value of $P_N(r)$ can be *approximated* by a Gaussian. Is a Gaussian a good approximation for small N? Is it necessary to do a Monte Carlo simulation to confirm that $R_N \sim N^{1/2}$ or can you give a simple argument for this dependence based on the form of P_N?

*PROBLEM 11.7 A persistent random walk

In a "persistent" random walk the *transition* or "jump" probability depends on the last transition. Consider a $d = 1$ walk for which steps are made to nearest neighbor sites only. Suppose that step $N - 1$ has been made. Then step N is made in the same direction with probability α; a step in the opposite direction occurs with probability $1 - \alpha$. A physical example of such a walk is a particle which is scattered by fixed scattering centers with anistropic cross sections. Another example of a persistent walk is discussed in part (c). Modify **Program random_walk** so that you can perform a Monte Carlo simulation of $<\Delta x_N^2>$ and $P_N(x)$. Note that it is necessary to specify both the initial position and initial state of the walker. What is the $\alpha = 1/2$ limit of the persistent random walk?

a. Consider the two cases $\alpha = 0.25$ and $\alpha = 0.75$ and determine $<\Delta x_N^2>$ for $N = 8$, 64, 256, and 512. Estimate the value of ν from the asymptotic N-dependence of $<\Delta x_N^2>$. Does ν depend on α? If $\nu \approx 1/2$, determine the self-diffusion constant D for $\alpha = 0.25$ and 0.75. Give a physical argument why $D(\alpha \neq 0.5)$ is greater (smaller) than $D(\alpha = 0.5)$.

b. Determine $P_N(x)$ as a function of x for $\alpha = 0.25$ and $N = 2$, 4, 6, and 10. Define a "speed of propagation" c by the relation $P_N(x) = 0$ for $x > cN$. Estimate c from a plot of the x-dependence of $P_N(x)$ for different values of N. Do your estimates of c approach a limiting value? Do a similar analysis for the usual random walk. Do your estimates of c approach a limiting value in this case?

c. A persistent random walk can also be considered as an example of a *multistate* walk in which the state of the walk is defined by the last transition. For example, consider the walker to be in one of two states; at each step the probabilities of remaining in the same state or switching states are α and $1 - \alpha$ respectively. One of the earliest applications of a two-state random walk was to the study of diffusion in a chromatographic column. Suppose that a molecule in a chromatographic column can be either in a mobile phase (constant velocity w) or a trapped phase (zero velocity). A quantity of experimental interest is the probability $P_N(x)$ that a molecule has traveled a distance x in N steps. Choose $w = 1$ and $\alpha = 0.75$ and compute the qualitative behavior of $P_N(x)$. Although the molecule cannot diffuse in either state, is it possible to define an effective diffusion constant for the molecule?

The fall of a raindrop considered in Problem 11.5e is an example of a restricted random walk, i.e. a walk in the presence of a boundary. In the following problem, we discuss in a more general context the effects of various types of restrictions or boundaries on random walks. Another example of a restricted random walk is given in Problem 11.16.

*PROBLEM 11.8 Restricted random walks

a. Consider a one-dimensional lattice which has "trap" sites at $x = 0$ and $x = a$ $(a > 0)$. A random walker begins at site x_0 $(0 < x_0 < a)$ and steps to nearest neighbor sites with equal probability. Do a Monte Carlo simulation and verify that the mean *first passage time* τ for the particle to be trapped is given by

$$\tau = (2D)^{-1}x_0(a - x_0) \quad . \tag{11.15}$$

D is the self-diffusion constant in the absence of the traps and the average is over all possible walks.

b. Random walk models in the presence of traps have had an important role in condensed matter science. For example, consider the following idealized model of energy transport in solids. The solid is represented as a lattice with two types of sites: hosts and traps. An incident photon is absorbed at a host site and excites the molecule. The excitation energy or *exciton* is transferred at random to one of its nearest neighbors and the original excited molecule returns to its ground state. The exciton wanders through the lattice until it reaches a trap site. The exciton is then trapped and a physical process such as a chemical reaction occurs.

One version of this energy transport model is a one-dimensional lattice with traps placed on a periodic sublattice. Since the traps are placed at regular intervals, we can replace the random walk on an infinite lattice by a random walk on a ring (see Fig. 11.5). Consider a ring of N host or non-trapping sites and one trap site. If a walker has the same probability of starting from any host site and has an equal probability of jumping to nearest neighbor sites, what is the N-dependence of the mean survival time τ (the mean number of steps taken before a trap site is reached)? Use the results of part (a) rather than doing another simulation.

c. A famous version of a first passage time problem is the "gambler's ruin." Suppose that two gamblers each begin with \$10 in capital and on each throw of the die, one gambler must win \$1 and the other must lose \$1. How

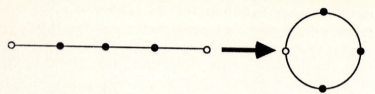

Fig. 11.5 Equivalency of a regular lattice of traps with periodicity four and a ring of $N = 3$ host sites with one trap site. The trap sites are denoted as open circles.

long can they play on the average until the capital of the loser is exhausted? How long can they play if they each begin with $100? (Unlike real life, neither gambler is allowed to go into debt.)

d. A crystalline solid is never perfect but contains a variety of *defects.* The simplest imperfection is a lattice vacancy, e.g. the absence of an atom from a lattice site and the placement of an additional atom on the surface. At finite temperature, a certain number of lattice vacancies are always present in an otherwise perfect crystal. In many cases the vacancy diffuses by exchanging places at random with neighboring atoms. Assume that at $t = 0$, a vacancy is at the center of a circle of radius r. Do a Monte Carlo simulation to determine the mean time for the vacancy to reach the surface of a metal a distance r away. What is the probability distribution for this first passage time?

e. Consider a one-dimensional lattice with reflecting sites at $x = -a$ and $x = a$. That is, if a walker reaches the reflecting site at $x = a$, it is reflected at the next step to $x = a - 1$. At $t = 0$, the walker starts at $x = 0$ and steps with equal probability to nearest neighbor sites. Write a Monte Carlo program to determine $P_N(x)$, the probability that the walker is at site x after N steps. Compare the form of $P_N(x)$ with and without the presence of the reflecting "walls." Can you distinguish the two probability distributions if N is the order of a? At what value of N can you first distinguish the two distributions?

Although all of the above problems involved random walks on a lattice, it was not necessary to store the positions of the lattice sites or the path of the walker. In the following problem, we consider a random walk model which requires us to store the lattice positions of a "gas" of random walkers.

*PROBLEM 11.9 Individual particle diffusion in a lattice gas

Consider a nonzero concentration c of random walkers (particles) on a square lattice. Each particle moves at random to *empty* nearest-neighbor sites but double occupancy of sites is excluded; otherwise the particles are noninteracting. Such a model is an example of a *lattice gas*. Note that the motion of an individual particle is correlated with the motion of the other particles. The physical motivation of this model arises from metal physics where diffusion is caused by thermal vacancies whose concentration depends on the temperature. The main physical quantity of interest is the self-diffusion constant D of an individual (tagged or tracer) particle. The algorithm for a Monte Carlo simulation of D can be stated as follows:

1. Occupy the lattice sites at random with a concentration c of particles. (Remember that $0 < c \leq 1$.) Tag each particle (i.e. distinguish it from the others) and record its initial position in an array.

2. At each step choose a particle at random and choose one of its neighboring sites. If the neighboring site is empty, the particle is moved to this site; otherwise the particle remains in its present position.

The measure of "time" in this context is arbitrary. The usual definition which we will use often is that one unit of time corresponds to one *Monte Carlo step per particle*. During one Monte Carlo step per particle, each particle attempts one jump *on the average*. The diffusion constant D is obtained as the limit $t \to \infty$ of $D(t)$, where $D(t)$ is given by

$$D(t) = \frac{1}{2dt} <\Delta R(t)^2> \tag{11.16}$$

and $<\Delta R(t)^2>$ is the net mean-square displacement per tagged particle after t units of time. An example of a program which implements this algorithm is given in the following.

```
PROGRAM lattice_gas
DIM site(30,30)
DIM x(200),y(200),xinitial(200),yinitial(200)
CALL initial(L,N,nmcs)
CALL lattice(L,N,site,x,y,xinitial,yinitial)
FOR t = 1 to nmcs
    CALL move(L,N,site,x,y,xinitial,yinitial)
    CALL data(L,N,t,x,y,xinitial,yinitial)
NEXT t
END
```

```
SUB initial(L,N,nmcs)
   RANDOMIZE
   LET L = 30                                    ! linear dimension of lattice
   INPUT prompt "number of particles = ": N      ! number of particles
   PRINT "concentration = "; N/(L*L)
   LET nmcs = 10                                 ! number of Monte Carlo steps per particle
   PRINT "time t","R2(t)"
END SUB

SUB lattice(L,N,site(,),x(),y(),xinitial(),yinitial())
   DO
      LET xadd = int(L*rnd + 1)
      LET yadd = int(L*rnd + 1)
      IF site(xadd,yadd) = 0 then
         LET i = i + 1                           ! number of particles added
         LET site(xadd,yadd) = -1                ! site occupied
         LET xinitial(i),x(i) = xadd             ! x-coordinate at t = 0
         LET yinitial(i),y(i) = yadd
      END IF
   LOOP until i = N
END SUB

SUB move(L,N,site(,),x(),y(),xinitial(),yinitial())
   FOR imove = 1 to N
      LET itrial = int(N*rnd + 1)
      LET xtrial = x(itrial)
      LET ytrial = y(itrial)
      CALL random(xtrial,ytrial,L)
      IF site(xtrial,ytrial) = 0 then            ! unoccupied site
         LET site(x(itrial),y(itrial)) = 0
         LET x(itrial) = xtrial
         LET y(itrial) = ytrial
         LET site(x(itrial),y(itrial)) = -1      ! new site occupied
      END IF
   NEXT imove
END SUB
```

```
SUB random(xtemp,ytemp,L)
    ! choose random direction and use periodic boundary conditions
    LET direction = int(4*rnd + 1)
    SELECT CASE direction
    CASE 1
        LET xtemp = xtemp + 1
        IF xtemp > L then LET xtemp = xtemp - L
    CASE 2
        LET xtemp = xtemp - 1
        IF xtemp < 1 then LET xtemp = L + xtemp
    CASE 3
        LET ytemp = ytemp + 1
        IF ytemp > L then LET ytemp = ytemp - L
    CASE 4
        LET ytemp = ytemp - 1
        IF ytemp < 1 then LET ytemp = L + ytemp
    END SELECT
END SUB


SUB separation(dx,dy,L)
    LET L2 = 0.5*L       ! use periodic boundary conditions to determine separation
    IF abs(dx) > L2 then LET dx = dx - sgn(dx)*L
    IF abs(dy) > L2 then LET dy = dy - sgn(dy)*L
END SUB


SUB data(L,N,t,x(),y(),xinitial(),yinitial())
    FOR i = 1 to N
        LET dx = x(i) - xinitial(i)
        LET dy = y(i) - yinitial(i)
        CALL separation(dx,dy,L)
        LET R2 = R2 + dx*dx + dy*dy
    NEXT i
    LET R2cum = R2cum + R2
    LET R2bar = R2cum/N
    PRINT t,R2bar
END SUB
```

a. Do a Monte Carlo simulation to determine D on a square lattice for $c = 0.1$, 0.2, 0.3, 0.5, and 0.7. Although D is defined as the limit $t \to \infty$ of (11.16), in practice $D(t)$ fluctuates with t and no improvement in accuracy is achieved by increasing t. Better statistics for D can be obtained by averaging D over as many tagged particles as possible and hence by considering a lattice with L, the linear dimension of the lattice, as large as possible. Why is it necessary to limit the number of Monte Carlo steps such that $<\Delta R(t)^2>$ be less than $(L/2)^2$? The accuracy of D can also be increased by averaging $<\Delta R(t)^2>$ over different initial starting times. Show that deviations of $D(t)$ from its correct value are proportional to the inverse square root of the total number of particles which enter into the average in (11.16).

b. Why is D a monotonically decreasing function of the concentration c? Determine the concentration dependence of the probability that if a particle jumps to a vacancy at time t, it returns to its original position at time $t + 1$. Try to determine a qualitative relation between the concentration dependence of D and this probability.

c. Consider a one-dimensional lattice model for which particles move at random but double occupancy of sites is excluded. The latter restriction implies that particles cannot pass by each other. Calculate $<\Delta x^2>$ as a function of t. Do the particles diffuse, i.e. is $<\Delta x^2>$ proportional to t? If not, what is the t-dependence of $<\Delta x^2>$?

PROBLEM 11.10 The central limit theorem

Consider a random variable x with probability density $f(x)$. The mth *moment* of $f(x)$ is defined as

$$<x^m> = \int dx \, x^m f(x) \quad . \tag{11.17}$$

The mean value $<x>$ is given by (11.17) with $m = 1$. The variance σ_x^2 of $f(x)$ is defined as

$$\sigma_x^2 = <x^2> - <x>^2 \quad . \tag{11.18}$$

Consider the sum y_n corresponding to the average of n values of x:

$$y_n = (x_1 + x_2 + \ldots + x_n)/n \quad . \tag{11.19}$$

We adopt the notation $y = y_n$. Suppose that we make many measurements of y. We know that the values of y will not be identical but will be distributed according to a probability density $P(y)$, where $P(y)\Delta y$ is the probability that the measured value of y is in the range y to $y + \Delta y$. The main quantities of interest are the mean $<y>$, the standard deviation $\sigma_y{}^2 = <y^2> - <y>^2$, and $P(y)$ itself.

a. Suppose that $f(x)$ is uniform in the interval $[-1, 1]$. Calculate $<x>$ and σ_x analytically. Use Monte Carlo methods to make a sufficient number of measurements of y to determine $P(y), <y>$ and σ_y with reasonable accuracy. (For example choose $n = 500$ and make 100 measurements of y.) Show that σ_y is approximately equal to $\sigma_x/\sqrt{n}$. Plot $P(y)$ versus y and discuss its qualitative form. Does the form of $P(y)$ change significantly if n is increased? Does the form of $P(y)$ change if the number of measurements of y is increased?

b. In order to test the generality of the results of part (a), consider the exponential probability density

$$f(x) = \begin{cases} exp(-x), & \text{if } x \geq 0; \\ 0, & \text{if } x < 0 \end{cases} \qquad (11.20)$$

Calculate $<x>$ and σ_x analytically. Modify the Monte Carlo program of part (a) to determine $P(y)$, $<y>$, and σ_y. Is σ_y related to σ_x as in part (a)? Plot $P(y)$ and discuss its qualitative form and its dependence on the number of measurements of y.

c. Let y be the Monte Carlo estimate of the integral

$$4 \int_0^1 dx \sqrt{1 - x^2} \qquad (11.21)$$

(See Problem 10.5a.) In this case y is found by sampling the integrand $f(x) = 4\sqrt{1 - x^2}$ n times. Choose $n = 1000$ and make 100 measurements of y. Show that the values of y are distributed according to a Gaussian. How is the standard deviation of $P(y)$ related to the standard deviation of $f(x)$?

d. Consider the Lorentzian probability density

$$f(x) = \frac{a}{\pi} \frac{1}{x^2 + a^2} \qquad (11.22)$$

with $a = 1$. What is the mean value $<x>$? Does the second moment and hence the variance of $f(x)$ exist? Perform a Monte Carlo calculation of $P(y)$, $<y>$, and σ_y. Plot $P(y)$ as a function of y and discuss its qualitative form. What is the dependence of $P(y)$ on the number of trials?

PROBLEM 11.11 Random walks with steps of variable length

a. Consider a random walk in one dimension with jumps of all lengths allowed. The probability that the length of a single step is magnitude j is denoted by $p(j)$. If the form of $p(j)$ is given by $p(j) = e^{-j}$, what is the form of $P_N(x)$? Suggestions: Use the inverse transform method discussed in Sec. 10.7 to generate step lengths according to the probability density $p(j)$. Then generate a walk of N-steps and determine the net displacement x. Generate many such walks and determine $P_N(x)$. Plot $P_N(x)$ versus x and confirm that the form of $P_N(x)$ is consistent with a Gaussian distribution. Is this random walk equivalent to a diffusion process?

b. Consider the lattice random walk of part (a) with the step probability $p(j)$ given by $p(j) = A/j^2$. Determine the normalization constant A using

$$\sum_{j=1}^{\infty} \frac{1}{j^2} = \frac{\pi^2}{6} \qquad (11.23)$$

and the requirement that $p(j)$ be normalized to unity. Does the second moment of $p(j)$ exist? Do you expect the probability $P_N(x)$ to be a Gaussian? Perform a Monte Carlo simulation as in part (a) and verify that the form of $P_N(x)$ is given by

$$P_N(x) \sim \frac{bN}{x^2 + b^2 N^2} \qquad (11.24)$$

What is the magnitude of the constant b? Does the variance of $P_N(x)$ exist? Is this random walk equivalent to a diffusion process?

Parts (a)–(d) of Problem 11.10 are examples of the *central limit theorem* which states that the probability distribution of a large number of measurements of y will be a Gaussian centered at $<y>$ with a standard deviation $1/\sqrt{n}$ times the standard deviation of $f(x)$. The only requirements are that $f(x)$ has finite first and second moments, that the measurements of y are statistically independent, and that n is large. Use the central limit theorem to explain your results in Problem 11.10 and in Problem 11.11(a). What is the relation of the present calculation of $P(y)$ to the calculations of the probability distribution in the random walk models considered earlier?

PROBLEM 11.12 The Gaussian distribution

Consider the sum

$$y = \sum_{i=1}^{12} r_i \tag{11.25}$$

where r_i is a uniform deviate in the interval $[0, 1]$. Make many "measurements" of y and show that the probability distribution of y approximates the Gaussian distribution with mean value 6 and variance 1. Discuss how to use this result to generate a Gaussian distribution with arbitrary mean and variance.

11.4 APPLICATIONS TO POLYMERS

There are few research areas in which random walk models play as important a role as in polymer physics (cf de Gennes). The earliest investigations (1934) of polymer configurations were phrased in terms of random walks. Over the past 50 years our understanding of the statistical properties of long, flexible polymer chains and of random walks has developed in parallel.

A polymer consists of N repeat units or monomers with N very large ($N \sim 10^3$—10^5). For example, the repeat unit for polyethylene can be represented as $\ldots - CH_2 - CH_2 - CH_2 - \ldots$. The detailed structure of the polymer is important for many practical applications. For example, if we want to improve the fabrication of rubber, a good understanding of the local motions of a rubber chain are essential. However if we are interested in the *global* properties of the polymer, the details of the chain structure can be ignored.

Let us consider a familiar example, a piece of spaghetti in warm water. After a short time the spaghetti becomes flexible and behaves as a polymer chain in a good solvent. That is, the spaghetti neither collapses into a little ball or becomes fully stretched. Rather it adopts a random structure as shown schematically in Fig. 11.6. We say that the spaghetti behaves as a dilute solution of polymer chains in a good solvent. The dilute nature of the solution implies that we can ignore entanglement effects of the chains and consider each chain individually. The presence of a "good" solvent implies that the polymers can move freely and hence adopt many different configurations. One fundamental geometrical property which can be used to characterize the polymer is the rms end-to-end distance R_N, where R_N is defined as in (11.13) and N is the number of monomers. It is known that for a dilute solution of polymer chains in a good solvent,

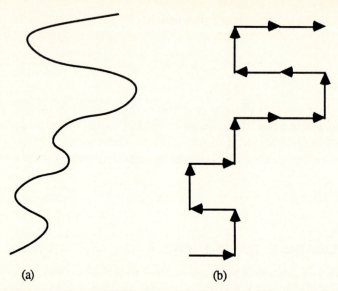

(a)   (b)

Fig. 11.6 (a) Schematic illustration of a linear polymer in a good
solvent. (b) Example of the corresponding walk on the square lattice.

the asymptotic dependence of R_N is given by (11.14) with the exponent $\nu \approx 3/5$
for *all* flexible chains in a good solvent. The result for ν in two dimensions is
known to be exactly $\nu = 3/4$. The prefactor a in (11.14) depends on the structure
of the monomers and on the solvent.

  We now discuss a random walk model which includes the global features of
linear polymers in solution. We have already discussed a model of a polymer
chain consisting of straight-line segments of the same size joined together at random angles (see Problem 11.6). A further idealization is to place the polymer
chain on a lattice see (Fig. 11.6b). If we ignore the interactions of the monomers,
we know that we obtain a Gaussian chain with $\nu = 1/2$ independent of dimension and the structure of the lattice. Since this result for ν is not in agreement
with experiment, we need to consider a more realistic model of a chain which
accounts for the most important physical feature of a polymer—two monomers
cannot occupy the same spatial position. This constraint, known as the "excluded volume" condition, implies that the walk cannot be adequately described
by a purely random walk model. The standard lattice model for a flexible polymer chain is known as the "self-avoiding" walk (SAW). Consider the set of all
N-step walks emanating from the origin subject to the global constraint that no
lattice site can be visited more than once in each walk; the constraint accounts
for the excluded volume condition. Calculation of the properties of the SAW is

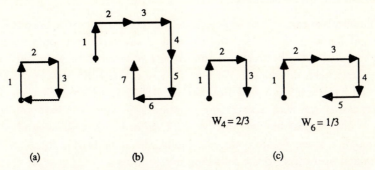

Fig. 11.7 Examples of self-avoiding walks on the square lattice. The origin is denoted by a filled circle. (a) The $N = 4$ walk is forbidden. (b) The $N = 8$ step leads to a self-intersection and the weight of the walk is zero. (c) Examples of weights of walks in the Rosenbluth enrichment method.

formidable and computer enumeration and Monte Carlo simulation have played an important role in our current understanding. We consider Monte Carlo simulations of the SAW in two dimensions in Problem 11.13.

PROBLEM 11.13 Monte Carlo simulation of the two-dimensional SAW

a. Consider the SAW on the square lattice. It is convenient to represent the lattice as a two-dimensional array; the array is used to record the sites which have been visited. Choose an arbitrary site as the origin and assume that the first step is "north," since the walks generated by the three other possible initial steps only differ by a rotation. Note that the second step can be in three possible directions. In order to obtain unbiased results, we generate a random integer $(1, 2$ or $3)$ to choose one of the three directions. Successive steps are generated in the same manner. Unfortunately the walk will not usually continue indefinitely in this manner. Consider the $N = 3$ walk shown in Fig. 11.7a. The next step shown in the figure leads to a self-intersection and hence violates the constraint. In order to obtain unbiased results, we must generate a random number $(1, 2, 3)$ as usual. If the next step leads to a self-intersection, the walk is terminated and a new walk is started at the origin. Write a program which implements this algorithm and record the fraction $f(N)$ of successful attempts to construct polymer chains with N total links (steps). What is the qualitative dependence of $f(N)$ on N?

What is the maximum value of N you can reasonably consider? Determine R_N for several different values of N.

b. The disadvantage of the above sampling method is that it becomes very inefficient for long chains, i.e. the fraction of successful attempts decreases exponentially fast. To overcome this attrition, several "enrichment" techniques have been developed. We first discuss a relatively simple procedure proposed by Rosenbluth and Rosenbluth (1955) in which each walk of N-steps is associated with a weighting function W_N. Since the first step to the north is always possible, we have $W_1 = 1$. In order that all allowed configurations of a given N are counted equally, the weights W_N for $N > 1$ are determined according to the following possibilities:

1. All three possible steps violate the self-intersection constraint (see for example Fig. 11.7b). The walk is terminated with a weight $W_N = 0$ and a new walk is generated at the origin.

2. All three steps are possible and $W_N = W_{N-1}$.

3. Only m steps are possible with $1 \leq m < 3$ (see Fig. 11.7c). Then $W_N = (m/3)W_{N-1}$ and a random number is used to choose one of the m possible steps.

The correct value of $<R_N^2>$ is obtained by weighting $R_{N,i}^2$, the value of R_N^2 obtained in the ith trial, by the value of W_N which we denote as $W_{N,i}$. Hence we have

$$<R_N^2> = \sum_i W_{N,i} R_{N,i}^2 / \sum_i W_{N,i} \qquad (11.26)$$

where the sum is over all trials. Incorporate the Rosenbluth method into your Monte Carlo program and calculate R_N for $N = 4, 8, 16$, and 32. Estimate the exponent ν from a log-log plot of R_N versus N. Can you distinguish your estimate for ν from its random walk value $\nu = 1/2$?

---

*PROBLEM 11.14 Application of the reptation method

One of the more efficient enrichment methods is the "reptation" method (see references). For simplicity, we discuss a model polymer chain in which all bond angles are 90°. As an example of this model, the five independent $N = 5$ polymer chains are shown in Fig. 11.8. (Other chains differ only by a rotation or a reflection.) The reptation method can be stated as follows:

1. Choose a chain at random and remove the tail link.

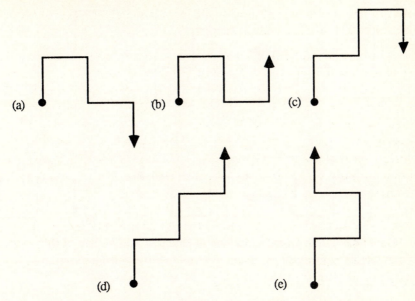

Fig. 11.8 The five independent possible walks of $N = 5$ steps on a square lattice with 90° bond angles. The tail and head of each walk are denoted by a circle and arrow respectively.

2. Attempt to add a link to the head of the chain. There is a maximum of two directions in which the new head link can be added.

3. If the attempt violates the self-intersection constraint, return to the original chain and interchange the head and tail. Include the chain in the statistical sample.

The above steps are repeated many times to obtain a statistical average of R_N^2.

As an example of the reptation method, suppose we choose chain a of Fig. 11.8. A new link can be added in two directions (see Fig. 11.9a) so that on the average we find, $a \rightarrow \frac{1}{2}c + \frac{1}{2}d$. In contrast, a link can be added to chain b in only one direction, and we obtain $b \rightarrow \frac{1}{2}e + \frac{1}{2}b$, where the tail and head of chain b have been interchanged (see Fig. 11.9b). Confirm that $c \rightarrow \frac{1}{2}e + \frac{1}{2}a$, $d \rightarrow \frac{1}{2}c + \frac{1}{2}d$, and $e \rightarrow \frac{1}{2}a + \frac{1}{2}b$, and that hence all five chains are equally probable. That is, the transformations in the reptation method preserve the proper statistical weights of the chains without attrition. There is just one problem: unless we begin with a double ended "cul-de-sac" configuration

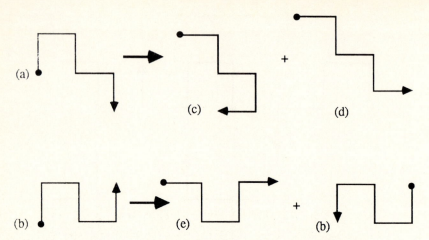

Fig. 11.9 The possible transformations of chains a and b. One of the two possible transformations of chain b violates the self-intersection restriction and so instead the head and tail are interchanged.

such as shown in Fig. 11.10, we will never obtain such a configuration using the above transformation. Hence we see that the reptation method introduces a small bias to our statistical sample and the calculated mean end-to-end distance will be slightly larger than if all configurations were considered. However the probability of such "trapped" configurations is very small, and the bias can be neglected for most purposes.

Adopt the 90° bond angle restriction and calculate by hand the exact value of $< R_N^2 >$ for $N = 5$. Then write a Monte Carlo program which implements the reptation method. Generate one walk of $N = 5$ and use the reptation method to generate a statistical sample of chains. As a check on your Monte Carlo program, compute $<R_N^2>$ and compare your two results for $<R_N^2>$. Then extend your Monte Carlo computations of $<R_N^2>$ to larger N.

A model which is easier to study and which describes the statistics of a special type of linear polymer in solution is the "true" self-avoiding walk (TSAW). The TSAW describes the path of a random walker which is constrained to avoid visiting a lattice site with a probability which is a function of the number of times

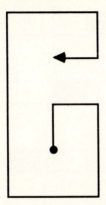

Fig. 11.10 Example of a double cul-de-sac configuration for the usual self-avoiding walk which cannot be obtained by the reptation method.

the site has already been visited. This constraint leads to a reduced excluded volume interaction in comparison to the usual self-avoiding walk. The TSAW is considered in Problem 11.15.

PROBLEM 11.15 The "true" self-avoiding walk in one dimension

The TSAW in one dimension corresponds to a walker who can "jump" to one of two nearest neighbors with a probability that depends on the number of times these neighbors have already been visited. Suppose that the walker is at site i at step t. The walker has already visited site $i + 1$ a number of times n_{i+1} and has already visited site $i - 1$ a number of times n_{i-1}. Then the probability that at step $t + 1$, the walker will jump to site $i + 1$ is given by

$$P_{i+1} = \frac{e^{-gn_{i+1}}}{e^{-gn_{i+1}} + e^{-gn_{i-1}}} \quad . \tag{11.27}$$

The probability of a jump to site $i - 1$ is $P_{i-1} = 1 - P_{i+1}$. The parameter g ($g > 0$) is a measure of the "desire" of the path to avoid itself. The first few steps of a typical TSAW walk are shown in Fig. 11.11. The main quantity of interest is the exponent ν. We know that $g = 0$ corresponds to the usual random walk with $\nu = 1/2$ and that the limit $g \to \infty$ corresponds to the self-avoiding walk. What is the value of ν for a self-avoiding walk in one

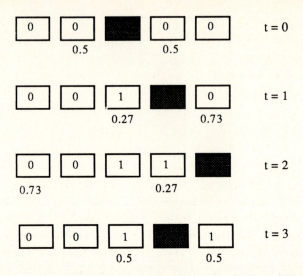

Fig. 11.11 Example of the time evolution of the true self-avoiding walk with $g = 1$. The shaded site represents the location of the walker at time t. The number of visits to each site are given within each site and the probability of a step to a nearest neighbor site is given below it.

dimension? Is the value of ν for any finite value of g different than these two limiting cases? We explore these questions in the following.

a. Write a program to do a Monte Carlo simulation of the one-dimensional TSAW. Keep a record of the total number of visits to every site. At each step calculate the probability P of a jump to the right. Generate a random number r and compare it to P. If $r \leq P$, then move the walker to the right; otherwise move the walker to the left. Use the same sequence of random numbers to compare the paths of the TSAW for $g = 0.1$ and for the usual random walk ($g = 0$).

b. Calculate $<\Delta x_N^2>$, where x is the distance of the walker from the origin, as a function of the number of steps N. Make a log-log plot of $<\Delta x_N^2>$ versus N and estimate ν. Can you distinguish ν from its random walk and self-avoiding walk values? Reasonable choices of parameters are $g = 0.1$ and a maximum N of 1000 steps. Averages over 100 trials will give qualitative results. For comparison, the published results of Bernasconi and Pietronero are for $N = 10,000$ steps and $1,000$ trials; extended results for $g = 2$ are given for 200,000 steps and 10,000 trials.

Many of the above problems have revealed the slow convergence of Monte Carlo simulations and the difficulty of obtaining quantitative results for asymptotic quantities such as the exponent ν. We conclude this section with a cautionary note and consider a "simple" problem for which straightforward Monte Carlo methods give misleading asymptotic results.

*PROBLEM 11.16 Random walk on lattices containing traps

a. We have already considered the mean survival time of a one-dimensional random walker in the presence of a periodic distribution of traps (see Problem 11.8b). Now suppose that trap sites are distributed at random on a one-dimensional lattice with concentration c. If a walker is placed at random at any non-trap site, determine its mean survival time τ, the mean number of steps taken before a trap site is reached. Assume that the walker has equal probability of moving to nearest neighbor sites at each step and use periodic boundary conditions. This problem is more difficult than it might appear initially, and indeed there are a number of pitfalls waiting for you! The major problem is that it is necessary to perform *three* averages: the distribution of traps, the initial position of the walker, and the different possible walks for a given initial position and distribution of traps. Choose reasonable values for the number of trials associated with each average and do a Monte Carlo simulation of the mean lifetime τ. If τ exhibits a power-law dependence, e.g. $\tau \approx \tau_0 c^{-z}$, estimate the exponent z. Think of a simple argument for the magnitude of z.

b. A seemingly straightforward extension of part (a) is to do a Monte Carlo simulation of the probability of survival P_n of an n-step random walk. Choose $c = 0.5$ and do a Monte Carlo simulation of P_n for n as large as possible. (Published results (Havlin et al.) are for $50,000$ trials and $2,000$ steps on lattices of $50,000$ sites.) Assume that for $n \gg 1$, the form of P_n is given by

$$ln\, P_n \sim -bn^{\alpha} \qquad (n \to \infty) \qquad (11.28)$$

where b is a constant which depends on concentration. Are your results consistent with the form (11.28)? Is it possible to make a meaningful estimate of the exponent α?

c. The object of part (b) is to convince you that in practice, it is not possible to use Monte Carlo methods to obtain the correct asymptotic behavior of P_n. The problem is that we are trying to estimate P_n in the asymptotic region

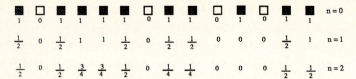

Fig. 11.12 An example of the exact enumeration of walks on a given configuration of traps. The filled and empty squares denote regular and trap sites respectively. At step $n = 0$, a walker is placed at each regular site. The numbers at each site i represent the number of walkers W_i. Periodic boundary conditions are used. The initial number of walkers in this example is $N_0 = 10$. The mean survival probability at step $n = 1$ and $n = 2$ is found to be 0.6 and 0.45 respectively.

where P_n is very small; the inherent fluctuations of the Monte Carlo method prevent us from obtaining meaningful results in a reasonable time. It has been proved using analytical methods, that the asymptotic n-dependence of P_n does have the form (11.28) but with $\alpha = 1/3$. Are your Monte Carlo results consistent with this value of α?

Fortunately there is a better approach which reduces the number of averages and which consequently reduces the fluctuations. The essence of the method is to determine exactly, for a given distribution of trap sites, the probability that the walker is at site i after n steps. The method is illustrated in Fig. 11.12. The first line represents a given configuration of traps distributed randomly on a one-dimensional lattice. In the second line, one walker is placed at each regular site; trap sites are assigned the value 0. Since each walker moves with probability 1/2 to each neighbor, the number of walkers $W_{n+1}(i)$ on site i at step $n + 1$ is given by

$$W_{n+1}(i) = \frac{1}{2}[W_n(i + 1) + W_n(i - 1)] \quad . \tag{11.29}$$

(Compare the relation (11.29) to the relation which you derived in Problem 11.1a.) The survival probability P_n after n steps for a given configuration of traps is given exactly by

$$P_n = \frac{1}{N_0} \sum_i W_n(i) \tag{11.30}$$

where N_0 is the initial number of walkers and the sum is over all sites in the lattice. Write a program to calculate P_n using this exact enumeration procedure and obtain the average $<P_n>$ over several configurations of traps. Choose $c = 0.5$ and determine the survival probability for $n = 32, 64, 128, 512,$ and 1024. Choose periodic boundary conditions and a lattice of sufficient size. How well can you estimate the exponent α? (For comparison, Havlin et al. consider a lattice of $50,000$ sites and values of n up to 10^7.)

11.5 THE CONTINUUM LIMIT

It is instructive to consider the continuum limit of the one-dimensional random walk model considered in Sec. 11.2. If there is an equal probability of taking a step to the right or left, the random walk can be written in terms of the simple "master" equation

$$P_n(i) = \frac{1}{2}P_{n-1}(i+1) + \frac{1}{2}P_{n-1}(i-1) \qquad (11.31)$$

where $P_n(i)$ is the probability that the walker is at site i after n steps. In order to obtain a differential equation for the probability density $P(x,t)$, we set $t = n\tau$, $x = ia$ and $P_n(i) = aP(x,t)$, where τ is the time between steps and a is the lattice spacing. This notation allows us to rewrite (11.31) in the equivalent form

$$P(x,t) = \frac{1}{2}P(x+a,t-\tau) + \frac{1}{2}P(x-a,t-\tau) \quad . \qquad (11.32)$$

We subtract $P(x, t - \tau)$ from both sides of (11.32), divide by τ, and rewrite (11.32) as

$$\frac{1}{\tau}[P(x,t) - P(x,t-\tau)] = \frac{a^2}{2\tau}[P(x+a,t-\tau) - 2P(x,t-\tau) + P(x-a,t-\tau)]a^{-2} \quad . \qquad (11.33)$$

By expanding $P(x, t - \tau)$ and $P(x \pm a, t - \tau)$ in a Taylor series and taking the limit $a \rightarrow 0$ and $\tau \rightarrow 0$ with the ratio $D = a^2/2\tau$ finite, we obtain the diffusion equation

$$\frac{\partial P(x,t)}{\partial t} = D\frac{\partial^2 P(x,t)}{\partial x^2} \quad . \qquad (11.34a)$$

The generalization of (11.34a) to three dimensions is

$$\frac{\partial P(x,y,z,t)}{\partial t} = D\nabla^2 P(x,y,z,t) \quad . \qquad (11.34b)$$

where $\nabla^2 = \partial^2/\partial x^2 + \partial^2/\partial y^2 + \partial^2/\partial x^2$ is the Laplacian operator. Equation (11.34) is known as the *diffusion* or *Fokker-Planck* equation and is frequently used to describe the dynamics of fluid molecules. As a "simple" exercise, follow a similar approach to find the form of the differential equation satisfied by $P(x,t)$ for $p \neq q$.

The solution of (11.34a) in free space can be shown to be a Gaussian whose width increases as $t^{1/2}$:

$$P(x,t) = (2\pi Dt)^{-1/2} e^{-x^2/4Dt} \tag{11.35}$$

where $P(x,t)$ is the probability density of finding the particle at point x at time t if the particle started at $x = 0$ at $t = 0$. You can verify that (11.35) is a solution to (11.34a) by direct substitution. We can use (11.35) to obtain

$$<x(t)> = \int_{-\infty}^{\infty} dx \, x P(x,t) = 0 \tag{11.36}$$

and

$$<x^2(t)> = \int_{-\infty}^{\infty} dx \, x^2 P(x,t) = 2Dt \quad . \tag{11.37}$$

We conclude that $<x^2(t)>$ is proportional to t as it is for a random walk on a lattice. The generalization of (11.37) to d dimensions is $<R^2(t)> = 2dDt$ (see (11.6)), where R^2 is the square of the displacement of the particle.

The numerical solution of the prototypical *parabolic* partial differential equation (11.33) is a non-trival problem in numerical analysis (cf Press et al and Koonin.) An indirect method of analysis of (11.34) is to use a Monte Carlo method, that is, replace (11.34) by a corresponding random walk on a lattice with discrete time steps. Since the asymptotic behavior of the partial differential equation and the random walk model are equivalent, this approach uses the Monte Carlo technique as a method of *numerical analysis.* In contrast if our goal is to understand a random walk lattice model directly, the Monte Carlo technique is a *simulation* method. The difference between simulation and numerical analysis sometimes is only in the eyes of the beholder.

11.6 RANDOM NUMBERS

So far we have blissfully used the random number generator supplied with our programming language to generate the desired "random" numbers for our Monte Carlo applications. In principle we might have generated these numbers from a random physical process, such as the decay of radioactive nuclei. However such a sequence of numbers is not reproducible and hence cannot be used to check our programs. Hence in practice we use a digital computer, a very deterministic machine, to generate sequences of "random" numbers according to a well-defined algorithm. Of course these sequences are not truly random and in fact are frequently referred to as *pseudorandom*. Still we call them random if they are uniformly distributed and satisfy all our criteria for randomness. In fact we will find that many of the tests of randomness can be stated in terms of random walks.

We will only summarize some of the features of a good random number generator here. Most random number generators yield a sequence in which each number is used to find the succeeding one according to a well-defined algorithm. Hence the sequence is determined by the *seed*, the first number of the sequence. All random number generators yield a sequence which repeats itself after some number of terms, the *period*. In the usual methods, the maximum possible period is related to the finite size of a computer memory "word". The most widely used random number generator is based on the *power residue* or *linear congruential* method. That is, given the seed x_0, each number in the sequence is determined by the "map"

$$x_n = (ax_{n-1} + c) \, mod \, m \tag{11.38}$$

where a, c, and m are integers. (The notation $y = z \, mod \, m$ means that m is subtracted from z until $0 \leq y \leq m$. For example, 412 mod 50 equals 12.) The map (11.38) is characterized by three parameters, the *multiplier a*, the *increment c* and the *modulus m*. Since m is the largest integer generated by (11.38), the maximum possible period is m. However in general the period depends on all three parameters. For example if $a = 3$, $c = 4$, $m = 32$, and $x_0 = 1$, the sequence generated by (11.38) is 1, 7, 25, 15, 17, 23, 9, 31, 1, 7, 25, ... and the period is 8 rather than the maximum possible value of 32. If we are careful to choose a, c and m such that the maximum period is obtained, then all possible integers between 0 and $m-1$ will occur in the sequence. Since we usually wish to have random numbers in the interval $[0, 1]$ rather than random integers, random number generators usually return the ratio x_{n+1}/m, which is always less than unity. (Note that $x_n = 0$ occurs once in the sequence.)

The advantage of the power residue method is that it is very fast. Some of its properties are explored in Problem 11.17. As the above example illustrates, we have to choose m, a and c carefully in order to achieve optimum results. Several rules have been developed (see Knuth) to obtain the longest period.

There is no necessary and sufficient test for the randomness of a finite sequence of numbers; the most that can be said about any finite sequence of numbers is that it is "apparently" random. Since no single statistical test is a reliable indicator, we consider several tests in the following problem.

PROBLEM 11.17 Statistical tests of randomness

a. One way to determine if the period is sufficiently long is to plot the net displacement of a random walk as a function of step number. The length of each successive step is ± 1 with equal probability. An example is shown in Fig. 11.13 using (11.38) with $a = 899$, $c = 0$, $m = 32768$, and $x_0 = 12$. Determine the period of the sequence generated by (11.38) using these values of a, c, and m. Also determine the period of the random number generator supplied with your programming language.

b. A random sequence should contain numbers distributed in the interval $[0, 1]$ with equal probability. However the consecutive numbers might not appear in a perfectly uniform way but instead exhibit a tendency to be clumped or correlated. One test of this correlation requires filling a simple cubic lattice of L^3 sites at random: Consider an array $n(x, y, z)$ which is initially empty, where $1 \leq x_i, y_i, z_i \leq L$. A point is selected randomly by choosing its three coordinates x_i, y_i, and z_i from three consecutive random numbers. If the site is empty, it is filled and $n(x_i, y_i, z_i) = 1$; otherwise it is not changed. This procedure is repeated tL^3 times, where t is the number of Monte Carlo steps per site. Since this process is analogous to the decay of radioactive nuclei, we expect that the fraction of empty lattice sites should decay as e^{-t}. Determine the fraction of unfilled sites using the random number generator supplied with your programming language for $L = 10$, 15, and 20. Are your results consistent with the expected fraction? If possible repeat the same test using (11.38) with $a = 65549$, $c = 0$, and $m = 231$.

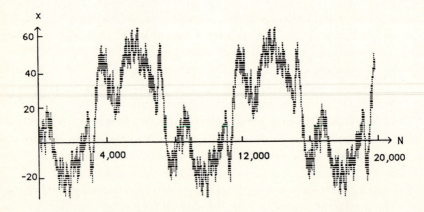

Fig. 11.13 A random walk generated by (11.38) with $a = 899$, $c = 0$ and $m = 32768$ with $x_0 = 12$.

c. Another test of uniformity is to divide the interval $[0, 1]$ into M equal size intervals or bins and place each member of the sequence into one of the bins. As an example consider the first $n = 10,000$ numbers generated by (11.37) with $a = 106$, $c = 1283$, and $m = 6075$ (see Press et al). Place each number into one of $M = 100$ bins. Is the distribution of numbers in the bins consistent with the laws of statistics? The most common test of this consistency is the *chi-square* or χ^2 test. Let y_i be the observed numbers in bin i and E_i be the expected values. In our example $E_i = 100$. The chi-square statistic is

$$\chi^2 = \frac{1}{M} \sum_{i=1}^{M} \frac{(y_i - E_i)^2}{E_i} \quad . \tag{11.39}$$

(Note that textbook definitions of χ^2 differ by a factor of M.) The number χ^2 is an indicator of the agreement between the observed and expected distributions. If $\chi^2 \simeq 0$, the agreement is perfect. If the number of bins is large or if the number of terms in a bin is large, then a value of $\chi^2 < 1$ indicates that the y_i are distributed according to the Gaussian distribution. Determine χ^2 for the values of a, c, and m given in the above and for the random number generator supplied with your programming language.

d. Another measure of short-term correlations is the autocorrelation function

$$C(k) = \frac{<x_i x_{i+k}> - <x_i><x_{i+k}>}{<x_i x_i> - <x_i><x_i>} \tag{11.40}$$

where x_i is the ith term in the sequence. The quantity $<x_i x_{i+k}>$ is found for a particular choice of k by forming all the possible products of $x_i x_{i+k}$ and dividing by the number of products. If x_i and x_{i+k} are not correlated, then $<x_i x_{i+k}> = <x_i><x_{i+k}>$ and $C(k) = 0$. Is $C(k)$ identically zero for any finite sequence? Calculate $C(k)$ for $a = 106$, $c = 1283$, and $m = 6075$.

*PROBLEM 11.18 An "improved" random number generator

One way to reduce sequential correlation and to lengthen the period is to "mix" or "shuffle" two different random number generators. The following procedure illustrates the approach for two random number generators which we denote as RAN1 and RAN2.

1. Make a list or table of 256 random numbers using RAN1. (The number 256 is arbitary, but should be less than the period of RAN1.)

2. Choose a random number x from this list by using RAN2 to generate a random index between 1 and 256.

3. Replace the number on the list with a new random number generated by RAN1.

The desired output is x. Consider two random number generators with relatively short periods and strong sequential correlation and show that the above shuffling scheme improves the quality of the random numbers.

REFERENCES AND SUGGESTIONS FOR ADDITIONAL READING

J. Bernasconi and L. Pietronero, "True self-avoiding walk in one dimension," *Phys. Rev.* B**29**, 5196 (1984). A research level paper. The authors present results for the exponent ν accurate to 1%.

S. Chandrasekhar, "Stochastic problems in physics and astronomy," *Rev. Mod. Phys.* **15**, 1 (1943). This article is reprinted in M. Wax, *Selected Papers on Noise and Stochastic Processes*, Dover Publications (1954).

A. K. Dewdney, "Computer Recreations (Five easy pieces for a do loop and random-number generator)," *Sci. Amer.* **252**, 20 (April 1985).

Robert Ehrlich, *Physics and Computers,* Houghton Mifflin (1973). Chapter 4 has a good discussion of the power residue method.

Pierre-Giles de Gennes, *Scaling Concepts in Polymer Physics,* Cornell University Press (1979). An important but difficult text.

Sholomo Havlin, George H. Weiss, James E. Kiefer and Menachem Dishon, "Exact enumeration of random walks with traps," *J. Phys. A: Math. Gen.* **17**, L347, (1984). The authors discuss a method based on exact enumeration for calculating the survival probability of random walkers on a lattice with randomly distributed traps.

Donald E. Knuth, *Seminumerical Algorithms,* 2nd ed., Vol. 2 of *The Art of Computer Programming,* Addison-Wesley (1981). The standard reference on random number generators.

Elliott W. Montroll and Michael F. Shlesinger, "On the wonderful world of random walks," in *Nonequilibrium Phenomena II: From Stochastics to Hydrodynamics,* J. L. Lebowitz and E. W. Montroll, eds. North-Holland Press (1984). The first part of this delightful review article chronicles the history of the random walk.

William H. Press, Brian P. Flannery, Saul A. Teukolsky and William T. Vetterling, *Numerical Recipes,* Cambridge University Press (1986).

F. Reif, *Fundamentals of Statistical and Thermal Physics*, McGraw-Hill (1965). This well known text on statistical physics has a good discussion on random walks (Chapter 1) and diffusion (Chapter 12).

Marshall N. Rosenbluth and Arianna W. Rosenbluth, "Monte Carlo calculation of the average extension of molecular chains," *J. Chem. Phys.* **23**, 356 (1955). One of the first Monte Carlo calculations for the self-avoiding walk.

John R. Taylor, *An Introduction to Error Analysis*, University Science Books, Oxford University Press (1982). See Chapter 12 for a discussion of the χ^2 test.

Frederick T. Wall and Frederic Mandel, "Macromolecular dimensions obtained by an efficient Monte Carlo method without sample attrition," *J. Chem. Phys.* **63**, 4592 (1975). An exposition of the "reptation" or "slithering snake" model.

George H. Weiss and Robert J. Rubin, "Random walks: Theory and Selected Applications," *Adv. Chem Phys.* **52**, 507 (1983). In spite of its research orientation, much of this review article can be understood by the motivated student.

George H. Weiss and Shlomo Havlin, "Trapping of random walks on the line," *J. Stat. Phys.* **37**, 17 (1984). The authors discuss an analytical approach to the asymptotic behavior of one-dimensional random walkers with randomly placed traps.

Charles A. Whitney, "Generating and Testing Pseudorandom Numbers," *Byte*, pp. 128-464 (October, 1984). An accessible and informative magazine article which includes tests of the rnd function in IBM BASICA.

APPENDIX 11A LEAST SQUARES FITS

In Problem 11.2 we computed the quantities $<x_N>$ and $<x_N^2>$ for $N = 8$, 16, 32, and 64. Our results are summarized in Table 11.1. Also shown is the rms displacement R_N given by $R_N = \sqrt{<x_N^2> - <x_N>^2}$ and the quantity $<x^4>$. It is easy to deduce from Table 11.1 that the general result $<x_N> = 0$ for $p = 1/2$ is consistent with our limited number of trials.

The main quantity of interest in Table 11.1 is the N-dependence of R_N. Since we suspect that R_N scales as N^ν for sufficiently large N, we can make a plot of $log\, R_N$ versus $log\, N$ and try to find the straight line which passes as closely as possible through the points. What value of the slope ν do you estimate from your results? Although frequently a visual fit can yield remarkably good results, it is desirable to make the fitting procedure more systematic.

TABLE 11.1 Monte Carlo results for $<x_N>$, $<x_N^2>$, $R_N = \sqrt{<x_N^2> - <x_N>^2}$, and $<x_N^4>$ for a random walk in one dimension. The quantities were averaged over 1,000 trials for each value of N. The step probability $p = 1/2$.

N	$<x_N>$	$<x_N^2>$	R_N	$<x_N^4>$
8	-0.010	7.980	2.825	183.984
16	-0.068	16.360	4.044	794.080
32	-0.006	30.284	6.830	2708.530
64	0.022	65.348	8.084	12118.900

The analytical method of finding the best straight line to fit a series of experimental points is called *linear regression* or *least squares*. Suppose we have n pairs of measurements (x_1, y_1), (x_2, y_2), ..., (x_n, y_n) and that the errors are entirely in the values of y. For the moment we will also assume that the uncertainties in y all have the same magnitude. Our goal is to obtain the best fit to the function

$$y = mx + b \quad . \tag{11.41}$$

The problem is to calculate the values of the parameters m and b for the best straight line through the n data points. If there were no errors in y_i, we would have $y_i - mx_i - b = 0$. The *residual* d_i is defined by the difference

$$d_i = y_i - mx_i - b \tag{11.42}$$

and is a measure of the error in y_i. Hence it is reasonable to assume that the best set of values of m and b are those which minimize the quantity

$$S = \sum_{i=1}^{n}(y_i - mx_i - b)^2 \quad . \tag{11.43}$$

In order to minimize S, we take the derivative of S with respect to b and m:

$$\frac{\partial S}{\partial m} = -2\sum_{i=1}^{n} x_i(y_i - mx_i - b) = 0 \tag{11.44}$$

$$\frac{\partial S}{\partial b} = -2\sum_{i=1}^{n}(y_i - mx_i - b) = 0 \quad . \tag{11.45}$$

(We omit the limits $i = 1$ to n in the following.) From (11.44) and (11.45) we obtain the two simultaneous equations:

$$m\sum x_i^2 + b\sum x_i = \sum x_i y_i \tag{11.46}$$

$$m\sum x_i + bn = \sum y_i \quad . \tag{11.47}$$

The solutions of (11.46) and (11.47) are

$$m = \frac{\sum(x_i - \bar{x})y_i}{\Delta} \tag{11.48}$$

$$b = \bar{y} - m\bar{x}. \tag{11.49}$$

where

$$\bar{x} = \frac{1}{n}\sum x_i \qquad \bar{y} = \frac{1}{n}\sum y_i \tag{11.50}$$

and

$$\Delta = \sum(x_i - \bar{x})^2 \quad . \tag{11.51}$$

Equations (11.48) and (11.49) determine the slope and intercept of the best straight line through the n data points.

For our random walk example, we can convert the non-linear relation $R_N = aN^\nu$ to the linear relation

$$ln\, R_N = ln\, a + \nu\, ln\, N \quad . \tag{11.52}$$

We use the values of R_N and N from Table 11.1 to obtain the values of $x = ln\, N$ and $y = ln\, R_N$ shown in Table 11.2 and Fig. 11.14.

TABLE 11.2 Computed values of $ln\ N$ and $ln\ R_N$ for a random walk in one dimension for $1,000$ trials.

$ln\ N$	$ln\ R_N$
2.079	1.039
2.773	1.397
3.466	1.921
4.159	2.090

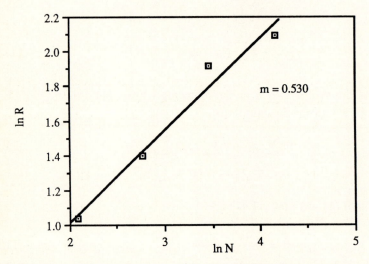

Fig. 11.14 Plot of $ln\ R_N$ versus $ln\ N$ for a random walk in one dimension. The values of $ln\ R_N$ are taken from Table 11.2. The straight line through the points is found by minimizing the sum (11.43).

From the values of $ln\ N$ and $ln\ R_N$ shown in Table 11.2, we find using (11.48)–(11.51) that $\bar{x} = 3.119$, $\bar{y} = 1.612$, $\Delta = 2.403$, $m = 0.530$, and $b = -0.043$. Hence we can conclude that our limited data for R_N yields the estimate $\nu = 0.53$ consistent with the exact result $\nu = 1/2$.

We give without proof the estimates for the probable range in m and b:

$$(\Delta m)^2 \approx \frac{1}{D} \frac{\sum d_i^2}{(n-2)} \tag{11.53}$$

$$(\Delta b)^2 \approx \left(\frac{1}{n} + \frac{\bar{x}^2}{\Delta}\right) \frac{\sum d_i^2}{n-2} \quad . \tag{11.54}$$

For our example $\Delta m = 0.07$, and we conclude that our best estimate for ν is $\nu = 0.53 \pm 0.07$.

If the values of y_i have different uncertainties σ_i, then the data points should be weighted by the quantity $w_i = 1/\sigma_i^2$. In this case it is necessary to minimize the quantity

$$S = \sum w_i(y_i - mx_i - b)^2 \quad . \tag{11.55}$$

The best estimates for m and b can be shown to be

$$m = \frac{1}{\Delta} \sum w_i(x_i - \bar{x})y_i \tag{11.56}$$

$$b = \bar{y} - m\bar{x} \tag{11.57}$$

$$\bar{x} = \frac{\sum w_i x_i}{\sum w_i} \qquad \bar{y} = \frac{\sum w_i y_i}{\sum w_i} \tag{11.58}$$

$$\Delta = \sum w_i(x_i - \bar{x})^2 \quad . \tag{11.59}$$

How can we estimate the error in $\ln R_N$? In Chapter 10 we found that the probable error of $<x_N>$ is given by $\sigma_x/\sqrt{n}$, where $\sigma_x{}^2 = <x_N^2> - <x_N>^2$. We can use similar arguments to show that the probable error of $<x_N^2>$ is given by $\tilde{\sigma}/\sqrt{n}$, where

$$\tilde{\sigma}^2 = <x_N^4> - <x_N^2>^2 \quad . \tag{11.60}$$

The computation of the errors in $\ln R_N$ is done in Problem 11.19.

*PROBLEM 11.19 Estimate of probable error of $\ln R_N$

a. Use the results for $<x_N^4>$ and $<x_N^2>$ to compute the standard deviation $\tilde{\sigma}$ and $\sigma_m = \tilde{\sigma}/\sqrt{n}$ for each value of N. The quantity σ_m is the most probable error in one measurement of $<x_N^2>$ consisting of n trials. Are the values of σ_m approximately equal for all N? If they are not, explain the qualitative behavior of σ_m. If it is desired to have approximately equal error estimates for all values of N, how many trials are needed for $N = 64$ relative to $N = 8$?

b. Since the quantity of interest is the *derived* quantity $\ln R_N$ rather than the *primary* quantity $<x_N^2>$, we need to relate the estimated error in the latter to the error in $\ln R_N$. It can be shown that if U is related to A by $U = A^p$, then the error ΔU is related to the error ΔA by

$$\frac{\Delta U}{U} = p \frac{\Delta A}{A} \quad . \tag{11.61}$$

(U and A are the average values.) Similarly if $U = \ln A$, then the errors are related by

$$\Delta U = \frac{\Delta A}{A} \quad . \tag{11.62}$$

Use (11.61) and (11.62) to estimate the error in $ln\, R_N$ for each value of N shown in Table 11.1. Since the values of $ln\, R_N$ have different errors, use the relations (11.56)–(11.59) to find a revised estimate for ν.

For the simple random walk considered here, the relation $R_N = AN^\nu$ holds for all N. However in many of the other random walk problems considered in this chapter, such a relation holds only asymptotically for large N. Hence it might be misleading to give more weight to small N results for R_N.

REFERENCES

William S. Cleveland and Robert McGill, "Graphical perception and graphical methods for analyzing scientific data," *Science* **229**, 828 (1985). There is more to analyzing data than least squares plots.

THE PERCOLATION PROBLEM

12

We introduce several concepts associated with critical phenomena in the context of *percolation*.

12.1 INTRODUCTION

This chapter on geometrical phase transitions requires little background in physics, e.g. no classical or quantum mechanics and little statistical physics. Indeed all that is required is some understanding of geometry and probability. Much of the appeal of geometrical phase transitions is their game-like aspects and their intuitive simplicity. Moreover these models serve as an excellent introduction to discrete computer models and the importance of graphical analysis. On the other hand a background in physics will make this chapter more meaningful and can serve as an introduction to problems in phase transitions and to important ideas such as scaling, critical exponents, and the renormalization group.

You might be familiar with the term "percolation" in the context of the brewing of coffee. However we will use this term in a more restrictive sense. In order to introduce the concept of percolation, we consider another example from the kitchen. Consider a large cookie sheet on which we randomly place drops of cookie batter. Then place the cookies in the oven to bake. During baking assume that each drop of cookie batter can spread to a maximum radius a. You might know from experience that if two cookies touch, they coalesce to form one cookie. What do you expect will happen? If you are not careful, you might find a very large cookie which will cover a significant portion of the cookie sheet (see Fig. 12.1).

Let us abstract this example in order to make the concept of percolation clearer. Imagine a very large chessboard rather than a cookie sheet. We will represent this chessboard as a square lattice and assume that every square or "site" on this lattice can be in either one of two states, "occupied" or "empty."

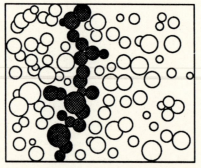

Fig. 12.1 Circles (cookies) of varying radii placed at random on a large sheet. Note that there is a path of overlapping circles (shaded) which connects the bottom and top sides of the "cookie sheet." If such a path exists, we say that the path "percolates" the lattice.

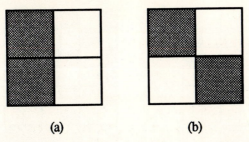

(a)   (b)

Fig. 12.2 An example of a site percolation cluster on a square lattice of linear dimension $L = 2$. The two nearest neighbor occupied sites (filled squares) in (a) are part of the same cluster; the two occupied sites in (b) are not nearest neighbor sites and do not belong to the same cluster.

Each site is occupied independently of its neighbors with probability p. This model of percolation is called *site* percolation. The occupied sites (the "cookies") are either isolated or form groups of nearest neighbors. We define a *cluster* as a group of occupied lattice sites which are connected by nearest neighbor distances (see Fig. 12.2). Two occupied sites belong to the same cluster if they are linked by a path of nearest-neighbor connections joining occupied sites.

One easy way to study percolation is to use the random number generator on a hand calculator. The procedure is to generate a random number and then occupy a lattice site if the random number is less than p. We perform this procedure for each site in the lattice. If the probability of site occupancy is small, we expect that only small isolated clusters will be present (see Fig. 12.3a). In contrast if $p \sim 1$, we expect that most of the occupied sites will form one large cluster which extends from one end of the lattice to the other (see Fig. 12.3d). Such a cluster is said to "span" the lattice and to be a *spanning cluster*. What happens for intermediate values of p, for example p between 0.4 and 0.7 (see Figs. 12.3b and c)? We shall see that in the limit of an infinite lattice, there exists a well defined "threshold" probability p_c such that:

For $p \geq p_c$, one spanning cluster or path exists.
For $p < p_c$, no spanning cluster exists and all clusters are finite.

We emphasize that the intrinsic characteristic of percolation is *connectedness*. Since the connectedness exhibits a qualitative change at a well-defined value of a parameter which can be changed continuously, we shall see that the

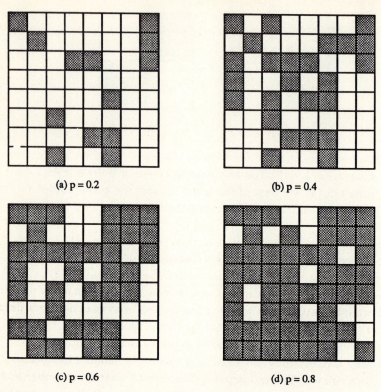

Fig. 12.3 Examples of site percolation clusters on a square lattice of linear dimension $L = 8$ for $p = 0.2$, 0.4, 0.6, and 0.8. On the average the fraction of occupied sites (black squares) is equal to p. Note that for $p = 0.6$, there exists a cluster which "spans" the lattice horizontally but not vertically; for $p = 0.8$ the cluster spans both vertically and horizontally.

transition from a state with no spanning cluster to a state with one spanning cluster is a type of *phase transition*.

Of course our real interest is not in large cookies or even in site percolation. An example of an application of percolation concepts is to the electrical conductivity of composite systems made of a mixture of metallic and insulating materials. An easy way to make such a system in the laboratory is to place a mixture of small plastic and metallic spheres of equal size into a container (see Fitzpatrick et al.). Care must be taken to pack the spheres at random. If the metallic domains constitute a small fraction of the volume of the system, electricity cannot be conducted and the composite system will be an insulator.

However, if the metallic domains comprise a sufficiently large fraction of the container, electricity will be able to flow from one domain to another and the composite system will be a conductor. The description of the conduction of electricity through composite materials can be made more precise by introducing the parameter ϕ, the volume fraction of the container which consists of metallic spheres. The transition between the two types of behavior (insulator and conductor) occurs abruptly as ϕ is increased and is associated with the non-existence or existence of a *connected path* of metallic spheres. More realistic composite systems are discussed in Zallen.

Percolation phenomena can also be observed in the laboratory with a piece of chicken wire or wire mesh. You might wish to do the experiment of Watson and Leath (1974) who measured the electrical conductivity of a large piece of uniform steel-wire screen mesh as a function of the fraction of the sites that were removed. The coordinates of the sites to be removed were provided by a random number generator. Watson and Leath found that the measured electrical conductivity is a rapidly decreasing function of the fraction of sites p still present and vanishes below a critical threshold. A related conductivity measurement on a sheet of conducting paper with random "holes" has also been performed recently (see Mehr et al.).

The applications of percolation phenomena range beyond metal-insulator transitions and the conductivity of chicken wire (a random resistor network) to include the spread of disease in a population, the behavior of magnets diluted by nonmagnetic impurities, and the characterization of gels. How does a bowl of jello differ from a bowl of broth? In the following we will concentrate on understanding several simple models of percolation which have an intuitive appeal of their own. Many of the applications of percolation concepts are discussed in the references.

12.2 THE PERCOLATION THRESHOLD

Since it is not convenient to generate percolation configurations using a hand calculator, we develop a simple program. Consider a square lattice of linear dimension L and associate a random number between zero and unity with each site in the lattice. A site is occupied if its random number is less than p. **Program site**, listed in the following, generates site percolation configurations and shows them on the screen where the clusters can be identified visually. The array r in the main program stores the random number associated with each site. Note that each lattice site has a random number attached to it, so that as p is increased, sites which are already occupied remain occupied.

```
PROGRAM site                        ! draw site percolation configurations
DIM r(50,50)
RANDOMIZE
CALL initial(L)                     ! define lattice and screen parameters
CALL lattice(L,r)                   ! assign random # to each site
CALL configuration(L,r)             ! occupy sites for given probability p
END

SUB initial(L)
    INPUT prompt "linear dimension of lattice = ": L
    LET aspect_ratio = 1.5          ! value for Macintosh
    LET margin = 0.1*L
    LET mx = aspect_ratio*margin
    LET bx = aspect_ratio*L
    SET window -mx,bx + mx,-margin,L + margin
    BOX LINES 0,L,0,L
END SUB

SUB lattice(L,r(,))
    FOR row = 1 to L                ! draw lattice sites
        LET y = row - 0.5
        ! associate box of linear dimension unity with each site
        FOR col = 1 to L
            LET x = col - 0.5
            LET r(col,row) = rnd     ! assign random number to each lattice site
            PLOT POINTS: x,y
        NEXT col
    NEXT row
END SUB
```

```
SUB configuration(L,r(,))
   DIM s(50,50)
   DO while p >= 0
      SET cursor 1,1
      INPUT prompt "probability p = ": p
      LET size = 0.4                      ! half length of box for occupied sites
      FOR row = 1 to L
         LET y = row - 0.5
         FOR col = 1 to L
            IF r(col,row) < p and s(col,row) <> 1 then      ! newly occupied site
               LET x = col - 0.5
               BOX AREA x - size,x + size, y - size,y + size
               LET s(col,row) = 1                  ! occupied site
            END IF
         NEXT col
      NEXT row
   LOOP
END SUB
```

The percolation threshold p_c is defined as the probability p at which an infinite cluster first appears in an infinite lattice. However for the finite lattices of linear dimension L which we can simulate on a computer, there is always a non-zero probability that there will be a spanning cluster that connects one side of the lattice to the other. For small p, this probability is of order p^L (see Fig. 12.4). As L becomes large, this probability goes to zero and for sufficiently small p, only finite clusters will exist. Since we need to adopt a "spanning" rule applicable to finite lattices, we define $p_c(L)$ as the average value of p at which a spanning cluster first appears. For a finite lattice the definition of spanning is arbitrary and hence the computed value of p_c depends on the spanning criteria. For example, we can define a connected path as one that (i) spans the lattice either horizontally or vertically, (ii) spans the lattice in a fixed direction (e.g. vertically); or (iii) spans the lattice both horizontally and vertically. All of these spanning rules should lead to the same extrapolated value for p_c in the limit $L \to \infty$. In the following problem we will obtain an approximate value for p_c which is accurate to about 10%. A more sophisticated analysis, called finite-sized scaling, allows us to extrapolate our results for $p_c(L)$ to $L \to \infty$. This analysis is discussed in Sec. 12.4.

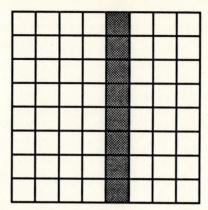

Fig. 12.4 An example of a spanning cluster of probability p^L on a finite $L = 8$ lattice. How many ways are there of realizing a spanning cluster of L sites?

PROBLEM 12.1 The percolation threshold on the square lattice

a. Use **Program Site** to generate random site configurations on the square lattice. Estimate p_c by finding the value of p at which a spanning cluster is first attained. First consider $L = 4$ and begin at a value of p for which you are confident that a spanning cluster is unlikely to be present. Then increase p in increments of 0.025 until you find a spanning cluster. Record the value of p for which spanning first occurs for each spanning criteria. Remember that each trial corresponds to a different set of random numbers. Repeat this process for a total of ten trials. Your estimate of p_c for $L = 4$ is the average of the ten trials. Are your results for p_c for each spanning criterion consistent with your expectations?

b. Repeat part (a) for $L = 16$ and 32. Is p_c better defined for larger L, that is, are the numerical values of p_c spread over a smaller range of values? How quickly can you visually determine the existence of a spanning cluster? Be as explicit as possible on the nature of your visual "algorithm" for determining if a spanning cluster exists.

The value of p_c depends on the symmetry of the lattice as well as its dimension. In addition to the square lattice, the most common lattice in two dimensions is the triangular lattice. As discussed in Chapter 11, the essential difference between the square and triangular lattices is the number of nearest neighbors.

PROBLEM 12.2 Site percolation on the triangular lattice

a. Modify **Program Site** to treat random site percolation configurations on the triangular lattice. One simple way to modify your program is to consider the sites to have the symmetry of the square lattice but to regard sites along one of the diagonal directions as nearest neighbors.

b. Assume that a connected path connects the top and bottom sides of the lattice (see Fig. 12.5). Do you expect p_c for the triangular lattice to be smaller or larger than the value of p_c for the square lattice? Estimate $p_c(L)$ for $L = 4$, 16, and 32. Are your results for p_c consistent with your expectations?

Another type of percolation is *bond* percolation. Imagine each lattice site to be occupied and there to be bonds or connections between nearest neighbor sites (see Fig. 12.6). In bond percolation, each bond is either occupied with probability p or not occupied with probability $1 - p$. A cluster is a group of sites connected by occupied bonds. A simple example of bond percolation is the wire mesh described in Sec. 12.1. This time we can imagine cutting the bonds between nodes rather than removing the nodes themselves. If we were to measure the electrical conductivity, we would find that the conductivity would

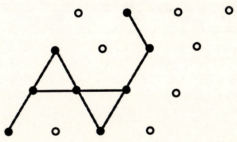

Fig. 12.5 Example of a spanning cluster on a $L = 4$ triangular lattice. The bonds between the occupied sites are drawn to clarify the nature of the lattice. Note that is sometimes convenient to associate the vertices of a lattice with the sites.

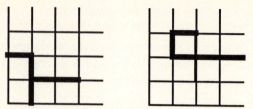

Fig. 12.6 Two examples of bond clusters. The occupied bonds are shown as bold lines.

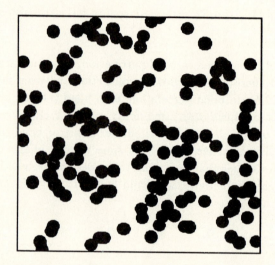

Fig. 12.7 A model of continuum percolation realized by placing disks of unit radius at random into a square box of linear dimension L. Is there a spanning cluster? The number of disks equals 150, $L = 20$, and the concentration of disks is $x = 150/(20)^2 = 0.375$.

be vanishingly small when the fraction of bonds present were less than or equal to approximately 0.5. Although bond percolation and other lattice percolation models are of interest, we shall consider only site percolation for simplicity.

In addition to lattice percolation models, we can also consider *continuum* percolation models. For example the following program places disks of unit radius at random in a box. Two disks are in the same cluster if they touch or overlap. A typical continuum percolation configuration is depicted in Fig. 12.7. We can again ask: "What is the minimum density of disks necessary for a connected path of disks to exist?"

```
PROGRAM continuum              ! draw continuum percolation configurations
RANDOMIZE
CALL initial(L)                ! see listing of subroutine in Program site
CALL disks(L)                  ! place disks at random inside box
END

SUB disks(L)
    LET r = 0.5                ! radius of disks
    LET area = L*L             ! L is linear dimension of box
    DO while n >= 0
       SET cursor 5,48
       INPUT prompt "# of new disks = ": n
       FOR i = 1 to n
          LET x = rnd*L        ! center of disk inside box
          LET y = rnd*L
          BOX CIRCLE x - r, x + r, y - r, y + r
       NEXT i
       LET number = number + n
       SET cursor 1,1
       PRINT "                                    ";    ! erase line
       SET cursor 1,1
       PRINT "density of disks ="; number/area;
    LOOP
END SUB
```

PROBLEM 12.3 Continuum percolation

a. Use **Program Continuum** to estimate the value of the percolation threshold x_c, where the parameter x is the number of disks per area.

*b. Consider a simple model of the "cookie sheet" problem discussed in Sec. 12.1 by modifying **Program continuum** so that disks of random sizes between 0 and 1 are placed at random into a square box. How is the value of x_c changed?

Our discussion of percolation has emphasized the existence of a percolation threshold p_c and the appearance of a spanning path or cluster for $p \geq p_c$. More information can be obtained from the *mean cluster-size distribution* $n_s(p)$ defined by

$$n_s(p) = \frac{average\ number\ of\ clusters\ of\ size\ s}{total\ number\ of\ sites\ in\ the\ lattice} \qquad (12.1)$$

For $p \geq p_c$, the spanning cluster is excluded from n_s. (For historical reasons, the *size* of a cluster refers to the *number* of sites in the cluster rather than to its spatial extent.) Inspection of Fig. 12.3a shows that $n_s(p = 0.2) = 5/64$, $1/64$, and $2/64$ for $s = 1$, 2, and 3 respectively, and is otherwise zero. Since $\sum_s sn_s$ is the total number of occupied sites and sn_s is the number of occupied sites in clusters of size s, the quantity

$$w_s = \frac{sn_s}{\sum_s n_s} \qquad (12.2)$$

is the probability that an occupied site chosen at random is part of an s-site cluster. Hence the *mean cluster size* S is given by

$$S = \sum_s sw_s = \frac{\sum_s s^2 n_s}{\sum_s sn_s} \qquad . \qquad (12.3)$$

As an example, the mean cluster size corresponding to the eight clusters in Fig. 12.3a is $S = 27/13$.

Another quantity which characterizes percolation is $P_\infty(p)$, the probability that an occupied site belongs to the spanning cluster. P_∞ is defined by

$$P_\infty = \frac{number\ of\ sites\ in\ the\ spanning\ cluster}{total\ number\ of\ occupied\ sites} \qquad . \qquad (12.4)$$

For an infinite lattice, $P_\infty(p) = 0$ for $p < p_c$ and $P_\infty(p) = 1$ for $p = 1$. Inspection of Fig. 12.3c shows that $P_\infty(p = 0.6) = 36/47$ for the particular configuration shown.

PROBLEM 12.4 Qualitative behavior of $n_s(p)$, $S(p)$, and $P_\infty(p)$

    a. Estimate the cluster-size distribution $n_s(p)$ on a square lattice for $L = 16$ and $p = 0.4$, $p = p_c$, and $p = 0.8$. Take $p_c = 0.5927$. Consider five trials for each value of p and average $n_s(p)$ over the five trials. Consistent results can be obtained by discarding configurations which have a spanning cluster for $p < p_c$ and which do not have a spanning cluster for $p \geq p_c$. Plot n_s as a function of s for each value of p and describe qualitatively the observed s-dependence. Does n_s decrease more rapidly with s for $p = p_c$ or for $p \neq p_c$?

b. Use the same configurations considered in part (a) to compute the mean cluster size S as a function of p. Remember that for $p > p_c$, the spanning cluster is excluded.

c. Compute $P_\infty(p)$ for $L = 16$ and various values of $p \geq p_c$. Plot $P(p)$ as a function of p and discuss its qualitative behavior.

*12.3 CLUSTER LABELING

Your visual algorithm for determining the existence of a connected path and counting the number of clusters is probably very sophisticated. Does it involve parallel processing? However the implementation of your algorithm is very tiring and time consuming, and we would rather have a computer do the job for us. As we will find in the following, this job is difficult for a computer also. The difficulty is that the assignment of a site to a cluster is a *global* rather than a *local* property of the site.

We consider the cluster multiple labeling method of Hoshen and Kopelman (cf references). The algorithm can best be described by an example. Consider the configuration of Fig. 12.8. We assign cluster labels to sites beginning at the lower left corner and continue from left to right. Since the $site(1, 1)$ is occupied,

(a)

7	7		9	3	3	
7				8	3	3
	6	3			3	3
6	6	5	5	3	3	3
		5		4	3	3
1	1			4	3	3
1		2	2		3	

(b)

7	7		3	3	3	
7				3	3	3
	3	3			3	3
3	3	3	3	3	3	3
		3		3	3	3
1	1			3	3	3
1		2	2		3	

Fig. 12.8 A percolation configuration on a square lattice with $L = 7$. Site coordinates are measured from the origin at the lower-left corner $(1, 1)$. Part (a) shows the improper cluster labels initially assigned by **Program cluster**, a modified implementation of the Hoshen-Kopelman algorithm. Part (b) shows the proper cluster labels.

we assign to it cluster label 1. The next site is empty and hence is not labeled. The next occupied site in the first row is $site(3,1)$. Since its left neighbor is unoccupied, we assign it the next available cluster label, label 2. The assignment of cluster labels to the remainder of the row is straightforward. We next proceed to $site(1,2)$ of the second row. Since this site is occupied and its nearest neighbor in the preceeding row is labeled 1, we assign label 1 to $site(1,2)$. We continue from left to right along the second row checking the occupancy of each site. If a site is occupied, we check the occupancy of its nearest neighbors in the previous row and column. If neither neighbor is occupied, we assign the next available cluster label. If only one nearest neighbor site is occupied, the site is assigned the label of its occupied neighbor. For example, $site(2,2)$ is assigned label 1 since its occupied neighbor, $site(1,2)$ has label 1.

The problem arises when we come to an occupied site at which two clusters coalesce and cluster labels need to be reassigned. This case first occurs at $site(6,2)$—its two neighbors in the previous row and column have labels 3 and 4, respectively. Clearly the *proper* cluster label assignment at $site(6,2)$ is the smaller of labels 3 and 4. Hence $site(6,2)$ is assigned cluster label 3 and label 4 should be reassigned to label 3. However since there might be further reassignments, we delay the reassignment of cluster labels until the entire lattice is surveyed. This reassignment is accomplished by distinguishing a *proper* label such as label 3 from an *improper* label such as label 4. We introduce an additional array $np(i)$ which distinguishes proper and improper labels and provides their connections. Let us return to the configuration shown in Fig. 12.8 to explain the use of this array. Before we came to $site(6,2)$, labels 1 through 4 were proper labels and we set

$$np(1) = 0, \qquad np(2) = 0, \qquad np(3) = 0, \qquad np(4) = 0 \quad .$$

However at $site(6,2)$ where labels 3 and 4 are linked, we set $np(4) = 3$. This nonzero reassignment of $np(4)$ tells us that label 4 is improper, and the numerical value of $np(4)$ tells us that label 4 is linked to label 3. Note that the argument of np is always larger than np itself.

The above procedure is not quite complete. What should we do when we come to a site with two previously labeled neighbors one or both of which are improper? For example consider $site(5,4)$ which has two occupied neighbors with labels 5 and 4. We might be tempted to assign $site(5,4)$ the label 4 and set $np(5) = 4$. However instead of assigning to a site the minimum label of its two neighbors, we should assign to it the minimum of the *proper* labels of the two neighboring sites. In addition if the two neighboring sites have different proper labels, then we should set np of the maximum proper label equal to the minimum proper label.

The above version of the Hoshen-Kopelman cluster assignment algorithm is implemented in **Program cluster** for the square lattice. The program also contains a "menu" so that various cluster-related quantities can be computed without writing another subroutine. In **SUB assign** random numbers are assigned to each site and stored in the array r. This subroutine is called by choices 1 and 11 in the menu. The occupancy of the sites is determined in **SUB occupy** and stored in the array s. The cluster label assignments are performed in subroutines **cluster_label**, **newcluster**, **neighbors**, **label_min**, and **proper**. The cluster labels assigned to each site are stored in the array cl and the relations of the cluster labels are stored in the one-dimensional array np. **SUB plot_label** draws either the proper or improper labels. **SUB plot_conf** draws the occupied sites, and **SUB plot_cluster** draws the positions of the sites in the cluster whose proper label is an argument of the subroutine.

After the clusters are labeled, we can obtain a number of geometrical quantities of interest. **SUB span** determines whether the configuration contains a vertically spanning cluster by checking for the existence of a common proper label in the bottom and top rows. The proper label of the spanning cluster is printed on the screen if it exists, otherwise the variable $ispan$ remains 0.

SUB compute_mass determines the size (the number of occupied sites) in each cluster. The cluster distribution n_s can be found by counting the number of clusters of size s and normalizing the results by dividing by L^2.

The probability of an occupied site belonging to the spanning cluster is determined in **SUB Pinfinity**. This subroutine uses the cluster label from the output of **SUB span** to determine the size of the spanning cluster and uses the cluster distribution output of **SUB mass** to determine the total number of occupied sites. The ratio of these two quantities is P_∞.

SUB mean_size uses the output of **SUB mass** to determine the mean cluster size S of the non-spanning clusters. In **SUB mean_size**, $ns(i)$ is the size of the cluster with proper label i. In order to obtain S, we sum over the proper labels rather than the size s as is done in the definition (12.3) of S. Convince yourself that the two methods of computing S are equivalent. Note that the spanning cluster is not included in the sums.

Program cluster is not the most efficient implementation of the Hoshen-Kopelman algorithm. A more efficient version written in Fortran has been given by Stauffer (see references). Although the Hoshen-Kopelman algorithm can be shown to be the most efficent cluster labeling approach for two-dimensional lattices, it is not clear that this approach is the most efficient in higher dimensions. Can you think of a different method for identifying the clusters?

```
PROGRAM cluster
DIM s(64,64),r(64,64),cl(64,64),np(1000),mass(1000)
RANDOMIZE
DO
  CLEAR
  CALL menu(choice)
  CLEAR
  SELECT CASE choice
  CASE 1                      ! generate new percolation configuration
    INPUT prompt "linear dimension of lattice = ": L
    INPUT prompt "site occupation probability = ": p
    CALL assign(L,r)          ! assign random number to each site
    CALL occupy(L,p,s,r)      ! check sites for occupancy
  CASE 2                      ! change p and retain random numbers
    INPUT prompt "new site occupation probability = " : p
    CALL occupy(L,p,s,r)
  CASE 3                      ! draw configuration
    CALL plot_setup(L)
    CALL draw_conf(L,s)
  CASE 4                      ! determine cluster labels
    CALL cluster_label(L,s,cl,np)          ! assign label to each cluster
  CASE 5                      ! list cluster distribution
    CALL compute_mass(L,cl,np,mass,nmax)   ! determine mass of each cluster
  CASE 6                      ! draw proper cluster labels
    CALL plot_setup(L)
    CALL print_label(L,cl,np,"y")          ! draw proper labels
  CASE 7                      ! draw cluster labels before reassignment
    CALL plot_setup(L)
    CALL print_label(L,cl,np,"n")          ! draw improper labels
  CASE 8                      ! determine spanning
    CALL span(L,cl,np,ispan)
    IF ispan <> 0 then
      PRINT "cluster label",ispan," spans vertically"
    ELSE
      PRINT "does not span vertically"
    END IF
```

```
    CASE 9                      ! compute radius of gyration
      INPUT prompt"label of cluster = ": label
      CALL radius_gyration(L,cl,np,label)
    CASE 10                     ! draw positions of desired cluster
      INPUT prompt"label of cluster = ": label
      CALL plot_cluster(L,cl,np,label)
    CASE 11                     ! estimate probability of first spanning
      CALL first_span(L,p,s,r,cl,np)
    CASE 12                     ! probability occupied site in spanning cluster
      CALL Pinfinity(mass,ispan,nmax,prob)
      PRINT "probability of site in infinite cluster = ", prob
    CASE 13                     ! compute mean cluster size
      CALL mean_size(mass,ispan,nmax,mean)
      PRINT "mean cluster size = ", mean
    CASE 14
      STOP
    CASE ELSE
    END SELECT
    PRINT "press space bar to see menu"
    DO
    LOOP until key input
  LOOP
END
```

```
SUB menu(choice)
    PRINT " enter one of the following choices"
    PRINT " 1. initialize lattice"
    PRINT " 2. change p, retain random numbers"
    PRINT " 3. draw occupied sites"
    PRINT " 4. determine cluster labels"
    PRINT " 5. list cluster distribution"
    PRINT " 6. draw proper cluster labels"
    PRINT " 7. draw bare cluster labels"
    PRINT " 8. determine (vertical) spanning"
    PRINT " 9. determine radius of gyration"
    PRINT "10. draw particular cluster"
    PRINT "11. determine first spanning probability"
    PRINT "12. obtain probability of site in spanning cluster"
    PRINT "13. obtain mean cluster size S of finite clusters"
    PRINT "14. stop"
    PRINT
    INPUT prompt "choice? ": choice
END SUB

SUB assign(L,r(,))
    ! assign random number to each site
    FOR col = 1 to L
        FOR row = 1 to L
            LET r(col,row) = rnd
        NEXT row
    NEXT col
END SUB

SUB occupy(L,p,s(,),r(,))
    FOR col = 1 to L
        FOR row = 1 to L
            IF r(col,row) < p then        ! occupy sites if p < r(i,j)
                LET s(col,row) = -1       ! occupied sites negative
            ELSE
                LET s(col,row) = 0
            END IF
        NEXT row
    NEXT col
END SUB
```

```
SUB cluster_label(L,s(,),cl(,),np())
   ! label sites
   MAT cl = 0
   MAT np = 0
   LET ncluster = 0                        ! cluster label
   IF s(1,1) < 0 then CALL newcluster(ncluster,cl,np,1,1)
   FOR col = 2 to L                        ! label bottom row first
      IF s(col,1) < 0 then
         LET col_left = col - 1
         IF s(col_left,1) < 0 then
            LET cl(col,1) = cl(col_left,1)
         ELSE
            CALL newcluster(ncluster,cl,np,col,1)
         END IF
      END IF
   NEXT col
   FOR row = 2 to L                        ! label clusters in remaining rows
      IF s(1,row) < 0 then                 ! treat first column separately
         LET row_down = row - 1            ! determine occupancy of site in lower row
         IF s(1,row_down) < 0 then
            LET cl(1,row) = cl(1,row_down)
         ELSE
            CALL newcluster(ncluster,cl,np,1,row)
         END IF
      END IF
      FOR col = 2 to L
         IF s(col,row) < 0 then
            LET row_down = row - 1
            LET col_left = col - 1
            IF cl(col,row_down) + cl(col_left,row) = 0 then
               CALL newcluster(ncluster,cl,np,col,row)
            ELSE
               CALL neighbor(s,cl,np,col,row)
            END IF
         END IF
      NEXT col
   NEXT row
END SUB
```

```
SUB cluster_label(L,s(,),cl(,),np())
   ! label sites
   MAT cl = 0
   MAT np = 0
   LET ncluster = 0                        ! cluster label
   IF s(1,1) < 0 then CALL newcluster(ncluster,cl,np,1,1)
   FOR col = 2 to L                        ! label bottom row first
      IF s(col,1) < 0 then
         LET col_left = col - 1
         IF s(col_left,1) < 0 then
            LET cl(col,1) = cl(col_left,1)
         ELSE
            CALL newcluster(ncluster,cl,np,col,1)
         END IF
      END IF
   NEXT col
   FOR row = 2 to L                        ! label clusters in remaining rows
      IF s(1,row) < 0 then                 ! treat first column separately
         LET row_down = row - 1           ! determine occupancy of site in lower row
         IF s(1,row_down) < 0 then
            LET cl(1,row) = cl(1,row_down)
         ELSE
            CALL newcluster(ncluster,cl,np,1,row)
         END IF
      END IF
      FOR col = 2 to L
         IF s(col,row) < 0 then
            LET row_down = row - 1
            LET col_left = col - 1
            IF cl(col,row_down) + cl(col_left,row) = 0 then
               CALL newcluster(ncluster,cl,np,col,row)
            ELSE
               CALL neighbor(s,cl,np,col,row)
            END IF
         END IF
      NEXT col
   NEXT row
END SUB
```

```
SUB newcluster(ncluster,cl(,),np(),col,row)
    LET ncluster = ncluster + 1
    LET cl(col,row) = ncluster
    LET np(ncluster) = 0                                    ! proper label
END SUB

SUB neighbor(s(,),cl(,),np(),col,row)              ! determine occupancy of neighbors
    LET row_down = row - 1
    LET col_left = col - 1
    IF s(col,row_down)*s(col_left,row) > 0 then        ! both neighbors occupied
      CALL label_min(cl,np,col,row,col_left,row_down)
      EXIT SUB
    END IF
    IF cl(col,row_down) > 0 then
      LET cl(col,row) = cl(col,row_down)
      EXIT SUB
    END IF
    ! neighbor to the left occupied
    LET cl(col,row) = cl(col_left,row)
END SUB

SUB label_min(cl(,),np(),col,row,col_left,row_down)
    ! both neighbors occupied, determine minimum cluster number
    IF cl(col_left,row) = cl(col,row_down) then
      ! both neighbors have same cluster label
      LET cl(col,row) = cl(col_left,row)
    ELSE
      ! determine minimum cluster label
      LET left = cl(col_left,row)
      LET down = cl(col,row_down)
      CALL proper(np,left)
      CALL proper(np,down)
      LET nmax = max(left,down)
      LET nmin = min(left,down)
      LET cl(col,row) = nmin
      IF nmin <> nmax then
        LET np(nmax) = nmin                    ! set improper label nmax = nmin
      END IF
    END IF
END SUB
```

```
SUB proper(np(),label)
    DO
        IF np(label) = 0 then EXIT SUB
        LET label = np(label)
    LOOP
END SUB

SUB plot_setup(L)
    ! window for plotting subroutines
    LET aspect_ratio = 1.5                    ! value for Macintosh
    LET margin = 0.1*L
    LET mx = aspect_ratio*margin
    LET Lx = aspect_ratio*L
    SET window -mx,Lx + mx,-margin,L + margin
END SUB


SUB print_label(L,cl(,),np(),proper$)
    LET size = 0.4
    FOR col = 1 to L
        LET x = col - 0.5
        FOR row = 1 to L
            LET y = row - 0.5
            LET label = cl(col,row)
            IF label > 0 then
                IF proper$ = "y" then CALL proper(np,label)
                BOX CLEAR x - size,x + size, y - size, y + size
                BOX LINES x - size,x + size, y - size, y + size
                PLOT TEXT, at x - 0.25,y - 0.25: using$("##",label)
            END IF
        NEXT row
    NEXT col
END SUB
```

```
SUB span(L,cl(,),np(),ispan)
    ! check for existence of vertical spanning cluster
    LET ispan = 0
    FOR side1 = 1 to L
        LET arg1 = side1
        LET arg2 = 1
        IF cl(arg1,arg2) > 0 then
            LET nbot = cl(arg1,arg2)
            CALL proper(np,nbot)              ! determine if label is proper
            FOR side2 = 1 to L
                LET arg1 = side2
                LET arg2 = L
                IF cl(arg1,arg2) > 0 then
                    LET ntop = cl(arg1,arg2)
                    CALL proper(np,ntop)
                    IF ntop = nbot then
                        LET ispan = ntop
                        EXIT SUB
                    END IF
                END IF
            NEXT side2
        END IF
    NEXT side1
END SUB


SUB compute_mass(L,cl(,),np(),mass(),nmax)
    ! array mass(i) is mass of cluster with proper label i
    FOR n = 1 to nmax
        LET mass(n) = 0
    NEXT n
    LET nmax = 0
    FOR row = 1 to L
        FOR col = 1 to L
            IF cl(col,row) > 0 then
                LET label = cl(col,row)
                CALL proper(np,label)              ! determine proper label
                IF label > nmax then LET nmax = label
                LET mass(label) = mass(label) + 1
            END IF
```

```
        NEXT col
     NEXT row
     PRINT "label", "mass"
     FOR i = 1 to nmax
        IF mass(i) > 0 then
           PRINT USING "#####": i,mass(i)
        END IF
     NEXT i
     PRINT
END SUB

SUB radius_gyration(L,cl(,),np(),label)
     FOR row = 1 to L
        FOR col = 1 to L
           IF cl(col,row) > 0 then
              LET label_temp = cl(col,row)
              CALL proper(np,label_temp)        ! determine proper label
              IF label_temp = label then        ! proper label
                 LET xcm = xcm + col
                 LET ycm = ycm + row
                 LET R2 = R2 + row*row + col*col
                 LET mass = mass + 1            ! number of sites in cluster
              END IF
           END IF
        NEXT col
     NEXT row
     IF mass > 0 then
        LET radius = sqr((R2/mass) - ((xcm*xcm + ycm*ycm)/(mass*mass)))
        PRINT "radius of gyration of cluster ";"label";label;" = ";radius
     ELSE
        PRINT "no cluster with that label"
     END IF
END SUB
```

```
SUB plot_cluster(L,cl(,),np(),label)
   CLEAR
   BOX LINES 0,L,0,L
   LET size = 0.4                          ! linear dimension of box drawn at each site
   FOR col = 1 to L
      LET x = col - 0.5          ! associate box of linear dimension 1 with each site
      FOR row = 1 to L
         LET y = row - 0.5
         BOX LINES x - size, x + size, y - size, y + size
         LET label_temp = cl(col,row)
         IF label_temp > 0 then
            CALL proper(np,label_temp)
            IF label_temp = label then        ! occupied site
               BOX AREA x - size, x + size, y - size, y + size
            END IF
         END IF
      NEXT row
   NEXT col
END SUB

SUB draw_conf(L,s(,))
   BOX LINES 0,L,0,L
   LET size = 0.4                       ! linear dimension of box drawn at each site
   FOR col = 1 to L
      LET x = col - 0.5     ! associate box of linear dimension 1 with each site
      FOR row = 1 to L
         LET y = row - 0.5
         PLOT POINTS: x,y                ! draw lattice sites
         IF s(col,row) = -1 then         ! occupied site
            BOX AREA x - size, x + size, y - size, y + size
         ELSE
            BOX LINES x - size, x + size, y - size, y + size
         END IF
      NEXT row
   NEXT col
END SUB
```

```
SUB first_span(L,p,s(,),r(,),cl(,),np())
    DIM prob(100)
    INPUT prompt "lattice size = ": L
    INPUT prompt "initial p = ": p0
    INPUT prompt "increment in p = ": dp
    INPUT prompt "number of trials = ": ntrial
    FOR itrial = 1 to ntrial
        LET p = p0
        LET ip = 1
        LET ispan = 0                    ! label of vertical spanning cluster
        CALL assign(L,r)
        DO
            CALL occupy(L,p,s,r)          ! occupy additional sites
            CALL cluster_label(L,s,cl,np)
            IF ispan = 0 then
                CALL span(L,cl,np,ispan)
                IF ispan <> 0 then LET prob(ip) = prob(ip) + 1
            END IF
            LET p = p + dp
            LET ip = ip + 1
        LOOP until ispan <> 0
    NEXT itrial
    LET p = p0
    LET ip = 1
    DO                             ! normalize first spanning probabilities
        IF prob(ip) <> 0 then
            LET prob(ip) = prob(ip)/ntrial
            PRINT "p","vertical"
            PRINT p,prob(ip)
        END IF
        LET p = p + dp
        LET ip = ip + 1
    LOOP until p > 0.9
END SUB
```

```
SUB Pinfinity(mass(),ispan,nmax,prob)
   ! probability of occupied site belonging to spanning cluster
   IF ispan = 0 then
      LET prob = 0
      EXIT SUB
   END IF
   LET sum = 0
   FOR i = 1 to nmax
      LET sum = sum + mass(i)
   NEXT i
   LET prob = mass(ispan)/sum
END SUB

SUB mean_size(mass(),ispan,nmax,mean)
   ! determine mean cluster size S
   LET sum = 0
   LET sum2 = 0
   FOR i = 1 to nmax
      IF i <> ispan then
         LET sum = sum + mass(i)
         LET sum2 = sum2 + mass(i)*mass(i)
      END IF
   NEXT i
   LET mean = sum2/sum
END SUB
```

In Problem 12.5 we apply the Hoshen-Kopelman cluster labeling algorithm to a more systematic study of site percolation. In Sec. 12.4 we will use a finite size scaling analysis to obtain quantitative results for relatively small systems. The subroutines which draw the configurations and cluster labels on the screen need to be used in Problem 12.5a only.

PROBLEM 12.5 Applications of the cluster labeling algorithm

a. Run **Program Cluster** and describe a few examples of the cluster labeling method. Explain in detail how the algorithm is implemented.

b. Compute $F(p)dp$, the probability of *first* spanning an $L \times L$ lattice in the range p to $p + dp$. Do a minimum of 100 trials for each value of L and plot

$F(p)$ change with increasing L? At what value of p have 50% of the trials already spanned for each of the spanning rules and for each lattice size? Call this value $p_c(L)$. Does $p_c(L)$ depend on L? How strongly does $p_c(L)$ depend on the spanning rule? (Note that you will have to modify **SUB span** and **SUB first_span** in order to compute $F(p)$ for different spanning rules.)

c. Modify **Program cluster** so that the quantity P_∞ is averaged over at least 100 trials for each value of p. Compute P_∞ for $p = p_c$, $p = 0.65$, $p = 0.75$, and $p = 0.9$ for $L = 4, 16$, and $L = 32$. Use either the estimated value of $p_c(L)$ determined in part (a) or the best known value $p_c = 0.5927$. What is the qualitative p-dependence of P_∞? Is $P_\infty(p = p_c)$ an increasing or decreasing function of L? Remember to discard those configurations which do not have a spanning cluster.

d. Write a subroutine to compute $n_s(p)$ from the array $ns(i)$ (i is the cluster label). Consider $p = p_c$ and $p = p_c \pm 0.1$ for $L = 4, 16$ and 32 and average over at least ten trials. Why is n_s a decreasing function of s? Does n_s decrease more quickly for $p = p_c$ or $p \neq p_c$?

e. Compute the mean cluster size S for $p = p_c$ and $p = p_c \pm 0.1$ for $L = 4, 16$ and 32. Average over at least ten trials. What is the qualitative p-dependence of $S(p)$? How does $S(p = p_c)$ depend on L? For $p < p_c$ discard the configurations which contain a spanning cluster and for $p > p_c$ discard the configurations which do not have a spanning cluster.

12.4 CRITICAL EXPONENTS AND FINITE-SIZE SCALING

We are familiar with the distinct phases of matter from our everyday experience. The most familiar example is water which can exist as a vapor, liquid or ice. It is well known that water changes from one phase to another at a well-defined temperature and pressure, e.g. the transition from ice to liquid water occurs at $0\,^\circ C$ at atmospheric pressure. Such a change of phase is an example of a *thermodynamic phase transition.* Most substances also exhibit a *critical point;* that is beyond a particular temperature and pressure, it is no longer possible to distinguish between the liquid and gaseous phases (cf Reif).

Another familiar but less well known example of a critical point occurs in magnetic systems at the Curie temperature T_c. We know that at low temperatures some substances exhibit ferromagnetism, a spontaneous magnetization in the absence of an external magnetic field. If we raise the temperature of a ferromagnet, the spontaneous magnetization decreases and vanishes continuously at a "critical" temperature T_c. For $T > T_c$ the system is a paramagnet. In Chapter 16 we use Monte Carlo methods to investigate the behavior of a magnetic system near the magnetic critical point.

Since an understanding of thermodynamic phase transitions requires a strong background in statistical physics, it is of interest to study the percolation phase transition. Of course percolation is an unusual phase transition since temperature is not involved. However we will find that the properties of the *geometrical* phase transition in the percolation problem are qualitatively similar to the qualitative properties of thermodynamic phase transitions. Hence the following analysis of the phase transition in percolation can serve as a simple introduction to thermodynamic phase transitions as well. A major conclusion will be that in the vicinity of a phase transition, the qualitative behavior of the system is governed by the appearance of long-range correlations.

We know that the essential physics near the percolation threshold is associated with the existence of large but finite clusters. For example for $p < p_c$, we found in Problem 12.5d that n_s decays exponentially with s; for $p > p_c$ n_s decreases more rapidly with s. However for $p = p_c$, the s-dependence of n_s is qualitatively different and n_s decreases much more slowly. This different behavior of n_s at p_c is due to the presence of all length scales, e.g. the "infinite" cluster and the finite clusters of all sizes.

A more direct way of observing the effects of the length of the clusters is to introduce a characteristic linear dimension or *mean connectedness length* $\xi(p)$. Two possible definitions of $\xi(p)$ are explored in Problem 12.6.

PROBLEM 12.6 The connectedness length

a. One operational definition of ξ is to identify it with the *radius of gyration* R_s. We write the radius of gyration R_s of a single cluster of s-particles as

$$R_s{}^2 = \frac{1}{s} \sum_{i=1}^{s} (\vec{r}_i - \bar{r})^2 \tag{12.5}$$

where

$$\bar{r} = \frac{1}{s} \sum_{i=1}^{s} \vec{r}_i \tag{12.6}$$

and $\vec{r}_i$ is the position of the ith site in the cluster. The quantity $\bar{r}$ is the familiar definition of the center of mass of the cluster. We associate ξ with the radius of gyration of the *largest* non-spanning cluster only, rather than with a

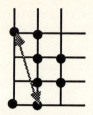

Fig. 12.9 The maximum separation between any two sites in the cluster shown is $\sqrt{10}$. The center of mass $(\bar{x}, \bar{y})$ and the radius of gyration of the cluster are given by $\bar{x} = 1$, $\bar{y} = 1.5$, and $R_s{}^2 = 14/8$.

weighted average of R_s over all non-spanning clusters. Generate a percolation configuration at a given value of p, compute R_s for the largest non-spanning cluster, and average R_s over several configurations. Consider values of p in steps of 0.01 in the intervals $[p_c - 0.05, p_c - 0.01]$ and $[p_c + 0.01, p_c + 0.05]$ with $p_c = 0.5927$. Choose $L = 32$ and consider a minimum of 50 configurations for each value of p. For $p < p_c$ discard those configurations which contain a spanning cluster, and for $p > p_c$ discard those configurations which do not have a spanning cluster. Plot ξ as a function of p and discuss its qualitative dependence on p. Is $\xi(p)$ a monotonically increasing or decreasing function of p for $p < p_c$ and $p > p_c$?

*b. Associate the connectedness length with the maximum separation between two sites in the largest non-spanning cluster (see Fig. 12.9). Modify **Program Cluster** so that the maximum separation can be computed and averaged over several trials. Use the same configurations as in part (a) and compute the mean maximum separation between two sites in the largest non-spanning cluster. Identify this length with ξ, plot $\xi(p)$ as a function of p, and discuss its qualitative dependence on p. Do the two definitions of ξ yield similar qualitative behavior?

On the basis of your results in Problem 12.6 for $\xi(p)$ on finite lattices, we can conclude that for large L, $\xi(p)$ is an increasing function of p for $p < p_c$ and a decreasing function of p for $p > p_c$ (see Fig. 12.10). Moreover we know that $\xi(p = p_c)$ is approximately equal to L and hence diverges as $L \to \infty$. This qualitative behavior of ξ is independent of the precise definition of $\xi(p)$ and is consistent with our physical picture of the clusters—as p approaches p_c, the probability that two occupied sites are in the same cluster increases. These qualitative considerations lead us to conjecture that in the limit $L \to \infty$, $\xi(p)$

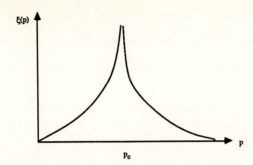

Fig. 12.10 Qualitative p-dependence of the mean connectedness length $\xi(p)$. The divergence of $\xi(p)$ in the critical region is characterized by the exponent ν (see (12.7)).

diverges in the *critical region*, $|p-p_c| \ll 1$. We can describe the divergence of $\xi(p)$ more quantitatively by introducing a *critical exponent* ν defined by the relation

$$\xi(p) \sim |p - p_c|^{-\nu} \quad . \tag{12.7}$$

Of course there is no *a priori* reason why the divergence of $\xi(p)$ can be characterized by a simple power-law. You might want to analyze your data for the p-dependence of $\xi(p)$ and attempt to estimate the value of ν. However since your data is limited by the relatively small lattices considered ("finite-size effects") and by the limited number of trials, your estimate for ν will be very approximate.

How do the other quantities that we have considered behave in the critical region in the limit $L \to \infty$? According to the definition (12.4) of P_∞, $P_\infty = 0$ for $p < p_c$ and is an increasing function of p for $p > p_c$. We conjecture that in the critical region, the increase of P_∞ with increasing p is characterized by another exponent β defined by the relation

$$P_\infty \sim (p_c - p)^\beta \quad . \tag{12.8}$$

In the language of critical phenomena, P_∞ is known as the *order parameter* of the system. The critical exponent β describes how the connectedness of the infinite cluster goes to zero at the percolation threshold. Another quantity of interest is the mean cluster size $S(p)$. The critical behavior of $S(p)$ can be written as

$$S(p) \sim |p - p_c|^{-\gamma} \tag{12.9}$$

which defines the critical exponent γ. The common critical exponents for percolation are summarized in Table 12.1. For comparison the analogous critical exponents of a magnetic critical point are also shown.

TABLE 12.1 Several of the critical exponents for the percolation and magnetism phase transitions in $d = 2$ and 3 dimensions. Rational numbers correspond to known exact results. The values of the magnetic exponents correspond to the Ising model (see Chapter 15.)

Quantity	Functional form	Exponent	$d = 2$	$d = 3$
Percolation				
order parameter	$P_\infty \sim (p - p_c)^\beta$	β	5/36	0.4
mean size of finite clusters	$S(p) \sim |p - p_c|^{-\gamma}$	γ	43/18	1.8
correlation length	$\xi(p) \sim |p - p_c|^{-\nu}$	ν	4/3	0.9
cluster numbers	$n_s \sim s^{-\tau}$	τ	187/91	2.2
Magnetism				
order parameter	$M(T) \sim (T_c - T)^\beta$	β	1/8	0.32
susceptibility	$\chi(T) \sim |T - T_c|^{-\gamma}$	γ	7/4	1.24
correlation length	$\xi(T) \sim |T - T_c|^{-\nu}$	ν	1	0.63

Since we can only simulate finite lattices, a direct fit of the measured quantities ξ, P_∞, and $S(p)$ to (12.7)–(12.9) will not yield good estimates for the corresponding exponents. The basic problem is that we cannot let p approach p_c too closely without obtaining finite size effects. In contrast, $\xi(p)$ is small in comparison to L for p far from p_c and the measured values of ξ, and hence the values of the other physical quantities are not affected by the finite size of the lattice. Hence for $p \ll p_c$ and $p \gg p_c$, the properties of the system are indistinguishable from the corresponding properties of a truly macroscopic system ($L \to \infty$). However if p is close to p_c, $\xi(p)$ is comparable to L and the behavior of the system differs from that of a macroscopic system. In particular a finite lattice cannot exhibit a true phase transition characterized by divergent physical quantities. Instead ξ and S reach a finite maximum at $p = p_c(L)$.

The effects of the finite size of the system can be made more quantitative by the following argument. Consider for example the conjectured critical behavior (12.8) of P_∞. As long as ξ is much less than L, the power law behavior given by (12.8) is expected to hold. However if ξ is comparable to L, ξ cannot change appreciably and (12.8) is no longer applicable. This qualitative change in the behavior of P_∞ and other physical quantities will occur for

$$\xi(p) \sim L \sim |p - p_c|^{-\nu} \quad . \tag{12.10}$$

Note that we can invert (12.10) and write

$$|p - p_c| \sim L^{-1/\nu} \quad . \tag{12.11}$$

Hence if ξ and L are approximately the same size, we can replace (12.8) by the relation

$$P_\infty(p = p_c) \sim L^{-\beta/\nu} \qquad (L \to \infty) \ . \tag{12.12}$$

The relation (12.12) between P_∞ and L at $p = p_c$ is consistent with the fact that a phase transition is defined only for infinite systems.

One implication of the relation (12.12) is that we can use it to determine the critical exponents. This method of analysis is known as *finite-size scaling* and is an important method for the analysis of critical exponents. Suppose that we generate percolation configurations at $p = p_c$ for different values of L and analyze P_∞ as a function of L. If L is sufficiently large, we can use the asymptotic relation (12.12) to estimate the ratio β/ν. A similar analysis can be used for $S(p)$ and other quantities of interest. We use this method in Problem 12.7.

*PROBLEM 12.7 Finite size scaling analysis of critical exponents

a. Use **Program Cluster** to compute P_∞ at $p = p_c$ for a minimum of 100 trials. Consider $L = 10, 20, 40,$ and 60. Include in your average only those configurations which have a spanning cluster. Although our qualitative arguments for the relation (12.12) do not specify whether we should choose p equal to $p_c(L)$ or $p_c(L \to \infty)$, best results are obtained using the latter value $p_c = 0.5927$ for a square lattice. Plot $\ln P_\infty$ versus $\ln L$, and estimate the ratio β/ν.

b. Use finite size scaling arguments to determine the dependence of the mean cluster size S on L at $p = p_c$. Modify **Program cluster** so that S is averaged over the same configurations as considered in part (a). Remember that S is the mean number of sites in the non-spanning clusters.

c. Find the mass (number of particles) M in the spanning cluster at $p = p_c$ as a function of L. Use the same configurations as in part (a). Determine an exponent from a plot of $\ln M$ vs $\ln L$. This exponent is called the fractal dimension of the cluster and is discussed in Chapter 13.

We found in Sec. 12.2 that the numerical value of the percolation threshold p_c depends on the symmetry and dimension of the lattice, e.g. $p_c \approx 0.5927$ for the square lattice and $p_c = 1/2$ for the triangular lattice. A remarkable feature of the power-law dependences summarized in Table 12.1 is that the values of the critical exponents do not depend on the symmetry of the lattice and are independent of the existence of the lattice itself, e.g. they are identical for the continuum percolation model discussed in Problem 12.3. Moreover it is not necessary to distinguish between the exponents for site and bond percolation. In the vocabulary of critical phenomena, we say that site, bond and continuum percolation all belong to the same *universality class* and that their critical exponents are identical.

Another important idea in critical phenomena is the existence of relations between the critical exponents. An example of such a *scaling law* is

$$2\beta + \gamma = \nu d \qquad (12.13)$$

where d is the dimension of the lattice. A more detailed discussion of finite size scaling and scaling laws can be found in the references.

12.5   THE RENORMALIZATION GROUP

In Sec. 12.4, we used the properties of cluster related quantities on different length scales to determine the values of the critical exponents. This idea of examining physical quantities near the critical point on different length scales can be extended beyond finite-size scaling and is the basis of the *renormalization group* method, probably the most important new method in theoretical physics during the past twenty years. The first renormalization group treatment of critical phenomena was published by K. G. Wilson in 1971. The author was honored in 1981 with the Nobel prize in physics for his contributions to the development of the renormalization group method. Although this method was first applied to thermodynamic phase transitions, it is simpler to introduce the method in the context of percolation. We will find that this method of analysis yields the critical exponents directly and in combination with Monte Carlo methods is frequently more powerful than Monte Carlo methods alone.

In order to introduce the method, let us consider a photograph of a percolation configuration generated at $p = p_0 < p_c$. If we view the photograph from longer and longer distances, what will we see? Convince yourself that when you are far from the photograph, you will not be able to distinguish sites which are adjacent to each other and will not be able to observe single site clusters. In addition, branches emanating from larger clusters and narrow bridges connecting large "blobs" will also be lost in your distant view of the photograph. Hence for $p_0 < p_c$, the distant photograph will look like a percolation configuration generated at a value of p equal to p_1 with $p_1 < p_0$. In addition the connectedness length $\xi(p_1)$ of the remaining clusters will be smaller than $\xi(p_0)$. If we move still further away from the photograph, the new clusters will look even smaller with a value of p equal to p_2 with $p_2 < p_1$. Eventually we will not be able to distinguish any clusters and the photograph will appear as if it were at the trivial *fixed point* $p = 0$.

Now consider what we would observe if $p_0 > p_c$. Close inspection of the photograph would reveal in general only small regions of unoccupied sites. As we move away from the photograph, these spaces would become less discernible and the configuration will look as though a larger percentage of the lattice were occupied. Hence the photograph will look like a configuration generated at a value of p equal to p_1 with $p_1 > p_0$ and $\xi(p_1) < \xi(p_0)$. We conclude that as we move further and further away from the photograph, it will eventually appear to be at the other trivial fixed point $p = 1$.

What happens if $p_0 = p_c$? We know that at the percolation threshold, all length scales are present and it does not matter what length scale we use to observe the system. Thus, the photograph will appear the same (although smaller overall) regardless of the distance at which we observe it. In this sense p_c is a special *non-trivial* fixed point.

We now consider an operational method of using a computer to change the configurations in a way that is similar to moving away from the photograph. Our treatment follows closely the paper by Reynolds et al. (see references). Consider a square lattice which is partitioned into *cells* or *blocks* which cover the lattice (see Fig. 12.11). If we view the lattice from the perspective in which the sites in a cell merge to become a new supersite or "renormalized" site, then the new lattice has the same symmetry as the original lattice. However the replacement of cells by the new sites has changed the length scale—all distances are now smaller by a factor of b, where b is the linear dimension of the cell. Thus the effect of a "renormalization" is to replace each cell with a single renormalized site and to rescale the connectedness length for the renormalized lattice by a factor of b.

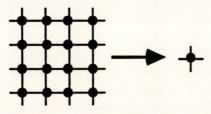

Fig. 12.11 An example of a $b = 4$ cell used on the square lattice. The cell contains b^2 sites which after a renormalization group transformation is rescaled to a single site.

How can we decide whether the renormalized site is occupied or not? Since we want to preserve the gross features of the original lattice and hence its connectedness, we assume that a renormalized site is occupied if the original group of sites spans the cell. We will adopt the vertical spanning rule for convenience. The effect of performing a scale transformation on typical percolation configurations for p above and below p_c is illustrated in Fig. 12.12a and Fig. 12.12b respectively. In both cases, the effect of the successive renormalization transformations is to move the system away from p_c. We see that for $p = 0.7$, the effect of the transformations is to drive the system toward $p = 1$. For $p = 0.5$, the trend is to drive the system toward $p = 0$. Of course since we began with a finite lattice, we cannot continue the renormalization transformation indefinitely.

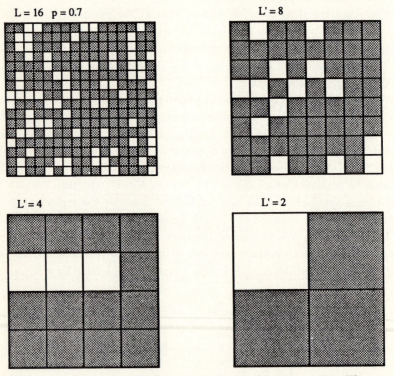

Fig. 12.12a A percolation configuration generated at $p = 0.7$. The original configuration has been renormalized three times using **Program rg** by transforming cells of four sites into one new supersite. What would be the effect of an additional transformation?

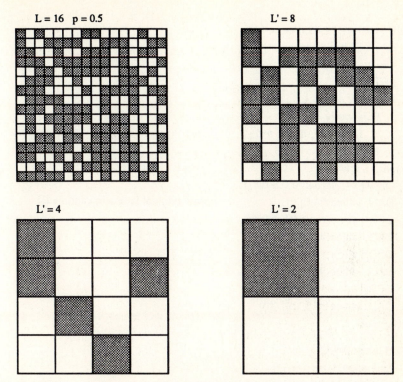

L = 16   p = 0.5   L' = 8

L' = 4   L' = 2

Fig. 12.12b A percolation configuration generated at $p = 0.5$. The original configuration has been renormalized three times using **Program rg** by transforming blocks of four sites into one new site. What would be the effect of an additional transformation?

Program rg, in conjunction with your visual intuition, generates the configurations of the type shown in Fig. 12.12 and provides a simple implementation of the renormalization group. The program divides the screen into four windows and draws the three renormalized lattices in windows 2 through 4.

```
PROGRAM rg
DIM r(16,16)
CALL initial(#1,#2,#3,#4,L,b,r)          ! assign random number to each site
CALL configuration(#1,#2,#3,#4,L,b,r)
END
```

```
SUB initial(#1,#2,#3,#4,L,b,r(,))
   RANDOMIZE
   LET L = 16
   LET b = 2
   FOR row = 1 to L
      FOR col = 1 to L
         LET r(col,row) = rnd          ! random number assigned to each site
      NEXT col
   NEXT row
   OPEN #1: screen 0,0.5,0.5,1
   CALL lattice(#1,L)                   ! draw original lattice in window #1
   OPEN #2: screen 0.5,1,0.5,1
   CALL lattice(#2,L/b)
   OPEN #3: screen 0,0.5,0,0.5
   CALL lattice(#3,L/(b*b))
   OPEN #4: screen 0.5,1,0,.5
   CALL lattice(#4,L/(b*b*b))
END SUB

SUB lattice(#1,L)
   LET aspect_ratio = 1.5
   LET margin = 0.2*L
   LET mx = aspect_ratio*margin
   LET bx = aspect_ratio*L
   SET window -mx,bx,-margin,L + margin
   BOX LINES 0,L,0,L
   FOR row = 1 to L
      FOR col = 1 to L
         PLOT POINTS: col - 0.5,row - 0.5
      NEXT col
   NEXT row
END SUB
```

```
SUB configuration(#1,#2,#3,#4,L,b,r(,))
  DIM s(16,16),s1(8,8),s2(4,4),s3(2,2)
  DO while p <=1
    WINDOW #1
    SET cursor 1,1
    PRINT "L ="; L;
    SET cursor 1,14
    PRINT "     "              ! erase previous value of p
    SET cursor 1,10
    INPUT prompt "p = ": p
    FOR row = 1 to L
      FOR col = 1 to L
        IF r(col,row) < p and s(col,row) <> 1 then
          CALL occupy(#1,col,row)
          LET s(col,row) = 1
        END IF
      NEXT col
    NEXT row
    CALL block(#2,L/b,s,s1)
    CALL block(#3,L/(b*b),s1,s2)
    CALL block(#4,L/(b*b*b),s2,s3)
  LOOP
END SUB

SUB block(#1,L,w(,),wr(,))
  WINDOW #1
  FOR row = 1 to L
    LET y = 2*row - 1
    FOR col = 1 to L
      LET x = 2*col - 1
      ! if cell spans vertically, then renormalized site occupied
      IF w(x,y)*w(x,y + 1) = 1 then LET wr(col,row) = 1
      IF w(x + 1,y)*w(x + 1,y + 1) = 1 then LET wr(col,row) = 1
      IF wr(col,row) = 1 then CALL occupy(#1,col,row)
    NEXT col
  NEXT row
  SET cursor 1,1
  PRINT "L' ="; L;
END SUB
```

```
SUB occupy(#1,col,row)
    LET x = 0.5
    LET d = 0.4
    BOX AREA col - x - d, col - x + d, row - x - d, row -x + d
END SUB
```

PROBLEM 12.8 Visual renormalization group

Use **Program rg** with $L = 32$ and $b = 2$ to estimate the value of the percolation threshold. For example show that for small p, e.g. $p \approx 0.4$, the renormalized lattice usually renormalizes to a nonspanning cluster. What happens for larger p, e.g. $p \approx 0.8$? How can you use the properties of the renormalized lattices to estimate p_c?

Although a visual implementation of the renormalization group allows us to roughly estimate p_c, it does not allow us to estimate the critical exponents. In the following we present an analysis based on the renormalization group method which allows us to obtain p_c and the critical exponent ν associated with the connectedness length. This analysis follows closely the method presented by Reynolds et al (see references).

The implementation of a renormalization group method consists of two parts: an average over the basic variables and a specification of the parameters which determine the renormalized configuration. We adopt the same average as before, i.e. we group the b^d sites within a cell of linear dimension b and replace the sites by a single site which represents whether or not the original lattice sites spanned the cell. The second step is to determine which parameters specify the

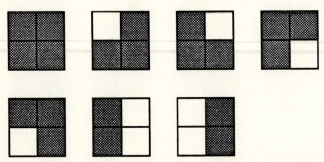

Fig. 12.13 The seven (vertically) spanning configurations on a $b = 2$ cell.

new configuration after the averaging. We make the simple approximation that each cell is independent of all the other cells and is characterized only by the probability p' that the cell is occupied. Since the renormalization transformation between p' and p must reflect the fact that the basic physics of percolation is connectednessnp, i.e. the formation of an infinite connected path, we define a cell to be occupied only if it contains a set of sites which "span" the cell. Hence if the sites are occupied with probability p, then the cells are occupied with probability p', where p' is given by a *recursion relation* or *renormalization transformation* of the form

$$p' = R(p) \quad . \tag{12.14}$$

$R(p)$ is the total probability that the sites form a spanning path. An example will make the formal relation (12.14) more clear. In Fig. 12.13, we show the seven vertically spanning site configurations for a $b = 2$ cell. The probability p' that the renormalized site is occupied is given by the sum of all the possibilities:

$$p' = R(p) = p^4 + 4p^3(1-p) + 2p^2(1-p)^2 \quad . \tag{12.15}$$

Note that in general the probability p' of the occupied renormalized sites is different than the occupation probability p of the original sites. For example suppose that we begin with $p = p_0 = 0.5$. After a single renormalization transformation, the value of p obtained from (12.15) becomes $p_1 = R(p_0 = 0.5) = 0.44$. If we perform a second renormalization transformation, we have $p_2 = R(p_1) = 0.35$. It is easy to conclude that further transformations will drive the system to the fixed point $p = 0$. Similarly if we begin with $p = p_0 = 0.7$, we will find that successive transformations will drive the system to the fixed point $p = 1$. In order to find the non-trivial fixed point associated with the critical threshold p_c, we need to find the special value of p such that

$$p^* = R(p^*) \quad . \tag{12.16}$$

For the recursion relation (12.15), we find that the solution of the fourth degree equation for p^* yields the two trivial fixed points $p^* = 0$ and $p^* = 1$ and the non-trivial fixed point $p^* = 0.61804$ which we associate with p_c. This calculated value of p^* for $b = 2$ should be compared with the best known estimate $p_c = 0.5927$.

In order to calculate the critical exponent ν from the renormalization transformation, we recall that on the renormalized lattice all lengths are reduced by a factor of b in comparison to the lengths in the original system. Hence the connectedness length transforms as

$$\xi' = \xi/b \quad . \tag{12.17}$$

Since $\xi(p) = const|p - p_c|^{-\nu}$ for $p \sim p_c$ and p_c corresponds to p^*, we have

$$|p' - p^*|^{-\nu} = b^{-1}|p - p^*|^{-\nu} \quad . \tag{12.18}$$

To find the relation between p' and p near p_c, we expand the renormalization transformation (12.14) about p^* and obtain to first order

$$p' - p^* = R(p) - R(p^*) \approx \lambda(p - p^*) \tag{12.19}$$

where

$$\lambda = \frac{dR}{dp}\Big|_{p=p^*} \quad . \tag{12.20}$$

We need to do a little algebra to obtain an explicit expression for ν. We first raise both sides of (12.19) to the $-\nu$ power and write

$$|p' - p^*|^{-\nu} = \lambda^{-\nu}|p - p^*|^{-\nu} \quad . \tag{12.21}$$

We then compare (12.21) and (12.18) and obtain

$$b^{-1} = \lambda^{-\nu} \quad . \tag{12.22}$$

Finally we take the logarithm of both sides of (12.22) and obtain the desired relation for the critical exponent ν:

$$\nu = \frac{\log b}{\log \lambda} \quad . \tag{12.23}$$

As an example we calculate λ for $b = 2$ by writing (12.15) in the form $R(p) = -p^4 + 2p^2$. The derivative of $R(p)$ with respect to p yields $\lambda = 4p(1-p^2) = 1.5279$ at $p = p^* = 0.61804$. We then use the relation (12.23) to obtain

$$\nu = \log 2 / \log 1.5279 = 1.635\ldots \quad . \tag{12.24}$$

The comparison of (12.24) with the exact result $\nu = 4/3$ in two dimensions shows remarkable agreement for such a simple calculation. What would we be able to conclude if we were to measure $\xi(p)$ directly on a 2×2 lattice? However our calculation of ν is uncontrolled, since we have no *a priori* estimate of the accuracy of our calculation. What is the nature of our approximations? Our basic assumption has been that the occupancy of each cell is independent of all other cells. This assumption is correct for the original sites but after one renormalization, we lose some of the original connecting paths and gain connecting paths which

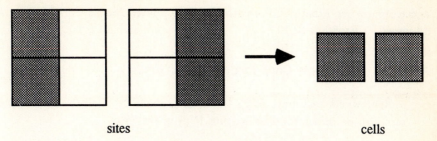

sites   cells

Fig. 12.14 Example of the interface problem between cells. The two cells are not connected at the original site level but are connected at the cell level.

are not present in the original lattice. An example of this "interface" problem is shown in Fig. 12.14. Since this surface effect becomes less probable with increasing cell size, one way to improve our renormalization group calculation is to consider larger cells. We consider a $b = 3$ calculation in Problem 12.9.

PROBLEM 12.9 Position space renormalization group method for small cells

a. Obtain the spanning configurations for a $b = 2$ spanning cell assuming that a cell spans if a spanning path exists in either the vertical or the horizontal directions. Obtain the recursion relation and solve for the fixed point p^*. The simplest way to solve (12.16) is by trial and error. Another way is to plot the function $R(p) - p$ versus p and to find the value of p at which $R(p) - p$ crosses the horizontal axis. How do p^* and ν compare to their values using the vertical spanning rule?

b. Enumerate the possible spanning configurations on a $b = 3$ cell, determine the probability of each configuration, and obtain the renormalization transformation $R(p)$. Assume that a cell is occupied if a cluster spans the cell vertically, and if a cluster spans the cell both vertically and horizontally. Then solve the recursion relation (12.16) for p^*. Once the value of p^* is known, the slope λ and the exponent ν can be determined analytically. Determine $p^*(b = 3)$ and $\nu(b = 3)$ for the two spanning rules. Are your results for p^* and ν closer to their known values than for $b = 2$?

It is possible to improve our results for $p_c(b)$ and $\nu(b)$ by enumerating the spanning clusters for much larger b. However since the 2^{b^2} possible configurations for a $b \times b$ cell increase rapidly with b, exact enumeration is not practical for $b > 5$

and we must use Monte Carlo methods. Two related Monte Carlo methods are discussed in Problem 12.10

discussed in Problem 12.10

*PROBLEM 12.10 Monte Carlo renormalization group

a. One way to estimate $R(p)$, the total probability of all the spanning clusters, can be understood by writing $R(p)$ in the form

$$R(p) = \sum_{n=1}^{N} \binom{N}{n} p^n q^{(N-n)} S(n) \qquad (12.25)$$

where $N = b^2$. The binominal coefficient $\binom{N}{n}$ represents the number of possible configurations of n-occupied sites and $(N-n)$-empty sites. The quantity $S(n)$ is the probability that a configuration with n occupied sites spans the cell. A comparison of (12.15) and (12.25) shows that for $b = 2$ and vertical spanning, $S(1) = 0$, $S(2) = 2/6$, $S(3) = 1$ and $S(4) = 1$. What are the values of $S(n)$ for $b = 3$?

Since $S(n)$ is a probability, we can estimate it by straightforward Monte Carlo methods. The simplest way to sample $S(n)$ is to add a particle at random to an unoccupied site and check to see if a spanning path exists. If a spanning path does not exist, add another particle at random to a previously unoccupied site. If a spanning path exists after s particles are added, then $S(n) = S(n)+1$ for $n \geq s$ and a new trial is begun. After a reasonable number of trials, the results for $S(n)$ can be normalized. Of course this procedure can be made more efficient by checking for a spanning cluster only after the total number of particles added is near $s \sim p^* N$ and by checking for spanning after adding several particles.

Write a Monte Carlo program to sample $S(n)$. Store the location of the unoccupied sites in an array. To check your program, first sample $S(n)$ for $b = 2$ and $b = 3$ and compare your results to the exact results for $S(n)$. Consider larger values of b and determine $S(n)$ for $b = 5, 8, 16$ and 32. For $b \simeq 16$, the function $R(p)$ can be found by using (12.25) and the Gaussian approximation

$$P_N(n) = \binom{N}{n} p^n q^{(N-n)} \approx (2\pi N pq)^{-1/2} exp(-(n - pN)^2/2N pq). \qquad (12.26)$$

Note that since $P_N(n)$ is sharply peaked for large b, it is necessary to sample $S(n)$ only near $n = p^* N$.

b. Note that in part (a), the number of particles rather than the occupation probability p was varied. An equivalent Monte Carlo procedure is to vary p and sample $F(p)dp$, the probability of *first* spanning a $b \times b$ cell in the range p to $p + dp$. Since the renormalization group transformation defines p' as the *total* probability of spanning at p, p' can be interpreted as the *cumulative distribution function* and hence is related to $F(p)$ by

$$p' = R(p) = \int_0^p F(p)\,dp \quad . \tag{12.27}$$

The sampling of $F(p)$ for finite width bins dp implies that the integral in (12.27) reduces to a sum. Since $\lambda = dR(p = p^*)/dp$, we have $\lambda = F(p^*)$. The simplest way to estimate λ is by setting $\lambda = F(p_{max})$, where p_{max} is the value of p at which $F(p)$ is a maximum. How does the value of p_c compare with p_{max}? Determine $p_c(b)$ and $\nu(b)$ for $b = 5, 8, 16$, and 32. How do your results compare with those found in part (a)? Which method yields smaller error estimates for p_c and ν?

c. It is possible to extrapolate the results for $p_c(b)$ and $\nu(b)$ to the limit $b \to \infty$. Use the asymptotic relations

$$\nu(b)^{-1} \approx \nu^{-1} - c_1/\ln b \tag{12.28a}$$

and

$$p^*(b) \approx p_c - c_2 b^{-\nu} \tag{12.28b}$$

to estimate the extrapolated values of ν and p_c. Note that it is necessary to consider cells on the order $b \approx 500$ and to do a more sophisticated analysis of $\nu(b)$ and $p^*(b)$ in order to obtain extrapolated results which are consistent with the exact value $\nu = 4/3$ and the best known estimate $p_c = 0.5927$.

REFERENCES AND SUGGESTIONS FOR ADDITIONAL READING

C. Domb, E. Stoll, and T. Schneider, "Percolation clusters," *Contemp. Phys.* **21**, 577 (1980). This review paper discusses the nature of the percolation transition using illustrations from a film of a Monte Carlo simulation of a percolation process.

J. W. Essam, "Percolation theory," *Reports on Progress in Physics* **53**, 833 (1980). A more mathematically oriented review paper.

J. P. Fitzpatrick, R. B. Malt, and F. Spaepen, "Percolation theory of the conductivity of random close packed mixtures of hard spheres," *Phys. Letts.* **A47**, 207 (1974). The authors describe a demonstration experiment done in a first year physics course at Harvard.

Edward T. Gawlinski and H. Eugene Stanley "Continuum percolation in two dimensions: Monte Carlo tests of scaling and universality for non-interacting discs," *J. Phys. A: Math. Gen.* **14**, L291 (1981). These workers show that within their Monte Carlo error the critical exponents of continuum percolation are the same as those for a two-dimensional lattice.

J. Hoshen and R. Kopelman, "Percolation and cluster distribution. I. Cluster multiple labeling technique and critical concentration algorithm," *Phys. Rev.* **B14**, 3438 (1976). The original paper on an efficient cluster labeling algorithm.

Ramit Mehr, Tal Grossman, N. Kristianpoller, and Yuval Gefen, "Simple percolation experiment in two dimensions," *Am. J. Phys.* **54**, 271 (1986). A simple experiment for an undergraduate physics laboratory is proposed.

Peter J. Reynolds, H. Eugene Stanley and W. Klein, "Large-cell Monte Carlo renormalization group for percolation," *Phys. Rev.* **B21**, 1223 (1980). An especially clearly written research paper. Our discussion on the renormalization group in Sec. 12.5 is based upon this paper.

D. Stauffer, "Percolation clusters as teaching aid for Monte Carlo simulation and critical exponents," *Am. J. Phys.* **45**, 1001 (1977).

D. Stauffer, "Scaling theory of percolation clusters," *Physics Reports* **54**, 1 (1979). An important review paper.

D. Stauffer, *Introduction to Percolation Theory*, Taylor & Francis (1985). A delightful little book by one of the leading workers in the field. An efficient Fortran implementation of the Hoshen-Kopelman algorithm is given in the appendix.

B. P. Watson and P. L. Leath, "Conductivity in the two-dimensional-site percolation problem," *Phys. Rev.* **B9**, 4893 (1974). A research paper on the conductivity of chicken wire.

Kenneth G. Wilson, "Problems in physics with many scales of length," *Sci. Am.* **241**, 158 (1979). An accessible article on the renormalization group method and its applications in particle and condensed matter physics. See also ibid. "The renormalization group and critical phenomena," *Rev. Mod. Phys.* **55**, 583 (1983). The latter article is the text of Wilson's lecture on the occasion of the presentation of the 1982 Nobel Prize in Physics. In this lecture he claims that he " ... found it very helpful to demand that a correctly formulated field theory be soluble by computer, the same way an ordinary differential equation can be solved on a computer ... ."

Richard Zallen, *The Physics of Amorphous Solids*, Wiley-Interscience (1983). Chapter Four of this very entertaining and informative book discusses many of the applications of percolation concepts to realistic systems.

FRACTALS, KINETIC GROWTH MODELS AND CELLULAR AUTOMATA

13

We introduce the concept of fractal dimension and discuss several percolation and kinetic growth models. Several cellular automata models are also introduced.

13.1   FRACTAL DIMENSION

One of the more interesting geometrical properties of objects is their shape.
As an example, we show in Fig. 13.1 a percolation cluster generated at the
percolation threshold. Although the visual description of the spanning cluster
is subjective, such clusters have been described as ramified, airy, tenuous, and
stringy. In contrast a percolation cluster would not be described as compact or
space-filling.

In recent years a new *fractal* geometry has been developed by Mandelbrot
and others (see references) to describe such ramified objects. One quantitative measure of the structure of these objects is the *fractal dimension* d_f. In
order to define d_f, we first review some simple ideas of ordinary Euclidean
geometry. Consider a circular or spherical object of mass M and radius R.
The object can be either solid (uniform density) or full of holes, but in either case we assume that the density does not depend on the size of the object (see Fig. 13.2). Hence if the radius of the object is increased from R to
$2R$, the mass of the object is increased by a factor of R^2 if the object is

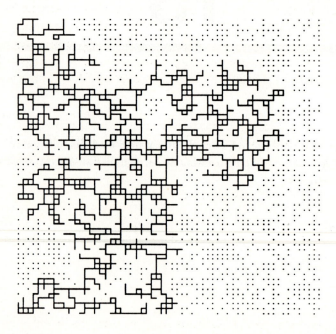

Fig. 13.1 Example of a percolation cluster generated at $p = 0.5927$
on an $L = 60$ square lattice. Occupied sites which are not part of the
spanning cluster are shown as points; unoccupied sites are not shown.

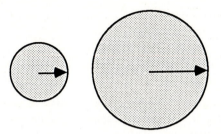

Fig. 13.2 The number of "dots" per unit area in each circle is uniform. How does the total number of dots (mass) vary with the radius of the circle?

circular or by R^3 if the object is spherical. We can write this relation between mass and length as

$$M(R) \sim R^d \tag{13.1}$$

where d is the spatial dimension. An object whose mass-length relation satisfies (13.1) is said to be "compact." Equation (13.1) implies that if the linear dimensions of a compact object is increased by a factor of R while preserving its shape, then the mass of the object is increased by R^d. This mass-length scaling relation is closely related to the intuitive idea of dimension and also provides a useful generalization to dimensions greater than three. Note that if the mass M and the length R are related by (13.1), the mass density $\rho = M/R^d$ scales as

$$\rho = R^0 \quad . \tag{13.2}$$

The relation of the mass of an object to its characteristic length R can be defined more generally than in (13.1). One way to define the fractal dimension d_f is by the relation

$$M(R) \sim R^{d_f} \quad . \tag{13.3}$$

We denote objects as "fractals" if they satisfy (13.3) with a value of d_f less than the spatial dimension d. Note that if an object satisfies (13.3), its density is not the same for all R but scales as

$$\rho(R) \sim M/R^d \sim R^{d_f - d} \quad . \tag{13.4}$$

Since $d_f < d$, a fractal object becomes less dense at larger length scales. This scale dependence of the density is a quantitative measure of the notion that fractals are ramified or stringy objects. Another way of describing a fractal object is to say that it has holes of all sizes.

The percolation cluster shown in Fig. 13.1 is an example of a *random* or statistical fractal since the mass-length relation (13.3) is satisfied only "on the average", e.g. if the relation $M(R)$ is averaged over many clusters and different origins in the cluster. In all real physical systems, the relation (13.3) does not extend over all length scales but is bounded by both upper and lower cut-off lengths. For example a lower cut-off length is provided by a microscopic distance such as a lattice spacing or the mean distance between the constituents of the object. In computer simulations an upper cut-off length is usually provided by the finite system size. The presence of these cut-offs complicates the estimation of the fractal dimension.

In Problem 13.1 we compute the fractal dimension of percolation clusters using straightforward Monte Carlo methods. A renormalization group method for estimating d_f is considered in Problem 13.2. Remember that data extending over several decades is required to obtain convincing evidence for a power law relationship between M and R and to determine reasonably accurate values for the exponent. Thus conclusions based on the limited simulations posed in the problems must be interpreted with caution.

PROBLEM 13.1 The fractal dimension of percolation clusters

a. Generate a percolation configuration at $p = 0.5927$, the best estimate for the percolation threshold on the square lattice. Consider the properties of the spanning cluster on a 61 × 61 lattice. Why might it be necessary to generate a number of configurations before a spanning cluster is obtained? First obtain a feel for the ramified nature of the spanning cluster by drawing the positions of the occupied sites in the spanning cluster as in Fig. 13.1. Does the percolation cluster have many dangling ends?

b. Choose a point on the cluster and count the number of points in the spanning cluster $M(b)$ within a square area b^2 centered about that point. Then double b and count the number of points within the larger box. Repeat this procedure until you can estimate the b-dependence of the number of points. Can you repeat this procedure indefinitely? Use the b-dependence of $M(b)$ to estimate d_f according to the definition (13.3). Choose another point in the spanning cluster and repeat this procedure. Are your results similar? A better estimate for d_f can be found by averaging over several origins in each cluster and over many spanning clusters.

c. If you have not already completed Problem 12.7c, compute d_f by determining the mean size (mass) M of the spanning cluster at $p = p_c$ as a function of the linear dimension L of the lattice. Consider $L = 10, 20, 40,$ and 60 and estimate d_f from a log-log plot of M versus L.

*d. Generate a percolation configuration for $p = 0.8$ on a 61×61 lattice. Is the spanning cluster a fractal?

PROBLEM 13.2 A renormalization group calculation of the fractal dimension

Compute $<s^2>$, the mean square number of occupied sites in the spanning cluster at $p = p_c$, and the quantity $<s'^2>$, the mean square number of occupied sites in the spanning cluster on the renormalized lattice of linear dimension $L' = L/b$. Since $<s^2> \sim R^{2d_f}$ and $<s'^2> \sim (R/b)^{2d_f}$, we can obtain d_f from the relation $b^{d_f} = <s^2>/<s'^2>$. Choose the length rescaling factor to be $b = 2$ and adopt the same blocking procedure as used in Sec. 12.5. An average over ten spanning clusters for $L = 16$ and $p = 0.5927$ is sufficient for qualitative results.

In Problems 13.1 and 13.2 we considered the properties of only the spanning cluster even though our algorithm for generating percolation configurations generates clusters of all sizes. There is a more efficient way of generating *single* percolation clusters due independently to Hammersley, Leath, and Alexandrowicz. This "growth" algorithm is equivalent to the following steps (see Fig. 13.3).

1. Occupy a single seed on the lattice. The four neighbors (on the square lattice) of the seed represent the *perimeter* sites.
2. Choose a perimeter site at random, and generate a random number r. If $r \le p$, the site is occupied; otherwise the site is not occupied. In order that sites be unoccupied with probability $1 - p$, this site is not tested again.
3. If the site is occupied, determine if there are any new perimeter sites, i.e. untested neighbors. Continue this procedure until a cluster of the desired size is grown or until there are no available sites to test for occupancy.

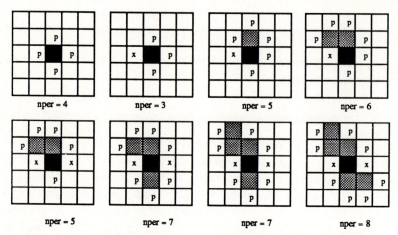

Fig. 13.3 Example of the "growth" of a percolation cluster. Sites are occupied with probability $p = 0.6$ and not occupied with probability $1 - p$. The seed site is black, perimeter sites are denoted by 'p', and tested unoccupied sites are marked by an 'x'. The number of perimeter sites *nper* is shown at each growth step.

Program single_cluster implements the growth algorithm and computes the number of occupied sites within a radius r of the seed particle. The "seed" site is placed at the origin and the lattice extends from $-L$ to $+L$ in each direction. Two one-dimensional arrays store the x and y positions of the perimeter sites.

```
PROGRAM single_cluster
! cluster generated by Hammersley, Leath, and Alexandrowicz algorithm
DIM num(1000)
CALL parameter(L,p)
CALL grow(L,num,p)
CALL mass_plot(num,L)
END

SUB parameter(L,p)
    INPUT prompt "value of L = ": L        ! lattice is (2L+1) x (2L+1)
    INPUT prompt "site occupation probability = ": p
END SUB
```

```
SUB grow(L,num(),p)                        ! generate single percolation cluster
   DIM perx(5000),pery(5000),site(-50 to 50,-50 to 50)
   DIM nx(4),ny(4)          ! positions of nearest neighbors of newly occupied site
   DATA 1,0,-1,0,0,1,0,-1
   LET site(0,0) = 1                       ! seed site at origin
   FOR i = 1 to 4
      READ perx(i),pery(i)                 ! positions of perimeter sites of seed
      LET nx(i) = perx(i)                  ! direction vector for perimeter sites
      LET ny(i) = pery(i)
   NEXT i
   LET nper = 4                            ! initial number of perimeter sites
   DO
      LET iper = int(rnd*nper + 1)         ! select random perimeter site
      LET x = perx(iper)                   ! coordinate of perimeter site
      LET y = pery(iper)
      IF rnd < p then                      ! site occupied
         LET site(x,y) = 1
         LET r = sqr(x*x + y*y)            ! distance from origin
         LET num(r) = num(r) + 1           ! number of sites at distance r
         LET n = n + 1                     ! number of occupied sites
         LET perx(iper) = perx(nper)       ! last perimeter site in list replaces
         LET pery(iper) = pery(nper)       ! newly occupied site in perx and pery
         LET nper = nper - 1
         FOR iz = 1 to 4                   ! find new perimeter sites
            LET xnew = x + nx(iz)
            LET ynew = y + ny(iz)
            IF site(xnew,ynew) = 0 and abs(xnew) <= L and abs(ynew) <= L then
               LET nper = nper + 1
               LET perx(nper) = xnew
               LET pery(nper) = ynew
            END IF
         NEXT iz
```

```
      ELSE                              ! site tested but not occupied
        LET site(x,y) = -1
        LET perx(iper) = perx(nper)
        LET pery(iper) = pery(nper)
        LET nper = nper - 1
      END IF
    LOOP until nper < 1               ! until all perimeter sites in lattice tested
  END SUB

  SUB mass_plot(num(),L)              ! plot ln M versus ln R
    LET ymax = 1 + int(log(4*L*L))    ! define axes for log-log plot
    LET xmax = 1 + int(log(L))
    SET window -1,xmax + 1,-1,ymax + 1
    PLOT LINES: 0,ymax;0,0;xmax,0
    PLOT TEXT, at 1,ymax: "Plot of log M versus log R"
    FOR x = 1 to xmax                 ! draw tick marks
       PLOT LINES: x,0;x,0.02*log(L)
    NEXT x
    FOR y = 1 to ymax
       PLOT LINES: 0,y; 0.01*log(L),y
    NEXT y
    LET numtot = 0
    FOR r = 1 to L
       IF num(r) = 0 then EXIT SUB
       LET numtot = numtot + num(r)
       LET lnR = log(r)
       LET lnM = log(numtot)
       BOX AREA lnR - 0.02,lnR + 0.02,lnM - 0.04,lnM + 0.04
    NEXT r
  END SUB
```

We use the growth algorithm in Problem 13.3 to generate single percolation clusters. The fractal dimension is determined by counting the number of sites M in the cluster within a distance r of the seed particle. A typical plot of $\ln M$ versus $\ln r$ is shown in Fig. 13.4. Note the curvature for small and large r. Since we do not expect the relation (13.3) to be valid for small r and for $r \sim L$, we should give more weight to the intermediate values of r. An eyeball estimate is sufficient for a rough estimate of d_f.

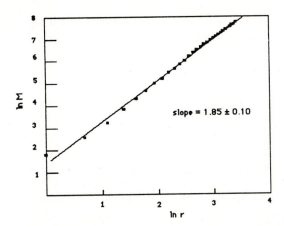

Fig. 13.4 Plot of $\ln M$ vs $\ln r$ for a percolation cluster generated at $p = 0.5927$ on a 61×61 lattice. The straight line is a visual fit to the data. The slope is an estimate of the fractal dimension. The plot was generated by **Program single_cluster**. The exact value of d_f for a percolation cluster is $d_f = 91/48 \approx 1.896$.

PROBLEM 13.3 Single cluster growth and the fractal dimension

a. Use **Program single_cluster** to grow single clusters on a $(2L + 1) \times (2L + 1)$ lattice using the growth algorithm. Consider a "spanning" cluster to be one whose mass is greater than a given minimum or one which connects the top and bottom rows of the lattice. Can you "grow" a spanning cluster for $p = 0.4$ or does the growth usually stop after a few sites are occupied?

b. Choose $p = 0.5927$ and $L = 30$, grow a cluster until no untested sites are available, and generate several pictures of spanning clusters. Note that some of your trials will not generate a spanning cluster. Determine the number of occupied sites $M(r)$ within a distance r of the seed site. (More correctly r should be measured from the center of mass of the cluster.) Determine M for several values of r and average $M(r)$ over at least ten spanning clusters. Estimate d_f from the log-log plot of M versus r (see Fig. 13.4). If time permits, generate percolation clusters on larger lattices.

c. Generate clusters at $p = 0.65$, a value of p slightly greater than p_c. Make a log-log plot of $M(r)$ versus r. Is the slope approximately equal to the value of d_f found in part (b)? Does the slope increase or decrease for larger r? Repeat for $p = 0.80$. Is a spanning cluster generated at $p > p_c$ a fractal?

d. The fractal dimension of percolation clusters is not an independent exponent but satisfies the scaling law

$$d_f = d - \beta/\nu \qquad (13.5)$$

where β and ν were defined in Table 12.1. The relation (13.5) can be understood by a finite-size scaling argument which we briefly summarize. The number of sites in the spanning cluster on a lattice of linear dimension L is given by

$$M(L) \sim P_\infty(L)L^d \qquad (13.6)$$

where P_∞ is the probability that an occupied site belongs to the spanning cluster and L^d is proportional to the total number of sites in the lattice. In the limit of an infinite lattice and p near p_c, we know that $P_\infty(p) \sim (p-p_c)^\beta$ and $\xi(p) \sim (p-p_c)^{-\nu}$ independent of L. For $L \sim \xi$ we can use finite-size scaling arguments to find that $P_\infty(L) \sim L^{-\beta\nu}$ (see (12.12)) and we have

$$M(L) \sim L^{-\beta/\nu}L^d \sim L^{d_f} \ . \qquad (13.7)$$

The relation (13.5) follows. Use the exact values of β and ν from Table 12.1 to find the exact value of d_f for $d = 2$. Is your estimate for d_f consistent with this value?

*e. Estimate the fractal dimension for percolation clusters on a simple cubic lattice. (Take $p_c = 0.3117$.)

Fractals have been used to describe the irregular shapes of such varied systems as turbulence, coastlines, mountain ranges, and clouds. A discussion of fractal geometry with many beautiful illustrations of computer generated fractals can be found in Mandelbrot's book (see references).

13.2 REGULAR FRACTALS AND SELF-SIMILARITY

One implication of (13.3) is that fractal objects are *self-similar*, i.e. they look the same on any length scale. How does a portion of the percolation cluster shown in Fig. 13.1 look under a magnifying glass? In order to clarify the meaning of self-similarity, we consider an example of a *regular* fractal, an object which is self-similar on all length scales. Begin with a line one unit long (see Fig. 13.5a). Suppose that we remove the middle third and replace it by two lines of length

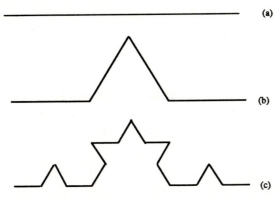

Fig. 13.5 Three stages (a)–(c) in the generation of a self-similar Koch curve. At each stage the displacement of the middle third of each segment is in the direction which increases the area under the curve. The curves were generated using **Program Koch**.

1/3 each so that the curve has a triangular bump in it and the total length of the curve is 4/3 (see Fig. 13.5b). In the next stage, each of the segments of length 1/3 is divided into lines of length 1/9 and the procedure is repeated (see Fig. 13.5c). What is the new length of the curve shown in Fig. 13.5c?

We can imagine that the three stages of generation shown in Fig. 13.5 can be extended an infinite number of times to produce an infinitely long curve containing an infinite number of infinitesimally small segments. Such a curve is known as the triadic Koch curve. A True BASIC program which uses a recursive procedure to draw this curve is given in the following.

```
PROGRAM Koch
! generate triadic Koch curve using recursion
CALL initial(x1,y1,x2,y2,n)
DO                              ! draw Koch curve for different number of iterations
   LET k = 0
   CALL draw(x1,y1,x2,y2,n)
   DO                           ! pause until any key is hit
      GET KEY k
   LOOP UNTIL k <> 0
   LET n = n + 1                ! number of stages of generation
   CLEAR
LOOP
END
```

```
SUB initial(x1,y1,x2,y2,n)
   LET n = 0
   LET x1 = 0                          ! coordinates at left end of line
   LET y1 = 0
   LET x2 = 10                         ! coordinates at right end of line
   LET y2 = 0
   SET window x1 - 1,x2 + 1,-1,7       ! arbitrary units
END SUB

SUB draw(x1,y1,x2,y2,n)
   IF n > 0 then
      LET dx = (x2 - x1)/3
      LET dy = (y2 - y1)/3
      LET x1n = x1 + dx
      LET y1n = y1 + dy
      LET x2n = x1 + 2*dx
      LET y2n = y1 + 2*dy
      ! rotate line segment (dx,dy) by 60 degrees and add to (x1n,y1n)
      LET xmid = dx*.5 - dy*.866 + x1n
      LET ymid = dy*.5 + dx*.866 + y1n
      CALL draw(x1,y1,x1n,y1n,n-1)
      CALL draw(x1n,y1n,xmid,ymid,n-1)
      CALL draw(xmid,ymid,x2n,y2n,n-1)
      CALL draw(x2n,y2n,x2,y2,n-1)
   ELSE
      PLOT LINES: x1,y1;x2,y2
   END IF
END SUB
```

Note that **SUB draw** calls itself. Use **Program Koch** to generate the curves shown in Fig. 13.5.

It is useful to discuss the fractal dimension in the context of regular fractals. First consider a one-dimensional curve of unit length which has been divided into N equal pieces of length ℓ so that $N = 1/\ell$ (see Fig. 13.6). As ℓ is decreased, N increases linearly—the expected result for a one-dimensional curve. Similarly if we divide a two-dimensional square of unit area into N equal subsquares of length ℓ, we have $N = 1/\ell^2$, the expected result for a two-dimensional object (see Fig. 13.6). In general we can state that $N = 1/\ell^d$, where d is the dimensionality of the object. Hence by taking the logarithm of both sides, we can express the

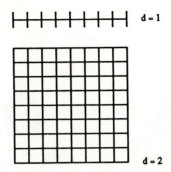

Fig. 13.6 Examples of one-dimensional and two-dimensional objects.

dimension as

$$d = log \, N / log(1/\ell) \quad . \qquad (13.8)$$

Now let us apply these ideas to the Koch curve. We found that each time the length ℓ of our measuring unit is reduced by a factor of 3, the number of segments is increased by 4. Thus we have $N = 4$ and $\ell = 1/3$ and the fractal dimension of the triadic Koch curve is given by

$$d_f = log \, 4 / log \, 3 \approx 1.2619 \quad . \qquad (13.9)$$

Hence we can say that the Koch curve has a dimensionality between that of a line and an area. Is this statement in accordance with your visual interpretation of the space-filling nature of the triadic Koch curve?

PROBLEM 13.4 The generation and fractal dimension of regular fractals

a. The concept of recursive programming as illustrated in **Program Koch** is probably one of the most difficult programming concepts you will encounter. Explain the nature of **Program Koch** and the nature of recursion.

b. Regular fractals can be generated from a pattern which can be used in a self-replicating manner. Write a program to generate the quadric Koch curve shown in Fig. 13.7a. What is its fractal dimension?

c. What is the fractal dimension of the Sierpiński gasket shown in Fig. 13.7b? Write a program which generates the next several iterations.

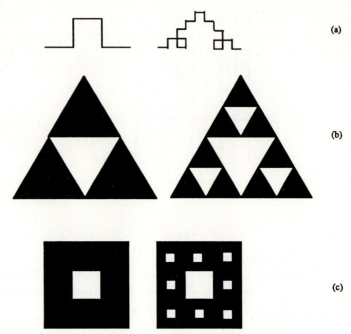

Fig. 13.7. (a) The first few iterations of the quadric Koch curve;
(b) The first few iterations of the Sierpiński gasket; (c) The first
few iterations of the Sierpiński carpet.

d. What is the fractal dimension of the Sierpiński carpet shown in Fig.
13.7c? How does the fractal dimension of the Sierpiński carpet compare to
the fractal dimension of a percolation cluster? Are the two fractals visually
similar?

13.3 FRACTAL GROWTH PROCESSES

We have mentioned that many systems occuring in nature exhibit fractal geometry. Why are fractal structures so common? How do fractal structures form?
In the following we will discuss several simple models which exhibit patterns
that can be described in terms of fractal geometry and that show a remarkable
similarity to forms observed in nature.

The Eden model. A simple example of a growth model was proposed by Eden in 1961 to simulate the growth of cell colonies. Although we will find that the resultant cluster is compact, the description of the Eden growth algorithm illustrates the nature of the fractal growth models we will discuss in the following.

Place a "seed" site at the center of the lattice. The unoccupied nearest neighbors of the occupied sites are denoted as *perimeter* sites. In the simplest version of the model, a perimeter site is chosen at random and occupied. The newly occupied site is removed from the list of perimeter sites and the new perimeter sites are added to the list of perimeter sites. This growth process is repeated many times until a large cluster of occupied sites are formed (see Fig. 13.8). Eden clusters are investigated in Problem 13.5.

		p					
	p	16	p				
	p	14	11	p			
p	17	10	2	p	18	p	
	p	6	1	3	13	p	
	p	9	5	4	7	12	p
	p	15	p	8	p	p	
		p					

Fig. 13.8 An example of a cluster grown on the square lattice according to the Eden model. The numbers on the sites denote the order in which these sites were occupied and the perimeter sites are denoted by the letter 'p'.

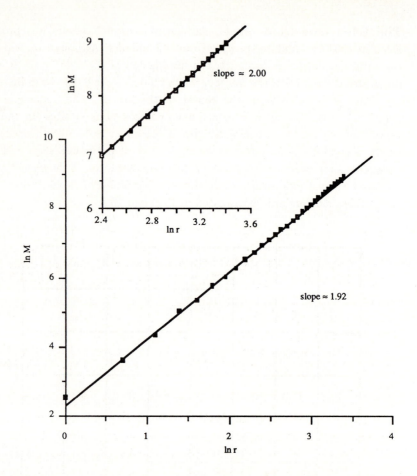

Fig. 13.9 Plot of ln M versus ln r for a Eden cluster generated on a
61×61 square lattice. A least squares fit to the data over the entire
range of r yields a slope of approximately 1.92. In this case elimination
of the small r data reduces the curvature and yields a slope closer to
2.0.

PROBLEM 13.5 Monte Carlo simulation of the Eden model

Modify **Program single_cluster** so that clusters are generated on the
square lattice according to the Eden model. A straightforward modification
is to occupy perimeter sites with probability $p = 1.0$ until the cluster reaches
the edge of the lattice. What happens if we continue to occupy perimeter
sites indefinitely? Follow the procedure of Problem 13.3 and determine the

number of occupied sites $M(r)$ within a distance r of the seed site. Assume that $M(r) \sim r^{d_f}$ and estimate d_f from the slope of a log-log plot of M versus r. A typical log-log plot is shown in Fig. 13.9. The corresponding slope is estimated to be 1.92. In order to eliminate possible small r curvature, we show a least squares fit to the same data in the range $12 \leq r \leq 30$. The slope is found to increase to approximately 2.0. A careful analysis of data averaged over many trials and over at least two decades of r is needed in order to conclude that the dimension of Eden clusters is equal to the dimension of the lattice. Can you conclude from your data that Eden clusters are compact?

Invasion percolation.   A dynamic process known as *invasion percolation* has been used to model the shape of the oil-water interface when water is forced into a porous media. In this process a cluster grows into a sample through paths of least resistance. Consider a lattice of size $L \times 2L$ with the water (the "invader") initially occupying the left edge (see Fig. 13.10). The resistance to the invader is given by random numbers between 0 and 1 which are assigned to each site in the lattice and are held fixed throughout the process. Sites which are neighbors of invader sites are the perimeter sites. At each time step, the perimeter site with the lowest random number is occupied by the invader and the oil (the "defender") is displaced.

Program invasion implements the invasion percolation growth process. The array $r(i,j)$ is used initially to store the random number for each site. If the site at (i,j) is occupied, then $r(i,j)$ is increased by 1. If the site (i,j) is a perimeter site, then $r(i,j)$ is increased by 2. Two sorting methods are used to sort the perimeter sites in order of the magnitude of the random number assigned to them. The invading cluster grows until a path forms which connects the left and right edges of the lattice. In order to minimize boundary effects, periodic boundary conditions are used for the top and bottom edges and all physical quantities are measured over the central $L \times L$ region of the lattice. The program draws the occupied ("wet") sites and computes the fraction of wet sites. The main quantity of interest is the probability $P(r)dr$ that a site with a random number between r and $r+dr$ is occupied. The properties of the invasion percolation model are explored in Problem 13.6.

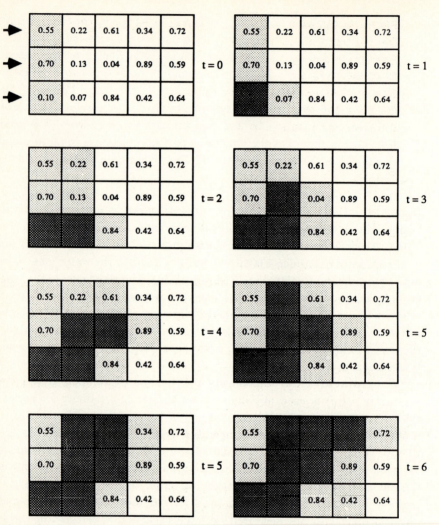

Fig. 13.10 Example of a cluster formed by invasion percolation. The lattice at $t = 0$ shows the random numbers which have been assigned to the sites. The darkly shaded sites are occupied by the invader which on the next step occupies the perimeter site (lightly shaded) with the smallest random number.

```
PROGRAM invasion                    ! compute invasion percolation cluster
DIM r(100,50),perx(500),pery(500)
RANDOMIZE
CALL initial(Lx,Ly)
CALL assign(r,perx,pery,Lx,Ly,s)
CALL invade(r,perx,pery,Lx,Ly,s)
CALL average(r,Lx,Ly)
END

SUB initial(Lx,Ly)
   INPUT prompt "lattice size in y direction = ": Ly
   LET Lx = 2*Ly
   SET window 0,Lx + 1,0,Ly + 2
END SUB

SUB assign(r(,),perx(),pery(),Lx,Ly,s)
   ! assign random numbers to each site and occupy first column
   ! sites in second column are initial perimeter sites
   LET s = 0.4                    ! half size of box drawn at filled site
   FOR row = 1 to Ly
      LET r(1,row) = 1            ! occupy first column
      BOX AREA 1 - s,1 + s,row - s,row + s
      FOR col = 2 to Lx           ! assign random numbers one row at a time
         LET r(col,row) = rnd
      NEXT col
      ! r(col,row) greater than 2 if perimeter site
      LET r(2,row) = 2 + r(2,row)
      LET nper = row              ! number of perimeter sites equals row number
      ! sort perimeter sites in second column
      CALL sort_shell(r,perx,pery,nper,2,row)            ! or call sort_insert
   NEXT row
END SUB
```

```
SUB sort_shell(r(,),perx(),pery(),nper,x0,y0)
    ! divide list into half and determine in which half random number belongs
    ! divide half list again and determine in which half number belongs
    ! continue this process until exact position of number is determined
    IF nper = 1 then                  ! only one perimeter site
       LET perx(nper) = x0
       LET pery(nper) = y0
       EXIT SUB
    END IF
    ! determine if random number of new site less than all previous numbers
    LET ix = perx(nper-1)
    LET iy = pery(nper-1)
    IF r(x0,y0) < r(ix,iy) then
       LET perx(nper) = x0
       LET pery(nper) = y0
       EXIT SUB
    END IF
    LET k1 = 1                        ! beginning of list
    LET k2 = nper-1                   ! end of list
    LET kmid = int((k1 + k2)/2)        ! middle of list
```

```
        DO                              ! begin shell sort
          LET ix = perx(kmid)
          LET iy = pery(kmid)
          ! determine which half of list new number located
          IF r(x0,y0) > r(ix,iy) then
              LET k2 = kmid              ! change upper end
          ELSE
              LET k1 = kmid             ! change lower end
          END IF
          LET kmid = int((k1 + k2)/2)
          IF (k1 = kmid) or (kmid = k2) then         ! exact position equal to k2
            FOR ilist = nper to k2 + 1 step -1       ! sites above k2 moved up one each
              LET perx(ilist) = perx(ilist-1)
              LET pery(ilist) = pery(ilist-1)
            NEXT ilist
            LET perx(k2) = x0                        ! new site inserted in list
            LET pery(k2) = y0
            EXIT SUB
          END IF
        LOOP
    END SUB

    SUB sort_insert(r(,),perx(),pery(),nper,x0,y0)          ! insertion sort method
        FOR iper = 1 to nper - 1
          LET ix = perx(iper)
          LET iy = pery(iper)
          IF r(x0,y0) > r(ix,iy) then                       ! insert new site
            FOR ilist = nper to iper + 1 step -1
              LET perx(ilist) = perx(ilist-1)
              LET pery(ilist) = pery(ilist-1)
            NEXT ilist
            LET perx(iper) = x0
            LET pery(iper) = y0
            EXIT SUB
          END IF
        NEXT iper
        LET perx(iper) = x0          ! new site smaller than all previous perimeter sites
        LET pery(iper) = y0
    END SUB
```

```
SUB invade(r(,),perx(),pery(),Lx,Ly,s)
   DIM nx(4),ny(4)              ! nx and ny designate positions of nearest neighbors
   DATA 1,0,-1,0,0,1,0,-1
   FOR iz = 1 to 4
      READ nx(iz),ny(iz)
   NEXT iz
   LET nper = Ly
   DO
      LET col = perx(nper)
      LET row = pery(nper)
      LET nper = nper - 1
      LET r(col,row) = r(col,row) - 1    ! occupied site between 1 and 2
      BOX AREA col - s,col + s,row - s,row + s
      FOR nn = 1 to 4                      ! find new perimeter sites
         LET xnew = col + nx(nn)
         LET ynew = row + ny(nn)
         IF ynew > Ly then                ! periodic boundary conditions in y
            LET ynew = 1
         ELSE IF ynew < 1 then
            LET ynew = Ly
         END IF
         IF r(xnew,ynew) < 1 then         ! new perimeter site
            LET r(xnew,ynew) = r(xnew,ynew) + 2
            LET nper = nper + 1
            CALL sort_shell(r,perx,pery,nper,xnew,ynew)    ! or call sort_insert
         END IF
      NEXT nn
   LOOP until col >= Lx                   ! stop when cluster reaches right boundary
END SUB
```

```
SUB average(r(,),Lx,Ly)
    ! compute probability density P(r)
    DIM P(0 to 20),nr(0 to 20)
    LET Lmin = Lx/3
    LET Lmax = 2*Lmin
    LET n = (Lmax - Lmin + 1)*Ly          ! number of sites in middle half of lattice
    LET dr = 0.05
    LET nbin = 1/dr
    FOR col = Lmin to Lmax
        FOR row = 1 to Ly
            LET ibin = nbin*(mod(r(col,row),1))
            LET nr(ibin) = nr(ibin) + 1
            IF (r(col,row) >= 1) and (r(col,row) < 2) then
                LET occupied = occupied + 1        ! total number of occupied sites
                LET P(ibin) = P(ibin) + 1
            END IF
        NEXT row
    NEXT col
    DO                               ! wait until key input to print results
    LOOP until key input
    CLEAR
    LET fraction = occupied/n
    PRINT "fraction of sites occupied = ",fraction
    PRINT " r","P(r)"
    PRINT
    FOR ibin = 0 to nbin
        LET rnum = dr*ibin
        IF nr(ibin) > 0 then PRINT rnum, p(ibin)/nr(ibin)
    NEXT ibin
END SUB
```

PROBLEM 13.6 Invasion percolation

a. Use **Program invasion** to generate an invasion percolation cluster on
the square lattice. What qualitative statements can you make about the
nature of the cluster? Explain the nature of the two sorting subroutines
given in the program. Which method yields the fastest results on a 20 × 40
lattice?

b. Modify **Program invasion** so that S_i, the fraction of the sites occupied by the invader at the time that the invader first reaches the right edge, is averaged over at least twenty trials. Assume that $S_i \sim L^{-\alpha}$ and estimate α from a plot of $\ln S_i$ versus $\ln L$. How is α related to the fractal dimension of the spanning cluster? Compare your estimate for the fractal dimension with that of ordinary percolation. (The published results for S_i by Wilkinson and Willemsen are for 2000 realizations each for L in the range 20 to 100.)

c. Determine the probability $P(r)dr$ that a site with a random number between r and $r + dr$ is occupied. It is sufficient to consider twenty intervals for the random numbers, i.e. $dr = 0.5$. Plot $P(r)$ versus r for $L = 10$ and larger values of L up to $L = 50$. Can you define a "critical value" of r near which $P(r)$ changes rapidly? How does this critical value of r compare to the value of p_c for ordinary site percolation on the square lattice?

*d. The invasion percolation model we have discussed is appropriate for the displacement of an infinitely compressible fluid by an incompressible one. In order to treat the displaced fluid (oil) as incompressible, we adopt a trapping mechanism so that once an oil cluster has become isolated, it can no longer be invaded. Unfortunately this trapping rule slows the simulation considerably, since it is necessary to check after every move whether a trap has occurred. Include the trapping mechanism and determine if there are any qualitative changes in α and $P(r)$.

Diffusion in disordered media. Suppose that we wish to understand the diffusion of an atom through a disordered solid or the conductivity of a random resistor network, e.g. the electrical conductivity of chicken wire with random missing nodes. One simple model of these phenomena is due to deGennes and is known as the "ant in the labyrinth." Consider a random walker (the ant) which moves at random only on the occupied sites of a percolation cluster. At each time step, the ant tosses a coin with four possible outcomes (on the square lattice). If the outcome corresponds to a step to an occupied site, the ant moves; otherwise it remains in its present position. In both cases the time is increased by one time unit. Suppose that the occupied sites of the percolation cluster occur with probability p. At $t = 0$ we place the ant at random on the cluster and at time t compute the square of the distance between its starting position and its end point. We then repeat the simulation many times to obtain the mean square displacement of the ant. How does R, the root mean square displacement of the ant, depend on p and t? How do the laws of diffusion change on a fractal lattice (the percolation cluster at $p = p_c$)? We consider these questions in Problem 13.7.

It might seem surprising at first that the random walk of an ant and the conductivity of a random resistor network are related problems. The connection between diffusion and conductivity was first found by Einstein. Consider a system of particles, e.g. a fluid. If we follow the individual motion of the particles in the absence of an external force, we can determine their mean square displacement and hence the self-diffusion constant D. Then if we apply a "small" force, we can measure the mean velocity in the direction of the force and deduce the *mobility* μ, the ratio of the mean velocity to the applied force. Einstein's contribution was to show that D and μ are proportional (cf Reif).

For a system of charged particles, we can extend the above reasoning to show that the mobility and the electrical conductivity are proportional. We can associate the applied force with the electric field and hence with the voltage and the mean velocity with the electrical current. Hence the mobility is proportional to the conductivity (the inverse resistivity) of the particles. Since the mobility is also proportional to D, we conclude that D and the conductivity are proportional. Hence we can use this relation to determine the p-dependence of the conductivity of a percolation cluster.

*PROBLEM 13.7 **The ant in the labyrinth**

a. For $p = 1$ the ant diffuses on a perfect lattice and $R \sim t^{1/2}$. Let us assume that $R \sim D(p)t^{1/2}$ for $p > p_c$. Generate a percolation cluster for $p > p_c$ using the growth algorithm considered in Problem 13.3. Choose the initial position of the ant to be the seed site and consider several random walks to find the root mean square displacement for a given cluster. Consider times long enough for R^2 to be approximately proportional to t, but short enough for $R < L$. Consider $p = 0.8, 0.7, 0.65,$ and 0.62 for $L = 60$ and estimate $D(p)$. Plot the ratio $D(p)/D(p = 1)$ as a function of p and discuss its qualitative behavior.

b. For $p < p_c$, the clusters are finite, $R(t)$ is bounded, and hence diffusion is impossible. Since $D(p) = 0$ for $p < p_c$ and is nonzero for $p > p_c$, we expect that $D(p) \sim (p - p_c)^z$ for p near p_c. Extend your calculations of part (a) to larger L and a greater range of p and estimate the dynamical exponent z. Since the conductivity is proportional to D, the exponent z also tells us how the conductivity vanishes near p_c. The chicken-wire measurements by Watson and Leath yield the estimate $z \approx 1.38 \pm 0.12$. Are your results for z consistent?

c. At $p = p_c$, we might expect a different type of t-dependence of $R(t)$ to be observed, e.g. $R(t) \sim t^k$ for large t. Do you expect k to be greater or less than $1/2$? Do a Monte Carlo simulation of $R(t)$ at $p = p_c$ and estimate the exponent k.

d. As discussed in Problem 11.16, a better method for treating random walks lattice is to use an exact enumeration approach rather than conventional Monte Carlo simulations. The essence of the exact enumeration method is that $W_{t+1}(i)$, the probability that the ant is at site i at time $t+1$, is determined solely by the probabilities of the ant being at the neighbors of site i at time t. Store the positions of the occupied sites in an array and introduce two arrays corresponding to $W_{t+1}(i)$ and $W_t(i)$ for all sites i in the cluster. Use the probabilities $W_t(i)$ to obtain $W_{t+1}(i)$ (see Fig. 13.11). Spatial averages such as the mean square distance can be calculated from the probability distribution function at different times. Details of the

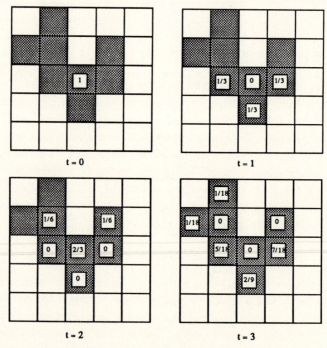

Fig. 13.11 The time evolution of the probability distribution function $W_t(i)$ for three successive units of time.

method and the results are discussed in Majid et al. (1984). These workers considered walks of 5000 steps on clusters with $\sim 10^3$ sites and averaged their results over 1000 different clusters.

Diffusion-limited aggregation (DLA). Many objects in nature grow by the random addition of subunits. Examples of such phenomena are snow flakes, lightning patterns and crack formation along a geological fault. It might seem unlikely that any unifying feature could exist for these phenomena. However in recent years we have found many clues to guide us towards their unification. One simple model which has provided much insight is called *diffusion limited aggregation* or DLA. The model is an example of how random motion can give rise to beautiful self-similar clusters. The first step is to occupy a site with a seed particle. A particle is then released from the perimeter of a large circle whose center coincides with the seed. The particle undergoes a random walk, i.e. diffuses, until it either leaves the circle or reaches a perimeter site of the seed and sticks. Then another random walker is released and allowed to walk until it reaches a perimeter site of one of the particles and sticks. The process is repeated many times (typically on the order of several thousand) until a large cluster is formed. A typical DLA cluster is shown in Fig. 13.12. Does the cluster remind you of any natural objects? Some of the properties of DLA clusters are explored in Problem 13.8.

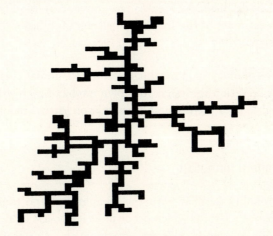

Fig. 13.12 An example of a DLA cluster of approximately 400 particles on a square lattice.

PROBLEM 13.8 Diffusion limited aggregation

a. Write a Monte Carlo program to generate clusters on the square lattice according to the diffusion limited aggregation algorithm. Suppose that each walker begins at a random site on a circle of radius $2R_{max}$, where R_{max} is the maximum radius of the cluster generated thus far. In order to reduce computer time, assume that walkers which reach a distance $3R_{max}$ from the seed are "removed" and that a new walker is placed at random on the launching circle. Begin with a lattice of linear dimension $L \sim 40$ and then consider as large a lattice as your hardware and patience permit. Limit the number of walkers so that the outer radius of the cluster does not grow too near the edge of the lattice. What is the visual appearance of DLA clusters? If they appear to be fractals, make a visual estimate of the fractal dimension. (Experts can make a visual estimate of d_f to within a few percent!)

*b. It is likely that your program generates DLA clusters inefficiently since most of the CPU time is spent in the random walker wandering far from the perimeter sites of the cluster. There are several ways of overcoming this problem. One way is to let the walker take bigger steps the further it is from the cluster. For example if the random walker is at a distance $R > R_{max}$, a step of length greater than or equal to $R - R_{max} - 2$ can be permitted if this distance is greater than one lattice unit. If the walker is very close to the cluster, the step length is one lattice unit. Other possible modifications are discussed by Meakin (see references). Modify your program and obtain an estimate of the fractal dimension of diffusion limited clusters in two dimensions.

DLA is only one of many models which lead to self-similar clusters. We invite you to use your imagination to design your own model of a growth process. You are also encouraged to read the research literature on growth models, since much of it is accessible.

*PROBLEM 13.9 Pattern formation

a. You are probably familiar with the complicated and random nature of electrical discharge patterns which occur in atmospheric lightning. Although this phenomenon known as *dielectric breakdown* is complicated, we will see that a simple but nontrival model leads to discharge patterns which are similar to those observed experimentally. Since lightning occurs in an inhomogeneous medium due to differences in the density, humidity and conductivity of air, we want to develop a model of an electrical discharge in an inhomogeneous insulator. We know that when an electrical discharge occurs, the electrical potential ϕ satisfies Laplace's equation $\nabla^2 \phi = 0$. The model (Family et al., Niemeyer et al.) is specified by the following rules (on the square lattice):

i. Consider a large circle of radius R and place a charge source at the origin. Choose the potential $\phi = 0$ at the origin and $\phi = 1$ for sites on the circumference of the circle (see Fig. 13.13). The radius R should be taken to be larger than the extent of the growing pattern.

ii. Associate a random number r ($0 \leq r \leq 1$) with each site within the circle. The random number r_i at site i represents a breakdown coefficient and the random nature of the insulator.

iii. Use the relaxation method (see Chapter 9) to obtain the values of the potential ϕ_i for sites within the circle.

iv. Choose the perimeter sites to be nearest-neighbor sites of the discharge pattern (black circles in Fig. 13.13). Let u_i denote the potential gradient at site i and form the product ru^a for each perimeter site, where a is an adjustable parameter.

v. The perimeter site $imax$ with the maximum value of the product ru^a breaks down, i.e. set $\phi_{imax} = 0$.

vi. Use the relaxation method to recalculate the values of the potential at the remaining "unoccupied" sites and repeat steps (v) and (vi).

Choose $a = \frac{1}{4}$ and analyze the structure of the discharge pattern. Does the pattern appear similar to lightning? Does the pattern appear to have a fractal geometry? Estimate the fractal dimension by counting $M(b)$, the average number of sites belonging to the discharge pattern which are within a $b \times b$ box. Consider other values of a, e.g. $a = \frac{1}{6}$ and $a = \frac{1}{3}$ and show that the patterns have a fractal structure with a tunable fractal dimension. Published results (Family et al.) are for patterns generated with 800 growth steps. Do you think that the nature of the pattern depends on the nature of the lattice? What type of pattern is formed in three dimensions?

b. Consider a deterministic growth model for which there is no need to assign a random number to each site. In this model *all* perimeter sites are tested for occupancy at each growth step. We adopt the same geometry and boundary conditions as in part (a) and use the relaxation method to

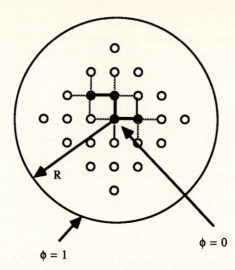

Fig. 13.13 Illustration of the dielectric breakdown model (Family et al.). The central site represents the charge source and the "ground" is represented by a circle at potential $\phi = 0$. The discharge pattern is indicated by the dark circles which are all at the potential $\phi = 0$. The dashed bonds connect the occupied sites to the perimeter sites.

solve Laplace's equation for ϕ. Then we find the perimeter site with the largest value of the potential gradient u and set this value equal to P_{max}. All the perimeter sites are then examined and only those sites for which the ratio u/P_{max} is larger than a parameter p are filled. After each growth step, the new perimeter sites are determined and the relaxation method is used to recalculate the values of ϕ at each unoccupied site. Choose $p = 0.35$ and determine the nature of the regular fractal pattern. What is the fractal dimension? Consider other values of p and determine the corresponding fractal dimension. These patterns have been termed *Laplace fractal carpets* (see Family et al.).

13.4 CELLULAR AUTOMATA

In this section we introduce another class of geometrical models called *cellular automata*. One of the distinguishing features of cellular automata is that they are completely discrete and hence lend themselves to exact simulation on a digital computer. Cellular automata were orginally introduced by von Neumann and Ulam in 1948 as a possible idealization of biological self-reproduction. Our main interest is that many cellular automata models are examples of simple dynamical systems which yield ordered patterns emerging from random initial conditions. You might convince yourself that the spatial patterns of many cellular automata resemble patterns observed in natural phenomena such as coagulation and crystal growth. However for the present, we will regard cellular automata as interesting computer models which hold tantalizing possibilities for the representation of physical systems.

Cellular automata are mathematical idealizations of physical systems in which space and time are discrete and physical quantities have a finite set of discrete values. Imagine a regular lattice (or "array") of sites ("cells") with each cell having a finite number of possible values, e.g. 0 or 1. The state of the system is completely specified by the values of the variables at each cell. The important characteristics of cellular automata include the following:

1. The value of each cell is updated in a sequence of *discrete* time steps.
2. The variables in each cell are updated *simultaneously* ("synchronously") based on the values of the variables at the previous time step.
3. The rule for the new value of a cell depends only on the values of a *local* neighborhood of cells near it.

We first consider one-dimensional automata with two possible values of the variables in each cell and with the neighborhood of a given cell assumed to be the cell itself and the cells immediately to the left and right of it. There are 256 possible rules for such "elementary" automata. Fig. 13.14 illustrates one

t:	111	110	101	100	011	010	001	000
t + 1:	0	1	0	1	1	0	1	0

Fig. 13.14 Example of a local rule for the time evolution of a one-dimensional cellular automaton. The variables at each cell can have values 0 or 1. The top row shows all $2^3 = 8$ possible combinations of three cells. The bottom row illustrates the rule for the time evolution and gives the value to be taken by the central cell on the next time step. This rule is termed 01011010 in binary notation (see the second row), the modulo-two rule, or rule 90 in Wolfram's notation. (Note that 90 is the base ten equivalent of the binary number 01011010, i.e. $90 = 2^1 + 2^3 + 2^4 + 2^6$.)

particular set of local rules. The properties of all 256 elementary one-dimensional cellular automata have been cataloged (see Wolfram). We explore some of the properties of one-dimensional cellular automata in Problem 13.10.

PROBLEM 13.10 One-dimensional cellular automata

a. Write a program to represent an elementary one-dimensional cellular automaton. The easiest way to update the cells simultaneously is to use separate arrays for the values of the cells at step t and step $t + 1$. Adopt the "modulo-two" rule shown in Fig. 13.14, i.e. the value of a cell at step $t + 1$ is the sum modulo 2 of its two neighbors at step t. Choose the initial configuration to be a single nonzero cell (seed). It is sufficient to consider the time evolution for approximately twenty time steps. Is the resulting pattern of nonzero cells self-similar? Can you characterize it by a fractal dimension?

b. Consider the properties of a similar rule for which the value of a cell at step $t+1$ is the sum modula 2 of the values of its neighbors *plus* its own value at step t. This rule is also termed rule 10010110 or $150 = 2^1 + 2^2 + 2^4 + 2^7$.

c. Choose an initial "disordered" configuration for which the independent probability for each cell to have value 1 is 50%. Consider the time evolution of rule 00010010 (rule $18 = 2^1 + 2^4$), rule 01001001 (rule $73 = 2^0 + 2^3 + 2^6$), rule 136 (10001000), rule 90, and rule 150. It is sufficient to consider 80 cells for 60 time steps. How sensitive are the patterns that are formed to changes in the initial conditions? Does the nature of the patterns depend on the use or nonuse of periodic boundary conditions? Group the qualitative behavior of the time evolution of these automata into one of four general classes:

1. A fixed, homogeneous state.

2. A pattern consisting of separated periodic regions.

3. A chaotic, aperiodic pattern.

4. Complex, localized structures.

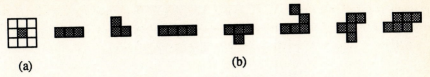

(a)   (b)

Fig. 13.15 (a) The "local" neighborhood of a cell is given by the sum of its eight neighbors. (b) Examples of initial configurations for the game of Life, some of which lead to interesting patterns. Live cells are shaded.

The results of Problem 13.10 suggest that an important feature of cellular automata is their capability for "self-organization." In the following problem, we consider a well known example of a two-dimensional cellular automata which exhibits self-organization.

*PROBLEM 13.11 The game of Life

The best known two-dimensional cellular automaton is the game of "Life" invented in 1970 by John Conway. The game is notorious for its many fascinating patterns and its ability to seduce people to use vast amounts of computer time to find more interesting patterns. The rules of the game are simple. For each cell determine the sum of the values of its four nearest and four next-nearest neighbors on a square lattice (see Fig. 13.15a). A "live" cell (value 1) remains alive only if the sum equals 2 or 3. If this sum is greater than 3, the cell will "die" (become value 0) due to overcrowding. If the sum is less than 2, the cell dies due to isolation. A dead cell will come to life in the next time step only if the sum equals 3. Write a program to implement the game of Life. Begin with a number of different initial configurations (random and ordered) and investigate the possible kinds of patterns that might emerge. Some suggested initial configurations are given in Fig. 13.15b.

PROBLEM 13.12 Examples of two-dimensional cellular automata models

a. Consider a simple *Boolean* automata for which each site is labeled by 1 ("on") and 0 ("off"). We adopt a "voting rule" such that the value of each cell at time $t + 1$ is determined by the vote of its four nearest neighbors (on a square lattice) at time t (see Vichniac). The rule is that a cell becomes "on" if 2, 3, or 4 of its four neighbors are on. Consider initial configurations for which 1-cells occur with probability p and 0-cells occur with probability

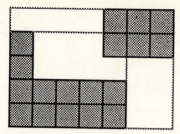

Fig. 13.16 Two rectanglar clusters of 1-cells overlap. What is the evolution of these clusters using the "two-out-of-four" rule (see Problem 13.12a)?

$1 - p$. Since the voting rule favors the growth of 1-cells, it is interesting to start with a minority of 1-cells. Choose $p = 0.1$. What happens to isolated 1-cells? How do they grow initially? For what shape (convex or concave) does a cluster of 1-cells stop growing? What happens to clusters of 1-cells such as those shown in Fig. 13.16? (If necessary, create such a configuration.) Show that for $p = 0.1$, the system eventually freezes in a pattern made of 1-cell rectangular islands in a sea of 0-cells. What happens for $p = 0.14$? Can you define a "critical density" p_c at which the behavior of the system changes. Consider lattices with linear dimension $L = 128$ and $L = 256$.

b. Consider a cellular automaton for which the value of the center cell at the next time step is decided by the value of the sum of the center cell *and* its eight neighbors (see Vichniac). In particular, suppose that the center cell equals 1 at the next time step if this sum equals 4 or more. Note that this rule favors the growth of 1-cells. This rule leads to a phenomenon similar to that found in part (a). Consider an initial configuration for which 1-cells occur with probability p and 0-cells occur with probability $1 - p$. Choose a 128×128 lattice and show that for $p = 0.2$, the system eventually freezes. What is the shape of the 1-clusters? Show that if a single 0-cell is changed to a 1-cell at the surface of the largest 1-cluster, the cluster of 1-cells grows. What is the eventual state of the system? What is the behavior of the system for $p = 0.3$? Is it possible to define a "critical density" p_c such that for $p \geq p_c$, the growth of the 1-clusters continues until the entire lattice turns to the 1-state. Consider larger lattices and show that the value of p_c appears to be insensitive to the size of the lattice. What is your estimated value of p_c in the limit of an infinite lattice?

c. There is one problem with the conclusions that you were able to reach in parts (a) and (b)—they are incorrect. The value of p_c is zero in the limit of an infinite lattice and the finite lattice results are misleading. The probability of *any* configuration of 1-cells is unity on an infinite lattice. Hence somehere in the lattice there will be a "critical cluster" which will grow indefinitely until the entire lattice changes to the 1-state. The moral of the story is "Do not trust a simulation without a theory" (a paraphrase of a quote usually attributed to Eddington).

13.5 OVERVIEW

We have seen that many of the models discussed in this chapter are presented in the form of a computer algorithm rather than in terms of a differential equation. These models are an example of the development of a "computer culture" (cf Vichniac) and are a reflection of the way that technology affects the way we think. Can you imagine many of the models discussed in this chapter without thinking about their computer implementation? Can you imagine understanding these models without the use of computer graphics?

The geometrical nature of the models discussed in Chapters 11–13 make them relatively accessible to those with relatively little background in physics. On the other hand there is much we cannot understand at this level. For example after we empirically "measure" an exponent, we might wonder: "Why does the exponent have this value? How do we know the exact values of the critical exponents for two-dimensional percolation? Can we find more unifying features for the many kinetic growth models that presently exist? Can geometrical models aid our understanding of other physical phenomena? What is the relation of these models to physical experiments? What other quantities in addition to the fractal dimension do we need to characterize the geometry of an object?"

In addition to the interest of physicists and others in geometrical models, such models are of interest to computational scientists. Indeed one of the major motivations for the study of cellular automata is their relation to theories of computation and the development of new computer architectures (cf Hillis).

REFERENCES AND SUGGESTIONS FOR ADDITIONAL READING

Fereydoon Family and David P. Landau, eds., *Kinetics of Aggregation and Gelation*, North-Holland (1984). A collection of research papers which give a wealth of information, pictures, and references on a variety of growth models.

J. M. Hammersley and D. C. Handscomb, *Monte Carlo Methods*, Methuen (1964). The chapter on percolation processes discusses the "growth" algorithm for percolation.

B. Hayes, "Computer recreations," *Sci. Amer.* **250**, 12 (March 1984). A simple introduction to cellular automata.

H. J. Herrmann, "Geometrical Cluster Growth Models and Kinetic Gelation," *Phys. Repts.* **136**, 154 (1986).

W. Daniel Hillis, *The Connection Machine*, MIT Press (1985). A discussion of a new "massively parallel" computer architecture influenced in part by physical models of the type discussed in this chapter.

Benoit B. Mandelbrot, *The Fractal Geometry of Nature*, W.H. Freeman (1983). An influential and beautifully illustrated book on fractals.

Imtiaz Majid, Daniel Ben-Avahram, Shlomo Havlin, and H. Eugene Stanley, "Exact-enumeration approach to random walks on percolation clusters in two dimensions," *Phys. Rev. B* **30**, 1626 (1984).

L. Niemeyer, L. Pietronero, and H. J. Wiesmann, "Fractal dimension of dielectric breakdown," *Phys. Rev. Letts.* **52**, 1033 (1984). See also Fereydoon Family, Y. C. Zhang, and Tamás Vicsek, "Invasion percolation in an external field: dielectric breakdown in random media," *J. Phys. A.* **19**, L733 (1986). A similar model has been proposed for the growth of snowflakes by the solidification of ice in supercooled vapor. See Fereydoon Family, Daniel E. Platt, and Tamás Vicsek, "Deterministic growth model of pattern formation in dendritic solidification," Emory University preprint (1987). In this preprint the authors also discuss the nature of Laplace fractal carpets.

H. 0. Peitgen and P. H. Richter, *The Beauty of Fractals*, Springer-Verlag (1986).

Luciano Pietronero and Erio Tosatti, eds., *Fractals in Physics*, North-Holland (1986). A collection of research papers many of which are accessible to the motivated reader.

William Poundstone, *The Recursive Universe*, Contemporary Books (1985). A book based on the game of Life which attempts to draw analogies between the patterns of Life and ideas of information theory and cosmology. Other references on Life include E.R. Berlekamp, J. H. Conway and R. K. Guy, *Winning Ways for Your Mathematical Plays*, Vol. 2, Academic Press (1984) and M. Gardner, *Wheels, Life and other Mathematical Amusements*, Freeman Press (1983).

Mark Przyborowski and Mark van Woerkom, "Diffusion of many interacting random walkers on a three-dimensional lattice with a personal computer," *Eur. J. Phys.* **6**, 242 (1985). This work was done while the authors were high school students in West Germany.

F. Reif, *Fundamentals of Statistical and Thermal Physics*, McGraw-Hill (1965). Einstein's relation between the diffusion and mobility is discussed in Chapter 15.

Leonard M. Sander, "Fractal growth," *Sci. Amer.* **256**, 94 (January, 1987). An accessible introduction to fractal growth models and their applications by one of the developers of the diffusion limited aggregation model (see Problem 13.8).

L. Schulman and P. Seiden, "Statistical mechanics of a dynamical system based on Conway's game of Life," *J. Stat. Phys.* **19**, 293 (1978).

H. Eugene Stanley and Nicole Ostrowsky, eds., *On Growth and Form*, Martinus Nijhoff Publishers, Netherlands (1986). A collection of research papers at approximately the same level as the Family and Landau collection. The article by Paul Meakin on DLA was referenced in the text.

David D. Thornburg, *Discovering Logo*, Addison-Wesley (1983). The book is more accurately described by its subtitle, *An Invitation to the Art and Pattern of Nature*. The nature of recursive procedures and fractals are discussed using many simple examples.

Gérard Y. Vichniac, "Cellular automata models of disorder and organization," in *Disordered Systems and Biological Organization*, E. Bienenstock, F. Fogelman Soulie, and G. Weisbuch, eds. Springer-Verlag (1986). See also Gérard Y. Vichniac, "Taking the computer seriously in teaching science (an introduction to cellular automata)," in *Microscience*, Proceedings of the UNESCO Workshop on Microcomputers in Science Education, G. Marx and P. Szucs, eds., (Balaton, Hungary, 1985).

Stephen Wolfram, ed., *Theory and Applications of Cellular Automata*, World Scientific, Singapore (1986). A collection of research papers on cellular automata which range in difficulty from straightforward to complex. An extensive annonated bibliography is also given.

David Wilkinson and Jorge F. Willemsen, "Invasion percolation: a new form of percolation theory," *J. Phys.* **A16**, 3365 (1983). One of the first articles on invasion percolation was by Roland Lenormand and Serge Bories, "Description of a bond percolation mechanism used for the simulation of drainage with trapping in porous idea" (in French), *C. R. Acad. Sci. Paris B* **291**, 279 (1980).

THE APPROACH
TO EQUILIBRIUM

14

We consider a simple model of a macroscopic system and introduce
the concepts of equilibrium and entropy.

14.1 INTRODUCTION

In this chapter we now use our knowledge of the laws of microscopic physics to understand the qualitative properties of macroscopic objects. Typical macroscopic systems encompass objects as diverse as gases, liquids, solids, polymers, gels, and biological organisms, and contain about 10^{20} to 10^{25} interacting molecules. Macroscopic systems exhibit a wide range of behavior such as the turbulent motion of a swiftly flowing brook, the melting of ice, and the self-reproduction of a living organism. The tremendous complexity inherent in macroscopic systems cannot be understood by the direct application of computers—the motion of 10^{20} interacting particles cannot be treated by even the most super of supercomputers. Moreover, detailed information on the behavior of the individual particles would not provide much insight into the essential features of the macroscopic system.

One of the most important features of macroscopic systems is their tendency toward disorder. That is, if the particles are initially ordered and the system is isolated from external influences, then after the removal of an internal constraint the particles will tend to become disordered. An example of this tendency can be seen by the addition of ink to a glass of water. Suppose that the ink has the same density as water and is carefully added to the surface of the water. The glass is left mechanically undisturbed and the environment is not changed. After some time has passed, we know that the ink and the water will become thoroughly mixed. Suppose we take a movie of the water-ink system and happen to watch the movie run backward. We would see that the random motion of the ink molecules has brought the ink to the surface. Our intuitive understanding of how nature works tells us that something is wrong—the movie is indeed being run backward. From our experience we can say that the natural tendency of macroscopic systems toward disorder defines the direction or "arrow" of time.

The water-ink mixture can be described by specifying its *microscopic state* or *microstate*. Such a description corresponds to the most complete specification, consistent with the laws of mechanics, of all the molecules in the system. According to classical mechanics such a description corresponds to specifying the positions and velocities of each molecule. On a larger scale, the *macroscopic state* or *macrostate* of the water-ink mixture can be described by specifying the average concentration of molecules in any small but finite region of the glass of water. The microscopic state of the system changes in a most complicated way. In contrast we know that after some time the macroscopic state does not change in time except for small random *fluctuations*. Such a state is said to be an *equilibrium* state.

14.2   A SIMPLE MODEL

The ideas of disorder and order, the direction of time, and the microscopic and macroscopic specification of a system can be illustrated by a simple model which we will consider in various contexts in this chapter. Consider an ideal gas of N identical particles for which the interaction between the particles can be ignored. Such a gas can be realized in the laboratory if the gas is sufficiently dilute. In this case the probability of their mutual interaction is small. We assume that the gas is confined within a box which is isolated (not influenced by an external system or force) and left undisturbed for a long time. Let us focus our attention on the distribution of the particles in space and imagine the box to be divided by a partition. The partition contains a small hole covered by a movable slide (see Fig. 14.1). Initially n particles are placed in the left half and n' in the right half of the box with $n + n' = N$. Then the hole is opened. Since the motion of each particle is independent of all the other particles, each particle has an equal chance of having a trajectory which leads it through the hole. We assume that one particle passes through the hole in one unit of time.

In order to define the microstates and macrostates for our model, we assume the particles to be distinguishable and labeled by a number from 1 to N. A microstate can be specified by the labels of the particles in the left side of the box since once we know the labels on the left, those on the right are determined as well. A macrostate is specified by the number of particles n in the left side.

What are the relevant questions we might ask about the behavior of the

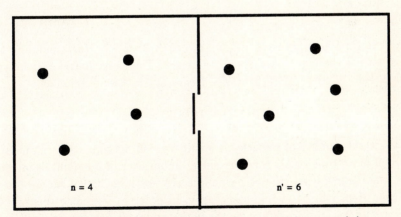

Fig. 14.1 A box divided into two equal halves by a partition containing a small hole with a movable slide. After the hole is opened, one particle moves through the hole in each time step.

simple "particles in a box" model? One obvious question is "Given n and n' at $t = 0$, what are n and n' at time t (after t moves)?" The answer to this question is clearly statistical in nature. We might rephrase the question and ask "What is the average number of particles in the left half at time t?" A more detailed question might require knowledge of $P_N(n, t)$, the probability that at time t there are n particles in the left out of a total of N particles.

14.3 EXACT ENUMERATION

Now that we understand the nature of the model and some of the relevant questions, what are the appropriate methods of solution? One way is to use *exact enumeration* and determine all the possibilities at each time step. For example suppose that at $t = 0$, $n = 10$ and $n' = 0$. At $t = 1$ the only possibility is $n = 9$ and $n' = 1$ and hence $P(n = 9, t = 1) = 1$. At $t = 2$ the possibilities are that one of the nine particles in the left moves to the right or the particle on the right returns to the left. Since the first possibility can occur in nine different ways, we have the non-zero probabilities

$$P(8, 2) = \frac{9}{10}, \qquad P(10, 2) = \frac{1}{10} \quad .$$

Hence at $t = 2$ the average number of particles on the left side of the box is

$$<n> = 8P(8, 2) + 10P(10, 2) = 8.2 \quad .$$

In the next time step we have $P(7, 3) = \frac{8}{10}P(8, 2) = \frac{72}{100}$, corresponding to a move of one of the eight particles to the right. The same considerations yield $P(9, 3) = \frac{10}{10}P(10, 2) + \frac{2}{10}P(8, 2) = \frac{28}{100}$. Hence at $t = 3$ we obtain

$$<n> = 7P(7, 3) + 9P(9, 3) = 7.56 \quad .$$

Since the total number of particles is small, we can continue this enumeration for several more time steps. However since the number of possibilities increases with t, the enumeration cannot be done easily for large t. For larger N even fewer time steps can be enumerated easily. In order to overcome this problem we can use a computer to determine the various possibilities. But for sufficiently large N or t, the number of possibilities becomes so huge that no computer can compute them.

14.4   MONTE CARLO METHOD

In contrast to the exact enumeration method, the "Monte Carlo" method is applicable to larger systems and longer times. In the Monte Carlo method we generate a sample of random moves and assume that our sample is representative of the set of all possible moves. Clearly the more samples we have, the closer we come to the exact result.

In order to implement the Monte Carlo method we require the probability that a particle in the left half of the box will go to the right. Since each particle has the same chance to be the next one to go through the hole, the probability per unit time of a move from left to right equals the number of particles in the left half at that time divided by the total number of particles. Thus the probability of a move from left to right is n/N. We can now simulate the time evolution of the model in a manner that is consistent with the above probability. The algorithm consists of the following steps:

1. Generate a random number r from a uniformly distributed set of random numbers with values between 0 and 1.
2. Compare r to the current value of the fraction of particles n/N in the left half of the box.
3. Move a particle from left to right if $r \leq n/N$; otherwise move a particle from right to left.

Program box implements this algorithm and plots the evolution of n.

```
PROGRAM box
RANDOMIZE
CALL initial(N,tmax)                    ! input data
CALL move(N,tmax)                       ! move particles through hole
END

SUB initial(N,tmax)
    INPUT prompt "number of particles = ": N        ! try N = 1000
    LET tmax = 10*N
    SET window -0.1*tmax,1.1*tmax,-0.1*N,1.1*N
    BOX LINES 0,tmax,0,N
    PLOT 0,N;
END SUB
```

```
SUB move(N,tmax)
   LET nl = N                              ! initially all particles on left side
   FOR itime = 1 to tmax
      LET prob = nl/N
      ! generate random number and move particle
      IF rnd <= prob then
         LET nl = nl - 1
      ELSE
         LET nl = nl + 1
      END IF
      PLOT itime,nl;
   NEXT itime
END SUB
```

PROBLEM 14.1 The "particles in the box" model

a. Describe the time evolution of the number of particles in the left half of the box. Consider $N = 10, 20, 40$, and 80 and assume that all N particles are initially in the left half.

b. What is the qualitative nature of equilibrium? Does the system evolve toward equilibrium? Can you determine a direction of time? What is the approximate time it takes for the system to reach equilibrium?

c. Modify **Program box** so that the number of particles on the left side is averaged over several trials. What is the implicit definition of the probability which is used to obtain the mean number $<n(t)>$ at each time step t? Is this definition identical to the definition used in the exact enumeration discussion of Sec. 14.3? If the two definitions are not identical, are they equivalent?

d. One way to verify your modified form of **Program box** is to compare the Monte Carlo results for $<n(t)>$ with the exact enumeration results. Choose a small value of N, e.g. $N = 4$, and use exact enumeration to calculate $<n(t)>$ exactly for several time steps. Then choose a sufficiently large number of trials to obtain a reasonable estimate for $<n(t)>$ and verify that your results are consistent.

e. Run your modified form of **Program box** for $N = 10$ with all particles initially in the left half of the box. Plot n, the number of particles in the left side, as a function of time for five different trials. Then plot n as a function of time averaged over the same five trials. How does the time-dependence of

n for one trial compare with the time-dependence of n averaged over several trials?

f. A measure of the equilibrium fluctuations is the variance σ^2 defined by

$$\sigma^2 = <(n- <n>)^2>$$
$$= <n^2> - <n>^2 \quad . \tag{14.1}$$

The brackets represent a time average taken after the system has reached equilibrium. The relative magnitude of the fluctuations is $\sigma/<n>$. Modify **Program box** so that the relative fluctuations in σ are computed after the system has reached equilibrium.

g. Determine the equilibration time, $<n>$, and $\sigma/<n>$ for $N = 20, 40,$ and 80. How do these various physical quantities depend on N?

14.5 ENTROPY

The simulations in Problem 14.1 illustrate a fundamental property of systems with many particles: if an isolated system is prepared in a nonrandom or ordered state, it will change in time so as to approach its most random state. In this most random state the macroscopic quantities are independent of time except for small fluctuations and the system is said to be in equilibrium.

Because of the simplicity of the model, we can calculate the number of microstates for each macrostate. We know that each particle can be in one of two states—left or right. In addition the location of each particle is independent of all the others. These two conditions imply that if there are N total particles, with n on the left and n' on the right, the number of microstates corresponding to each macrostate is given by $N!/n!n'!$, the Binomial distribution. In Table 14.1 we give the number of microstates Ω_n for $N = 10$ and the different values of n. Note that the maximum number of microstates occurs for $n = 5$.

We can give a more quantitative measure of order and disorder. In Problem 14.1 we found that for $N = 10$, the equilibrium macrostate is $n = 5$, the macrostate with the greatest number of microstates. We say that this macrostate corresponds to the state of "maximum disorder." In contrast the $n = 0$ macrostate corresponds to a state of zero disorder since the system is found in only one microstate. It is convenient to measure the degree of disorder by introducing the *entropy* S such that the entropy is equal to zero if there is only one microstate

TABLE 14.1 The number of microstates Ω_n and the entropy $S_n = log\,\Omega_n$ for the "particles in the box" model with $N = 10$. The macrostate is specified by the number of particles on the left side and is fixed at n. The total number of microstates for $N = 10$ is $2^{10} = 1024$.

n	Ω_n	$log\,\Omega_n$
0	1	0.00
1	10	2.30
2	45	3.81
3	120	4.79
4	210	5.35
5	252	5.53
6	210	5.35
7	120	4.79
8	45	3.81
9	10	2.30
10	1	0.00

and increases as the number of microstates increases. A definition of S due to Boltzmann for a system in a definite macostate n is (cf Reif)

$$S_n/k_B = ln\,\Omega_n \tag{14.2}$$

where Ω_n is the total number of possible microstates corresponding to n. The constant k_B is included to make the definition (14.2) consistent with the thermodyamic definition of S. Since its inclusion is irrelevant here, we measure S in units of k_B, i.e. we set k_B equal to unity.

According to (14.2), the entropy of a system is a logarithmic measure of the number of microstates corresponding to a macrostate. The entropy associated with each macrostate is shown in Table 14.1. We see that S_n is a maximum for $n = 5$. Such a state is said to be the most random since the number of microstates corresponding to this macrostate is a maximum.

The definition (14.2) of the entropy requires the enumeration of all possible microstates, an impossible task in general. It is desirable to have a method for measuring the entropy which is based on the observable properties of the system rather than on an idealized definition involving the enumeration of all possible microstates. A definition of the entropy which lends itself to direct measurement by computer simulation is due to Ma (see references). This definition of the entropy uses the fact that a system evolving in time will eventually duplicate a microstate (or a similar microstate). The longer it takes for there to be a coincidence of two uncorrelated microstates, the fewer microstates there are and hence

TABLE 14.2 Sequence of twenty microstates for macrostate $n = 1$. Each of the twenty microstates are specified by the particle label on the left side.

8	7	5	10	7	2	4	6	2	10	3	4	3	9	6	5	2	9	2	4

the lower the entropy of the system. A quantity that we can directly measure is the coincidence rate R_n defined as the ratio of the number of comparisons of duplicate microstates to the total number of comparisons of two microstates. The entropy is defined in terms of R_n by

$$S_n/k_B = ln \frac{1}{R_n} \quad . \tag{14.3}$$

The relation (14.3) is the basis of the method of coincidences method. The measurement of R_n should be taken over a relatively long time. As we increase the time our results should converge to the exact result for R_n.

In order to understand the implementation of the definition (14.3) of S, we apply it to the "particles in the box" model. Since (14.3) is applicable only to a system in a definite macrostate, we must set the number of particles on each side equal to a constant. The simplest modification of our algorithm which is consistent with this constraint is to assume the system evolves by the *exchange* of a particle on the left with a particle on the right. In contrast our earlier simulation allowed n to fluctuate by the random *moves* of particles from one side to the other.

In Table 14.2 we show a sequence of twenty exchanges for $n = 1$; the particle labels represent the label of the particle on the left side. Since there are a total of twenty exchanges, there are $20(20 - 1)/2 = 190$ possible comparisons of microstates. The number of coincidences for each microstate is $m(m - 1)/2$, where m is the number of occurences of a particular microstate. From Table 14.2 we see that $m = 4$ for microstate 2 and hence the number of possible coincidences of this microstate is $(4)(3)/2 = 6$. The number of coincidences for the microstates is given in Table 14.3. Since the total number of coincidences is fifteen, the coincidence rate is found to be $R = 15/190$ and hence $S \sim ln\,190/15 \approx 2.5$. This approximate result for S is consistent with the exact result, $S = ln\,10 \approx 2.3$, given in Table 14.1.

TABLE 14.3 Coincidences of the ten possible microstates associated with the macrostate $n = 1$ (one particle on left side of box) for a sequence of twenty exchanges. The total number of coincidences for this sequence is found to be fifteen.

microstate	number of occurences	number of coincidences
1	0	0
2	4	6
3	2	1
4	3	3
5	2	1
6	2	1
7	2	1
8	1	0
9	2	1
10	2	1

TABLE 14.4 A sequence of twenty microstates for macrostate $n = 2$. A microstate is specified uniquely by the quantity $micro = 2^{L_1} + 2^{L_2}$, where L_1 and L_2 are the particle labels of the two particles on the left side.

trial	L_1	L_2	micro	trial	L_1	L_2	micro
1	6	9	576	11	3	10	1032
2	4	9	528	12	3	5	40
3	4	10	1040	13	5	7	160
4	3	10	1032	14	5	6	96
5	2	10	1028	15	5	10	1056
6	2	3	12	16	5	7	160
7	3	10	1032	17	5	6	96
8	5	10	1056	18	5	8	288
9	1	5	34	19	2	5	36
10	1	10	1026	20	2	8	260

We note that for $n = 2$ there are approximately four times the number of possible microstates as for $n = 1$. Thus we need a simple method of labeling and comparing microstates. One method is to specify a microstate by the quantity *micro* defined as

$$micro = \sum 2^L \tag{14.4}$$

where L is the particle label for each particle, and the sum is over all particles on the left. Note that the sum (14.4) can be thought of as a binary number

1032 three times and equals 1056, 96 and 160 twice each.) Hence $R = 6/190$ and $S \sim ln\,190/6 \approx 3.45$. This estimate for S is within 10% of the exact value $S = ln\,45 \approx 3.81$ (see Table 14.1).

The following program computes the entropy for general n using the above procedure for the comparison of microstates.

```
PROGRAM entropy
DIM left(10),right(10),micro(0 to 2000)
RANDOMIZE
! input parameters and choose initial configuration of particles
CALL initial(nl,nr,left,right,micro,nexch)
CALL exchange(nl,nr,nexch,left,right,micro)         ! exchange particles
CALL output(nexch,micro)                    ! compute coincidence rate and entropy
END

SUB initial(nl,nr,left(),right(),micro(),nexch)
    ! fix macrostate
    INPUT prompt "total number of particles = ": N
    INPUT prompt "number of particles on the left = ": nl
    LET nr = N - nl                      ! number of particles on the right
    LET micro(0) = 0
    FOR il = 1 to nl
        LET left(il) = il                       ! list of particle numbers on left side
        LET micro(0) = micro(0) + 2^il                      ! initial microstate
    NEXT il
    FOR ir = 1 to nr
        LET right(ir) = ir + nl          ! list of particle numbers on right side
    NEXT ir
    INPUT prompt "number of exchanges = ": nexch
END SUB
```

```
SUB exchange(nl,nr,nexch,left(),right(),micro())
    ! exchange particle number on left corresponding to lindex
    ! with particle on right corresponding to rindex
    FOR iexch = 1 to nexch
        ! randomly choose array indexes
        LET lindex = int(rnd*nl + 1)                    ! left index of array
        LET rindex = int(rnd*nr + 1)                     ! right index of array
        LET left_particle = left(lindex)
        LET right_particle = right(rindex)
        LET left(lindex) = right_particle       ! new particle number in left array
        LET right(rindex) = left_particle        ! new particle number in right array
        LET micro(iexch) = micro(iexch - 1) + 2^right_particle
        LET micro(iexch) = micro(iexch) - 2^left_particle           ! new microstate
    NEXT iexch
END SUB

SUB output(nexch,micro())
    ! compute coincidence rate and entropy
    LET ncomparisons = nexch*(nexch - 1)/2        ! total number of comparisons
    ! compare microstates
    FOR iexch = 1 to nexch - 1
        FOR jexch = iexch + 1 to nexch
            IF micro(iexch) = micro(jexch) then
                LET ncoincidences = ncoincidences + 1        ! number of coincidences
            END IF
        NEXT jexch
    NEXT iexch
    LET rate = ncoincidences/ncomparisons           ! coincidence rate
    IF rate > 0 then LET S = log(1/rate)
    PRINT "estimate of entropy = ",S
END SUB
```

PROBLEM 14.2 Dynamical determination of the entropy

a. Choose $N = 10$ and use **Program entropy** to compute the coincidence rate R_n and the entropy S_n for each of the macrostates of the particles in the box model.

b. Compare your approximate results for S_n to the exact results given in Table 14.1.

c. Estimate the error associated with your computation of S_n by running the program for longer sequences.

d. If possible repeat the above measurements for larger N. What is the largest value of N that is possible to consider using the quantity *micro* defined in (14.4) and in **Program entropy**? Is there a practical upper limit to the value of N that can be considered?

In **Program entropy** the generation of the configurations is much faster than the computation of the coincidences. The former is proportional to the number of exchanges, but the latter is proportional to the square of the number of exchanges. Thus it might be convenient to save the values of *micro* generated by **SUB exchange** in a separate file. In this way we can separate the analysis of the data from its generation and if necessary use various methods of analysis. In True BASIC we open a file with the statement:

```
OPEN #1: name "data1", access output, create new
```

The values of *micro* are written in file #1 using the statement:

```
PRINT #1: micro(iexch)
```

We close file #1 with the statement:

```
CLOSE #1
```

In order to read the data we use the statements:

```
OPEN #1: name 'data1", access input
INPUT #1, micro(iexch)
CLOSE #1
```

14.6 EFFECT OF CORRELATIONS

You might have noticed that in Table 14.4, particle 5 is on the left side for
a relatively long time. For this particular example, this short-time correlation
is due to correlations in the random number generator (not the one in True
BASIC). This type of short-time correlation also occurs in real systems. However
the utility of the definition (14.3) of the entropy depends on the microstates
being uncorrelated. We should only compare microstates that are separated by
a time which is longer than the *correlation time*, the average time between two
microstates such that they are uncorrelated. For our example the correlation
time is the number of exchanges required for the system to evolve from one
microstate to another where the latter has almost no particles in common with
the former. One estimate of the correlation time is the time it takes for system
to reach equilibrium. In the following problem we look at whether correlations
are an important factor in our simple model calculation of the entropy.

*PROBLEM 14.3 Entropy and correlations

> **a.** Modify **Program entropy** so that no comparisons are made between
> states which are separated in time by less than the equilibration time (see
> Problem 14.1). Compute S_n for $N = 10$ and different n taking into account
> the effect of correlations.

> **b.** What do your results in part (a) tell you about the correlation time if
> the entropy found in part (a) is the same as that found in Problem 14.2?

14.7 THE EQUILIBRIUM ENTROPY

The definition (14.3) of the entropy is applicable to a system known to be in a
definite macrostate. However in our original formulation of the particles in a box
model, we allowed the particles to move from one side to the other at random and
hence n was allowed to fluctuate. In order to compute the entropy of a system at
equilibrium where the macrostate is not fixed, we generalize the definition (14.3)
and write

$$S = \sum_n P_n S_n \qquad (14.5)$$

where P_n is the equilibrium probability of occurence of the macrostate n; the
sum is over all macrostates.

PROBLEM 14.4 The equilibrium entropy

a. For the particles in a box model the equilibrium probability P_n is the probability of a macrostate occuring with n particles on the left. P_n can be calculated exactly by enumerating the number of microstates corresponding to the macrostate n and dividing by the total number of possible microstates. Use the results given in Table 14.1 to calculate P_n for $N = 10$.

b. A simple procedure for computing P_n from a sequence of states is to count the number of times a macrostate occurs and divide this sum by the total number of occurences. Modify **Program box** so that P_n is computed. Choose $N = 10$ and compare your results to the exact results for P_n found in part (a).

c. Compute the equilibrium entropy using the relation (14.5) and the probabilities P_n and S_n computed in part (b) and Problem 14.2 respectively.

d. How does your result for S found in part (c) compare with the entropy S_n for $n = 5$? How would the equilibrium entropy compare to S_n for $n = N/2$ if $N \gg 1$?

We emphasize that the practical measurement of the entropy remains a difficult problem of much current interest. The method of coincidences is applicable only to relatively small systems or to small independent parts of a larger system.

*14.8 ENTROPY AND CHAOS

In Chapter 7 we discussed a simple period doubling model which exhibits behavior suggestive of the approach to chaos in turbulent systems. The model is determined by the difference equation

$$x_{n+1} = 4rx_n(1 - x_n) \quad . \tag{14.6}$$

We found that the map (14.6) exhibits periodic or chaotic behavior depending on the value of the control parameter r. It might be possible to apply Ma's method of computing the entropy to gain additional insight into the nature of the chaotic region. We divide the interval $[0,1]$ into N equal intervals and define a microstate of the model by the value of x; a macroscopic state of the model is characterized by the parameter r. The entropy is computed by counting the number of coincidences. For $r < r_c$ and N sufficiently large, we expect that the entropy will reach a limiting value independent of N. What is the N-dependence of the entropy for $r > r_c$? If a microscopic state is never duplicated, we expect that the entropy will be an increasing function of N and not reach a limiting value.

PROBLEM 14.5 Entropy of a period doubling system

a. Write a program which computes the coincidence rate for the quadratic map (14.6). Choose a value of r such that x_n is periodic, e.g. $r = 0.85$, and verify that Ma's coincidence method correctly determines the number of possible values of x_n. Show that for large N, the entropy is independent of N. Does the finite number of digits retained by your computer affect your results?

b. Consider the macrostate $r = 1$ for which it is known that there are no regions between $x = 0$ to 1 that x_n does not visit. This choice of r corresponds to the "most" chaotic region. Determine the entropy as a function of N.

c. For certain values of $r > r_c$ (e.g. $r = 0.91$), the trajectory of x appears chaotic but there might exist regions of x which might not be visited. Determine the entropy in this region as a function of N. Does the finite number of digits retained by your computer affect your results in this region? A detailed and careful analysis would be required to differentiate a truly chaotic region from an "almost" chaotic region.

REFERENCES AND SUGGESTIONS FOR ADDITIONAL READING

P. W. Atkins, *The Second Law*, W. H. Freeman (1984). A beautifully illustrated book which discusses the concepts entropy and disorder in a variety of contexts.

Ralph Baierlein, *Atoms and Information Theory*, W. H. Freeman (1971). An advanced undergraduate text which develops statistical mechanics from the point of view of information theory.

Robert M. Eisberg, *Applied Mathematical Physics with Programmable Pocket Calculators*, McGraw-Hill (1976). Chapter 7 discusses entropy and the arrow of time.

Robert M. Eisberg and Lawrence S. Lerner, *Physics*, Vol. II, McGraw-Hill (1981). See Chapter 18 for a discussion of disorder and entropy.

Shang-keng Ma, "Calculation of entropy from data of motion," *J. Stat. Phys.* **26**, 221, (1981). See also Chapter 25 of Ma's graduate level text, *Statistical Mechanics,* World Scientific (1985). Note that the coincidence rate is related to the recurrence time for a finite system to return to an arbitrarily small neighborhood of almost any given initial state.

F. Reif, *Statistical and Thermal Physics,* Berkeley Physics, Vol. 5, McGraw-Hill (1965).

C. Ray Smith and W. T. Grandt, Jr., eds., "Maximum-Entropy and Bayesian Methods in Inverse Problems," D. Reidel (1985). A collection of articles on applications of the entropy maximum principle. One of the more accessible articles is on the reconstruction of images.

TABLE 15.1 The sixteen possible microstates for a system of $N = 4$ noninteracting particles moving in one dimension. Each particle can have velocity v_0 or $-v_0$. The letter R denotes a particle moving to the right and the letter L denotes a particle moving to the left. The mass of the particles is taken to be unity and the total (kinetic) energy $E = 4(v_0^2/2)$.

L L L L	L L L R	L L R R	L R R R	R R R R
	L L R L	L R L R	R L R R	
	L R L L	L R R L	R R L R	
	R L L L	R L L R	R R R L	
		R L R L		
		R R L L		

in state tails. Since Ω, the total number of coin states, equals two, we have from (15.1) that $P_h = 1/2$. We expect that the two methods for calculating P_h would yield the same result.

To illustrate these ideas in a more physical context, consider a model in which the particles are distinguishable, non-interacting and have only two possible velocities v_0 and $-v_0$. Since the particles are non-interacting, the size of the system and the positions of the particles are irrelevant. In Table 15.1 we show the ensemble of systems consistent with $N = 4$ and $E = 2v_0^2$. The mass of the particles is taken to be unity.

The enumeration of the sixteen systems in the ensemble allows us to calculate ensemble averages for the physical quantities of the system. For example inspection of Table 15.1 shows that P_n, the probability that the number of particles moving to the right is n, is given by 1/16, 4/16, 6/16, 4/16, 1/16 for $n = 0$, 1, 2, 3, and 4 respectively. Hence the mean number of particles moving to the right is

$$\langle n \rangle = \sum n P_n$$
$$= (0 \times 1 + 1 \times 4 + 2 \times 6 + 3 \times 4 + 4 \times 1)/16 = 2 \quad .$$

15.3 MONTE CARLO SIMULATION

We have found in Chapter 6 that we can simulate a system of many particles with N, V and E fixed by integrating the equations of motion for each particle and calculating the time-averaged value of the physical quantities of interest. How can we do an ensemble average at fixed N, V and E? One way might

THE MICROCANONICAL ENSEMBLE

15

We simulate the microcanonical ensemble and "discover" the Boltzmann distribution for systems in thermal contact with a heat reservoir.

15.1 INTRODUCTION

The molecular dynamics simulations in Chapter 6 and the "particles in the box" problem of Chapter 14 have given us insight into some of the important qualitative features of macroscopic systems, e.g. the irreversible approach to equilibrium and the existence of equilibrium fluctuations in macroscopic quantities. In this chapter we apply Monte Carlo methods to the simulation of the equilibrium properties of systems with many degrees of freedom. This application will allow us to explore the methodology of statistical mechanics and to introduce the concept of temperature.

Due in part to the impact of computer simulation, statistical mechanics has had many exciting developments in recent years. Applications of statistical mechanics have expanded from the traditional areas of dense gases and liquids to the study of phase transitions, particle physics and theories of the early universe. In fact the algorithm used in this chapter was developed by a physicist interested in using computer simulation to make predictions of experimentally verifiable quantities from "lattice gauge theories," theories used to describe the fundamental interactions of elementary particles.

15.2 THE MICROCANONICAL ENSEMBLE

We first discuss a *closed* system for which the number of particles N, the volume V, and the total energy E are fixed. We also assume that the system is *isolated*, i.e. that the influence of external parameters such as gravitational and magnetic fields can be ignored. We know that in general a closed macroscopic system tends to a time-independent equilibrium state of maximum randomness or entropy. The *macrostate* of the system is specified by the values of N, V and E. At the microscopic level there are in general a large number of different ways or *configurations* in which the macrostate (N, V, E) can be realized. A particular configuration or *microstate* is *accessible* if its properties are consistent with the specifed macrostate.

All we know about the accessible microstates is that their properties are consistent with the known physical quantities of the system. Since we have no reason to prefer one microstate over another, it is reasonable to postulate that at any given time, the system is *equally* likely to be in any one of its accessible microstates. In order to make this postulate of *equal a priori probabilities* more precise, imagine an isolated system with Ω accessible states. The probability P_s of finding the system in microstate s is

$$P_s = \begin{cases} 1/\Omega, & \text{if } s \text{ is accessible} \\ 0, & \text{otherwise} \end{cases} \qquad (15.1)$$

The sum of P_s over all Ω states is equal to unity.

The averages of physical quantities can be determined in two ways. In the usual laboratory experiment, physical quantities are measured over a span of time sufficiently long to allow the system to sample a large number of its accessible microstates. We already performed such time averages in Chapter 6 where we used the method of molecular dynamics to compute the time-averaged values of quantities such as the temperature and pressure. An interpretation of the probabilities in (15.1) which is consistent with such a time average is that during a sequence of observations, P_s yields the fraction of times that a single system is found in a given microscopic state.

In spite of the conceptual simplicity of time-averages, it is convenient to formulate statistical averages at a given instant of time. Instead of performing measurements on a single system, imagine a collection or *ensemble* of systems which are identical mental replicas characterized by the same macrostate. The number of systems in the ensemble equals the number of possible microstates. In this interpretation, the probabilities in (15.1) describe an ensemble of identical systems. An ensemble of systems specified by E, N, V which is described by the probability distribution of the form (15.1) is called a *microcanonical* ensemble.

Suppose that a physical quantity A has the value A_s when the system is in the state s. Then the ensemble average of A is given by

$$<A> = \sum_s A_s P_s \qquad (15.2)$$

where P_s is given by (15.1).

Since the above discussion of time averages and ensemble averages is still formal, we consider a simple example. Suppose we have a coin and want to know the probability P_h that a coin toss yields "heads." We can find P_h by tossing a single coin N times and calculating the fraction

$$P_h = \frac{n_h}{N} \qquad (15.3)$$

where n_h is the total number of heads which are observed. Do we expect to obtain the same value of P_h each time we toss the coin N times? Alternatively we can consider an ensemble of 2 identical coins, one in state heads and the other

TABLE 15.1 The sixteen possible microstates for a system of $N = 4$ noninteracting particles moving in one dimension. Each particle can have velocity v_0 or $-v_0$. The letter R denotes a particle moving to the right and the letter L denotes a particle moving to the left. The mass of the particles is taken to be unity and the total (kinetic) energy $E = 4(v_0{}^2/2)$.

L L L L	L L L R	L L R R	L R R R	R R R R
	L L R L	L R L R	R L R R	
	L R L L	L R R L	R R L R	
	R L L L	R L L R	R R R L	
		R L R L		
		R R L L		

in state tails. Since Ω, the total number of coin states, equals two, we have from (15.1) that $P_h = 1/2$. We expect that the two methods for calculating P_h would yield the same result.

To illustrate these ideas in a more physical context, consider a model in which the particles are distinguishable, non-interacting and have only two possible velocities v_0 and $-v_0$. Since the particles are non-interacting, the size of the system and the positions of the particles are irrelevant. In Table 15.1 we show the ensemble of systems consistent with $N = 4$ and $E = 2v_0{}^2$. The mass of the particles is taken to be unity.

The enumeration of the sixteen systems in the ensemble allows us to calculate ensemble averages for the physical quantities of the system. For example inspection of Table 15.1 shows that P_n, the probability that the number of particles moving to the right is n, is given by 1/16, 4/16, 6/16, 4/16, 1/16 for $n = 0$, 1, 2, 3, and 4 respectively. Hence the mean number of particles moving to the right is

$$<n> = \sum n P_n$$
$$= (0 \times 1 + 1 \times 4 + 2 \times 6 + 3 \times 4 + 4 \times 1)/16 = 2 \quad .$$

15.3 MONTE CARLO SIMULATION

We have found in Chapter 6 that we can simulate a system of many particles with N, V and E fixed by integrating the equations of motion for each particle and calculating the time-averaged value of the physical quantities of interest. How can we do an ensemble average at fixed N, V and E? One way might be to enumerate all the microstates and calculate the ensemble averages of the desired physical quantities as we did in our examples. However this approach is usually not practical, since the number of microstates for even a small system is much too large to enumerate. In the spirit of Monte Carlo, we wish to develop a practical method of obtaining a representative sample of the total number of microstates. An obvious procedure is to fix N and V, change the positions and velocities of the individual particles at random, and retain the configuration if it has the desired total energy. However this procedure is very inefficient, since in general most configurations will not have the desired total energy and must be discarded.

There is an efficient Monte Carlo procedure which has been proposed by Michael Creutz and coworkers. Imagine a macroscopic system which is divided into two "subsystems," i.e. the original system of interest, referred to as the *system,* and a *subsystem* which has one member. For historical reasons, this extra degree of freedom is called a "demon." The demon travels about the system transfering energy as it attempts to change the dynamical variables of the system. If the demon has sufficient energy in its sack, it gives energy to any member of the system who requires energy to make the desired change. Conversely if the desired change lowers the energy of the system, then the excess energy is given to the demon. The only limitation on the demon is that it cannot have negative energy. The algorithm is summarized in the following:

a. choose a particle at random and make a trial change in its coordinates;
b. compute the change in the energy of the system due to the change in coordinates;
c. if the trial change decreases the energy of the system, the system gives its energy to the demon and the new configuration is accepted;
d. if the trial change increases the energy of the system, the new configuration is accepted if the demon has sufficient energy to give to the system. Otherwise the new configuration is rejected and the particle retains its old coordinates;
e. if the trial change does not change the energy of the system, the new configuration is accepted.

The above procedure is repeated until a representative sample of states is obtained. After a period of time for equilibration, the demon and the system will reach a compromise and agree on an average energy for each. The total energy remains constant, and since the demon is only one degree of freedom in comparison to the many degrees of freedom of the system, we expect that the energy fluctuations of the system will be small.

How do we know that this Monte Carlo simulation of the microcanonical ensemble will yield results equivalent to the time-averaged results of molecular dynamics? The assumption that the two averages yield equivalent results is called the *ergodic* hypothesis (or more accurately the quasi-ergodic hypothesis). Although these two averages cannot be shown to be identical in general, they have been found to yield equivalent results in all cases of practical interest.

15.4   ONE DIMENSIONAL CLASSICAL IDEAL GAS

We first apply the demon algorithm to the classical ideal gas. In this case the particle velocities are continuous and unbounded. The energy of a configuration is independent of the positions of the particles, and the total energy is the sum of the kinetic energies of the individual particles. Hence for an ideal gas the only coordinates of interest are the velocity coordinates. In order to change a configuration, we choose a particle at random and change its velocity by a random amount. For simplicity only the motion of particles in one dimension is considered.

Of course we do not need to use the demon algorithm for an ideal gas since a reduction in the energy of one particle can be easily compensated by the corresponding increase in the energy of another particle. However it is usually a good idea to consider a simple case first.

Program ideal_demon listed in the following is an example of a microcanonical Monte Carlo simulation of a one dimensional ideal classical gas. The particles are chosen to have equal initial velocities. The variables *vinitial* and *dvmax* defined in **SUB initial** determine the velocity scale and the maximum change of velocity in one attempt. The variable *nmcs*, the number of Monte Carlo steps per particle, plays an important role in Monte Carlo simulations. The interpretation of *nmcs* is that on the average the demon attempts to change the velocity of a particle *nmcs* times in one run.

```
PROGRAM ideal_demon
! demon algorithm for the one-dimensional ideal classical gas
DIM vel(100)
RANDOMIZE
CALL initial(N,nmcs,esystem,edemon,vel,vtot,dvmax)
FOR imcs = 1 to nmcs
    CALL changes(N,esystem,edemon,vel,vtot,escum,vcum,edcum,dvmax,accept)
NEXT imcs
CALL averages(N,nmcs,escum,vcum,edcum,accept)
END

SUB initial(N,nmcs,esystem,edemon,vel(),vtot,dvmax)
    INPUT prompt  "number of particles = ": N
    INPUT prompt  "number of Monte Carlo steps per particle = ": nmcs
    INPUT prompt  "initial energy of system = ": esystem
    LET edemon = 0                     ! initial demon energy
    INPUT prompt  "maximum change in velocity = ": dvmax
    LET vinitial = sqr(2*esystem/N)    ! divide energy equally among particles
    ! all particles same initial velocities
    FOR ipart = 1 to N
        LET vel(ipart) = vinitial
        LET vtot = vtot + vinitial     ! total velocity of system
    NEXT ipart
END SUB

SUB changes(N,esystem,edemon,vel(),vtot,escum,vcum,edcum,dvmax,accept)
    FOR i = 1 to N
        LET dv = (2*rnd - 1)*dvmax      ! trial change in velocity
        LET ipart = int(rnd*N + 1)      ! select random particle
        LET vtrial = vel(ipart) + dv    ! trial velocity
        LET de = .5*(vtrial*vtrial - vel(ipart)*vel(ipart))   ! trial energy change
```

```
        IF de <= edemon then
           LET vel(ipart) = vtrial
           LET vtot = vtot + dv              ! total velocity of system
           LET accept = accept + 1
           LET edemon = edemon - de
           LET esystem = esystem + de
        END IF
        ! accumulate data after each trial change
        CALL data(esystem,edemon,vtot,escum,vcum,edcum)
     NEXT i
END SUB

SUB data(esystem,edemon,vtot,escum,vcum,edcum)
   LET edcum = edcum + edemon
   LET escum = escum + esystem
   LET vcum = vcum + vtot
END SUB

SUB averages(N,nmcs,escum,vcum,edcum,accept)
   LET norm = 1/(nmcs*N)
   LET edave = edcum*norm            ! average demon energy
   LET accept = accept*norm          ! ratio of acceptances
   ! system averages per particle
   LET norm = norm/N
   LET esysave = escum*norm          ! mean energy per system particle
   LET vave = vcum*norm              ! mean velocity per system particle
   PRINT "mean demon energy = "; edave
   PRINT "mean system energy per particle = "; esysave
   PRINT "mean velocity per particle = "; vave
   PRINT "acceptance ratio = "; accept
END SUB
```

PROBLEM 15.1 Monte Carlo simulation of the ideal gas

a. Use **Program ideal_demon** with the initial condition that all particles
have the same velocity. The mass of the particles is set equal to unity. Choose
the numerical values $N = 20$, the initial total energy $esystem = 10$, $dvmax =$
2, and $nmcs = 50$ for your initial runs. Increase $nmcs$, the number of Monte
Carlo steps per particle, until the desired averages are constant to within a
few percent.

b. What is the initial mean velocity per particle? What is the equilibrium value of the mean velocity per particle?

c. Compute the mean energy of the demon and the mean system energy per particle. Do your results in parts (b) and (c) depend on whether the particles are chosen randomly or sequentially?

d. Choose *esystem* $= 20$ and find the value of *dvmax* which yields an acceptance ratio of approximately 50%. Compute the mean demon energy and mean system energy per particle after equilibrium has been established. Then consider *esystem* $= 40$ and obtain an approximate relation between the mean demon energy and the mean system energy per particle.

e. The Monte Carlo simulation of the microcanonical ensemble is done at fixed total energy with no reference to temperature. Define the temperature by the relation $\frac{1}{2}m <v^2> = \frac{1}{2}k_B T_{kin}$, where $\frac{1}{2}m <v^2>$ is the mean kinetic energy per particle. Set Boltzmann's constant k_B equal to unity. Use this relation to obtain T_{kin}. Is T_{kin} related to the mean demon energy?

f. What is the meaning of the "acceptance ratio" defined in **Program ideal_demon**? What is the empirical relation between the acceptance ratio and *dvmax/vinitial*?

15.5 TEMPERATURE AND THE CANONICAL ENSEMBLE

Although the microcanonical ensemble is conceptually simple, it does not represent the situation found in the laboratory. That is, laboratory systems are not closed but are in thermal contact with their environment. This thermal contact allows energy to be exchanged between the laboratory system and its environment in the form of heat. The laboratory system is usually small relative to its environment. The larger system with many more degrees of freedom is referred to as the *heat reservoir* or *heat bath*.

We now consider the more realistic case for which the total energy of the *composite* system consisting of the laboratory system and the heat reservoir is constrained to be constant, but the energy of the laboratory system can vary. Imagine a large number of mental copies of the laboratory system and the heat reservoir. Considered together the laboratory system plus the heat reservoir are isolated and can be described by the microcanonical ensemble. However since we are interested in the equilibrium values of the physical quantities describing the laboratory system, we wish to know the probability P_s of finding the laboratory system in the state s with energy E_s. The ensemble which describes the probability distribution of the laboratory system in thermal equilibrium with a heat reservoir is known as the *canonical* ensemble.

In general the laboratory system can be any macroscopic system which is much smaller than the heat reservoir. For example it might be a sunken treasure in an ocean, the latter acting as the heat reservoir. The laboratory system can be as small as an individual particle if it can be clearly distinguished from the particles of the reservoir. An example of such a laboratory system is the demon. Hence we can consider the demon to be a laboratory system whose microstate is specified only by its energy.

Our strategy for finding the form of the probability distribution of the canonical ensemble is to do a computer simulation of a demon which can exchange energy with an ideal gas of N particles. The ideal gas will serve as the heat bath and we will determine the probability $P(E_d)$ that the demon has energy E_d. We will find in Problem 15.2 that the form of $P(E_d)$ is given by

$$P(E_d) = \frac{1}{Z} e^{-E_d/k_B T} \tag{15.4}$$

where Z is a normalization constant such that the sum over all states of the demon is unity. The parameter T in (15.4) is called the *absolute temperature*. If T is measured in degrees Kelvin, Boltzmann's constant k_B is given by $k_B = 1.38 \times 10^{-16} \, erg \, deg^{-1}$. The probability distribution (15.4) is called the *Boltzmann* or the *canonical distribution*.

Note that the Boltzmann distribution is specified by the temperature. If we assume that the form (15.4) is applicable to any laboratory system in thermal equilibrium with a heat bath, we see that a macrostate in the canonical ensemble is specified by T, N, and V. In contrast, a macrostate in the microcanonical ensemble is specified by E, N, and V.

The form (15.4) of the Boltzmann distribution provides a simple way of computing T from the mean energy $<E_d>$ of the demon. Since $<E_d>$ is given by

$$<E_d> = \frac{\int dE \, E \, e^{-E/k_B T}}{\int dE \, e^{-E/k_B T}} = k_B T \quad . \tag{15.5}$$

we see that T is simply the average demon energy divided by k_B. Note that the result $<E_d> = k_B T$ in (15.5) holds only if the energy of the demon can take on a continuum of values.

PROBLEM 15.2 The Boltzmann probability distribution

a. Add a subroutine to **Program ideal_demon** which computes the probability distribution $P(E_d)$ of the demon and its mean energy. Plot the logarithm of $P(E_d)$ versus E_d and verify the form (15.4) for the Boltzmann distribution. What is the slope of this plot? Choose units such that k_B equals unity and estimate the corresponding magnitude of T. Choose the same parameters as were used in Problem 15.1.

b. Determine the magnitude of T from the relation (15.5). Are your two estimates of T consistent?

c. Compare the value of T obtained in parts (a) or (b) with the value of T found in Problem 15.1 using the kinetic definition of the temperature. Is the demon in thermal equilibrium with its heat bath?

15.6   THE ISING MODEL

The simplest and most popular model of a system of interacting variables in statistical physics is the *Ising* model. The Ising model has a rich history which has been reviewed by Brush (see references). The model was proposed by Lenz and investigated by his graduate student, Ising, to study the phase transition from a paramagnet to a ferromagnet. Ising computed its thermodynamic properties in one dimension and found that the model does not have a phase transition. However, for two and three dimensions the Ising model does exhibit a transition. The nature of the phase transition in two dimensions and the applications of the Ising model to systems as diverse as ferromagnets and antiferromagnets, binary alloys, fluids and nonmagnetic systems are discussed in Chapter 16.

In order to introduce the Ising model, consider a lattice containing N sites and assume that each lattice site i has associated with it a number s_i, where $s_i = +1$ for an "up" spin and $s_i = -1$ for a "down" spin. A particular configuration or microstate of the lattice is specified by the set of variables $\{s_1, s_2, \ldots s_N\}$ for all lattice sites.

Fig. 15.1 The interaction energy between nearest neighbor spins in the absence of an external magnetic field.

We know that the macroscopic properties of a system are determined by the nature of the accessible microstates. Hence it is necessary to know the dependence of the energy E on the configuration of spins. The total energy in the presence of a uniform magnetic field h is given in the Ising model by

$$E = -J \sum_{<ij>} s_i s_j - h \sum_{i=1}^{N} s_i \qquad (15.6)$$

where the first summation in (15.6) is over all nearest neighbor pairs and the second summation is over all spins in the lattice. The *exchange constant J* is a measure of the strength of the interaction between nearest neighbor spins (see Fig. 15.1). If $J > 0$, then the states ↑↑ and ↓↓ for which nearest neighbor spins in one dimension are aligned is energetically favored in comparison to the states ↑↓ and ↓↑ for which they are not aligned. Hence for $J > 0$, we expect that the state of lowest total energy is *ferromagnetic*, i.e. the average net number of spins pointing in one direction is nonzero. If $J < 0$, the states ↑↓ and ↓↑ for which nearest neighbors are anti-aligned is favored and the state of lowest energy is expected to be *antiferromagnetic*, i.e. alternate spins are aligned. If we subject the spins to an external "magnetic field" h directed upward, the spins ↑ and ↓ possess an additional internal energy which is given by $-h$ and $+h$ respectively. Note that the units of h are such that the magnetic moment per spin is unity.

An important virtue of the Ising model is its simplicity. Some of its simplifying features are that the kinetic energy of the atoms associated with the lattice sites has been neglected, only nearest neighbor contributions to the interaction energy have been included, and the spins are allowed to have only two discrete values. In spite of the simplicity of the model, we will find that it exhibits interesting behavior.

For the familiar case of classical particles whose position and velocity coordinates can have a continuum of values, the dynamics is given by Newton's laws. In the Ising model the dependence (15.6) of the energy on the spin configuration is not sufficient to determine the time-dependent properties of the system. That is, the relation (15.6) does not tell us how the system changes from one spin configuration to another and we have to introduce the dynamics separately. The most common dynamics for Ising spin systems is called "spin flip" dynamics. In this dynamics, a spin is chosen at random and the trial change corresponds to a flip of the spin from ↑ to ↓ or ↓ to ↑. Another dynamics for the Ising model is discussed in Chapter 16.

We now apply the demon algorithm to the simulation of the Ising model in the microcanonical ensemble. In the one-dimensional Ising model the demon must choose the spins randomly in order to avoid configurations periodically repeating themselves. Since we are interested in the properties of an infinite system, we have to consider the boundary conditions. The simplest boundary condition is to choose a "free surface" so that the spins at sites 1 and N each have one nearest neighbor interaction only. In general a better choice is periodic (toroidal) boundary conditions. For this choice the lattice becomes a ring and the spins at sites 1 and N interact with one another and hence have the same number of interactions as do the other spins.

What are some of the averages of physical quantities that we wish to compute? An obvious physical quantity is the net magnetic moment or *magnetization* M given by

$$M = \sum_{i=1}^{N} s_i \quad .$$
(15.7)

(Remember that we have set the magnetic moment per spin equal to unity.) Usually we are interested in the average values $< M >$ and the fluctuations $<M^2> - <M>^2$ as a function of the temperature of the system and the applied magnetic field. We can determine the temperature as a function of the energy of the system in two ways. One way is to measure the probability that the demon has energy E_d. Since we know that this probability is proportional to $exp(-E_d/k_BT)$, we can determine the temperature from a plot of the logarithm of the probability as a function of E_d. An easier way to determine the temperature is to measure the mean demon energy. However, since the values of the demon energy are not continuous for the Ising model, the temperature is not proportional to the mean demon energy as it is for the ideal gas. We show in Appendix 15A that in the limit of an infinite system, the temperature for $h = 0$ is related to E_d by

$$k_BT/J = \frac{4}{ln(1 + 4J/E_d)} \quad .$$
(15.8)

The result (15.8) comes from replacing the integrals in (15.5) by sums over the possible demon energies. Note that in the limit $|J/E_d| \ll 1$, (15.8) reduces to $k_BT = E_d$ as expected.

Program Ising_demon implements the microcanonical simulation of the Ising model in one dimension using periodic boundary conditions and spin flip dynamics. Once the initial configuration is chosen, the demon algorithm is similar to that described in Sec. 15.3. However in contrast to the ideal gas, the spins in the one-dimensional Ising model must be chosen randomly.

```
PROGRAM Ising_demon
! demon algorithm for the one-dimensional Ising model
DIM s(1000)
RANDOMIZE
CALL initial(N,nmcs,esystem,edemon,s,J,h,mag)
FOR imcs = 1 to nmcs
    FOR i = 1 to N
        CALL changes(N,esystem,edemon,s,J,h,mag,accept)
        ! accumulate data after every attempted flip
        CALL data(esystem,edemon,mag,escum,magcum,mag2cum,edcum)
    NEXT i
NEXT imcs
CALL averages(N,nmcs,J,escum,magcum,mag2cum,edcum,accept)
END


SUB initial(N,nmcs,esystem,edemon,s(),J,h,mag)
    INPUT prompt "number of spins = ": N
    INPUT prompt "number of Monte Carlo steps per spin = ": nmcs
    LET h = 0                       ! external magnetic field
    INPUT prompt "coupling constant = ": J
    INPUT prompt "desired total energy = ": esi
    ! initial configuration of spins in minimum energy state
    FOR ispin = 1 to N
        LET s(ispin) = 1
    NEXT ispin
    LET mag = N                     ! net magnetization
    ! compute initial system energy
    LET esystem = -(J + h)*N
    LET edemon = 4*J*int((esi - esystem)/(4*J))
    PRINT "total energy = "; esystem + edemon
END SUB
```

```
SUB changes(N,esystem,edemon,s(),J,h,mag,accept)
   LET ispin = int(rnd*N + 1)          ! random spin
   ! determine neighboring spin values using periodic boundary conditions
   IF ispin = 1 then
      LET left = s(N)
   ELSE
      LET left = s(ispin - 1)
   END IF
   IF ispin = N then
      LET right = s(1)
   ELSE
      LET right = s(ispin + 1)
   END IF
   ! spin flip dynamics
   LET de = 2*s(ispin)*(-h + J*(left + right))          ! trial energy change
   IF de <= edemon then
      LET s(ispin) = -s(ispin)
      LET mag = mag + 2*s(ispin)
      LET accept = accept + 1          ! number of changes accepted
      LET edemon = edemon - de
      LET esystem = esystem + de
   END IF
END SUB

SUB data(esystem,edemon,mag,escum,magcum,mag2cum,edcum)
   ! accumulate data
   LET edcum = edcum + edemon
   LET escum = escum + esystem
   LET magcum = magcum + mag
   LET mag2cum = mag2cum + mag*mag
END SUB
```

```
SUB averages(N,nmcs,J,escum,magcum,mag2cum,edcum,accept)
    LET norm = 1/(N*nmcs)          ! collected data after every attempt
    LET edave = edcum*norm
    LET accept = accept*norm        ! acceptance ratio
    ! averages per spin
    LET norm = norm/N
    LET es_ave = escum*norm
    LET magave = magcum*norm
    LET mag2ave = mag2cum*norm
    PRINT "mean demon energy = ";edave
    PRINT "mean system energy per spin = "; es_ave
    PRINT "mean magnetization per spin = "; magave
    PRINT "mean magnetization squared per spin = "; mag2ave
    PRINT "acceptance ratio = ";accept
    LET temperature = 4*J/log(1 + 4*J/edave)
    PRINT "temperature = "; temperature
END SUB
```

Note that for $h = 0$, the change in energy due to a spin flip is either 0 or $\pm 4J$. Hence the initial energy of the system plus the demon must be an integer multiple of $4J$. Since the spins are interacting, it is difficult to choose an initial configuration of spins with precisely the desired energy. The procedure followed in **SUB initial** is to choose the initial configuration to be all spins "up," a minimum energy configuration. The advantage of this configuration is that the total energy can be easily computed. The demon energy is then chosen so that the total energy of the system plus the demon is equal to the desired multiple of $4J$.

PROBLEM 15.3 The one-dimensional Ising model

a. Use **Program Ising_demon** with $N = 100$, $J = 1$, $h = 0$, and a desired total energy $esi = -20$. What is the initial energy assigned to the demon in **SUB initial**? The physical quantities drift as the demon's energy is distributed over the N spins. Compute a running average of the demon energy and M as a function of the number of Monte Carlo steps per spin (the "time"). Note that the data is taken after every attempt rather than after every Monte Carlo step per spin. What is the approximate time necessary for these quantities to approach their equilibrium values? Modify the program so that nonequilibrium configurations are not used to determine the averages of physical quantities. What are the mean equilibrium values of $<E_d>$, $<M>$, and $<M^2>$? The choice of $nmcs = 100$ is appropriate for testing the program and yields results of approximately 20% accuracy. To obtain better than 5% results, $nmcs$ should be the order of 1000.

b. Use the relation (15.8) to determine the equilibrium temperature T for the system parameters considered in part (a). Measure E in units of J. What is the corresponding energy of the system?

c. Compute T and E for the three cases $N = 100$, $J = 1$ and $esi = -40$, -60, and -80. Compare your results to the exact result for an infinite one-dimensional lattice, $E/N = -tanh(J/k_BT)$. How do your computed results for E/N depend on the number of spins N and the number of Monte Carlo steps per spin?

d. Use the same runs to compute $<M^2>$ as a function of T. Does $<M^2>$ increase or decrease with T?

e. Modify **Program Ising_demon** and verify the Boltzmann form (15.4) for the probability distribution of the demon.

*f. Include a nonzero magnetic field h and compute $<E_d>$, $<M>$, and $<M^2>$ as a function of h for fixed total E. Are the possible values of E arbitrary? Read the discussion in Appendix 15A and determine the relation of $<E_d>$ to the temperature for $h \neq 0$. Is the equilibrium temperature higher or lower for the same total energy?

*PROBLEM 15.4 The two-dimensional Ising model

a. Extend **Program Ising_demon** to simulate the two-dimensional Ising model on a square lattice with spin-flip dynamics. Take the length of one side of the lattice to be L. The total number of spins N is given by $N = L^2$. Use periodic boundary conditions as shown in Fig. 15.2 so that spins in the left-hand column interact with spins in the right-hand column, etc.

b. Unlike the one-dimensional case, the spins in higher dimensional lattices can be chosen sequentially or randomly. Compute the average demon energy and $<M^2>$ as a function of E. Convenient initial choices of parameters are $L = 5$ and $h = 0$. Use (15.8) to determine the dependence of the temperature on the system energy.

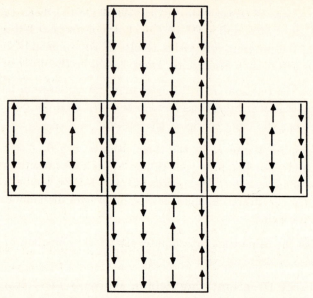

Fig. 15.2 One of the 2^N possible configurations of a system of $N = 16$ Ising spins on a square lattice. Also shown are four periodic images of the central cell. An "up" spin is denoted by ↑ and a "down" spin is denoted by ↓. Note that the number of nearest neighbors on a square lattice is four. With periodic boundary conditions the energy of this configuration is $E = -8J + 4h$.

c. Modify your program to make some "snapshots" of the spin configurations. Describe qualitatively the nature of the configurations at different energies or temperatures. Are they ordered or disordered? Are there domains of up or down spins?

*15.7 HEAT FLOW

In the above problems one demon shared its energy equally with all the spins. As a result the spins all attained the same mean energy of interaction. Many interesting questions arise when the system is not spatially uniform and is in a non-equilibrium but time-independent (steady) state.

Consider the problem of heat flow in a one-dimensional Ising model. Suppose that instead of all the sites sharing energy with one demon, each site has its own demon. We can study the flow of heat through such a system by requiring the demons at sites 1 and N to satisfy different conditions from the demons at the remaining sites. The demon at site 1 adds energy to the system by flipping spin 1 so that it is always in its highest energy state—in the opposite direction of spin 2. The demon at site N removes energy from the system by flipping spin N so that spin N is in its lowest energy state—in the same direction as spin $N - 1$. A consequence of these assumptions is that energy flows from site 1 to site N via the demons associated with the other sites. In order that energy not build up at the "hot" end of the Ising chain, we require that spin 1 can only add energy to the system if spin N simultaneously removes energy from the system. Since the demons at the two ends of the lattice satisfy different conditions than the other demons, it is necessary to remove the periodic boundary condition.

The temperature of the system is internally determined by the generalization of the relation (15.8), i.e. the temperature at site i is related to the mean energy of the demon at site i. To control the temperature gradient, we can update the end spins at a rate different than the other spins. The maximum temperature gradient occurs if we update the end spins after every update of an internal spin. A smaller temperature gradient occurs if we update the end spins less frequently. The temperature gradient between any two spins can be determined from the "temperature profile," the spatial dependence of the temperature. The energy flow can be determined by computing the magnitude of the energy per unit time which enters the lattice at site 1.

To implement this procedure we modify **Program Ising_demon** by converting *edemon* and *edcum* to arrays. We do the usual updating procedure for spins 2 through $N - 1$ and visit spins 1 and N at regular intervals denoted by *nheat*. Since little new information about *each* spin is obtained until each spin has attemped one flip, we obtain data in **Program conduct** only after each Monte Carlo step per spin rather than after each attempted flip.

```
PROGRAM conduct            ! many demon algorithm for d = 1 Ising model
! heat added at spin 1 and subtracted at spin N
DIM s(1000),edemon(1000),edcum(1000),magcum(1000)
RANDOMIZE
CALL initial(N,nmcs,s,J,nheat)
FOR imcs = 1 to nmcs
   FOR ispin = 1 to N - 2
      LET istep = (imcs - 1)*(N - 2) + ispin          ! # of attempted flips
      IF (mod(istep,nheat) = 0) then CALL heat(N,J,s,edcum)
      CALL change(N,edemon,s,J,accept)
   NEXT ispin
   CALL data(N,s,edemon,magcum,edcum)
NEXT imcs
CALL average(N,nmcs,J,magcum,edcum,accept)
END

SUB initial(N,nmcs,s(),J,nheat)
   INPUT prompt "number of spins = ": N
   INPUT prompt "number of MC steps per spin = ": nmcs
   INPUT prompt "coupling constant = ": J
   INPUT prompt "Monte Carlo steps between updates of end spins = ": nheat
   FOR i = 1 to N                          ! initial random configuration
      IF rnd > 0.5 then
         LET s(i) = 1
      ELSE
         LET s(i) = -1
      END IF
   NEXT i
END SUB

SUB change(N,edemon(),s(),J,accept)                      ! spin flip dynamics
   LET ispin = int(rnd*(N - 2) + 2) ! pick spin at random from spins 2 to N - 1
   LET de = 2*s(ispin)*J*(s(ispin - 1) + s(ispin + 1))       ! trial energy change
   IF de <= edemon(ispin) then
      LET s(ispin) = - s(ispin)
      LET accept = accept + 1
      LET edemon(ispin) = edemon(ispin) - de
   END IF
END SUB
```

```
SUB data(N,s(),edemon(),magcum(),edcum())
    FOR i = 2 to N - 1
        LET edcum(i) = edcum(i) + edemon(i)
        LET magcum(i) = magcum(i) + s(i)
    NEXT i
END SUB

SUB average(N,nmcs,J,magcum(),edcum(),accept)
    INPUT prompt "name of output file = ": out$
    OPEN #1: name out$, access output, create new
    LET norm = 1/nmcs
    LET accept = accept*norm/(N - 2)
    PRINT "acceptance ratio = "; accept
    PRINT #1: "acceptance ratio = "; accept
    PRINT "edave(1) = heat in, edave(N) = energy out"
    PRINT tab(2);"i";tab(16);"edave";tab(35);"T";tab(45);"magnetization"
    PRINT
    PRINT #1: "edave(1) = heat in, edave(N) = energy out"
    PRINT #1: tab(2);"i";tab(16);"edave";tab(35);"T";tab(45);"magnetization"
    PRINT #1
    FOR i = 1 to N
        LET edave = edcum(i)*norm
        LET temperature = 0
        IF edave <> 0 then
            IF (1 + 4*J/edave) > 0 then
                LET temperature = 4*J/log(1 + 4*J/edave)
            END IF
        END IF
        LET mag = magcum(i)*norm
        PRINT i,edave,temperature,mag
        PRINT #1: i,edave,temperature,mag
    NEXT i
    CLOSE #1
END SUB
```

```
SUB heat(N,J,s(),edcum())
    ! attempt to add heat at spin 1 and remove it at spin N
    ! success if spins 1 and 2 are aligned and spin N and N - 1 are not aligned
    IF (s(1)*s(2) = 1) and (s(N)*s(N-1) = -1) then
        LET edcum(1) = edcum(1) + 2*J
        LET edcum(N) = edcum(N) - 2*J
        LET s(1) = -s(1)
        LET s(N) = -s(N)
    END IF
END SUB
```

*PROBLEM 15.5 One-dimensional heat flow

a. Modify **Program conduct** so that all the demons are equivalent, i.e. impose periodic boundary conditions and do not use **SUB heat**. Compute the mean energy of the demon at each site and use (15.8) to define a local site temperature. Use $N = 22$, $nmcs = 1000$, and $J = 1$. Is the local temperature uniform? How do your results compare with the one demon case?

b. In **Program conduct** energy is added to the system at site 1 and is removed at site N. Use $N = 22$, $J = 1$, $nmcs = 1000$, and $nheat = 100$. Determine the mean demon energy for each site and obtain the corresponding local temperature. Draw the temperature profile by plotting the temperature as a function of site number. The temperature gradient is the difference in temperature from site $N-1$ to site 2 divided by the distance between them. (Remember that the distance between neighboring sites is taken to be unity.) Because of local temperature fluctuations and edge effects, the temperature gradient should be estimated by fitting the temperature profile in the middle of the lattice to a straight line. Also determine the mean temperature of the system.

c. The heat flux Q is the energy flow per unit length per unit time. The energy flow is the amount of energy demon 1 adds to the system at site 1. "Time" is conveniently measured in units of Monte Carlo steps per spin. Determine Q for the parameters used in part (b).

d. If the temperature gradient $\partial T/\partial x$ is not too large, the heat flux Q is proportional to $\partial T/\partial x$. We can determine the *thermal conductivity* κ by the relation

$$Q = -\kappa \frac{\partial T}{\partial x} \ . \tag{15.9}$$

Use your results for $\partial T/\partial x$ and Q to estimate κ. Because of the limited number of spins and Monte Carlo steps, your results should be accurate to only about 20%. More accurate results would require a system of at least $N = 50$ spins and $10,000$ to $100,000$ Monte Carlo steps per spin. However unless special programming techniques are used (see Sec. 15.8) such a run would require a mainframe computer.

e. The maximum heat flux and temperature gradient can be obtained for $nheat = 1$. Determine Q, the temperature profile, and the mean temperature for different values of $nheat$. Is the temperature profile linear for all $nheat$? If the temperature profile is linear, estimate $\partial T/\partial x$ and determine κ. Does κ depend on the mean temperature?

Note that in Problem 15.5 we were able to compute a temperature profile by using an algorithm which manipulated only integer numbers. The conventional approach would be to solve a heat equation similar in form to the diffusion equation (11.34).

*PROBLEM 15.6 Magnetization profile

a. Modify **Program conduct** by removing **SUB heat** and constraining spins 1 and N to be $+1$ and -1 respectively. Estimate the magnetization profile by plotting the mean value of the spin at each site versus the site number. Choose $N = 22$, $nmcs = 1000$, and $J = 1$. How do your results vary as you increase N?

b. Compute the mean demon energy and hence the local temperature at each site. Does the system have a uniform temperature even though the magnetization is not uniform? Is the system in thermal equilibrium?

c. The effect of this constraint is easier to observe for two and three dimensions than in one dimension. Write a program for a two-dimensional Ising model on a $L \times L$ square lattice. Constrain the spins at site (i, j) to be $+1$ and -1 for $i = 1$ and $i = L$ respectively. Use periodic boundary conditions in the y direction. How do your results compare with the one-dimensional case?

d. Remove the periodic boundary conditions in the y direction and constrain all the boundary spins from $i = 1$ to $L/2$ to be $+1$ and the other boundary spins to be -1. Choose an initial configuration where all the spins on the left half of the system are $+1$ and the others are -1. Do the simulation and draw a configuration of the spins once the system has reached equilibrium. Draw a line between each pair of spins of opposite sign. Describe the curve separating the +1 spins from the −1 spins. Describe the nature of this curve. Begin with $L = 20$ and determine what happens as L is increased.

15.8 COMMENTS

The advantage of the microcanonical ensemble is the disarming simplicity of the postulate of equal *a priori* probabilities. The main advantage of performing computer simulations using the microcanonical ensemble rather than other ensembles is that the demon need not make any demands on the random number generator. Creutz and coworkers have been able to develop very fast algorithms by using one computer bit per spin and using multiple demons. Of course there are also several disadvantages of the demon algorithm. One disadvantage is the difficulty of establishing a system at the desired value of the energy. However the most important disadvantage for us is conceptual. That is, it is more natural for us to think of the behavior of macroscopic physical quantities as functions of temperature rather than the total energy. Hence we consider further properties of the Ising model in Chapter 16 in the context of the canonical ensemble.

REFERENCES AND SUGGESTIONS FOR ADDITIONAL READING

S. G. Brush, "History of the Lenz-Ising Model," *Rev. Mod. Phys.* **39**, 883 (1967).

Michael Creutz, "Deterministic Ising dynamics," *Ann. Phys.* **167**, 62 (1986). The author presents a deterministic cellular automaton rule which simulates the Ising model and allows study of nonequilibrium phenomena.

Michael Creutz, "Microcanonical Monte Carlo Simulation," *Phys. Rev. Letts.* **50**, 1411 (1983). See also Gyan Bhanot, Michael Creutz, and Herbert Neuberger, "Microcanonical simulation of Ising systems," *Nuc. Phys.* **235**, 417 (1984).

APPENDIX 15A RELATION OF THE MEAN DEMON ENERGY TO THE TEMPERATURE

We know that the energy of the demon, E_d, is constrained to be positive and is given by $E_d = E - E_s$, where E_s is the energy of the system and E is the total energy. We have found in Problems 15.2 and 15.3 that the probability for the demon to have energy E_d is proportional to $exp(-E_d/k_B T)$. We assume that the same form of the probability distribution holds for any macroscopic system in thermodynamic equilibrium. Hence $<E_d>$ is given by

$$<E_d> = \frac{\sum E_d\, e^{-E_d/k_B T}}{\sum e^{-E_d/k_B T}} \tag{15.10}$$

where the summations in (15.10) are over the possible values of E_d. If an Ising spin is flipped in zero magnetic field, the minimum non-zero decrease in energy of the system is $4J$ (see Fig. 15.3). Hence the possible energies of the demon are $0, 4J, 8J, 12J, \ldots$. If we write $x = 4J/k_B T$, we can perform the summations in (15.10) and obtain

$$<E_d/k_B T> = \frac{0 + xe^{-x} + 2xe^{-2x} + \ldots}{1 + e^{-x} + e^{-2x} + \ldots} = \frac{x}{e^x - 1}\,. \tag{15.11}$$

The form (15.8) can be obtained by solving (15.11) for T in terms of E_d. Convince yourself that the relation (15.11) is independent of dimension for lattices with an even number of nearest neighbors.

If the magnetic field is nonzero, the possible values of the demon energy are $0, 2h, 4J - 2h, 4J + 2h, \ldots$. If J is a multiple of h, then the result is the

before   after

Fig. 15.3 The change in energy due to a change in orientation of the central spin is $4J$. In general the change in energy due to a spin flip equals $+2sJ + 2h$, where s is the net spin of the four nearest neighbor spins.

same as before with $4J$ replaced by $2h$, since the possible energy values for the demon are multiples of $2h$. Otherwise we must sum separately the numerator and denominator of (15.10) for all possible demon energies. The simplest procedure is to use a computer to perform the sums directly and to make a table of E_d versus T for a few values of h. It will usually be sufficient to keep on the order of ten to twenty terms in each sum.

MONTE CARLO SIMULATION OF THE CANONICAL ENSEMBLE

16

We develop Monte Carlo methods for simulating systems in equilibrium with a heat bath. Applications are made to models of magnetism and fluids.

16.1   THE CANONICAL ENSEMBLE

Most physical systems are not isolated but exchange energy with their environment. Since such a system is usually small in comparison to its environment, we assume that any change in the energy of the smaller system does not have a significant effect on the temperature of the larger system. Hence the larger system acts as a *heat reservoir* or *heat bath* at a fixed absolute temperature T. If a small but macroscopic system is placed in thermal contact with a heat bath, the system reaches thermal equilibrium by exchanging energy with the heat bath until the system attains the temperature of the bath.

Imagine an infinitely large number of mental copies of the system and the heat bath. In Chapter 15 we verified that P_s, the probability that the *system* is in microstate s with energy E_s, is given by

$$P_s = \frac{1}{Z} e^{-E_s/k_B T} \tag{16.1}$$

where Z is a normalization constant. The ensemble defined by (16.1) is known as the *canonical* ensemble. Since $\sum P_s = 1$, Z is given by

$$Z = \sum_{s=1}^{M} e^{-E_s/k_B T} \quad . \tag{16.2}$$

The summation in (16.2) is over all M microstates of the system. The quantity Z is known as the *partition function* of the system.

We can use (16.1) to obtain the ensemble average of physical quantities of interest. For example the mean energy is given by

$$\langle E\rangle = \sum_s E_s P_s = \frac{1}{Z} \sum_s E_s e^{-\beta E_s} \quad . \tag{16.3}$$

Note that the energy can fluctuate in the canonical ensemble.

16.2   THE METROPOLIS ALGORITHM

How can we simulate a system of N particles confined in a volume V at a fixed temperature T? Since we can generate only a finite number m of the total number of M configurations, we might hope to obtain an estimate for the mean value $<A>$ from

$$<A> = \sum_s^M A_s e^{-\beta E_s} / \sum_s^M e^{-\beta E_s} \tag{16.4}$$

$$\approx \sum_s^m A_s e^{-\beta E_s} / \sum_s^m e^{-\beta E_s} \tag{16.5}$$

where E_s and A_s are the total energy and value of the physical quantity A in configuration s. A crude Monte Carlo procedure is to generate a configuration at random, calculate E_s, A_s, and the product $A_s e^{-\beta E_s}$ and evaluate the corresponding contribution of the configuration to the sums in (16.5). However such a configuration would likely be very improbable and hence contribute little to the sum. Instead as we have seen in a variety of contexts, we must use an *importance sampling* method and generate configurations according to a probability distribution function π_s. Since we will average over the m configurations of a biased sample, we must weight each configuration by $1/\pi_s$ to eliminate the bias:

$$<A> \approx \sum_s^m A_s \frac{1}{\pi_s} e^{-\beta E_s} / \sum_s^m \frac{1}{\pi_s} e^{-\beta E_s} \quad . \tag{16.6}$$

Inspection of the form of (16.6) will convince you that a reasonable choice of π_s is the Boltzmann probability itself, i.e.

$$\pi_s = \frac{e^{-\beta E_s}}{\sum_s e^{-\beta E_s}} \quad . \tag{16.7}$$

This choice of π_s implies that $<A>$ can be written as

$$<A> \approx \frac{1}{m} \sum_s A_s \quad . \tag{16.8}$$

The choice (16.7) for π_s is due to Metropolis et al. (see references).

In the context of statistical mechanics, the expressions "Monte Carlo" and the "Metropolis" sampling method are almost synonymous. Although we discussed the Metropolis sampling method in Chapter 10 in the context of the numerical evaluation of integrals, it can be introduced easily in the present (and original) context. In the following we give the most common form of the Metropolis algorithm in the context of a system of spins or particles.

0. Establish an initial configuration.
1. Make a random trial change in the initial configuration. For example choose a spin at random and attempt to flip it. Or choose a particle at random and attempt to displace it a random distance.
2. Compute ΔE, the change in the energy of the system due to the trial change.
3. If ΔE is less than or equal to zero, accept the new configuration and go to step 7.
4. If ΔE is positive, compute the "transition probability" $W = e^{-\Delta E / k_B T}$.
5. Generate a random number r in the interval $[0,1]$.
6. If $r \le W$, accept the new configuration; otherwise retain the previous configuration.
7. Determine the value of the desired physical quantities.
8. Repeat steps (1) through (7) to obtain a sufficient number of configurations or "trials."
9. Compute averages over configurations which are statistically independent of each other.

The above steps can be interpreted as a random walk. Let the different configurations be numbered as "points" $i = 1, 2, 3, \ldots$ and consider a random walker on these points. Steps 2 through 6 give the conditional probability that the walker be at point i at "time" $t + 1$ given that it was at point j at time t. Since it is necessary to evaluate only the ratio $P(i)/P(j)$, it is not necessary to normalize $P(i)$ to unity. Note that since the configurations are generated with a probability proportional to the desired probability, all averages become arithmetic averages as in (16.8). However, since the constant of proportionality is not known, it is not possible to estimate the partition function Z in this manner.

The proof that, after a sufficient number of steps, the Metropolis algorithm generates states with a probability proportional to the Boltzmann probability distribution does not add much to our physical understanding of the algorithm. Instead we will first apply the algorithm to the ideal classical gas and a classical magnet in a magnetic field, and find that the Metroplois algorithm does indeed yield the Boltzmann distribution after sufficient "time" has elapsed.

Although we choose π_s to be the Boltzmann distribution, other choices such as $\pi_s = w_s e^{-\beta E_s}$ are possible. The adoption of a different distribution, i.e. w_s not a constant, is useful in some contexts (see references). In addition, the above choice of the transition probability W is not the only one which leads to the Boltzmann distribution in the asymptotic limit. It can be shown that the only requirement is that W satisfy the "detailed balance" condition:

$$W(1 \to 2)e^{-E_1/k_B T} = W(2 \to 1)e^{-E_2/k_B T} \tag{16.9}$$

where $W(1 \rightarrow 2)$ is the probability per unit time for the system to make a transition from configuration 1 to configuration 2.

16.3 VERIFICATION OF THE BOLTZMANN DISTRIBUTION

We first consider an ideal classical gas and demonstrate that the Metropolis algorithm leads to the Boltzmann distribution for the individual microstates. Since the energy of an ideal gas depends only on the velocity of the particles, a microstate of this system is completely described by a specification of the velocity (or momentum) of each particle. However since the velocity is a continuous variable, it is necessary to describe the possible microstates so that they are countable. In the usual way we subdivide the ranges of the velocity into arbitrarily small discrete intervals. Suppose we have $N = 10$ particles and divide the possible values of the velocity into twenty intervals. Then the total number of microstates would be 20^{10}. Not only would it be difficult to label these 20^{10} states, it would take a prohibitively long time to obtain an accurate estimate for the probability of any one of them.

In order to avoid this problem, we first consider the Monte Carlo simulation of a single classical particle moving in one dimension. The array P in **Program Boltzmann** stores the probability $P(E)dE$ that the system has energy between E and $E + dE$. Note that our units for temperature are such that $k_B = 1$ and thus temperature is measured in units of energy.

```
PROGRAM Boltzmann
! Metropolis algorithm for a classical particle in one dimension
DIM P(0 to 500)
RANDOMIZE
CALL initial(nmcs,nequil,beta,vel,E,dvmax,nbin,del_E)
FOR imcs = 1 to nmcs + nequil
    CALL Metropolis(beta,vel,E,dvmax,accept)
    ! accumulate data after each trial change
    IF imcs > nequil then CALL data(E,vel,Ecum,E2cum,vcum,P,nbin,del_E)
NEXT imcs
CALL averages(nmcs,vcum,Ecum,E2cum,P,accept,beta,nbin)
END
```

```
SUB initial(nmcs,nequil,beta,vel,E,dvmax,nbin,del_E)
    INPUT prompt "number of Monte Carlo steps = ": nmcs
    INPUT prompt "absolute temperature = ": T
    INPUT prompt "vinitial = ": vel
    INPUT prompt "maximum change in velocity = ": dvmax
    LET beta = 1/T
    LET nequil = 0.1*nmcs
    LET E = 0.5*vel*vel
    LET del_E = 0.05                        ! energy subinterval
    LET nbin = 4*T/del_E                     ! maximum number of bins
END SUB

SUB Metropolis(beta,vel,E,dvmax,accept)
    LET dv = (2*rnd - 1)*dvmax           ! trial change in velocity
    LET vtrial = vel + dv                ! trial velocity
    LET de = 0.5*(vtrial*vtrial - vel*vel)   ! trial energy change
    IF de > 0 then
      IF exp(-beta*de) < rnd then
        EXIT SUB                         ! step not accepted
      END IF
    END IF
    LET vel = vtrial
    LET accept = accept + 1
    LET E = E + de
END SUB

SUB data(E,vel,Ecum,E2cum,vcum,P(),nbin,del_E)
    LET Ecum = Ecum + E
    LET E2cum = E2cum + E*E
    LET vcum = vcum + vel
    CALL probability(E,P,nbin,del_E)
END SUB

SUB probability(E,P(),nbin,del_E)
    LET ibin = E/del_E
    IF ibin > nbin then LET ibin = nbin
    LET P(ibin) = P(ibin) + 1
END SUB
```

```
SUB averages(nmcs,vcum,Ecum,E2cum,P(),accept,beta,nbin)
    LET norm = 1/nmcs
    LET accept = accept*norm          ! ratio of acceptances
    LET Eave = Ecum*norm              ! mean energy
    LET E2ave = E2cum*norm
    LET vave = vcum*norm              ! mean velocity
    PRINT "mean energy ="; Eave
    LET sigma2 = E2ave - Eave*Eave
    PRINT "mean velocity ="; vave
    PRINT "acceptance ratio ="; accept
    PRINT "sigma = "; sqr(sigma2)
    PRINT "bin","P(E)","log P(E)"
    FOR ibin = 0 to nbin
        IF P(ibin) > 0.01*norm then    ! only print P if appreciable
            LET prob = p(ibin)*norm
            PRINT ibin,prob,log(prob)
        END IF
    NEXT ibin
END SUB
```

PROBLEM 16.1 The Boltzmann distribution

a. We consider the motion of only a single particle so that its microstates can be labeled by its energy. Strictly speaking there are two microstates for each energy. Why? Use **Program Boltzmann** to determine the form of the probability distribution that is generated by the Metroplis algorithm. Choose $T = 1.0$, $dvmax = 2.0$, $nmcs = 1000$, $vinitial = 0$, and compute the mean energy, the mean velocity, and the probability density $P(E)$.

b. Is $P(E)$ an increasing or decreasing function of E? A plot of $ln\,P(E)$ versus E should yield a straight line with a slope equal to $-1/T$. Increase $nmcs$ until the exponential form of $P(E)$ is at least approximately verified.

c. How well do your results for the mean energy and the mean velocity with $nmcs = 1000$ compare with the corresponding exact values? Is it necessary to choose $nmcs$ as large as in part (b) to obtain reasonable accuracy?

d. To insure that your results are not a function of the initial conditions, set $vinitial = 2$ and compute the mean energy and velocity. Does the value of $dvmax$ make any difference?

*PROBLEM 16.2 Planar spin in an external magnetic field

a. Consider a classical planar magnet with magnetic moment μ_0. The magnet can be oriented in any direction in the x-y plane. The energy of interaction between the spin and an external magnetic field B pointing in the y-direction is $-\mu_0 B \cos \phi$, where ϕ is the angle between the moment and $\vec{B}$. What are the possible microstates of this system? Write a Monte Carlo program which samples the configurations of this system in thermal equilibrium with a heat bath at temperature T. Compute the mean energy as a function of the ratio $\mu_0 B / k_B T$.

b. Compute the probability density $P(E)$ and analyze your results in the same way as in Problem 16.1.

PROBLEM 16.3 Simulation of a classical ideal gas in one dimension

a. Modify **Program Boltzmann** to simulate an ideal gas of N particles in one dimension. Choose $N = 20$, $T = 100$, and $nmcs = 200$. Give all particles the same initial velocity *vinitial* and choose *vinitial* $= 10$ for your first run. Determine the value of *dvmax*, the maximum change in the velocities, so that the acceptance ratio is approximately 50%. What is the mean kinetic energy and mean velocity of the particles?

b. We might expect the total energy of an ideal gas to remain constant since the particles do not interact with one another and hence cannot exchange energy directly. What is the value of the initial energy of the system for *vinitial* $= 10$? Does the total energy remain constant? If the energy does not remain constant, explain how the energy changes. Explain why the measured mean particle velocity is approximately zero even though the initial particle velocities are not zero.

c. What is a simple criterion for "thermal equilibrium"? Estimate the number of Monte Carlo steps per particle necessary for the system to reach thermal equilibrium. What choice of the initial velocities allows the system to reach thermal equilibrium at temperature T as quickly as possible?

d. Compute the mean energy per particle for $T = 10$, 100, and 400. In order to compute the averages after the system has reached thermal equilibrium, call **SUB data** only after equilibrium has been achieved. Increase the number of Monte Carlo steps until the desired averages do not change appreciably. What is the approximate value of *nmcs* necessary for thermal equilibrium for $N = 10$ and $T = 100$ and for $N = 40$ and $T = 100$? If the value of *nmcs* is different in the two cases, explain the reason for this difference.

e. Compute the probability $P(E)dE$ for the system of N particles to have a total energy between E and $E+dE$. Do you expect $P(E)$ to be proportional to e^{-E/k_BT}? Plot $P(E)$ as a function of E and describe the qualitative behavior of $P(E)$. Does the plot of $ln\,P(E)$ versus E yield a straight line? Describe the qualitative features of a plot of $ln\,P(E)$ versus E.

f. Compute the mean energy for $T = 10$, 20, 30, 90, 100, and 110 and estimate the heat capacity.

g. Compute the mean square energy fluctuations $<\Delta E^2> = <E^2> - <E>^2$ for $T = 10$ and $T = 40$. Compare the magnitude of the ratio $<\Delta E^2>/T^2$ with the heat capacity determined in part (f).

You might have been surprised to find in Problem 16.3e that the form of $P(E)$ is a Gaussian centered about the mean energy of the system. That is, if the *microscopic* states of the system are distributed according to the Boltzmann distribution, then the distribution function of a *macroscopic* quantity such as the total energy is sharply peaked about its average value.

We now consider the simulation of the Ising model in equilibrium with a heat bath. As discussed in Chapter 15, the energy of the Ising model is given by

$$E = -J \sum_{<ij>} s_i s_j - \mu_0 H \sum_i s_i \qquad (16.10)$$

where $s = \pm 1$, J is a measure of the strength of the interaction between spins, and the first sum is over all pairs of spins which are nearest neighbors. The second term in (16.10) is the energy of interaction of the magnetic moment with an external magnetic field.

In Problem 16.4 we use the Metropolis algorithm and spin flip dynamics to simulate the one-dimensional Ising model. In this dynamics the possible trial change is the flip of a spin, $s_i \rightarrow -s_i$. Note that the parameters J, k_B, and T do not appear separately but appear in the dimensionless ratio J/k_BT. Unless otherwise stated we will measure temperature in units such that $J/k_B = 1$. Most of our simulations will be done for $H = 0$.

PROBLEM 16.4 One-dimensional Ising model

a. Write a Monte Carlo program which simulates the one-dimensional Ising model in equilibrium with a heat bath. Suggestions: modify **SUB changes** in **Program Ising_demon** (see Chapter 15) or see **Program Ising** in Sec. 16.4 in which the Metropolis algorithm for the two-dimensional Ising model is implemented. Consider only zero magnetic field. Your program should compute the mean energy and magnetization of the lattice and draw the microscopic state of the system after each Monte Carlo step per spin. Use periodic boundary conditions.

b. Choose $N = 20$, $T = 1.0$, $nmcs = 30$, and all spins initially "up," i.e. $s_i = +1$. What is the initial "temperature" of the system? Visually inspect the microscopic state of the system after each Monte Carlo step and estimate the time it takes for the system to reach equilibrium.

c. Change the initial condition so that all spins are initially random. What is the initial "temperature" of the system? Visually inspect the microscopic state of the system after each Monte Carlo step and estimate the time it takes for the system to reach equilibrium.

d. Choose $N = 20$ and equilibrate the system for 100 Monte Carlo steps per spin. Use at least 200 Monte Carlo steps per spin to determine the mean energy $<E>$ and magnetization $<M>$ as a function of T in the range $T = 0.5$ to 5.0. Plot $<E>$ as a function of T and discuss its qualitative features. Compare your computed results for mean energy to the exact result (for zero magnetic field)

$$<E> = -N \tanh \frac{J}{k_B T} \quad . \tag{16.11}$$

What are your results for $<M>$? Do they depend on the initial configuration?

e. Is the acceptance ratio an increasing or decreasing function of T? Does the Metropolis algorithm become more or less efficient at low temperatures?

f. Compute the probability density $P(E)$ for a system of 50 spins with $T = 1.0$. Choose $nmcs = 200$. Plot $\ln P(E)$ versus $(E - <E>)^2$ and discuss its qualitative features.

*PROBLEM 16.5 Alternative choice of W

Another choice of transition probability that is consistent with the detailed balance condition (16.9) is given by

$$W'(1 \rightarrow 2) = \frac{e^{-E_2/k_B T}}{e^{-E_1/k_B T} + e^{-E_2/k_B T}} \quad . \tag{16.12}$$

To implement this symmetric form of the transition rate, we compute the quantity

$$W' = \frac{e^{-\Delta E/k_B T}}{e^{-\Delta E/k_B T} + 1} \quad . \tag{16.13}$$

Note that if $\Delta E = 0$, then $W' = 1/2$ and the trial configuration has an equal probability of being accepted. If $J/k_B T \gg 1$, which form of W leads to the system reaching equilibrium more quickly? Does the same conclusion hold for $J/k_B T \ll 1$?

16.4 SIMULATION OF THE TWO-DIMENSIONAL ISING MODEL

One of the more interesting natural phenomena in nature is ferromagnetism. You are probably familiar with materials such as iron and nickel which exhibit a spontaneous magnetization in the absence of an applied magnetic field. This nonzero magnetization occurs only if the temperature is lower than a well-defined temperature known as the Curie or critical temperature T_c. For temperatures $T > T_c$, the magnetization vanishes. Hence T_c separates the disordered phase for $T > T_c$ from the ferromagnetic phase for $T < T_c$.

Although the origin of ferromagnetism is quantum mechanical in nature and an area of much current experimental and theoretical research, the study of the classical Ising model in two and three dimensions has provided much insight into the properties of magnetic systems in the neighborhood of the phase transition. However, due to its classical nature and the neglect of the other spin components, the Ising model does not give a complete description of ferromagnetism, especially at temperatures well below T_c. In particular, the Ising model assumes that the individual moments are localized and hence the Ising model does not apply to metals such as iron and nickel.

In order to explore the properties of the Ising model, we need to specify the physical properties of interest and develop a program to compute them. The equilibrium quantities of interest include the mean energy $<E>$, the mean magnetization $<M>$, the heat capacity C, and the magnetic susceptibility χ. One way to measure C at constant external magnetic field is from the definition

$$C = \frac{\partial <E>}{\partial T} \quad . \tag{16.14a}$$

Another way to measure C is to use its relation to the statistical fluctuations of the total energy in the canonical ensemble:

$$C = \frac{1}{k_B T^2}(<E^2> - <E>^2) \quad . \tag{16.14b}$$

The magnetic susceptibility χ is another example of a "response function," since it measures the ability of a spin to "respond" or flip due to a change in an external magnetic field. The zero field isothermal magnetic susceptibility is defined by the thermodynamic derivative

$$\chi = \lim_{H \to 0} \frac{\partial <M>}{\partial H} \quad . \tag{16.15a}$$

The zero field susceptibility can be related to the magnetization fluctuations in the system:

$$\chi = \frac{1}{k_B T}(<M^2> - <M>^2) \tag{16.15b}$$

where $<M>$ and $<M^2>$ are zero field values. Relations (16.14b) and (16.15b) are examples of a general relation between response functions and equilibrium fluctuations. For completeness they are derived in Appendix 16A.

Now that we have specified several equilibrium quantities of interest, we wish to implement the Metropolis algorithm. This algorithm was stated in Sec. 16.2 as a recipe for generating states with the desired Boltzmann probability. However, the algorithm with "spin flip" dynamics is a reasonable approximation to the real dynamics of an anisotropic magnet whose spins are coupled to the vibrations of the lattice. In this case the coupling leads to random spin flips and we expect that one Monte Carlo step per spin is proportional to the average time between spin flips observed in the laboratory. Hence we can regard spin flip dynamics as a true time-dependent process and observe the relaxation to equilibrium after sufficiently long times.

In the following we develop **Program Ising** for the Monte Carlo simulation of the two-dimensional Ising model in contact with a heat bath. One of the most time consuming aspects of the Metropolis algorithm is the calculation of the exponential function $e^{-\beta \Delta E}$, where $\beta = 1/T$. However as indicated in Fig. 16.1, there are only a small number of possible values of $\beta \Delta E$ for the Ising model. Hence to save computer time, we store the small number of different probabilities for spin flips in an array w. Note that if a flip is rejected and the old configuration is retained, thermal equilibrium is not described properly unless the old configuration is included again in calculating the averages. Note also that in **SUB data**, the values of the physical observables are recorded after each Monte Carlo step; the optimum time for "sampling" physical quantities is explored in Problem 16.8.

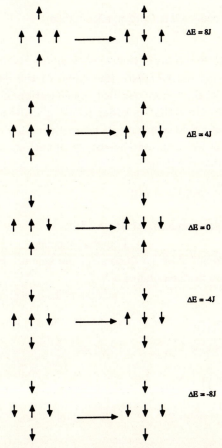

Fig. 16.1 The five possible transitions of the Ising model on the square lattice with spin flip dynamics. The change in energy is $8J$, $4J$, 0, $-4J$, and $-8J$ respectively.

```
PROGRAM Ising
! Metropolis algorithm for the two-dimensional Ising model on the square lattice
DIM spin(32,32),w(-4 to 4)
CALL initial(N,L,T,nmcs,spin,E,M,w)
FOR imcs = 1 to nmcs
    CALL Metropolis(N,L,spin,E,M,w,ratio)
    CALL data(E,M,ecum,e2cum,mcum,m2cum)
NEXT imcs
CALL output(N,nmcs,ecum,e2cum,mcum,m2cum,ratio)
END
```

We choose the initial directions of the spins, compute the initial value of the energy and magnetization, and calculate the values of the different transition probabilities in **SUB initial**. A more detailed consideration of initial conditions is given in Problem 16.6. Note that in order to calculate the total energy, we consider the interaction of a spin only with its nearest neighbor spins to the north and the east. In this way we compute the energy of each spin-spin interaction only once and avoid double counting.

```
SUB initial(N,L,T,nmcs,spin(,),E,M,w())
    RANDOMIZE
    INPUT prompt "linear dimension of lattice = ": L
    LET N = L*L                          ! number of spins
    INPUT prompt "number of Monte Carlo steps per spin = ": nmcs
    INPUT prompt "reduced temperature = ": T
    FOR y = 1 to L                       ! random initial configuration
        FOR x = 1 to L
            IF rnd < 0.5 then
                LET spin(x,y) = 1        ! spin up
            ELSE
                LET spin(x,y) = -1
            END IF
            LET M = M + spin(x,y)        ! net magnetization
        NEXT x
    NEXT y
```

```
FOR y = 1 to L                        ! compute initial energy E
  IF y = L then
    LET up = 1                        ! periodic boundary conditions
  ELSE
    LET up = y + 1
  END IF
  FOR x = 1 to L
    IF x = L then
      LET right = 1
    ELSE
      LET right = x + 1
    END IF
    LET sum = spin(x,up) + spin(right,y)
    LET E = E - spin(x,y)*sum   ! total energy
  NEXT x
NEXT y
! compute Boltzmann probability ratios if energy increases
! index of array w equals the sum of nearest neighbor spin values
LET e4 = exp(-4/T)
LET e8 = e4*e4
LET w(4) = e8
LET w(-4) = e8
LET w(2) = e4
LET w(-2) = e4
END SUB
```

We can implement the Metropolis algorithm in two steps. First we determine if $\Delta E \leq 0$ and then accept the trial flip if this condition is met. If this condition is not satisfied, we generate a random number and compare it to $e^{-\beta \Delta E}$. The trial flip is accepted if the random number is less than or equal to the transition probability.

```
SUB Metropolis(N,L,spin(,),E,M,w(),ratio)
    FOR ispin = 1 to N
        LET x = int(L*rnd + 1)          ! randomly select x coordinate
        LET y = int(L*rnd + 1)          ! randomly select y coordinate
        ! determine neighbor spins using periodic boundary conditions
        CALL periodic(x,y,L,spin,sum)        ! compute sum of 4 nearest neighbors
        IF spin(x,y)*sum <= 0 then
            CALL accept(x,y,M,E,sum,spin,ratio)
        ELSE IF rnd < w(sum) then
            CALL accept(x,y,M,E,sum,spin,ratio)
        END IF
    NEXT ispin
END SUB
```

A typical laboratory system has at least 10^{23} spins. In contrast the number of spins studied in computer simulations typically ranges from 32^2 to 600^3. As we have discussed in other contexts, the use of periodic boundary conditions minimizes finite size effects. However, a disadvantage of periodic boundary conditions is that they reduce the maximum separation between spins to one-half the length of the system. More sophisticated boundary conditions are also possible. For example, we can imagine giving the surface spins extra neighbors, whose direction is related to the mean spin of the configuration at that time. We adopt the simpler periodic boundary conditions in **SUB periodic**.

```
SUB periodic(x,y,L,spin(,),sum)
    IF x = 1 then
        LET left = spin(L,y)
    ELSE
        LET left = spin(x - 1,y)
    END IF
    IF x = L then
        LET right = spin(1,y)
    ELSE
        LET right = spin(x + 1,y)
    END IF
    IF y = 1 then
        LET down = spin(x,L)
    ELSE
        LET down = spin(x,y - 1)
    END IF
```

```
    IF y = L then
       LET up = spin(x,1)
    ELSE
       LET up = spin(x,y + 1)
    END IF
    LET sum = left + right + up + down
END SUB

SUB accept(x,y,M,E,sum,spin(,),ratio)
    LET spin(x,y) = -spin(x,y)
    LET ratio = ratio + 1          ! normalize later to determine acceptance ratio
    LET M = M + 2*spin(x,y)
    LET E = E - 2*spin(x,y)*sum
END SUB

SUB data(E,M,ecum,e2cum,mcum,m2cum)
    ! accumulate data after every Monte Carlo step per spin
    LET ecum = ecum + E
    LET e2cum = e2cum + E*E
    LET mcum = mcum + M
    LET m2cum = m2cum + M*M
END SUB

SUB output(N,nmcs,ecum,e2cum,mcum,m2cum,ratio)
    LET norm = 1/(nmcs*N)                    ! averages per spin
    LET ratio = ratio*norm
    LET eave = ecum*norm
    LET e2ave = e2cum*norm
    LET mave = mcum*norm
    LET m2ave = m2cum*norm
    PRINT "acceptance ratio = ",ratio
    PRINT "mean energy per spin = ",eave
    PRINT "mean square energy per spin = ",e2ave
    PRINT "mean magnetization = ", mave
    PRINT "mean square magnetization = ",m2ave
END SUB
```

In some simulations the process of equilibration can account for a substantial fraction of the total computer time. The most practical choice of initial conditions is an "equilibrium" configuration from a previous run which is at a temperature close to the desired temperature. The following subroutine saves the last configuration of a run and can be included after **SUB output** in **Program Ising**.

```
SUB save_config(N,L,T,spin(,))
    INPUT prompt "name of file for last configuration = ": file$
    OPEN #2: name file$, access output, create new
    PRINT #2: T
    FOR y = 1 to L
        FOR x = 1 to L
            PRINT #2: spin(x,y)
        NEXT x
    NEXT y
    CLOSE #2
END SUB
```

A previous configuration can be used in a later run by adding the following statements to **SUB initial**.

```
INPUT prompt "old configuration (y/n)?": old$
IF old$ = "y" or new$ = "Y" then
    INPUT prompt "filename?": file$
    OPEN #1: name file$, access input
    INPUT #1: T
    FOR y = 1 to L
        FOR x = 1 to L
            INPUT #1: spin(x,y)
        NEXT x
    NEXT y
    CLOSE #1
END IF
```

PROBLEM 16.6 Equilibration of the two-dimensional Ising model

a. The input parameters of **Program Ising** are L, the linear dimension of the lattice, the number $nmcs$ of Monte Carlo steps per spin, and the temperature T of the heat bath. Run **Program Ising** with $L = 8$ and $T = 2$ and choose the initial spins to be all up. What is the initial "temperature" of the system? Plot the variation of the energy and magnetization with "time" (the number of Monte Carlo steps per spin). How much time is necessary for the system to reach equilibrium? After the system has reached equilibrium, save a typical configuration.

b. Visually inspect several equilibrium configurations. Is the system "ordered" or "disordered"?

c. Run **Program Ising** with $L = 8$ and $T = 1.5$ and choose the initial spin configuration to be the same as in part (a), i.e. all spins up. How long does it take for the system to reach equilibrium? Now choose the initial configuration to be the one saved in part (a) with $T = 2.0$. Compare the relative times to reach equilibrium with the two configurations.

d. Visually inspect several equilibrium configurations for $T = 1.5$. Are the configurations more or less ordered than the configurations in part (a)?

Now that we have obtained typical equilibrium configurations, we wish to compute the mean values of several physical quantities of interest. Suppose we wish to compute the mean value of the physical quantity A. In general the calculation of A is time consuming and hence we do not want to calculate its value more often than necessary. Clearly we do not want to compute A after the flip of only one spin, since the values of A in the two configurations would be almost the same. Ideally we wish to compute A for configurations which are statistically independent. However, since we do not know the "correlation time" of the configurations *a priori*, we have to estimate the correlation time in our preliminary computations.

One way to determine the time intervals over which configurations are correlated is to compute the time-dependent *autocorrelation* functions $C_M(t)$ and $C_E(t)$ defined by

$$C_M(t) = <M(t)M(0)> - <M>^2 \qquad (16.16a)$$

and

$$C_E(t) = <E(t)E(0)> - <E>^2 \quad . \qquad (16.16b)$$

$M(t)$ and $E(t)$ are the values of the magnetization and total energy of the system at "time" t, the number of Monte Carlo steps per spin. Note that at $t = 0$, $C_M(0)$ is proportional to the susceptibility and $C_E(0)$ is proportional to the heat capacity. For sufficiently large t, $M(t)$ and $M(0)$ will become uncorrelated and $<M(t)M(0)> \rightarrow <M(t)><M(0)> = <M>^2$. Hence $C_M(t)$ and $C_E(t)$ should vanish for $t \rightarrow \infty$. In general we expect $C_M(t)$ and $C_E(t)$ to decay exponentially with time. The time it takes $C(t)$ to decay to $1/e$ of its value at $t = 0$ is an estimate of the correlation time τ. Since configurations separated by times less than τ are statistically correlated, we will compute the desired physical quantities for time intervals on the order of τ rather than after each Monte Carlo step per spin.

PROBLEM 16.7 The correlation time

a. Modify **Program Ising** so that the equilibrium values of $C_M(t)$ and $C_E(t)$ are computed. Consider $L = 8$ with $T = 3.0$ (high T), $T = 2.3$, and $T = 1.5$ (low T). Use an equilibrium configuration generated in Problem 16.6 as the initial state of the simulation. Estimate the correlation time τ for the energy and the magnetization fluctuations. Are the correlation times comparable for the two fluctuations? How do your estimates for τ compare with your estimates of the relaxation time found in Problem 16.6?

*b. In order to describe the relaxation towards equilibrium as realistically as possible, we randomly selected the spins to be flipped. However if we are only interested in equilibrium properties, it might be possible to save computer time if the spins are selected sequentially. Determine if the correlation time is greater, smaller, or about the same if the spins are chosen sequentially rather than randomly. If the correlation time is greater, does it still save cpu time to choose spins sequentially? Why is it not desirable to choose spins sequentially in the one-dimensional Ising model?

PROBLEM 16.8 Comparison with exact results

Since in general Monte Carlo programs yield exact answers only after an
infinite number of configurations have been sampled, how can we be sure that
the algorithm and our program works correctly? There is no general rule for
the necessary number of statistical samples or the time of equilibration. But
since systemmatic programming and typing errors are easily overlooked, we
should ensure that our program is able to reproduce exact results in known
limits. One way to test **Program Ising** is to consider a small system for
which the partition function and thus the mean energy and magnetization
can be calculated analytically.

a. Calculate analytically the T-dependence of E, M, C and χ for the two-
dimensional Ising model with $L = 2$ and periodic boundary conditions. (A
summary of the calculation is given in Appendix 16B.)

b. Use **Program Ising** with $L = 2$ and estimate E, M, C, and χ for
$J/k_BT = 2.0$ and 3.0. Use the relations (16.14b) and (16.15b) to compute
C and χ respectively. Compare your estimated values to the exact results
found in part (a). How many Monte Carlo steps per spin are necessary to
obtain E and M to within 1%? How many Monte Carlo steps per spin are
necessary to obtain C and χ to within 1%?

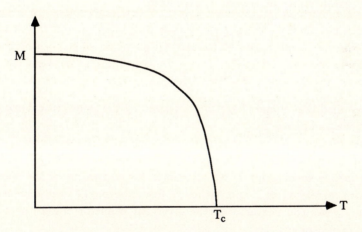

Fig. 16.2 Qualitative temperature-dependence of $m(T)$, the magnetization per spin, for a continuous phase transition.

16.5   THE ISING PHASE TRANSITION

Now that we have tested our program for the two-dimensional Ising model in various contexts, we are ready to explore its properties. We first summarize some of the qualitative properties of ferromagnetic systems in zero external field. We know that at $T = 0$, the spins are perfectly aligned in either direction, i.e. the mean magnetization per spin $m(T) = <M>/N$ is given by $m(T = 0) = \pm 1$. As T is increased, the magnitude of $m(T)$ decreases continuously until at $T = T_c$, $m(T)$ vanishes completely (see Fig. 16.2). Since $m(T)$ vanishes continuously rather than abruptly, the transition is termed *continuous* rather than discontinuous. (The term *first-order* describes the latter type of transition.)

How can we characterize a continuous magnetic phase transition? The same way we characterized the vicinity of the percolation threshold. Since $m \neq 0$ implies that a net number of spins are spontaneously aligned, we designate m as the *order parameter* of the system. Near T_c we can characterize the behavior of many physical quantities by power-law behavior (see Table 12.1). For example we can write m near T_c as

$$m(T) \sim (T_c - T)^\beta \tag{16.17}$$

where β is a critical exponent (not to be confused with the quantity $1/k_B T$). Although $m(T)$ vanishes at T_c, thermodynamic derivatives such as the heat capacity and susceptibility diverge at T_c. We write

$$\chi \sim |T - T_c|^{-\gamma} \tag{16.18}$$

and

$$C \sim |T - T_c|^{-\alpha} \quad . \tag{16.19}$$

We have assumed that χ and C are characterized by the same critical exponents γ and α above and below T_c.

Another measure of the magnetic fluctuations is the linear dimension $\xi(T)$ of a typical magnetic domain. We expect the *correlation length* $\xi(T)$ to be the order of a lattice spacing for $T >> T_c$. Since the alignment of the spins will become more correlated as T approaches T_c from above, $\xi(T)$ will increase as T approaches T_c. We can characterize the divergent behavior of $\xi(T)$ near T_c by the critical exponent ν

$$\xi(T) \sim |T - T_c|^{-\nu} \quad . \tag{16.20}$$

As we found in our discussion of percolation in Chapter 12, a finite system cannot exhibit a true phase transition. Nevertheless we expect that if the $\xi(T)$ is less than the linear dimension L of the system, then a finite system will be an accurate representation of the infinite system. In other words, our simulations should yield results comparable to an infinite system if T is not too close to T_c. In the following problem, we obtain preliminary data for the T-dependence of m, $<E>$, C, and χ. This data will help us understand the qualitative nature of the ferromagnetic phase transition in the two-dimensional Ising model.

PROBLEM 16.9 Qualitative behavior of the two-dimensional Ising model

a. Modify **Program Ising** so that the values of the physical quantities of interest are computed for configurations which are statistically independent. Since we will consider the Ising model for lattices of different values of L, it will be convenient to compute intensive quantities such as the mean energy per spin, the specific heat (per spin) and the susceptibility per spin. In order to simplify the notation, we will retain the same notation for both the extensive and corresponding intensive quantities.

b. Use your modified program to compute the magnetization per spin m, the mean energy per spin $<E>$, the specific heat C and the susceptibility per spin χ. Choose $L = 4$ and consider $T = 1.5$ to 3.5 in steps of 0.2. Choose the initial condition for $T = 1.5$ to be all spins up. Use an equilibrium configuration from a previous run at temperature T as the initial configuration for a run at temperature $T + \Delta T$. Since all the spins might overturn and the magnetization change sign during the course of your observation, estimate the mean value of $|m|$ rather than m. Use at least 200 Monte Carlo steps per spin and estimate the number of equilibrium configurations needed for approximately 5% accuracy for m and $<E>$. Plot $<E>$, $|m|$, C, and χ as a function of T and describe their qualitative dependence on the temperature. Do you see any evidence of a phase transition? Note that it is possible to save time by using the same random numbers for lattices at different temperatures.

c. Repeat the calculations of part (b) for $L = 8$ and $L = 16$. Plot your estimates for $<E>$, $|m|$, C and χ as a function of T and describe their qualitative dependence on the temperature. Do you see any evidence of a phase transition? For comparison the published Monte Carlo results by Landau (see references) for the two-dimensional Ising model are in the range $L = 4$ to $L = 60$ with 10^4 to 2×10^3 Monte Carlo steps per spin.

d. For a given value of L, e.g. $L = 16$, choose a value of T which you believe corresponds to a temperature well below T_c. Instead of choosing an initial configuration corresponding to all spins up, choose the directions of the spins

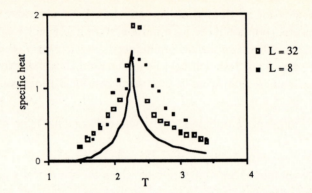

Fig. 16.3 The temperature-dependence of the specific heat (per spin) on a $L \times L$ square Ising model with periodic boundary conditions. One thousand Monte Carlo steps per spin were used for each value of the temperature. The continuous line represents the temperature dependence of the specific heat in the limit of an infinite lattice.

randomly. What is the initial "temperature" of the system? Observe the spins evolve in time. Do you see several domains with positive and negative spontaneous magnetization? How does the magnetization evolve with time? Does it exhibit large fluctuations? Describe an equilibrium configuration of the system. Does it exhibit many domains or only one? Why did we suggest in part (b) that you begin at a low temperature and gradually "warm" the system?

e. Since all our simulations have been for zero external magnetic field, all directions are equivalent. Hence for $T < T_c$ where a spontaneous magnetization is expected to be present, we might expect to observe both positive and negative values of the magnetization. Suppose the initial configuration corresponds to all spins up and $T < T_c$. Do you expect to observe negative values of M? Why or why not? Are you more or less likely to observe negative values of M for bigger or smaller values of L? If you had started with an initial state of all spins down, would you expect to observe positive or negative values of M?

The most serious limitation of a computer simulation study of phase transitions is the relatively small size of our systems. Nevertheless we observed in Problem 16.9 that even systems as small as $L = 4$ exhibit behavior which is reminiscent of a phase transition. In Fig. 16.3 we show our Monte Carlo data for the T-dependence of the specific heat of the two-dimensional Ising model for $L = 8$ and $L = 32$. We see that C exhibits a broad maximum which becomes more marked for larger L. Does your data for C exhibit similar behavior?

Since we can simulate only finite lattices, it is difficult to obtain estimates for α, β and γ by using the definitions (16.17)–(16.19) directly. Instead as we learned in Chapter 12, we can do a *finite-size scaling analysis* to extrapolate our finite L results to $L \to \infty$. For example, we see from Fig. 16.3 that the temperature at which C exhibits a maximum becomes better defined for larger L. This behavior provides a simple definition of the transition temperature $T_c(L)$ of a finite system. According to finite-size scaling theory, the critical temperature $T_c(L)$ scales as

$$T_c(L) - T_c(L = \infty) \sim aL^{-1/\nu} \tag{16.21}$$

where a is a constant and ν is defined in (16.20). Since we expect the finite size of the lattice to be important for

$$\xi(T) \sim L \sim |T - T_c|^{-\nu} \tag{16.22}$$

we expect that the T-dependence of M, C and χ to be replaced for finite L by

$$m(T) \sim (T_c - T)^{\beta} \to L^{-\beta/\nu} \tag{16.23}$$

$$C(T) \sim |T - T_c|^{-\alpha} \to L^{\alpha/\nu} \tag{16.24}$$

$$\chi(T) \sim |T - T_c|^{-\gamma} \to L^{\gamma/\nu} \quad . \tag{16.25}$$

In Problem 16.10 we use the relations (16.23)–(16.25) to estimate the critical exponents.

PROBLEM 16.10 Finite-size scaling and the estimate of critical properties of the two-dimensional Ising model

a. Use the relation (16.21) together with the exact result $\nu = 1$ to estimate the value of T_c on a infinite square lattice. Since it is difficult to obtain a precise value for T_c with small lattices, we will use the exact result $k_B T_c/J = 2/ln(1 + \sqrt{2}) \approx 2.269$ in the remaining parts of this problem.

b. Determine the specific heat C, $|m|$, and the susceptibility χ at $T_c = 2.269$ for $L = 2$, 4, 8, and 16. Use as many Monte Carlo steps per spin as is practical. Plot the logarithm of the values of $|m|$ and χ versus L and use the scaling relations (16.23)–(16.25) to determine the critical exponents β

and γ. Assume the exact result $\nu = 1$. Do your log-log plots of $|m|$ and χ yield reasonably straight lines? Compare your estimates for β and γ with the exact values given in Table 12.1.

b. Make a log-log plot of C versus L. If your data for C is sufficiently accurate, you will find that the log-log plot of C versus L is not a straight line but shows curvature. The reason for this curvature is that α in (16.19) equals zero for the two-dimensional Ising model and hence (16.24) needs to be interpreted as

$$C \sim C_0 \ln L \quad . \tag{16.26}$$

Is your data for C consistent with (16.26)? The exact result for the proportionality constant C_0 in (16.26) is approximately 0.4995.

So far we have performed all our Ising model simulations on the square lattice. Since nature is not square, you might wish to determine if the critical temperature and the critical exponents depend on the symmetry and the dimension of the lattice. Based on your experience with the percolation transition in Chapter 12, you might already know the answer. Do you think that T_c (at fixed J) for the triangular lattice is greater than or smaller than for the square lattice?

*PROBLEM 16.11 **The effects of symmetry and dimension on the critical properties of the Ising model**

a. The nature of the triangular lattice is discussed in Chapter 11 (see Fig. 11.3). The main difference between the triangular lattice and the square lattice is the coordination number. Make the necessary modifications in your Ising program, e.g. determine the possible transitions and the values of the transition rate. Compute C and χ for different values of T in the interval $[1.0, 5.0]$. Assume that $\nu = 1$ and use finite-size scaling to estimate T_c in the limit of an infinite triangular lattice. Compare your estimate of T_c to the known value (to three decimal places) $k_B T_c / J = 3.641$. (The simulation of Ising models on the triangular lattice is relevant to the understanding of the experimentally observed phases of materials which can be absorbed on the surface of graphite.)

b. Since no exact results are available for the Ising model in three dimensions, there has been much interest in Monte Carlo simulations of the three-dimensional Ising model. Write a Monte Carlo program to simulate the Ising model on the simple cubic lattice (coordination number six). Compute C and χ for $T = 3.2$ to 5.0 in steps of 0.2 for different values of L. Estimate $T_c(L)$

from the maximum of C and χ. Does $T_c(L)$ determined from $C(T)$ have a stronger L-dependence than $T_c(L)$ determined from $\chi(T)$? Use the values of $T_c(L)$ which exhibit a stronger L-dependence and plot $T_c(L)$ versus $L^{-1/\nu}$ for different values of ν in the range 0.5 to 1.0. Show that the extrapolated value of $T_c(L = \infty)$ is almost independent of the value of ν. Compare your estimate for $T_c(L = \infty)$ to the best known value (to four decimal places) $k_B T_c / J = 4.5108$.

c. Compute $|m|$, C, and χ at $T_c = 4.5108$ for different values of L on a simple cubic lattice. Do a finite-size scaling analysis to estimate the ratios, β/ν, α/ν, and γ/ν. The values of the critical exponents for the three dimensional Ising model are given in Table 12.1. Note that Landau (see references) considered the finite-size behavior of the simple cubic Ising lattice for $L = 6$ to $L = 20$; 2000–5000 Monte Carlo steps per spin were used for calculating the averages after equilibrium had been reached.

*PROBLEM 16.12 Critical slowing down

a. Consider the two-dimensional Ising model on a square lattice with $L = 16$. Compute the correlation time τ for $T = 2.5$, 2.4, and 2.3. Show that τ increases as the critical temperature is approached, a physical effect known as *critical slowing down*.

b. Since τ diverges near T_c for an infinite lattice, it is possible to define a "dynamic critical exponent" Δ by the relation $\tau \sim (T - T_c)^{-\Delta}$. On a finite lattice we have the relation $\tau \sim L^z$ at $T = T_c$. Use finite-size scaling arguments to obtain the relation of z to Δ. Compute τ for different values of L on a square lattice at $T = T_c$ and estimate z.

c. The magnitude of τ found in parts (a) and (b) depend in part on our choice of "dynamics." Although we have generated a trial change by the attempted flip of one spin, it is possible that other types of trial changes, e.g. the simultaneous flip of two or more spins, might be more efficient and lead to smaller correlation times. Since critical slowing down hampers the Monte Carlo study of phase transitions, a problem of much current interest is the development of more efficient algorithms near phase transitions.

16.6   OTHER APPLICATIONS OF THE ISING MODEL

Since the applications of the Ising model are so extensive and wide ranging, we can mention only a few applications here. In the following, we briefly describe applications of the Ising model to first-order phase transitions, lattice gases, antiferromagnetism, and the order-disorder transition in binary alloys.

So far we have investigated continuous phase transitions in the Ising model and have found that the energy and magnetization vary continuously with the temperature, but thermodynamic derivatives such as the specific heat and the susceptibility diverge near T_c in the limit of an infinite lattice. In Problem 16.13 we discuss a simple example of a *first-order* phase transition. Such transitions are accompanied by finite *discontinuous* changes in thermodynamic quantities such as the energy and the magnetization.

*PROBLEM 16.13 The two-dimensional Ising model in an external magnetic field

a. Modify your two-dimensional Ising program so that the energy of interaction with an external magnetic field H is included. It is convenient to measure H in terms of the quantity $h = \mu_0 H / k_B$. We wish to compute m, the mean magnetization per spin, as a function of h for $T < T_c$. Consider a square lattice with $L = 16$ and equilibrate the system at $T = 1.8$ and $h = 0$. Adopt the following procedure to obtain $m(h)$.

i. Use an equilibrium configuration at $h = 0$ as the initial configuration for $h_1 = \Delta h = 0.2$.

ii. Run the system for 20 time steps (Monte Carlo steps per spin) before computing averages.

iii. Average m over 80 time steps.

iv. Use the last configuration for $h_n = n\Delta h$ as the initial configuration for $h_{n+1} = h_n + \Delta h$.

vi. Repeat steps (ii)–(iv) until $m \sim 0.95$

Make a plot of m versus h. Do the measured values of m correspond to equilibrium averages?

b. Decrease h by $\Delta h = -0.2$ until h passes through zero and $m \sim -0.95$. Does m remain positive for small negative h? Do the measured values of m for negative h correspond to equilibrium averages? Draw the spin configurations for several values of h. Do you see evidence of domains? Extend your plot of m versus h to negative h values.

c. Increase h until the m versus h curve forms a closed loop. What is the value of m at $h = 0$? This value of m is the spontaneous magnetization.

d. A first-order phase transition is characterized by a discontinuity (for an infinite lattice) in the order parameter. In the present case the transition is characterized by the behavior of m as a function of h. What is your measured value of m for $h = 0.2$? If $m(h)$ is double-valued, which value of m corresponds to the equilibrium state, an absolute minima in the free energy? Which value of m corresponds to a *metastable* state, a relative minima in the free energy? What are the equilibrium and metastable values of m for $h = -0.2$? Why is the transition from positive m to negative m a first-order transition? Note that first-order transitions exhibit *hysteresis* and the properties of the system depend on the history of the system, e.g. whether h is an increasing or decreasing function. Because of the long lifetime of metastable states near a phase transition, such states can mistakenly be confused with an equilibrium state. Since near a continuous phase transition, the relaxation to equilibrium becomes very long (see Problem 16.12), a system with a continuous phase transition can behave as if it were effectively in a metastable state. Hence it is very difficult to distinguish the nature of a phase transition using computer simulations alone.

e. Repeat the above simulation for $T = 3.0$, a temperature above T_c. Why do your results differ from the simulations in parts (a)–(c) done for $T < T_c$?

The Ising model can describe other systems which might appear to have little in common with ferromagnetism. For example we can interpret the Ising model as a "lattice gas," where "down" represents a lattice site occupied by an atom and "up" represents an empty site. Each lattice site can be occupied by one atom at most. The "spins" interact with their nearest neighbors as before. The lattice gas represents a crude model of the behavior of a real gas of atoms and is of historical importance as a model for the gas-liquid transition and the critical point. What properties does the lattice gas have in common with a real gas? What properties of real gases does the lattice gas omit?

An important difference between a ferromagnet and a lattice gas is that the total number of atoms is fixed in the latter, whereas the number of "up" and "down" spins can change in the ferromagnet. Hence we can no longer use spin flip dynamics for the lattice gas. A choice of dynamics which does conserve the number of down and up spins is known as *spin exchange dynamics*. In this dynamics a trial *interchange* of two nearest neighbor spins is made and the change in energy ΔE is calculated. The criterion for the acceptance or rejection of the trial change is the same as before. What physical process occurs in a lattice gas if a down spin and an up spin are interchanged?

*PROBLEM 16.14 Simulation of a lattice gas

a. Modify your Ising program so that spin exchange dynamics rather than spin flip dynamics is used. For example, determine the possible values of ΔE on the square lattice, the possible values of the transition probability array w, and change the way a trial move is made. Note that the number of occupied sites is a conserved variable and must be specified initially. If we are interested only in the mean value of static quantities such as the total energy, we can reduce the computation time by not interchanging like spins. For example we can keep a list of "bonds" between occupied and empty sites and make trial moves by choosing bonds at random from this list. However, since we will consider only small lattices, we recommend that you not bother to keep such a list and choose a trial move by simply choosing a spin and one of its nearest neighbors at random.

b. Consider a square lattice with $L = 8$ and with 32 sites initially occupied. Determine the mean energy for T in the range 1.0 to 4.0. Plot the mean energy as a function of temperature. Does the energy appear to vary continuously?

c. Repeat the calculations of part (b) with 44 sites initially occupied. Plot the mean energy as a function of T. Does the energy vary continuously? Do you see any evidence of a first-order phase transition?

d. Since the spins correspond to atoms, we can compute the equilibrium single-particle diffusion constant of the atoms. (See Problem 11.9 for a similar simulation.) Use an array to record the position of each spin (atom) as a function of time. After equilibrium has been reached, choose the origin of time and compute $<R(t)^2>$, the net mean-square displacement per atom after t units of time. If the atoms undergo a random walk, the self-diffusion constant D is defined as $D = (1/2dt) <R(t)^2>$ in the limit $t \to \infty$. Estimate D for different temperatures and numbers of occupied sites.

Although you are probably more familiar with ferromagnetism, nature actually provides more examples of antiferromagnetism. In the language of the Ising model, antiferromagnetism means that nearest neighbor spins prefer to be aligned in opposite directions and the interaction parameter J is negative. As we will see in Problem 16.15, the properties of the antiferromagnetic Ising model on a square lattice are similar to the ferromagnetic Ising model. For example the energy and specific heat are identical at all temperatures in zero magnetic field and the system exhibits a phase transition at the Néel temperature T_N. On the other hand the total magnetization and susceptibility for the antiferromagnet do not exhibit any critical behavior near T_N. However we can define two sublattices for the square lattice as shown in Fig. 16.4 and introduce the "staggered magnetization" M_s equal to the difference of the magnetization on the two sublattices. The temperature dependence of M_s and the corresponding staggered susceptibility χ_s are identical to the analogous quantities in the ferromagnetic Ising model.

*PROBLEM 16.15 Antiferromagnetic Ising model

Since J does not appear explicitly in **Program Ising**, we need to change the sign of the energy calculations to model an Ising antiferromagnet. This change can be made by letting $spin(x, y)*sum \rightarrow -spin(x, y)*sum$ wherever it occurs. To compute the staggered magnetization on a square lattice, we

Fig. 16.4 The black and white squares correspond to two sublattices.

define one sublattice to be the sites (x, y) for which $mod(x, 2)+mod(y, 2) = 1$; the other sublattice corresponds to the remaining sites.

a. Modify **Program Ising** to simulate the antiferromagnetic Ising model on the square lattice. Consider $L = 16$, $h = 0$, and choose the initial condition to be all spins up. What configuration of spins corresponds to the state of lowest energy? Compute the temperature dependence of the mean energy, specific heat, magnetization, and susceptibility. Does the temperature dependence of any of these quantities show evidence of a phase transition?

b. Compute the temperature dependence of M_s and the staggered susceptibility χ_s defined as (see (16.15b))

$$\chi_s = \frac{1}{k_B T}[<M_s{}^2> - <M_s>^2] \quad . \tag{16.27}$$

Verify that the temperature dependence of M_s for the antiferromagnetic Ising model is the same as the temperature dependence of M for the Ising ferromagnet. Could you have predicted this similarity without doing the simulation?

c. In part (a) you might have noticed that χ shows a cusp. Compute χ for different values of L at $T = T_N = 2.269$. Do a finite-size scaling analysis to show that χ does not diverge.

d. Consider the behavior of the antiferromagnetic Ising model on a triangular lattice. Choose $L = 16$ and compute the same quantities as in part (a). Do you see any evidence of a phase transition? Draw several configurations of the system at different temperatures. Do you see evidence of many small domains at low temperatures? Can you draw the ground state configuration? Is there a unique ground state? If you cannot find a unique ground state, you share the same frustration as do the individual spins in the triangular antiferromagnetic Ising model. (The term *frustration* is a technical term which describes the fact that there is no configuration on the triangular lattice such that spins alternate in sign along any axis.)

Another important application of the Ising model is the study of phase separation in a binary A-B alloy. As an example the alloy known as β-brass has a low temperature ordered phase in which the two components (copper and zinc) have equal concentrations and form a cesium chloride structure (cf Kittel). As the temperature is increased, some zinc atoms exchange positions with copper atoms, but the system is still "ordered." However above the critical temperature

$T_c = 742\,K$, the zinc and copper atoms become mixed and the system is "disordered." This transition is an example of an *order-disorder* transition. How can you apply the Ising model to an order-disorder transition?

The Ising model is only one of several models of magnetism. The Heisenberg, Potts, x-y, and Ashkin-Teller models are examples of other models of magnetic materials familiar to condensed matter scientists. Monte Carlo simulations of these models and others have been important in the development of our understanding of phase transitions in both magnetic and non-magnetic materials.

16.7 SIMULATION OF CLASSICAL FLUIDS

The existence of matter in three different phases, solid, liquid and gas, is familiar to our everyday experience (see Fig. 16.5). From this experience we can distinguish the properties of the three phases. For example, solids are rigid in contrast to gases and liquids which flow under a shear stress. Our goal in this section is to use Monte Carlo methods to gain additional insight into the qualitative differences between the three phases.

Monte Carlo simulations of classical fluids are considerably simplified by the fact that the velocity (momentum) variables are irrelevant. For example, the contribution of the velocity coordinates to the mean energy is $\frac{1}{2}k_B T$ per degree of freedom. Thus we need to sample only the positions of the molecules, i.e.

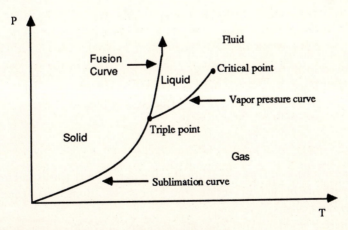

Fig. 16.5 Phase diagram for a simple substance.

the "configurational" degrees of freedom. Is such a simplification possible for quantum systems?

The physically relevant quantities of a fluid include the mean energy, specific heat and equation of state. Another interesting quantity is the *pair correlation function* $g(r)$ which we define as follows. Suppose that N particles are contained in a region of volume V with the mean number density $\rho = N/V$. (In two and one dimension, we replace V by the area and length respectively.) Choose one of the particles, the reference particle, to be the origin of a coordinate system. Then the probability of finding a second particle in the interval between r and $r + dr$ is given by $\rho g(r)d\vec{r}$, where the "volume" element $d\vec{r} = 4\pi r^2 dr$ ($d = 3$), $2\pi r dr$ ($d = 2$), and $2dr$ ($d = 1$). We expect that $g(r) \to 0$ as $r \to 0$, since particles cannot penetrate one another. We also expect that $g(r) \to 1$ as $r \to \infty$, since the inhomogeneity near a particle is limited to a finite region. Note that if we integrate $\rho g(r)d\vec{r}$ over $d\vec{r}$, we obtain $N - 1$, the total number of particles in the system minus the reference particle. We will find in Problems 16.16–16.18 that $g(r)$ is a probe of the density fluctuations and hence of the local "order" in the system.

Several thermodynamic properties can also be obtained from $g(r)$. For example if only two-body forces are present, it can be shown that the mean potential energy per particle can be expressed as

$$\frac{U}{N} = \frac{\rho}{2} \int g(r)V(r)\, d\vec{r} \quad . \tag{16.28}$$

We can also use the force virial (see Chapter 6) to write the equation of state as

$$\frac{\beta P}{\rho} = 1 - \frac{\beta \rho}{2d} \int g(r)\, r \frac{dV(r)}{dr}\, d\vec{r} \quad . \tag{16.29}$$

Hard spheres in d dimensions.   In order to separate the effects of the short-range repulsive interaction from the longer range attractive interaction, we first investigate a model of *hard spheres* with the interparticle interaction

$$V(r) = \begin{cases} +\infty, & r < \sigma \\ 0, & r \geq \sigma \end{cases} \quad . \tag{16.30}$$

Such a model has been extensively studied using both Monte Carlo and molecular dynamics methods in one dimension (hard-rods), two dimensions (hard disks) and in three dimensions.

Since there is no attractive interaction present in (16.30), there is no transition from a gas to a liquid. Is there a phase transition between a fluid phase at low densities and a solid at high densities? Can a solid form in the absence of an attractive interaction? We investigate these questions in the following.

What are the physically relevant quantities for a system of hard spheres? There are no thermal quantities such as the mean potential energy since this quantity is always zero for hard spheres. The major quantity of interest is $g(r)$, since it yields information on the correlations of the particles and the equation of state. If the potential is given by (16.30), it can be shown that (16.29) reduces to

$$\frac{\beta P}{\rho} = 1 + \frac{2\pi}{3}\rho\sigma^3 g(\sigma) \qquad d = 3 \qquad (16.31a)$$

$$= 1 + \frac{\pi}{2}\rho\sigma^2 g(\sigma) \qquad d = 2 \qquad (16.31b)$$

$$= 1 + \rho\sigma g(\sigma) \qquad d = 1 \quad . \qquad (16.31c)$$

We will calculate $g(r)$ for different values of r and then extrapolate our results to $r = \sigma$.

An easy way to implement the Metropolis algorithm for a hard sphere system is to choose a particle at random and move it to a new trial position. If the new position overlaps another particle, the move is rejected and the old configuration is retained; otherwise the move is accepted. A reasonable, although not necessarily optimum, choice for the maximum displacement δ is to choose δ so that approximately one-half of all trial states are accepted. The major difficulty in implementing this algorithm is determining the overlap of two particles. If the number of particles is not too large, it is sufficient to compute the distances between the trial particle and all the other particles. **Program hard_disk** uses this straightforward procedure for a system of hard disks. For larger systems this procedure is too time consuming. As discussed in Chapter 6, a better procedure is to divide the system into "cells" and to only check particles in the same and neighboring cells.

```
PROGRAM hard_disk                        ! Metropolis algorithm for hard disks
DIM x(50),y(50),gcum(100)
RANDOMIZE
CALL initial(N,x,y,nmcs,Lx,Ly,kx,ky,dr,bin,dxmax,dymax)
FOR imcs = 1 to nmcs
    CALL move(N,x,y,Lx,Ly,kx,ky,dxmax,dymax,accept)
    CALL correl(N,x,y,gcum,Lx,Ly,kx,ky,bin)
NEXT imcs
CALL output(N,nmcs,gcum,Lx,Ly,dr,bin,accept)
CALL save_config(N,Lx,Ly,x,y)
END
```

The choice of initial positions for the disks is more complicated that it might first appear. One strategy is to place the disks at random in the box. If a disk overlaps a disk already present, simply throw it down somewhere else. If the density is low, a possible initial configuration can be computed fairly quickly in this way. In order to reach higher densities, we might imagine moving the walls inward toward the center of the box until one of the walls just touches one of the disks. Then the disks are moved a number of Monte Carlo steps and the walls are moved inward again. Clearly this procedure becomes more difficult as the density increases.

An alternative procedure is to begin the particles in an ordered set of positions. For example, we can start the disks on a triangular lattice at the highest density of interest. Then we can expand the lattice and proportionately change the coordinates of the disks. In this way no overlap of disks will occur in the new configuration. We follow this latter procedure in **SUB initial**. Note that in order to satisfy the condition that each disk have the same number of nearest neighbors, it is necessary to consider only an even number of particles. It is convenient to choose units such that all distances are measures in terms of the hard core radius σ. The reduced density is $\rho^* = \rho/\sigma^d$ where d is the dimension of the system.

```
SUB initial(N,x(),y(),nmcs,Lx,Ly,kx,ky,dr,bin,dxmax,dymax)
    INPUT prompt "number of particles (even) = ": N
    INPUT prompt "number of rows = ": Ny
    LET Nx = N/Ny                      ! Nx must be an integer
    INPUT prompt "length of box = ": Lx
    INPUT prompt "width of box = ": Ly
    INPUT prompt "number of Monte Carlo steps per particle = ": nmcs
    INPUT prompt "r interval dr = ": dr       ! use dr to compute g(r)
    LET bin = 1/dr
    INPUT prompt "maximum move in x direction = ": dxmax
    INPUT prompt "maximum move in y direction = ": dymax
    LET kx = 2/Lx                      ! use for periodic boundary conditions
    LET ky = 2/Ly
    INPUT prompt "old configuration (y/n)? ": old$
    IF old$ = "y" or old$ = "Y" then
       INPUT prompt "What is the filename? ": fnm$
       OPEN #1: name fnm$, access input
       INPUT #1: Lxold,Lyold
       LET xexpand = Lx/Lxold
       LET yexpand = Ly/Lyold
       FOR i = 1 to N
          INPUT #1: x(i),y(i)
          LET x(i) = x(i)*xexpand       ! expand old box
          LET y(i) = y(i)*yexpand
       NEXT i
       CLOSE #1
    ELSE                               ! create new triangular lattice
       LET dx = Lx/Nx                  ! dx and dy must be greater than unity
       LET dy = Ly/Ny
       FOR j = 1 to Ny step 2
          FOR i = 1 to Nx
             LET m = m + 2
             LET x(m - 1) = (i - 0.75)*dx
             LET y(m - 1) = (j - 0.5)*dy
             LET x(m) = (i - 0.25)*dx
             LET y(m) = (j + 0.5)*dy
          NEXT i
       NEXT j
    END IF
END SUB
```

In **SUB move** a particle is chosen at random, its trial coordinates are generated and corrected for periodic boundary conditions and the overlap with other disks is determined.

```
SUB move(N,x(),y(),Lx,Ly,kx,ky,dxmax,dymax,accept)
    FOR i = 1 to N
        LET itrial = int(N*rnd + 1)              ! # of particle chosen at random
        LET xtrial = x(itrial) + (2*rnd - 1)*dxmax      ! trial x position
        LET ytrial = y(itrial) + (2*rnd - 1)*dymax      ! trial y position
        CALL cell(xtrial,ytrial,Lx,Ly,kx,ky)
        CALL overlap(N,itrial,xtrial,ytrial,x,y,Lx,Ly,kx,ky,accept)
    NEXT i
END SUB
```

There are at least two ways of treating the periodic boundary conditions. So far we have tested the position of a particle using **IF** statements. We use an alternative method in **SUB cell** and **SUB separation**. The method uses the properties of the **truncate** function in True BASIC. This function truncates all decimal places when its second argument equals 0. Thus $truncate(9.3, 0) = 9$, $truncate(-9.3, 0) = -9$, and $truncate(9.7, 0) = 9$. It is left as an exercise for the reader to determine which method is faster on your computer.

Note that the **int(x)** function in FORTRAN is equivalent to the **truncate(x,0)** function in True BASIC. In contrast the **int** function in True BASIC returns the largest integer less than its argument. Hence $int(9.3) = 9$, $int(-9.3) = -10$, and $int(9.7) = 9$ in True BASIC.

```
SUB cell(xtrial,ytrial,Lx,Ly,kx,ky)
    ! Lx width of box, Ly length of box
    ! true positions of particles between 0 and L
    LET xtrial = xtrial - Lx*truncate(xtrial*kx - 1,0)
    LET ytrial = ytrial - Ly*truncate(ytrial*ky - 1,0)
END SUB
```

```
SUB separation(dx,dy,Lx,Ly,kx,ky)
    ! true separations between 0 and L/2
    LET dx = dx - Lx*truncate(kx*dx,0)
    LET dy = dy - Ly*truncate(ky*dy,0)
END SUB
```

Now that we have determined the "true" location of the trial move, we call

SUB overlap to determine if the trial move overlaps the position of any other disks.

```
SUB overlap(N,itrial,xtrial,ytrial,x(),y(),Lx,Ly,kx,ky,accept)
    ! disks overlap if distance < 1
    FOR j = 1 to N
      IF itrial <> j then
        LET dx = x(j) - xtrial
        LET dy = y(j) - ytrial
        CALL separation(dx,dy,Lx,Ly,kx,ky)        ! true separation
        LET R2 = dx*dx + dy*dy
        IF  R2 < 1 then EXIT SUB                   ! disks overlap
      END IF
    NEXT j
    LET accept = accept + 1
    LET x(itrial) = xtrial
    LET y(itrial) = ytrial
END SUB
```

In **SUB correl** we calculate the array $gcum$, the total number of particles which are in the interval r to $r + \Delta r$ from a given reference particle. Note that $gcum$ is found for $\frac{1}{2}N$ reference particles. Although **SUB correl** is called after each Monte Carlo step, it might be more appropriate to calculate the correlations less frequently.

```
SUB correl(N,x(),y(),gcum(),Lx,Ly,kx,ky,bin)
    ! bin equals the inverse of dr, the distance between shells
    FOR i = 1 to N - 1
      FOR j = i +1 to N
        LET dx = x(i) - x(j)
        LET dy = y(i) - y(j)
        CALL separation(dx,dy,Lx,Ly,kx,ky)
        LET R2 = dx*dx + dy*dy
        LET r = truncate(bin*sqr(R2),0)
        LET gcum(r) = gcum(r) + 1
      NEXT j
    NEXT i
END SUB
```

In **SUB output** we obtain the normalized pair correlation function $g(r)$ by dividing $gcum$ by the number of samples, the density, and the area $2\pi r dr$ of the ring a distance r away from the reference particle. Since *gcum* is found for $\frac{1}{2}N$ reference particles, we also divide by $\frac{1}{2}N$ to avoid double counting.

```
SUB output(N,nmcs,gcum(),Lx,Ly,dr,bin,accept)
    ! obtain normalized g(r) and print results
    ! maximum separation of particles is Ly/2
    LET rmax = bin*min(Lx/2, Ly/2)
    LET density = N/(Lx*Ly)                         ! number density
    PRINT "number density = "; density
    LET accept = accept/(nmcs*N)
    PRINT "acceptance ratio = "; accept
    ! g(r) is calculated after each Monte Carlo step per particle
    LET norm = 2.0/(density*nmcs*N)                 ! normalization for g(r)
    FOR ir = 1 to rmax
        IF gcum(ir) > 0 then
            LET r = ir*dr + 0.5*dr                  ! compute r in middle of shell
            LET area = 2*pi*r*dr                    ! area of shell
            LET g = gcum(ir)*norm/area
            PRINT r,g
        END IF
    NEXT ir
END SUB
```

The last configuration of a previous run should be saved in a file to be used as the initial configuration of a later run.

```
SUB save_config(N,Lx,Ly,x(),y())
    INPUT prompt "Name of file for last configuration = ": fnm$
    OPEN #2: name fnm$, access output, create new
    PRINT #2: Lx, ",", Ly
    FOR i = 1 to N
        PRINT #2: x(i), ",", y(i)
    NEXT i
END SUB
```

As a check on **Program hard_disk** we first consider a one-dimensional system of hard_rods. Because of the simplicity of this system, the equation of state and $g(r)$ can be calculated exactly. For example the equation of state is given by

$$\frac{P}{Nk_BT} = \frac{1}{L - N\sigma} \tag{16.32}$$

where the density $\rho = N/L$. Since hard rods cannot pass through one another, it is easy to see that the excluded volume is $N\sigma$ and hence that the available volume is $L - N\sigma$. Note that the form (16.32) of the equation of state is the same as the van der Waals equation (see Chapter 6) with the contribution from the attractive part of the interaction set equal to zero.

PROBLEM 16.16 Monte Carlo simulation of hard rods

a. Modify **Program hard_disk** so that it is applicable to a system of hard rods. Choose $L = 12$ and $N = 10$. How does the density compare to the maximum possible density? Choose the initial positions to be on a one-dimensional grid. What is the acceptance ratio for the choice $dxmax = 0.1$? Approximately how many Monte Carlo steps per particle are necessary to reach equilibrium? Compute the pair correlation function $g(r)$ with $r = |x|$. Remember that r is measured in units of σ.

b. Plot $g(r)$ as a function of r. Why does $g(r) = 0$ for $r < 1$? Why are values of $g(r)$ for $r > L/2$ not meaningful? What is the physical interpretation of the peaks in $g(r)$? Determine the pressure by extrapolating your results for $g(r)$ to $r = 1$ and using (16.31).

c. Compute $g(r)$ at several lower densities by using an equilibrium configuration from a previous run and increasing L. How do the size and the location of the peaks in $g(r)$ change?

PROBLEM 16.17 Monte Carlo simulation of hard disks

a. Our main goal in this problem is to compute $g(r)$ as a function of the density. What is the maximum possible density of hard disks, that is, how many disks can be packed together in a box of area A? We begin by simulating a system at a density slightly lower than the maximum density. Choose $N = 16$ with $L_x = 4.41$ and $L_y = 0.5*\sqrt{3}*L_x$. Calculate the reduced density ρ^* and compare it to the maximum possible density. What is the mean distance between particles? Choose the initial positions of the particles to be on a triangular lattice. A reasonable first choice for the trial step lengths is $dxmax = dymax = 0.1$. Does such a choice yield an acceptance ratio of approximately 50%? Compute $g(r)$ for $\rho^* = 0.95, 0.92, 0.88, 0.85, 0.80, 0.70,$ $0.60,$ and 0.30. Keep the same ratio of L_x/L_y and use the last configuration of the previous run to be the first configuration of the new run at lower

ρ^*. Allow at least twenty Monte Carlo steps per particle for the system to equilibrate and average $g(r)$ for $nmcs \geq 100$.

b. What is the qualitative behavior of $g(r)$ at high and low densities? For example describe the number and height of the peaks of $g(r)$.

c. Compute the pressure as a function of ρ^* by using the relation (16.31b). Plot the ratio PV/Nk_BT as a function of ρ^*. The "volume" $V = L_x L_y$. Is the ratio PV/Nk_BT an increasing or decreasing function of ρ^*? At low densities we might expect the system to act like an ideal gas with the volume replaced by $(V - N\sigma)$. Compare your lowest density results with this prediction.

d. Take "snapshots" of the disks at intervals of ten to twenty Monte Carlo steps per particle. Do you see any evidence of the solid melting to a fluid at lower densities?

*e. Compute an "effective diffusion constant" D by determining the net mean square displacement $<R(t)^2>$ of the particles after equilibrium is reached. The "time" t can be identified with the number of Monte Carlo steps per particle. Define D by the relation $D = <R(t)^2>/4t$ and estimate D for the densities considered in part (a). Plot the product $\rho^* D$ as a function of ρ^*. What is the dependence of D on ρ^* for a dilute gas? Try to identify a region of ρ^* where D drops abruptly. Do you observe any evidence of a phase transition?

Continuous potentials. Our computer simulations of hard disks led us to the tentative conclusion that there is a phase transition from a fluid at low densities to a solid at higher densities. This conclusion is consistent with molecular dynamics and Monte Carlo studies on larger systems. Although the existence of a fluid-solid transition for hard sphere systems is well accepted, the relatively small numbers of particles used in any computer simulation should remind us that results of this type cannot be taken as proof independent of any theoretical justification.

The existence of a fluid-solid transition for hard spheres indicates that the fluid-solid transition is primarily determined by the repulsive part of the potential. We now consider a system with both a repulsive and an attractive contribution. Our primary goal will be to determine the influence of the attractive potential on the structure of a liquid.

We adopt as our model potential the Lennard-Jones interparticle potential

$$V(r) = 4\epsilon[(\frac{\sigma}{r})^{12} - (\frac{\sigma}{r})^6] \quad . \tag{16.33}$$

The nature of this potential was described in Chapter 6. The Lennard-Jones parameters for argon are $\sigma = 3.405 \, \mathring{A}$ and $\epsilon/k_B = 119.8 \, K$. It is convenient to introduce the dimensionless temperature and pressure by the relations $T^* = k_B T/\epsilon$ and $P^* = P\sigma^2/\epsilon$.

We now apply the Metropolis method to a continuous potential. The major change we need to make in **Program hard_disk** is to replace **SUB overlap** with **SUB test**. In the latter subroutine the main quantity of interest is *petest*, the new potential energy of interaction of particle *itrial* at its trial position $(xtrial, ytrial)$. For simplicity the potential energy of particle *itrial* is computed by considering the energy of interaction with all the other $N - 1$ particles rather than only with the particles that are in the range of the potential ($\sim 2.3\,\sigma$). The quantity *petest* is compared to *peold*, the potential energy of interaction of particle *itrial* at the position $x(itrial), y(itrial)$. Note that *pe* must be computed initially and passed to **SUB test**.

```
SUB test(N,itrial,xtrial,ytrial,x(),y(),pe,beta,Lx,Ly,kx,ky,accept)
   ! Metropolis algorithm for continuous potentials
   DECLARE DEF V
   ! particle number itrial chosen at random in SUB move
   LET petest = 0
   LET peold = 0
   FOR j = 1 to N
      IF itrial <> j then
         LET dx = x(j) - xtrial
         LET dy = y(j) - ytrial
         CALL separation(dx,dy,Lx,Ly,kx,ky)        ! compute true separation
         LET R2 = dx*dx + dy*dy
         LET r = sqr(R2)
         ! petest trial energy of interaction of particle itrial with other particles
         LET petest = petest + V(r)
      END IF
   NEXT j
   FOR j = 1 to N
      IF itrial <> j then
         LET dx = x(j) - x(itrial)
         LET dy = y(j) - y(itrial)
         CALL separation(dx,dy,Lx,Ly,kx,ky)
         LET R2 = dx*dx + dy*dy
         LET r = sqr(R2)
         LET peold = peold + V(r)
      END IF
   NEXT j
   LET de = petest - peold
   IF de > 0 then
      IF exp(-beta*de) < rnd then
         EXIT SUB                          ! trial configuration not accepted
      END IF
   END IF
   LET accept = accept + 1
   LET x(itrial) = xtrial                   ! itrial denotes particle label
   LET y(itrial) = ytrial
   LET pe = pe + de
END SUB
```

PROBLEM 16.18 Monte Carlo simulation of simple liquids and solids

a. Consider a simple model of an interacting many-particle system with the potential energy of interaction (16.33). Such a model is frequently termed "Lennard-Jonesium" to distinguish it from more realistic models of liquids. Modify **Program hard_disk** so that the mean energy, pressure, and pair correlation function of Lennard-Jonesium in two dimensions can be computed using the Metropolis algorithm. (Be sure to write a subroutine to compute the initial potential energy of interaction.) For simplicity compute the averages after every Monte Carlo step per particle. Use the dimensionless units $E^* = E/\epsilon$, $T^* = k_B T/\epsilon$, and $\rho^* = \rho/\sigma^2$. What is an appropriate definition of P^*? (Remember that $PV = Nk_B T$ for an ideal gas.)

b. Before we apply the Metropolis algorithm at $T^* \neq 0$, we wish to find E_0^*, the ground state energy per particle at $T^* = 0$. In order to do this calculation using your program developed in part (a), place comment characters (!) before statements which include the variable *beta*. Moves will be accepted only if the potential energy is decreased. Choose $N = 16$, $Lx = 4.5$, $Ly = 6.0*sqrt(3)/2$, and place the particles on a triangular lattice. Since these positions are close to the equilibrium configuration, it is not necessary to average E_0^* for more than ten Monte Carlo steps per particle.

c. Use the same initial conditions as in part (b) but take $T^* = 1.5$. Choose $dxmax = dymax = 0.15$, $nmcs \geq 100$, and $dr = 0.1$. Compute the mean energy per particle E^*. Repeat the simulation for $T^* = 2.5$ and $T^* = 3.5$. The harmonic theory of solids predicts that the total energy of a system is due to the $T = 0$ contribution plus a term due to the harmonic oscillation of the atoms. The contribution of this latter part should be proportional to the temperature. Compare your results for the temperature-dependence of E^* with this prediction.

d. Describe the qualitative nature of $g(r)$ for a Lennard-Jones solid. How does it compare with your hard disk results for $g(r)$? Use (16.29) to determine the mean pressure.

e. What is the corresponding temperature, energy, and pressure in cgs units for the above simulations for solid argon?

f. Decrease the density by multiplying Lx, Ly and all the particle coordinates by 1.5. Estimate the number of Monte Carlo steps per particle necessary for 10% accuracy for P^* and E^* for $T^* = 3.5$. Compare P^* and E^* to their ideal gas values. Is the total energy positive or negative? Follow the method discussed in Problem 16.17 and compute an effective diffusion constant. Is the system a liquid or a solid? Plot $g(r)$ versus r/σ and compare $g(r)$ to your results for hard disks at the same density. The simulation of a larger system allows us to compute $g(r)$ for larger r. If time permits, consider $N = 36$ and compute $g(r)$ at the same density and temperature. What is the qualitative behavior of $g(r)$? What is the interpretation of the peaks in $g(r)$ in terms of the structure of the liquid?

g. Compute the mean energy, pressure, and $g(r)$ for $Lx = 10$, $Ly = 10$, $dr = 0.1$, $dxmax = dymax = 1.0$, $nmcs \geq 100$, and $T^* = 3.0$. These conditions correspond to a dilute gas. How do your results for the pressure compare with the ideal gas result? How does $g(r)$ compare with the results you obtained for the liquid?

*PROBLEM 16.19 The inverse power law potential

Consider the inverse power law potential

$$V(r) = V_0(\sigma/r)^n \quad . \tag{16.34}$$

The hard-sphere system is a special case of (16.34) with $n \to \infty$. What phases do you expect to occur for arbitrary n? Compare the qualitative features of $g(r)$ for a "soft" potential such as $n = 4$ to the hard disk case at the same density.

16.8   OTHER APPLICATIONS

You probably do not need to be convinced that Monte Carlo methods are powerful, flexible, and applicable to a wide variety of systems. Extensions to the Monte Carlo methods which we have not discussed include multiparticle moves, biased moves where particles tend to move in the direction of the force on them, manipulation of bits for Ising-like models, use of special processors for specific systems, and the use of array processors to allow different parts of a large system to be updated simultaneously.

Another application which we have not described is the simulation of systems with long-range potentials such as Coulombic systems. For these potentials, it is necessary to devise methods to include the interactions of the particles in the center cell with the infinite set of periodic images. One of the more recent exciting applications of Monte Carlo methods has been the analysis of the behavior of lattice gauge theories, theories which hold much promise for understanding the fundamental interactions of matter.

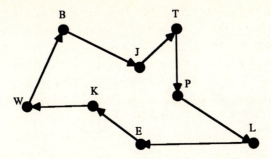

Fig. 16.6 What is the optimum route for this random arrangement of
$N = 8$ cities? The route begins and ends at city **W**. A possible route
is shown.

We conclude this chapter with a discussion of Monte Carlo methods in a context
which might appear to have little in common with the types of problems we
have discussed. This context is called *multivariate* or *combinatorial optimization*,
a fancy way of saying, "How do you find the minimum of a function which
depends on many parameters?" We explain the nature of this type of problem
by an example known as the *traveling salesman problem*, which we rename as
the *peddler problem.*

The peddler problem can be stated as follows. Suppose a peddler wishes to
visit N cities and follow a route such that no city is visited more than once, the
end of the trip coincides with the beginning, and the total distance traveled is a
minimum. What is the optimum route? An example of N cities and a possible
route is shown in Fig. 16.6. Problems of this type arise in all areas of scheduling
and design. All known exact methods for determining the optimal route require
a computing time which increases as e^N. Hence in practice, an exact solution can
be found only for problems involving a few hundred cities or less. The peddler
problem belongs to a large class of problems known as NP-complete, a term you
can use to impress your friends. Use pencil and paper to find the optimum route
for a random arrangement of eight cities. What is a reasonable estimate for the
limit on the number of cities you can consider without the use of a computer?

In order to understand the nature of the different approaches to the peddler problem, consider the plot in Fig. 16.7 of the "energy" function $E(a)$. We
can associate $E(a)$ with the length of the route and interpret a as a parameter which represents the order in which the cities are visited. In general $E(a)$

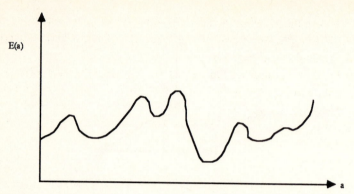

Fig. 16.7 Plot of the function $E(a)$ as a function of the parameter a.

has several local minima and an absolute minimum. What is a good strategy for finding the absolute minimum of $E(a)$? One way is by exact enumeration. That is, vary a and find the value of E everywhere. This method would correspond to determining the length of the route of the peddler for each possible route, clearly an impossible task if the number of cities is large. Hence we must use a *heuristic method,* i.e. an approximate method for finding a route which is close to the absolute minimum. One strategy is to choose a value of a, generate a small random change δa, and accept this change if $E(a + \delta a)$ is less than or equal to $E(a)$. This iterative improvement strategy corresponds to a search for steps which lead downhill. Since this search usually becomes stuck in a local and not a global minimum, it is customary to begin from several initial choices of a and to keep the best result. What would be the application of this type of strategy to the peddler problem?

Now let us consider a seemingly unrelated problem. Suppose we wish to make a perfect single crystal. You probably know that we should first melt the substance, and then lower the temperature very slowly to the desired low temperature. If we lower the temperature too quickly (a rapid "quench"), the resulting crystal will have many defects or not become a crystal at all. The gradual lowering of the temperature is known as *annealing.*

How can we apply the method of annealing to the problem of finding the minimum of $E(a)$? Let us choose a value of a, generate a small random change δa, and calculate $E(a + \delta a)$. If $E(a + \delta a)$ is less than or equal to $E(a)$, we accept the change as before. However if $\Delta E = E(a + \delta a) - E(a) > 0$, we accept the change with a probability $P = e^{-\Delta E / k_B T}$, where T is an effective temperature. This procedure is the familiar Metropolis algorithm with the temperature having the role of a control parameter. The *simulated annealing* process consists of first "melting" the system, and then gradually lowering the temperature. At each temperature, the simulation should last long enough for the system to reach a steady state. The annealing schedule, i.e. the rate of temperature decrease, determines the quality of the solution.

The strategy of the simulated annealing method is clear—sometimes it is necessary to climb a hill to reach a valley. The first application of the method of simulated annealing was to the optimal design of computers. Perhaps you can think of other applications. In Problem 16.20 we apply this method to the peddler problem.

*PROBLEM 16.20 Simulated annealing and the peddler problem

Generate a random arrangement of eight cities in a square of length $10^{1/2}$ and do a hand calculation to find the optimum route. Then write a program which applies the method of simulated annealing to this problem. For example, use an array to store the coordinates of each city and an array to store the distances between them. The state of the system, i.e. the route represented by a sequence of cities, can be stored in another array. The length of this route is associated with the energy of an imaginary thermal system. What is a reasonable criterion for the initial temperature of the system? How can we generate random rearrangements of the route? One method is to choose two cities at random and to interchange the order of visit. Choose this method or one that you devise and find a reasonable annealing schedule. Compare your annealing results to exact results whenever possible. Extend your results to larger N, e.g. $N = 12$ and 24 and 48. For a given annealing schedule, determine the probability of finding a route of a given length.

REFERENCES AND SUGGESTIONS FOR ADDITIONAL READING

K. Binder, ed. *Monte Carlo Methods in Statistical Physics*, second edition, Springer-Verlag (1986). Also see K. Binder, ed. *Applications of the Monte Carlo Method in Statistical Physics*, Springer-Verlag (1984).

Marvin Bishop and C. Bruin, "The pair correlation function: a probe of molecular order," *Am. J. Phys.* **52**, 1106 (1984). The authors compute the pair correlation function for a two-dimensional Lennard-Jones model.

J. Kertsz, J. Cserti and J. Szp, "Monte Carlo simulation programs for micro-computer," *Eur. J. Phys.* **6**, 232 (1985).

Charles Kittel, *Introduction to Solid State Physics*, 6th ed., John Wiley & Sons (1986). A discussion of ferromagnetism and antiferromagnetism is found in Chapter 16 of this classic text.

S. Kirkpatrick, C. D. Gelatt, M. P. Vecchi, "Optimization by simulated annealing," *Science* **220**, 671 (1983). See also S. Kirkpatrick and G. Toulouse,
"Configuration space analysis of traveling salesman problems," *J. Physique* **46**,
1277 (1985).

D. P. Landau, "Finite-size behavior of the Ising square lattice," *Phys. Rev.*
B13, 2997 (1976). A clearly written paper on a finite-size scaling analysis of
Monte Carlo data. See also D. P. Landau, "Finite-size behavior of the simple-
cubic Ising lattice," *Phys. Rev.* **B14**, 255 (1976).

D. P. Landau and R. Alben, "Monte Carlo calculations as an aid in teaching
statistical mechanics," *Am. J. Phys.* **41**, 394 (1973).

N. Metropolis, A. W. Rosenbluth, M. N. Rosenbluth, A. H. Teller, and E.
Keller, "Equation of state calculations for fast computing machines," *J. Chem.
Phys.* **6**, 1087 (1953).

J. Marro and R. Toral, "Microscopic observations on a kinetic Ising model,"
Am. J. Phys. **54**, 1114 (1986).

Ole G. Mouritsen, *Computer Studies of Phase Transitions and Critical Phenomena*, Springer-Verlag (1984).

H. Eugene Stanley, *Introduction to Phase Transitions and Critical Phenomena*, Oxford University Press (1971). See Appendix B for a clear discussion of
the exact solution of the zero-field Ising model for a two-dimensional lattice.

J. P. Valleau and S. G. Whittington, "A guide to Monte Carlo for statistical
mechanics: 1. Highways," in *Statistical Mechanics, Part A*, Bruce J. Berne, ed.,
Plenum Press (1977). See also J. P. Valleau and G. M. Torrie, "A guide to Monte
Carlo for statistical mechanics: 2. Byways," *ibid.*

APPENDIX 16A FLUCTUATIONS IN THE CANONICAL ENSEM-BLE

We first obtain the relation of the constant volume heat capacity to the energy
fluctuations in the canonical ensemble. For simplicity we adopt the notation
$U = <E>$. From the definition (16.14a) of the heat capacity we have

$$C = \frac{\partial U}{\partial T} = -\frac{1}{k_B T^2}\frac{\partial U}{\partial \beta} \quad . \tag{16.35}$$

From (16.3) we have

$$U = -\frac{\partial}{\partial \beta}\ln Z \tag{16.36}$$

and

$$\frac{\partial U}{\partial \beta} = -\frac{1}{Z^2}\frac{\partial Z}{\partial \beta}\sum_s E_s\, e^{-\beta E_s} - \frac{1}{Z}\sum_s E_s^2\, e^{-\beta E_s}$$

$$= <E>^2 - <E^2> \quad . \tag{16.37}$$

The relation (16.14b) follows from (16.35) and (16.37). Note that the heat capacity is at constant volume since the partial derivatives were performed with the energy levels E_s kept constant.

The relation of the magnetic susceptibility to the fluctuations of the magnetization can be obtained in a similar way. We assume that the energy can be written as

$$E_s = E_{0,s} - H M_s \tag{16.38}$$

where $E_{0,s}$ is the energy in the absence of a magnetic field, H is the external applied field, and M_s is the magnetization in the s state. The mean magnetization is given by

$$<M>' = \frac{1}{Z}\sum M_s\, e^{-\beta E_s} \quad . \tag{16.39}$$

Since $\partial E_s/\partial H = -M_s$, we have

$$\frac{\partial Z}{\partial H} = \sum_s \beta M_s\, e^{-\beta E_s} \quad . \tag{16.40}$$

Hence we obtain

$$<M> = \frac{1}{\beta}\frac{\partial}{\partial H} \ln Z \quad . \tag{16.41}$$

If we use (16.39) and (16.41), we find

$$\frac{\partial <M>}{\partial H} = -\frac{1}{Z^2}\frac{\partial Z}{\partial H}\sum_s M_s\, e^{-\beta E_s} + \frac{1}{Z}\sum_s \beta M_s^2\, e^{-\beta E_s}$$

$$= -\beta <M>^2 + \beta <M^2> \quad . \tag{16.42}$$

The relation (16.15b) for the zero-field susceptibility follows from (16.42) and the definition

$$\chi = \lim_{H \to 0}\frac{\partial <M>}{\partial H} \quad . \tag{16.43}$$

APPENDIX 16B EXACT ENUMERATION OF THE ISING MODEL ON A 2×2 LATTICE

Since the number of possible states or configurations of the Ising model increases as 2^N, we can only enumerate the possible configurations for small N. As an

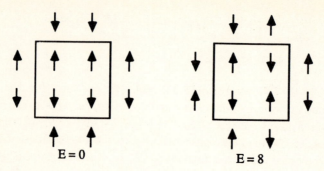

Fig. 16.8 Examples of Ising configurations on a 2 × 2 square lattice. Note the use of periodic boundary conditions.

TABLE 16.1 The energy and magnetization of the 2^4 states of the zero-field Ising model on the 2×2 square lattice.

No. spins up	Degeneracy	Energy	Magnetization
4	1	-8	4
3	4	0	2
2	4	0	0
2	2	8	0
1	4	0	-2
0	1	-8	-4

example, we calculate the various quantities of interest for a 2 × 2 Ising model on the square lattice. Two different configurations with 2 spins up are shown in Fig. 16.8. In Table 16.1 we group the states according to their total energy and magnetization. We can now compute all the quantities of interest using Table 16.1. The partition function is given by

$$Z = 2e^{8\beta J} + 12 + 2e^{-8\beta J} \tag{16.44}$$

If we use (16.36) and (16.44), we find

$$U = -\frac{1}{Z}[2(8)e^{8\beta J} + 2(-8)e^{-8\beta J}] \tag{16.45}$$

Since the other quantities of interest can be found in a similar manner, we only give the results:

$$<E^2> = \frac{1}{Z}[2(64)e^{8\beta J} + 2(64)e^{-8\beta J}] \tag{16.46}$$

$$<M> = \frac{1}{Z}(0) = 0 \tag{16.47}$$

$$<|M|> = \frac{1}{Z}[2(4)e^{8\beta J} + 8(2)] \tag{16.48}$$

$$<M^2> = \frac{1}{Z}[2(16)e^{8\beta J} + 8(4)] \tag{16.49}$$

The dependence of C and χ on βJ can be found by using (16.45) and (16.46) and (16.47) and (16.49) respectively.

QUANTUM SYSTEMS

17

We study numerical solutions of the time-independent Schrödinger equation using the Euler-Cromer algorithm. The motion of wave packets is generated using the stationary state solutions and the superposition principle. We then describe a random walk approach to the time-independent Schrödinger equation and a Monte Carlo variational calculation of the ground state properties.

17.1 INTRODUCTION

Thus far we have simulated the behavior of physical systems using both Monte Carlo methods and molecular dynamics. In the latter method, the classical trajectory (position and momentum) of each particle is calculated as a function of time. However, in quantum systems it is impossible to use molecular dynamics methods, since the position and momentum of a particle cannot be specified simultaneously. Since a fundamental description of nature is intrinsically quantum mechanical, we have a problem—we cannot ultimately simulate nature on a computer!

Of course quantum mechanics does allow us to *analyze* the probabilities. In order to understand the difficulties associated with such an analysis, let us first consider a simple probabilistic system described by the one-dimensional diffusion equation (see Chapter 11)

$$\frac{\partial P(x,t)}{\partial t} = D\,\frac{\partial^2 P(x,t)}{\partial x^2} \tag{17.1}$$

where $P(x,t)$ is the probability density of a particle being at position x at time t. One way to compute $P(x,t)$ is to make x and t discrete variables. Suppose we choose a mesh size for x such that the probability is given at m values of x. If we choose m to be order 10^3, then we see that a straightforward calculation of $P(x,t)$ requires approximately 10^3 data points for each value of t. In contrast, the corresponding molecular dynamics calculation using Newton's second law would require one data point.

The difficulty of the direct computational approach becomes even more apparent if we have many degrees of freedom. For example with N particles in one dimension, we have to calculate the probability $P(x_1, x_2, \ldots, x_N, t)$, where x_i is the coordinate of particle i. Since we need to choose a mesh of m-points for each x_i, we need to specify N^m configurations at each time t. Usually we choose m to be of the same order as N, since the probability at each point in space represents useful information. Hence we would need to compute on the order of N^N configurations to obtain the desired probability at each time interval. Consequently a doubling of the size of the system, $N \to 2N$, would lead to an exponential growth in the calculation time and in the memory requirements.

Although the direct computational approach is limited to systems with a few degrees of freedom, the simplicity of this approach will aid our understanding of the behavior of one-dimensional quantum systems. After a summary of the general features of quantum mechanical systems in Sec. 17.2, we consider this approach to the time-independent Schrödinger equation in Sec. 17.3. In Sec.

17.4, we use the stationary state solutions and the principle of superposition to generate wave packet solutions to the time-dependent Schrödinger equation.

Are there other ways of approaching probabilistic systems? Since we have already learned that (17.1) can be formulated as a random walk problem, it might not surprise you that Schrödinger's equation can be analyzed in a similar way. We introduce quantum Monte Carlo methods in Sec. 17.5. Monte Carlo methods are also used in Sec. 17.6 to obtain variational solutions of the ground state.

17.2 REVIEW OF QUANTUM THEORY

For simplicity we consider one-dimensional, non-relativistic quantum systems consisting of one particle. The state of the system is completely characterized by a *wave function* $\Psi(x, t)$, which is interpreted as a *probability amplitude*. Since the possible positions of the particle can vary continuously, the probability $P(x, t)dx$ of the particle being in a "volume" element dx centered about the position x at time t is equal to

$$P(x, t)\, dx = C|\Psi(x, t)|^2 dx \tag{17.2}$$

where C is a normalization constant. This probabilistic interpretation of $\Psi(x, t)$ implies that it is convenient to use normalized wave functions such that

$$\int_{-\infty}^{\infty} dx\ \Psi^*(x, t)\Psi(x, t) = 1 \tag{17.3}$$

where $\Psi^*(x, t)$ is the complex conjugate of $\Psi(x, t)$. The constant C in (17.2) is then equal to 1.

If the particle is subject to the influence of a potential $V(x, t)$, the time evolution of $\Psi(x, t)$ is given by the time-dependent Schrödinger equation

$$i\hbar \frac{\partial \Psi(x, t)}{\partial t} = -\frac{\hbar^2}{2m} \frac{\partial^2 \Psi(x, t)}{\partial x^2} + V(x, t)\Psi(x, t) \tag{17.4}$$

where m is the mass of the particle and $\hbar$ is Plank's constant divided by 2π.

Physical quantities such as the momentum can be represented as operators. The expectation or average value of an observable A is given by

$$<A> = \int dx\ \Psi^*(x, t)A_{op}\Psi(x, t) \tag{17.5}$$

where A_{op} is the operator corresponding to the quantity A. For example, the momentum operator corresponding to the linear momentum p is $p_{op} = -i\hbar\partial/\partial x$.

If the potential is independent of time, we can obtain solutions of (17.4) of the form

$$\Psi(x, t) = \phi(x)e^{-iEt/\hbar} \quad . \tag{17.6}$$

A particle in the state (17.6) has a well-defined energy E. If we substitute (17.6) into (17.3), we obtain the time-independent Schrödinger equation

$$-\frac{\hbar^2}{2m}\frac{d^2\phi(x)}{dx^2} + V(x)\phi(x) = E_n\phi(x) \quad . \tag{17.7}$$

Note that $\phi(x)$ is an *eigenfunction* of the Hamiltonian operator

$$H_{op} = -\frac{\hbar^2}{2m}\frac{\partial^2}{\partial x^2} + V(x) \tag{17.8}$$

with the *eigenvalue* E. That is

$$H_{op}\,\phi(x) = E\,\phi(x) \quad . \tag{17.9}$$

In order to distinguish between the various possible values of the energy E, we label the states ϕ with an index n.

The general form of $\Psi(x, t)$ can be expressed as a superposition of the eigenfunctions of the operator corresponding to any physical observable. For example if H is independent of time, we can write

$$\Psi(x, t) = \sum_n c_n\phi_n(x)e^{-iE_nt/\hbar} \tag{17.10}$$

where ϕ_n is an eigenfunction of H and Σ represents a sum over the discrete states and an integral over the continuum states. The coefficients c_n in (17.10) can be determined from the value of $\Psi(x, t)$ at any time t. For example if we know $\Psi(x, t)$ at $t = 0$, we can use the orthonormality property of the eigenfunctions of any physical operator to obtain

$$c_n = \int dx\,\phi_n^*(x)\Psi(x, 0) \quad . \tag{17.11}$$

The coefficient c_n can be interpreted as the probability amplitude of a measurement of the total energy yielding the value E_n.

17.3   THE TIME-INDEPENDENT SCHRODINGER EQUATION

We consider bound-state solutions of the time-independent Schrödinger equation (17.7). Our main result will be that acceptable solutions to (17.7) exist only if the eigenvalues are quantized, i.e. restricted to a discrete set of energies. To be an acceptable solution, $\phi_n(x)$ must be finite for all x and bounded for large $|x|$ so that $\phi_n(x)$ can be normalized. For finite $V(x)$, $\phi_n(x)$ and $\phi_n' = d\phi_n(x)/dx$ are required to be continuous, finite, and single-valued for all x.

Since the time-independent Schrödinger equation is a second-order differential equation, two boundary conditions must be specified in general to uniquely specify the solution. In order to simplify the analysis, we consider symmetric potentials which satisfy the condition

$$V(x) = V(-x) \quad . \tag{17.12}$$

The condition (17.12) implies that $\phi(x)$ can be chosen to have definite parity. For even parity solutions, $\phi(-x) = \phi(x)$; odd parity solutions satisfy $\phi(-x) = -\phi(x)$. The definite parity of $\phi(x)$ allows us to specify either ϕ or ϕ' at $x = 0$.

In order to guide our choice of a suitable algorithm for the numerical solution of (17.7), recall that the solution of (17.7) with $V(x) = 0$ can be expressed as a linear combination of sine and cosine functions. The oscillatory nature of this solution leads us to expect that the Euler-Cromer algorithm introduced in Chapter 3 will yield satisfactory results for $V(x) \neq 0$. The implementation of the Euler-Cromer algorithm proceeds as follows:

1. Divide the range of x into N intervals of width Δx. Adopt the notation $x_r = r\Delta x$, $\phi_r = \phi(x_r)$, and $\phi_r' = \phi'(x_r)$.
2. Specify the parity of $\phi(x)$. For an even parity solution choose $\phi(0) = 1$ and $\phi' = 0$; for an odd parity solution choose $\phi(0) = 0$ and $\phi' = 1$. The non-zero value of $\phi(0)$ or ϕ' is arbitrary.
3. Guess a value for E.
4. Compute ϕ_{r+1}' and ϕ_{r+1} using the algorithm:

$$\phi_{r+1}' = \phi_r' + \phi_r''\Delta x \tag{17.13a}$$
$$\phi_{r+1} = \phi_r + \phi_{r+1}'\Delta x \quad . \tag{17.13b}$$

4. Iterate $\phi(x)$ toward increasing x until $\phi(x)$ diverges.
5. Change E and repeat steps (2) to (4). Bracket the value of E by changing E until ϕ diverges in one direction if E is made slightly smaller and diverges in the opposite direction if E is made slightly larger.

Program eigen implements this procedure for a square well potential given by

$$V(x) = \begin{cases} 0 & \text{for } |x| \leq a \\ V_0 & \text{for } |x| > a \end{cases} \tag{17.14}$$

The input parameters are V_0 and a, the parity of the eigenfunction, the assumed value of the energy E, the step size Δx, and $xmax$, the maximum value of x to be plotted.

```
PROGRAM eigen
CALL parameters(V0,a,xmax,dx)
CALL plot_potential(V0,a,xmax)
CALL Euler(V0,a,dx,xmax)
END

SUB parameters(V0,a,xmax,dx)
   INPUT prompt "well height = ": V0
   INPUT prompt "half width of well = ": a
   INPUT prompt "step size dx = ": dx
   INPUT prompt "maximum value of x to be plotted = ": xmax
END SUB

SUB plot_potential(V0,a,xmax)
   SET window -xmax,xmax,-10,10
   PLOT LINES: -xmax,-6; -a,-6; -a,-9; a,-9; a,-6; xmax,-6
END SUB

SUB Euler(V0,a,dx,xmax)
   DECLARE DEF V
   INPUT prompt "even or odd parity (1 or -1) ": parity
   DO
      INPUT prompt "E = ": E
      IF E = 0 then EXIT SUB
      IF parity = -1 then
         LET phi = 0                    ! initial values at x = 0
         LET dphi = 1
```

```
        ELSE
          LET phi = 1
          LET dphi = 0
        END IF
        LET x = 0
        DO                           ! compute wave function
          LET x = x + dx
          LET d2phi = 2*(V(x,V0,a) - E)*phi      ! dimensionless units
          LET dphi = dphi + d2phi*dx
          LET phi = phi + dphi*dx
          PLOT POINTS: x,phi; -x,phi*parity      ! plot wave function
        LOOP until x > xmax or abs(phi) > 10
      LOOP
    END SUB

    DEF V(x,V0,a)                    ! potential function V(x)
      IF abs(x) > a then
        LET V = V0
      ELSE
        LET V = 0
      END IF
    END DEF
```

PROBLEM 17.1 The infinite square well

a. Consider the infinite square well or the "particle in a box problem" with $V(x)$ given by (17.14) with $V_0 \to \infty$. Show analytically that the energy eigenvalues are given by $E_n = n^2\pi^2\hbar^2/8ma^2$, where n is a positive integer. Also show that the normalized eigenfunctions have the form

$$\phi_n(x) = \frac{1}{\sqrt{a}} \cos \frac{n\pi x}{a} \qquad (even\,parity, n = 1, 3, \ldots) \qquad (17.15a)$$

$$\phi_n(x) = \frac{1}{\sqrt{a}} \sin \frac{n\pi x}{a} \qquad (odd\,parity, n = 2, 4, \ldots) \quad . \qquad (17.15b)$$

What is the parity of the ground state solution? Why does the ground state wave function have no nodes?

b. Choose $a = 1$ and $V_0 = 150$ and use **Program eigen** to find the ground state energy E_1 of a particle in an infinite square well. We will choose units in all the problems such that $m = \hbar = 1$. Choose $\Delta x = 0.01$ and $xmax = 5$;

the number of intervals N is given by $N = xmax/dx$. Try the initial guesses $E = 1.5$ and $E = 1.0$. How do you know that the ground state energy is between these two values of E? How many guesses do you need to obtain E_1 to two decimal places?

c. Is your numerical result for E_1 affected by your choice of Δx? Determine a value of Δx which yields E_1 to three decimal places. Is V_0 sufficiently large that your value for E_1 approximates that of an infinite square well? Does your result for E_1 depend on the magnitude of ϕ at $x = 0$?

d. Write a program to normalize ϕ. What is the value of ϕ at $x = 0$? Compare your numerical result for the ground state eigenfunction with the analytical solution.

e. If we count the number of nodes (zeros) of ϕ, we can find the excited state eigenfunctions and eigenvalues in a way similar to that used for the ground state. For example, the first excited state corresponds to one node and quantum number $n = 2$. Modify **Program eigen** so that it computes the number of nodes and find the first two excited states of the infinite square well.

f. Suppose you wish to find the eigenvalue corresponding to the tenth excited state of the particle in a box problem. Can you use the same value of V_0 that was used in part (b)?

Note that it is not possible to obtain a numerical solution for ϕ that does not diverge at sufficiently large x. That is, since we can compute ϕ only to finite accuracy, the computed ϕ will always diverge if a sufficiently large number of iterations are performed. However we can always calculate ϕ to the desired accuracy by choosing an appropriate algorithm and a sufficiently small step size.

PROBLEM 17.2 The effect of a small perturbation on the ground state of an infinite square well

a. Determine the effect of a small perturbation on the eigenstates and eigenvalues of the infinite square well. Place a small rectangular bump of half-width b and height V_b symmetrically about $x = 0$ (see Fig. 17.1). Choose $V_b \ll V_0$ and $b \ll a$ and determine how the ground state energy and eigenfunction change with V_b and b. What is the relative change in E_1 for $V_b = 10$, $b = 0.1$ and $V_b = 20$, $b = 0.1$? (Set $V_0 = 150$ and $a = 1$.) Let ϕ_b denote the

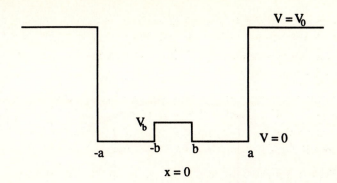

Fig. 17.1 A square well with a potential bump of height V_b in the middle.

ground state eigenfunction for $b \neq 0$ and ϕ_0 denote the ground state function for $b = 0$. What is the relative change of the product

$$\int_0^a dx \, \phi_b(x)\phi_0(x) \quad . \tag{17.16}$$

How does this change compare to the relative change in the energy?

b. Compute the ground state energy for $V_b = 20$ and $b = 0.05$. How does the value of E_1 compare to that found in part (a) for $V_b = 10$ and $b = 0.1$?

PROBLEM 17.3 Finite square well

a. Consider a finite square well with $V_0 = 10$ and $a = 1$. Compute the ground state eigenvalue and eigenfunction by determining a value of E such that $\phi(x)$ has no nodes and is approximately zero for large x. In Fig. 17.2 we show the x-dependence of ϕ for two different choices of E. Note that ϕ diverges to $+\infty$ for $E = 0.77$ and diverges to $-\infty$ for $E = 0.87$.

b. Since the well depth at $x = |a|$ is finite, ϕ is nonzero in the classically forbidden region for which $E < V_0$ and $x > |a|$. Define the "penetration distance" as the distance from $x = a$ to a point where ϕ is $\sim 1/e \approx 0.37$ of its maximum value. Determine the qualitative dependence of the penetration distance on the magnitude of V_0.

c. Compute the excited eigenstates and eigenvalues. What is the total number of excited states? Why is the total number of bound states finite?

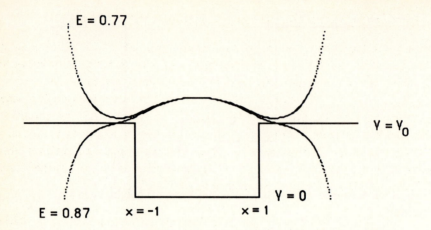

Fig. 17.2 Two numerical solutions of the time-independent Schrödinger equation for the guesses $E = 0.77$ and $E = 0.87$. The system is a square well potential with $V_0 = 10$ and $a = 1$.

PROBLEM 17.4 Other one-dimensional potentials

a. Obtain numerical solutions for the first several eigenvalues and eigenfunctions of the harmonic oscillator with $V(x) = \frac{1}{2}x^2$. What value of Δx is needed for 0.1% accuracy for the ground state energy?

b. Obtain a numerical solution of the anharmonic oscillator with $V(x) = \frac{1}{2}x^2 + bx^4$. In this case there are no analytical solutions and numerical solutions are of much interest. Compute the ground state energy for $b = 0.1, 0.2$, and 0.5. How does the ground state energy depend on b for small b? How does the ground state eigenfunction depend on b?

c. Obtain a numerical solution for the ground state of the linear potential:

$$V(x) = |x| \quad . \tag{17.17}$$

The quantum mechanical treatment of this potential can be used to study the energy spectrum of a bound quark-antiquark system known as quarkonium.

17.4   THE TIME-DEPENDENT SCHRODINGER EQUATION

Although we found that the integration of the "ordinary" differential equation (17.7) could be done by using numerical methods, the numerical solution of the time-dependent Schrödinger equation (17.4) is not as straightforward.

The first step in the "naive" approach to the numerical solution of the time-dependent Schrödinger equation is to introduce a mesh for the time coordinate as well as for the spatial coordinate. We use the notation $t_n = t_0 + n\Delta t$, $x_r = x_0 + r\Delta x$, and $\Psi_r(n) \equiv \Psi(x_r, t_n)$. The problem is to develop an algorithm which relates $\Psi_r(n+1)$ to the value of $\Psi_r(n)$ for each value of x_r. An example of an algorithm which has first-order accuracy in time is given by

$$\frac{1}{\Delta t}[\Psi_r(n+1) - \Psi_r(n)] = \frac{1}{(\Delta x)^2}\delta^2\Psi_r(n) \qquad (17.18)$$

where $\delta^2\Psi_r(n)$ represents a finite difference approximation to the second derivative of Ψ with respect to x:

$$\delta^2\Psi_r(n) = \Psi_{r+1}(n) - 2\Psi_r(n) + \Psi_{r-1}(n) \quad . \qquad (17.19)$$

Such an approach is an example of an *explicit* scheme since given Ψ at time t_n, we can calculate Ψ at time t_{n+1}. Unfortunately this explicit approach leads to unstable solutions, that is, the numerical value of Ψ diverges from the exact solution (cf Koonin).

One way to avoid this difficulty is to retain the same form as (17.18), but to evaluate the spatial derivative on the right-hand side of (17.18) at time t_{n+1} rather than time t_n:

$$\frac{1}{\Delta t}[\Psi_r(n+1) - \Psi_r(n)] = \frac{1}{(\Delta x)^2}\delta^2\Psi_r(n+1) \quad . \qquad (17.20)$$

Equation (17.20) is now an *implicit* method since the unknown function $\Psi_r(n+1)$ appears on both sides. In order to obtain $\Psi_r(n+1)$, it is necessary to solve a set of linear equations at each time step. More details of this approach and the demonstration that (17.20) leads to stable solutions can be found in the references.

In lieu of this direct numerical approach, we will assume that we already know the eigenfunctions and eigenvalues of the time-independent Schrödinger equation. Our approach will be to use these eigenfunctions and eigenvalues together with the principle of superposition to obtain the time-dependent behavior. The application of interest will be the motion of a wave packet in the vicinity of a potential.

We know that if $V(x)$ is independent of time, we can express an arbitrary solution of the time-dependent Schrödinger equation in the form (17.10) where the functions $\phi_n(x)$ are stationary state solutions of Schrödinger's equation with the potential $V(x)$. We first consider the motion of a free particle. In this case the eigenfunctions are characterized by the wave vector k and are proportional to e^{ikx} and e^{-ikx}. We wish to construct a wave packet corresponding to a particle localized about $x = x_0$ with a mean momentum $\hbar k_0$ to the right. One way to construct such a wave packet is to sum a linear combination of plane waves with the weighting function

$$c_k = Ne^{-i(k-k_0)x_0}e^{-\alpha(k-k_0)^2} \quad . \tag{17.21}$$

The quantity N is a normalization constant. The reasons for this form of c_k and the interpretation of α will be discussed in Problem 17.5. Since we can include only a finite number of plane waves n_k, the approximate form of the wave packet at $t = 0$ is given by

$$\Psi(x, 0) \approx \sum_k c_k e^{ikx} \tag{17.22}$$

where the sum is over $k_n = k_0 + n\Delta k$ with $-n_k/2 \leq n \leq n_k/2$. Since the eigenvalues of the free-particle Hamiltonian are given by $E_k = \hbar^2 k^2/2m$, the time-evolution of $\Psi(x, t)$ is given by the approximate relation

$$\Psi(x, t) \approx \sum_k c_k e^{i(kx - k^2 t/2)} \quad . \tag{17.23}$$

In **Program wavepacket** we use (17.21) and (17.23) to observe a wave packet evolve in time in the absence of a potential. Because of the presence of complex numbers, it is necessary in True BASIC to treat the real and imaginary parts of c_k and Ψ separately and to use the relation

$$e^{ikx} = \cos kx + i \sin kx \quad . \tag{17.24}$$

The input parameters in **Program wavepacket** include $x0$, the value of the center of the wave packet at $t = 0$, $delta\_x$, the initial width of the packet in coordinate space, $k0$, the mean momentum of the wave packet, and n_k, the number of k vectors which are included in the sum in (17.23). For a given value of t, the values of $\Psi(x, t)$ are computed at $x_r = x_0 + rdx$, where dx is an input parameter and $-\frac{1}{2}n_x < r < \frac{1}{2}n_x$. The program draws the values of $|\Psi(x, t)|^2$ at intervals of dt for times between $t = 0$ and $t = tmax$ and for values of x between $xmin$ and $xmax$.

```
PROGRAM wavepacket
! compute motion of Gaussian wave packet
DIM Re_c(-50 to 50),Im_c(-50 to 50),prob(-50 to 50)
DIM Re_phi(-50 to 50,-50 to 50)
DIM Im_phi(-50 to 50,-50 to 50)
CALL parameters(k0,delta_x,x0,xmin,dx,dk,dt,tmax,n_k,n_x)
CALL packet(delta_x,x0,n_k,dk,Re_c,Im_c)
CALL free(n_k,n_x,k0,dk,dx,Re_c,Im_c,Re_phi,Im_phi)
DO
   LET t = t + dt
   CALL move(t,n_k,n_x,k0,dk,dx,Re_phi,Im_phi,prob)
   CALL plot(prob,xmin,n_x,dx)
LOOP until t > tmax
END

SUB parameters(k0,delta_x,x0,xmin,dx,dk,dt,tmax,n_k,n_x)
   INPUT prompt "minimum value of x = ": xmin
   INPUT prompt "maximum value of x = ": xmax
   INPUT prompt "initial position of packet = ": x0
   INPUT prompt "width of wave packet in x space = ": delta_x
   INPUT prompt "step length = ": dx      ! do not confuse with delta_x
   LET n_x = (xmax - xmin)/dx              ! number of positions psi calculated
   INPUT prompt "central wave vector of packet = ": k0
   INPUT prompt "number of wave vectors = ": n_k
   LET dk = 2/(delta_x*n_k)
   LET n_k = n_k/2
   LET n_x = n_x/2
   INPUT prompt "time interval = ": dt
   INPUT prompt "total time = ": tmax
   LET ymax = 0.5
   SET window xmin,xmax,-0.1,ymax
END SUB
```

```
SUB packet(delta_x,x0,n_k,dk,Re_c(),Im_c())
    ! compute coefficients c(k)
    LET sum = 0                         ! used to normalize c(k)
    FOR ik = -n_k to n_k
        LET delta_k = ik*dk             ! difference between k and k0
        LET c = exp(-delta_k*delta_k*delta_x*delta_x/4)
        ! phase due to starting at x0 not equal to 0
        LET Re_c(ik) = c*cos(-delta_k*x0)
        LET Im_c(ik) = c*sin(-delta_k*x0)
        LET sum = sum + Im_c(ik)*Im_c(ik)
        LET sum = sum + Re_c(ik)*Re_c(ik)
    NEXT ik
    LET norm = dk*sqr(1/sum)
    FOR ik = -n_k to n_k
        LET Re_c(ik) = norm*Re_c(ik)
        LET Im_c(ik) = norm*Im_c(ik)
    NEXT ik
END SUB

SUB free(n_k,n_x,k0,dk,dx,Re_c(),Im_c(),Re_phi(,),Im_phi(,))
    ! compute a(k)exp(ikx)
    FOR ik = -n_k to n_k
        LET k = k0 +ik*dk
        FOR ix = -n_x to n_x
            LET arg = k*ix*dx
            LET fr = cos(arg)
            LET fi = sin(arg)
            LET Re_phi(ik,ix) = fr*Re_c(ik) - fi*Im_c(ik)
            LET Im_phi(ik,ix) = fr*Im_c(ik) + fi*Re_c(ik)
        NEXT ix
    NEXT ik
END SUB
```

```
SUB move(t,n_k,n_x,k0,dk,dx,Re_phi(,),Im_phi(,),prob())
    ! compute sum over k of psi(k,x)exp(-iEt) and calculate psi(x,t)
    FOR ix = -n_x to n_x
        LET Re_psi = 0
        LET Im_psi = 0
        FOR ik = -n_k to n_k
            LET k = k0 + ik*dk
            LET arg = -0.5*k*k*t
            LET fr = cos(arg)
            LET fi = sin(arg)
            ! compute real and imaginary parts of psi
            LET Re_psi = Re_psi + Re_phi(ik,ix)*fr
            LET Re_psi = Re_psi - Im_phi(ik,ix)*fi
            LET Im_psi = Im_psi + Re_phi(ik,ix)*fi
            LET Im_psi = Im_psi + Im_phi(ik,ix)*fr
        NEXT ik
        LET prob(ix) = Re_psi*Re_psi + Im_psi*Im_psi
    NEXT ix
END SUB

SUB plot(prob(),xmin,n_x,dx)
    CLEAR
    FOR i = -n_x to n_x                 ! draw probability
        LET x = i*dx
        PLOT x,prob(i);
    NEXT i
    PLOT
    LET xmax = x
    PLOT LINES: xmin,0;xmax,0
    FOR i = -n_x to n_x                 ! draw tick marks
        LET x = i*dx
        PLOT LINES: x,0; x,0.01
    NEXT i
END SUB
```

PROBLEM 17.5 Motion of a free wavepacket

a. What is the explicit form of c_k used in **Program wavepacket**? At what value of k is c_k a maximum? At what value of k is $|c_k|^2$ equal to $1/e$ of its maximum value? What is a reasonable criterion for the width of $|c_k|^2$? How does **Program wavepacket** determine the width of the wave packet in k-space? What is the basis of the relation $dk = 2/delta\_x * n\_k$ which is used in **Program wavepacket**? Note we have adopted units such that $\hbar = m = 1$.

b. Use **Program wavepacket** to follow the motion of a free particle in a potential free region. Choose $xmin = -10$, $xmax = 10$, $x_0 = -7$, $delta\_x = 1$, $dx = 0.5$, $k0 = 2$, $n\_k = 20$, $dt = 0.5$, and $tmax = 10$. What is the shape of the wave packet at different times? Does the shape of the wave packet depend on your choice of the parameters dx and n_k?

c. Modify **Program wavepacket** so that the quantities $x_0(t)$ and $\Delta x(t)$, the position and width of the wave packet as a function of time, can be measured directly. What is a reasonable definition of $\Delta x(t)$? (Choose a definition such that $\Delta x(t = 0) = delta\_x$.) What is the qualitative dependence of $x_0(t)$ and $\Delta x(t)$ on t? How are your results changed if the initial width of the packet is reduced by a factor of four?

Now let us follow the motion of a wave packet in the presence of a potential. It is necessary to change the eigenfunctions in (17.23) from e^{ikx} to the eigenfunctions of $H = p^2/2m + V(x)$. Let us consider the one-dimensional potential step at $x = 0$ given by

$$V(x) = \begin{cases} 0, & x \leq 0 \\ V_0, & x > 0 \end{cases} \quad . \tag{17.25}$$

The eigenfunctions for $E > V_0$ are

$$\phi(x) = \begin{cases} e^{ik_1x} + Be^{-ik_1x}, & x \leq 0 \\ Se^{ik_2x}, & x > 0 \end{cases} \tag{17.26a}$$

where

$$k_1{}^2 = \frac{2mE}{\hbar^2}$$

$$k_2{}^2 = \frac{2m(E - V_0)}{\hbar^2}$$

$$B = \frac{k_1 - k_2}{k_1 + k_2}$$

$$S = \frac{2k_1}{(k_1 + k_2)} \quad . \tag{17.26b}$$

If $E < V_0$, the solution is the analytic continuation of (17.26) with $k_2 \to i\kappa$. The major change we need to make in **Program wavepacket** is to replace **SUB free** by **SUB step**. Note that in **SUB step**, the form of the eigenfunctions depends on the position and the energy of the wave packet relative to the barrier.

```
SUB step(n_k,n_x,k0,dk,dx,Re_c(),Im_c(),Re_phi(,),Im_phi(,))
   ! compute c(k)[exp(ik1x) + Bexp(-ik1x)] for x <= 0
   ! c(k) S exp(ik2x) for x > 0
   PRINT "barrier at x = 0"
   INPUT prompt "barrier height = ": V0
   FOR ik = -n_k to n_k
      LET k1 = k0 +ik*dk
      LET E = .5*k1*k1                        ! unit mass
      IF E > V0 then
         LET k2 = sqr(2*(E - V0))
         LET Re_B = (k1 - k2)/(k1 + k2)
         LET Im_B = 0
         LET Re_S = 2*k1/(k1 + k2)
         LET Im_S = 0
      ELSE
         LET k2 = sqr(2*(V0 - E))
         LET denom = k1*k1 + k2*k2
         LET Re_B = (k1*k1 - k2*k2)/denom
         LET Im_B = 2*k1*k2/denom
         LET Re_S = 2*k1*k1/denom
         LET Im_S = -2*k1*k2/denom
      END IF
      ! compute psi(k,x t = 0)
      FOR ix = -n_x to 0
         LET arg = k1*ix*dx
         LET cs = cos(arg)
         LET si = sin(arg)
         ! use sin(-kx) = -sin(kx) and cos(-kx) = cos(kx)
         LET Re_g = cs + Re_B*cs + Im_B*si
         LET Im_g = si + Im_B*cs - Re_B*si
         LET Re_phi(ik,ix) = Re_g*Re_c(ik) - Im_g*Im_c(ik)
         LET Im_phi(ik,ix) = Re_g*Im_c(ik) + Im_g*Re_c(ik)
      NEXT ix
```

```
    FOR ix = 1 to n_x
        LET arg = k2*ix*dx
        IF E > V0 then                  ! oscillatory wave function
            LET cs = cos(arg)
            LET si = sin(arg)
        ELSE
            LET cs = exp(-arg)          ! decaying exponential
            LET si = 0
        END IF
        LET Re_g = Re_S*cs - Im_S*si
        LET Im_g = Im_S*cs + Re_S*si
        LET Re_phi(ik,ix) = Re_g*Re_c(ik)-Im_g*Im_c(ik)
        LET Im_phi(ik,ix) = Re_g*Im_c(ik)+Im_g*Re_c(ik)
    NEXT ix
  NEXT ik
END SUB
```

PROBLEM 17.6 Motion of a wave packet incident on a potential step

a. Use **Program wavepacket** with **SUB free** replaced by **SUB step** to compute the motion of a wave packet incident on a potential step at $x = 0$. Choose $xmin = -10$, $xmax = 10$, $x0 = -7$, $delta\_x = 1$, $dx = 0.5$, $k0 = 2$, $n\_k = 20$, $dt = 0.5$, $tmax = 10$, and step height $V0 = 2$. Give a qualitative description of the motion of the wave packet. Does the shape of the wave packet remain a Gaussian for all t? Measure the height and width of the reflected and transmitted wave packets. Determine the time t_i for the incident wave to hit the barrier at $x = 0$. Does the particle break up into pieces at $x = 0$? Determine the time t_r for the reflected wave to return to $x = -x_0$. Is $t_r = t_i$? If these times are not equal, explain the cause of the difference.

b. Repeat the above analysis for $V_0 = 10$. Is $t_r \approx t_i$ in this case?

c. What is the motion of a classical particle with a kinetic energy corresponding to the central wave vector $k = k_0$?

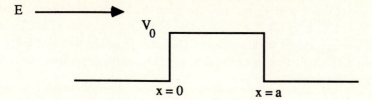

Fig. 17.3 A potential barrier of height V_0 between $x = 0$ and $x = a$.

PROBLEM 17.7 Scattering of a wave packet from a potential barrier

a. Consider a potential barrier of the form (see Fig. 17.3)

$$V(x) = \begin{cases} 0, & x < 0 \\ V_0, & 0 \le x \le a \\ 0, & x > a \end{cases} \qquad (17.27)$$

The eigenfunctions for $E < V_0$ have the form (for a particle incident from the left)

$$\phi(x) = \begin{cases} e^{ikx} + Be^{-ikx}, & x < 0 \\ Ce^{-\kappa x} + De^{\kappa x}, & 0 \le x \le a \\ Ee^{ikx}, & x > a \end{cases} \qquad (17.28a)$$

where

$$k^2 = \frac{2mE}{\hbar^2}$$

$$\kappa^2 = \frac{2m(V_0 - E)}{\hbar^2}$$

$$B = \frac{i(k^2 + \kappa^2)\sinh \kappa a}{\Delta}$$

$$C = \frac{k(ik + \kappa)e^{-\kappa a}}{\Delta}$$

$$D = \frac{-k(ik - \kappa)e^{\kappa a}}{\Delta}$$

$$E = \frac{2k\kappa e^{-ika}}{\Delta}$$

$$\Delta = 2k\kappa \cosh \kappa a - i(k^2 - \kappa^2)\sinh \kappa a \qquad (17.28b)$$

Use these eigenfunctions to make the appropriate modifications in **SUB** step. Generate a series of "snapshots" which show the packet approaching the barrier and then interacting with it to generate reflected and transmitted packets. Set $a = 1$ and $V_0 = 2$ and consider the behavior of the wave packet for $k_0 = 1$, 1.5, 2, and 3. For what values of k_0 is the motion of the packet in qualitative agreement with a classical particle? Does the width of the packet increase with time? How does the change of the width depend on the incident energy of the packet?

b. Consider a square well with $V_0 = -2$ and consider the same questions as in part (a).

PROBLEM 17.8 Motion of a wave packet inside an infinite well

a. Consider the motion of a wave packet which is restricted to be within an infinite well of width $2a$. Construct a wave packet using the first ten eigenfunctions of the infinite well. Locate the center of the wave packet at $x = 0$, choose the form of c_k to be a Gaussian, and set the width of $|c_k|^2$ equal to a. Include both positive and negative wave vectors in the sum. Note that the values of k are not continuous, but must equal $n\pi/2a$. Describe the time evolution of the wave packet. What is the corresponding classical motion of a particle in a box?

b. Choose the initial width of the packet to be much smaller than $2a$. How does the motion of the wave packet differ from part (a)?

c. Repeat part (a) with only positive wave vectors. Is the motion of the wave packet changed?

17.5 RANDOM WALK ANALYSIS OF QUANTUM SYSTEMS

We now introduce a Monte Carlo approach based on the relation of the Schrödinger equation to a diffusion process in imaginary time. Our approach follows that of Andersen (see references). In order to understand this relation, we substitute $\tau = it/\hbar$ into the time-dependent Schrödinger equation for a free particle and obtain

$$\frac{\partial \Psi(x, \tau)}{\partial \tau} = \frac{\hbar^2}{2m} \frac{\partial^2 \Psi(x, \tau)}{\partial x^2} \quad . \tag{17.29}$$

Note that (17.29) is similar in form to the diffusion equation (17.1) and hence we can interpret the wave function as a probability density in a diffusion process with a diffusion constant $D = \hbar^2/2m$.

The formal similarity between a diffusion process and the free-particle Schrödinger equation might seem to make the solution of the latter more complex.
However, recall from our discussion in Chapter 11 that it is possible to use a
random walk process to simulate the solution of a diffusion equation. Hence instead of solving Schrödinger's equation directly, we can replace it by an equivalent
random walk problem.

Since Schrödinger's equation is linear, we can imagine not one but many
non-interacting random walkers. How can we interpret the role of the potential
energy $V(x)$? Let us rewrite Schrödinger's equation as

$$\frac{\partial \Psi(x,\tau)}{\partial \tau} = \frac{\hbar^2}{2m}\frac{\partial^2 \Psi(x,\tau)}{\partial x^2} - V(x)\Psi(x,\tau) \quad . \tag{17.30}$$

If the $V\Psi$ term were absent, (17.30) would be the usual diffusion equation.
On the other hand, if the $V\Psi$ term was the only term present on the right-
hand side, (17.30) could be interpreted as a rate equation describing branching
processes such as radioactive decay or exponential birth and death processes in
a population. Hence the complete equation can be treated as a combination of
diffusion and branching processes in which the number of walkers increases or
decreases at a point x depending on the sign of $V(x)$. Note that the diffusion
interpretation requires that the probability amplitude be non-negative.

Now that we have begun to understand the rules of the game, let us see how
we can determine the ground state wave function and energy. We know that if
we substitute $\tau = it/\hbar$, the general solution of Schrödinger's equation can be
written as (see (17.10))

$$\Psi(x,\tau) = \sum_n c_n \phi_n(x) e^{-E_n \tau} \quad . \tag{17.31}$$

For sufficiently large τ, the dominant term in the sum in (17.31) comes from the
term representing the eigenvalue of lowest energy. Hence we have

$$\Psi(x,\tau) \rightarrow c_0 \phi_0(x) e^{-E_0 \tau} \quad . \tag{17.32}$$

From (17.32) we see that the spatial dependence of the large τ probability distribution of the random walkers is proportional to the ground state eigenfunction
ϕ_0. However, we also see that the probability density $\Psi(x,t)$ that a walker is at
x eventually decays to zero unless E_0 equals zero. This problem can be avoided
by measuring E_0 from an arbitrary reference energy V_{ref}, which is adjusted so
that an approximate steady state distribution is reached.

We now develop a method for finding the ground state energy. Although
we can attempt to fit the t-dependence of the computed probability distribution

of random walkers to (17.32) and extract E_0, this procedure would not yield accurate values of E_0. We show in the following that E_0 can be found from the relation

$$E_0 = <V> = \frac{\sum n_i V(x_i)}{\sum n_i} \tag{17.33}$$

where n_i is the number of walkers at x_i at time τ. An estimate for E_0 can then be found by computing the sum in (17.33) for several values of τ once a steady state distribution has been reached.

In order to derive (17.33), we rewrite (17.30) and (17.32) by explicitly introducing the reference potential V_{ref}:

$$\frac{\partial \Psi(x, \tau)}{\partial \tau} = \frac{\hbar^2}{2m} \frac{\partial^2 \Psi(x, \tau)}{\partial x^2} - [V(x) - V_{ref}]\Psi(x, \tau) \tag{17.34}$$

and

$$\Psi(x, \tau) \approx c_0 \phi_0(x) e^{-(E_0 - V_{ref})\tau} \quad . \tag{17.35}$$

Let us first integrate (17.34) with respect to x. Since $\partial \Psi / \partial x$ vanishes in the limit $|x| \to \infty$, we obtain

$$\int \frac{\partial \Psi(x, \tau)}{\partial \tau} \, dx = -\int V(x)\Psi(x, \tau) \, dx + V_{ref} \int \Psi(x, \tau) \, dx \quad . \tag{17.36}$$

If we differentiate (17.35) with respect to τ, we obtain the relation

$$\frac{\partial \Psi(x, \tau)}{\partial \tau} = (V_{ref} - E_0)\Psi(x, \tau) \quad . \tag{17.37}$$

We substitute (17.37) for $\partial \Psi / \partial \tau$ into (17.36) and find

$$\int (V_{ref} - E_0)\Psi(x, \tau) \, dx = -\int V(x)\Psi(x, \tau) \, dx + V_{ref} \int \Psi(x, \tau) \, dx \quad . \tag{17.38}$$

Hence if we cancel the V_{ref} terms in (17.38), we find

$$E_0 \int \Psi(x, \tau) \, dx = \int V(x)\Psi(x, \tau) \, dx \tag{17.39}$$

or

$$E_0 = \frac{\int V(x)\Psi(x, \tau) \, dx}{\int \Psi(x, \tau) \, dx} \quad . \tag{17.40}$$

The desired result (17.33) follows by making the connection between $\Psi(x)$ and the number of walkers at the point x.

Although the derivation of (17.33) might seem rather involved, the rules of the random walk are straightforward:

1. Place N_0 walkers at the initial set of locations x_i, where the x_i need not be on a grid.
2. Compute the initial reference energy, $V_{ref} = \frac{1}{N_0}\sum_i V_i$.
3. Randomly move a walker to the right or left by a fixed step length Δs. The step length Δs is related to the time step $\Delta \tau$ by $(\Delta s)^2 = D\Delta \tau$. (Note that $D = \frac{1}{2}$ in units such that $\hbar = m = 1$.)
4. Compute $\Delta V = [V(x) - V_{ref}]\Delta \tau$ and a random number r in the interval $[0, 1]$. If $\Delta V > 0$ and $r < \Delta V$, then remove the walker. If $\Delta V < 0$ and $r < -\Delta V$, then add another walker at x. (This procedure is accurate only in the limit of a very small time step.)
5. Repeat steps 3–4 for each of the N_0 walkers. Then change the reference potential to

$$V_{ref} = <V> - \frac{1}{N_0}(N - N_0)\Delta \tau \qquad (17.41)$$

where N is the new number of walkers and $<V>$ is the mean potential energy of the N walkers. The average of V is an estimate of the ground state energy.
6. Repeat steps 3–5 until the estimates of the ground state energy have reached a steady state value with random fluctuations. Then average these estimates over many trials to compute the mean energy eigenvalue and compute the distribution of random walkers.

Program qmwalk implements this algorithm for the harmonic oscillator potential. The walkers are randomly distributed within a distance *srange* of the origin. Other input parameters are N, the desired number of walkers, *ntrial*, the number of trials per walker, and *ds*, the step size. The program lists ten values of the energy with each value being an average over one-tenth of the trials. The first ten percent of the trials are discarded in the averages.

```
PROGRAM qmwalk
DIM xsite(2000)
RANDOMIZE
CALL initial(N,srange,ds,ntrials,Vref,xsite)
CALL walk(N,srange,ds,ntrials,Vref,xsite)
END
```

```
SUB initial(N,srange,ds,ntrials,Vref,xsite())
    DECLARE DEF V
    INPUT prompt "desired number of walkers = ": N
    INPUT prompt "enter step length = ": ds
    INPUT prompt "number of trials = ": ntrials
    INPUT prompt "initial region of walkers = ": srange
    FOR i = 1 to N
        LET xsite(i) = srange*(0.5 - rnd)     ! position of ith walker
        LET Vref = Vref + V(xsite(i))
    NEXT i
    LET Vref = Vref/N
    PRINT "energy","# walkers","reference potential"
    PRINT
END SUB

SUB walk(N,srange,ds,ntrials,Vref,xsite())
    DECLARE DEF V
    DIM psi(-500 to 500)
    LET ninitial = N              ! # of walkers at beginning of trial
    LET nwalker = N               ! # of walkers during a trial
    LET dt = ds*ds                ! time step
    LET nbar = 10                 ! # times averages calculated
    LET nave = ntrials/nbar       ! # trials averaged in each output of energy
    LET nequil = 0.1*ntrials      ! # trials before "steady state"
    LET dx_plot = 0.2             ! distance between points on plot of wave function
    LET scale = srange/dx_plot        ! scaling for index of array psi
    FOR itrial = 1 to ntrials
        LET vsum = 0.0            ! total potential energy
        FOR iwalker = ninitial to 1 step -1
            IF rnd < 0.5 then
                LET xsite(iwalker) = xsite(iwalker) + ds
            ELSE
                LET xsite(iwalker) = xsite(iwalker) - ds
            END IF
```

```
            LET potential = V(xsite(iwalker))        ! potential at xsite
            LET dv = potential - Vref
            IF dv < 0.0 then  ! check to add walker
                IF rnd < -dv*dt then
                    LET nwalker = nwalker + 1
                    LET xsite(nwalker) = xsite(iwalker)        ! new walker
                    LET vsum = vsum + 2*potential
                ELSE
                    LET vsum = vsum + potential        ! only do old walker
                END IF
            ELSE
                IF rnd < dv*dt then                    ! check to remove walker
                    ! replace walker by nwalker
                    LET xsite(iwalker) = xsite(nwalker)
                    LET nwalker = nwalker - 1
                ELSE
                    LET vsum = vsum + potential
                END IF
            END IF
        NEXT iwalker
        LET vave = vsum/nwalker                    ! mean potential
        ! decide to print averages
        IF mod(itrial,nave) = 0 then
            LET Eave = (vave + esum)/nave
            PRINT Eave,nwalker,Vref
            LET esum = 0
        ELSE
            LET esum = esum + vave
        END IF
        IF ntrials > nequil then
            FOR iwalker = 1 to ninitial
                LET x = xsite(iwalker)*scale
                LET psi(x) = psi(x) + 1        ! number of walkers at each site
            NEXT iwalker
        END IF
        LET Vref = vave - (nwalker - N)/(N*dt)        ! new ref energy
        LET ninitial = nwalker
    NEXT itrial
    CALL wave_function(psi,scale)
END SUB
```

```
SUB wave_function(psi(),scale)
    INPUT prompt "plot wave function ?": choice$
    IF choice$ = "y" then
        FOR i = -100 to 100
            LET sum = sum + psi(i)*psi(i)
        NEXT i
        LET norm = sqr(sum/scale)
        SET window -100,100,-0.5,2
        PLOT LINES: -100,0;100,0
        PLOT LINES: -scale,-0.1;-scale,0.1       ! draw tick mark at xsite = -1
        PLOT LINES: scale,-0.1;scale,0.1         ! draw tick mark at xsite = 1
        FOR i = -99 to 100
            PLOT LINES: i - 1,psi(i-1)/norm;i,psi(i)/norm
        NEXT i
    END IF
END SUB


DEF V(xsite)
    LET V = 0.5*xsite*xsite
END DEF
```

PROBLEM 17.9 Ground state of the harmonic and anharmonic oscillator

a. Use **Program qmwalk** to determine the ground state energy and eigenfunction for $V(x) = \frac{1}{2}x^2$. Choose the initial number of walkers $N = 50$, step length $ds = 0.1$, and $ntrials = 100$. Place the walkers at random within the region $-1 < x < 1$, i.e. set $srange = 2$. Compare your Monte Carlo estimate for E_0 to the exact result $E_0 = 0.5$.

b. Choose $ntrials = 400$. How much improvement does this choice make for the estimate of E_0? How many trials are needed for 1% accuracy for E_0? Plot the spatial distribution of the random walkers and compare it to the exact result for the ground state wave function.

c. Obtain a numerical solution of the anharmonic oscillator with

$$V(x) = \frac{1}{2}x^2 + bx^3 \quad (b \ll 1) \quad . \tag{17.42}$$

Consider $b = 0.1$, 0.2 and 0.5. For this potential there are no analytical solutions and numerical solutions are of much interest. Calculation of the effect of the x^3 term is necessary for the study of the anharmonicity of the vibrations of a physical system, e.g. the vibrational spectrum of diatomic molecules.

PROBLEM 17.10 Ground state of a square well

a. Use **Program qmwalk** to find the ground state energy and wave function for the square well potential (17.14). Choose $V_0 = 5$, $N = 100$, $ds = 0.1$, $srange = 2$, and $ntrials = 300$.

b. Increase V_0 and find the ground state energy as a function of V_0. Use your results to estimate the limiting value of the ground state energy for $V_0 \to \infty$.

c. Modify the potential so that $V(x) = V_b$ for $|x| \leq 0.2$, $V(x) = 0$ for $0.2 < |x| \leq 1$ and $V(x) = V_0$ for $|x| > 1$. Choose $V_0 = 10$ and $V_b = 2$. How does this modification change the ground state energy and eigenfunction?

PROBLEM 17.11 Ground state of a cylindrical box

Compute the ground state energy and wave function of a two-dimensional circular box with the potential

$$V(r) = \begin{cases} 0 & r \leq 1 \\ -V_0, & r > 1 \end{cases} \tag{17.43}$$

where $r^2 = x^2 + y^2$. Modify **Program qmwalk** by using Cartesian coordinates in two dimensions, e.g. add an array $ysite$ to store the positions of the y coordinates of the walkers. What happens if you begin with an initial distribution of walkers which is not cylindrically symmetric?

It is possible to improve the above random walk algorithm by introducing an importance sampling method. The idea is to use an initial guess for the wave function to guide the walkers to spend more time in the important regions of $V(x)$. If we write $f(x, \tau) = \Psi(x, \tau)\phi_T(x, \tau)$, it can be shown that the equation of motion for $f(x, \tau)$ is similar in form to the original Schrödinger equation and can be analyzed in terms of a random walk process with a superimposed drift and a branching term. The use of a good trial wave function ϕ_T reduces the variance and makes it possible to solve the Schrödinger equation for several hundred particles. Another improvement of the random walk method is to reformulate the diffusion process so that no systematic errors are made due to the finite step size. Such a formulation is called Green's function Monte Carlo. Details of the importance sampling and Green's function Monte Carlo can be found in the references.

17.6 VARIATIONAL QUANTUM MONTE CARLO METHODS

Another approach to quantum systems is to use a variational method to obtain upper bounds for the ground state energy. Such a variational method has numerous applications, especially in atomic and molecular physics, nuclear physics, and condensed matter physics. Since the variational method is discussed in several textbooks, we only summarize the method here. We then discuss several Monte Carlo methods for implementing the variational method.

Consider a physical system whose Hamiltonian operator H_{op} is given by (17.8). Assume the eigenvalues E_n and corresponding eigenstates ϕ_n are not known. The variational principle states that for an arbitrary function $\phi(x)$

$$<H> = \frac{\int \phi^*(x) H_{op} \phi(x)\, dx}{\int \phi^*(x) \phi(x)\, dx} \geq E_0 \qquad (17.44)$$

where E_0 is the ground state energy of the system. This inequality reduces to an equality only if ϕ is an eigenfunction of H with the eigenvalue E_0. The quantity $<H>$ can be interpreted as the expectation value of the total energy for the approximate state function $\phi(x)$.

The inequality (17.44) is the basis of the variational method. The procedure is to choose a trial wave function $\phi(x)$ whose form is physically reasonable and which depends on one or more parameters. The quantity $<H>$ is calculated and the parameters are varied until a minimum of $<H>$ is obtained. This value of $<H>$ is an upper bound to the true ground state energy.

We first describe a Monte Carlo method for obtaining trial wave functions for low-dimensional systems. For simplicity consider a one-dimensional system and introduce a grid of mesh size Δx such that ϕ is defined only at the points $x_r = r\Delta x$. The Monte Carlo procedure can be stated as follows:

1. Choose reasonable values for ϕ at the points x_r.
2. Choose a point x_r at random and change the value of $\phi_r = \phi(x_r)$ by a random amount in the interval $[-\delta, \delta]$.
3. Compute the change ΔE in $<H>$. If $\Delta E \leq 0$, then accept the change in ϕ_r; otherwise reject the change.
4. Repeat steps 2 and 3 until $<H>$ does not change significantly.

Program **variation** implements this procedure for one-dimensional symmetric potentials. The kinetic energy contribution at $x = x_r$ is approximated by $\phi_r(2\phi_r - \phi_{r+1} - \phi_{r-1})/(2(\Delta x)^2)$. Note that since the kinetic energy depends on the curvature of ϕ, a change in ϕ at $x = x_r$ changes the kinetic energy at $x = x_r$ and also at $x = x_{r-1}$ and $x = x_{r+1}$.

```
PROGRAM variation          ! find ground state using variational principle
! vary wave function and accept change only if energy is lowered
DIM phi(-200 to 200)
CALL initial(dx,N,delta,E,norm,phi,nmove)
CALL changes(dx,N,delta,E,norm,phi,nmove)
END

SUB initial(dx,N,delta,E,norm,phi(),nmove)
    DECLARE DEF V
    INPUT prompt "maximum value of x = ": xmax
    INPUT  prompt "number of points in each direction = ": N
    LET dx = xmax/N
    INPUT prompt "maximum change in wave function = ": delta
    SET window -xmax,xmax,-0.5,1
    LET delta = 2*delta
    LET nmove = 10*N                        ! number of trials between plots
    FOR i = 1  to N
       LET x = i*dx
       LET phi(i) = exp(-.5*x*x)            ! initial guess
       LET phi(-i) = phi(i)
       LET norm = norm + 2*phi(i)*phi(i)    ! normalization
    NEXT i
    LET phi(0) = 1      ! "integration" factor dx omitted in pe, ke, and normalization
    LET norm = norm + phi(0)*phi(0)
    FOR i = 1 to N                          ! calculate initial energy
       LET x = i*dx
       LET pe = phi(i)*phi(i)*V(x)
       LET ke = .5*phi(i)*(2*phi(i) - phi(i+1) - phi(i-1))/(dx*dx)
       LET E = E + 2*(pe + ke)             ! factor of 2 for phi(i) and phi(-i)
    NEXT i
    LET E = E + V(0)*phi(0)^2
    LET E = E + 0.5*phi(0)*(2*phi(0) - phi(1) - phi(-1))/(dx*dx)
END SUB
```

```
SUB changes(dx,N,delta,E,norm,phi(),nmove)
   DECLARE DEF V
   DO
      LET Ecum = 0
        FOR imove = 1 to nmove
           LET i = int(N*rnd + 1)                  ! position
           LET dphi = (rnd - 0.5)*delta            ! change in wave function
           LET phi_trial = phi(i) + dphi           ! new wave function at site i
           LET dphi2 = phi_trial*phi_trial - phi(i)*phi(i)
           ! dV change in potential energy,
           ! dK change in kinetic energy
           ! dK includes change in kinetic energy at "sites" i + 1 and 1 - 1 due
           ! to change in wave function at i
           LET dV = dphi2*V(i*dx)
           LET dK = (dphi2 - dphi*(phi(i+1) + phi(i-1)))/dx^2
           IF i = 0 then
              LET Etrial = E + dK+ dV              ! trial energy
              LET norm_trial = norm + dphi2        ! new normalization constant
           ELSE                 ! include change due to phi(i) and phi(-i)
              LET Etrial = E + 2*(dv + dk)         ! new energy
              LET norm_trial = norm + 2*dphi2      ! new normalization constant
           END IF
           LET dE = (Etrial/norm_trial) - (E/norm)
           IF dE < 0  then             ! accept phi_trial if energy decreased
              LET phi(i) = phi_trial
              LET phi(-i) = phi_trial
              LET norm = norm_trial
              LET E = Etrial
           END IF
           LET Ecum = Ecum + E/norm              ! accumulate energy values
        NEXT imove
        LET Eave = Ecum/nmove                     ! average energy
        PRINT "mean value of ground state energy ="; Eave
        INPUT prompt "plot,stop,or continue (p/s/c) ": choice$
        IF choice$ = "p" then CALL plot_phi(phi,N,dx,norm)
   LOOP UNTIL choice$ = "s"
END SUB
```

```
SUB plot_phi(phi(),N,dx,norm)
   DECLARE DEF V
   ! plot wave function and potential
   CLEAR
   LET dy = 0.01                    ! height of hash marks
   PLOT LINES: -N*dx,0;N*dx,0
   PLOT
   FOR i = -N to N                  ! draw hash marks
      LET x = i*dx
      PLOT LINES: x,0; x,dy
      PLOT LINES: -x,0; -x,dy
   NEXT i
   PLOT
   LET scale = 0.025                ! depends on height of potential
   FOR i = -N to N
      LET x = i*dx
      PLOT POINTS: x,V(x)*scale
   NEXT i
   LET norm_phi = 1/sqr(norm)       ! normalization for phi
   PLOT
   FOR i = -N to N                  ! plot wave function
      LET x = i*dx
      LET iabs = abs(i)
      PLOT x,phi(iabs)*norm_phi;
   NEXT i
END SUB

DEF V(x)
   LET V = 0.5*x*x                  ! harmonic oscillator potential
END DEF
```

PROBLEM 17.12 Monte Carlo calculation of the ground state of the harmonic and anharmonic oscillators

a. Use **Program variation** to obtain the ground state energy of the harmonic oscillator. The input parameters include N, the number of points at which the trial wave function ϕ is evaluated, and $xmax$, the maximum value of x. The quantity $delta$ is the maximum change in ϕ. The program prints $<E>$ and plots ϕ after every $100N$ trials. Choose $N = 40$, $xmax = 4$, and *delta* = 0.1. What is the initial form of the trial ground wave function in **Program variation**?

b. Choose the trial wave function to be $\phi(x) = \cos x$. How many trials are required to obtain an estimate of the ground state energy to within 1%? What is the overall accuracy of the computed trial wave function?

c. Choose the trial wave function to be $\phi(x) = 1$. How many trials are required to obtain an estimate of the ground state energy to within 1%? Which form of ϕ yields more rapidly convergent results?

d. Consider the anharmonic potential $V(x) = \frac{1}{2}x^2 + bx^4$. Plot $V(x)$ as a function of x for $b = 1/8$. Use first-order perturbation theory to calculate the lowest order change in the ground state energy due to the x^4 term. Then use **Program variation** to obtain E_0 and compare your result with the harmonic oscillator result ($b = 0$). Choose N and *xmax* such that your results yield 1% accuracy for the energy. What is a reasonable criterion for your choice of *delta*?

e. Consider the anharmonic potential of part (d) with $b = -1/8$. Plot $V(x)$ as a function of x. Use first-order perturbation theory to calculate the lowest order change in the ground state energy due to the x^4 term. Then use **Program variation** to obtain an estimate for E_0. Do your estimates for E_0 have a lower bound? Why or why not?

PROGRAM 17.13 Monte Carlo calculations of square well potentials

a. Use **Program variation** to estimate the ground state energy of the square well potential (17.14) with $V_0 = 2$ and $a = 1$. Choose $xmax = 2$, $N = 40$, and *delta* = 0.1, and consider the the initial trial wave functions $\phi(x) = \cos x$, $e^{-x^2/2}$, and 1. Which initial guess for ϕ yields more rapidly convergent results? What is the "penetration depth" of the computed wave function?

b. Modify $V(x)$ so that

$$V(x) = \begin{cases} V_b, & |x| \leq 0.2 \\ 0, & 0.2 < |x| \leq 1 \\ 2, & |x| > 1 \end{cases} \qquad (17.45)$$

How do you expect the ground state energy to depend on V_b? Assume that $V_b \ll V_0$ and find the new eigenfunction and eigenvalue starting from an initial $\phi(x) = \cos x$. How do your computed results compare with your expectations? Is the penetration depth into the region $|x| > 1$ changed by the modification of V?

c. Consider the following double well ($x > 0$) potential

$$V(x) = \begin{cases} +40, & |x| > 4 \\ -40, & 3 \le |x| \le 4 \\ 0, & 2 < |x| < 3 \\ -20, & 1 \le |x| \le 2 \\ 0, & |x| < 1 \end{cases} \qquad (17.46)$$

Plot $V(x)$ as a function of x and sketch your guess of the form of the ground state wave function on the same graph. Compute the ground state using $xmax = 4.5$, $N = 45$, $delta = 0.05$, and the initial guess $\phi = 1$ for $|x| \le 1.5$ and $\phi = 0$ for $|x| > 1.5$. Plot your resulting estimate for the trial wave function and compare it to your expected form for ϕ. Why did you not obtain a reasonable estimate for ϕ?

d. Repeat the computation of part (c) but with the initial guess $\phi = e^{-x^2}$ (choose $delta = 0.05$). Explain why your results for $<H>$ and ϕ are different than that found in (c). Think of another method for making trial changes in ϕ, e.g. simultaneous changes in ϕ at multiple values of x, which leads to rapidly convergent results even for a poor choice of initial trial wave function.

Instead of computing ϕ on a grid, we can base the variational approach on the expansion of ϕ in terms of a complete set of basis functions f_n:

$$\phi = \sum_n c_n f_n \qquad (17.47)$$

Our Monte Carlo approach will be to retain a finite number of terms in (17.47) and to vary the unknown coefficients c_n until a reasonable estimate of the minimum of $<H>$ is found. Although this approach would be useful in higher dimensions, we only discuss the one-dimensional case. In order to implement this procedure we need to calculate the matrix elements

$$T_{nm} = <n|T|m> \qquad (17.48a)$$
$$V_{nm} = <n|V|m> \qquad (17.48b)$$

where T and V represent the kinetic and potential energy operators respectively. For completeness we note that the matrix elements $<n|A|m>$ of the operator A are given in one dimension by

$$<n|A|m> = \int dx\, f_n^* A f_m \quad .$$ (17.49)

For higher dimensions we can use Monte Carlo methods to compute the matrix elements. Once the matrix elements are known, the expectation value $<H>$ is given by

$$<H> = \frac{\sum_{n,m} c_n^* c_m (T_{nm} + V_{nm})}{\sum_{n,m} c_n^* c_m} \quad .$$ (17.50)

We apply this Monte Carlo approach in Problem 17.14.

*PROBLEM 17.14 Monte Carlo calculation of the ground state energy of the Morse potential

Consider the Morse potential

$$V(x) = (1 - e^{-x})^2$$ (17.51)

for which an analytical solution for the eigenvalues and wave function can be calculated. Since $V(x) \approx x^2$ for small x, it is reasonable to choose the basis set to be the solutions to the corresponding harmonic oscillator problem:

$$\phi_n = N_n H_n e^{-x^2/2} \quad .$$ (17.52)

The Hermite polynomials $H_n(x)$ have the form

$$H_n(x) = (-1)^n e^{x^2} \frac{\partial^n}{\partial x^n} e^{-x^2} \quad .$$ (17.53)

The normalization constant N_n is given by

$$N_n = \left(\frac{1}{\pi^{\frac{1}{2}} 2^n n!}\right)^{\frac{1}{2}} \quad .$$ (17.54)

The matrix elements T_{nm} can be evaluated analytically for this choice of basis set. The result is

$$<n|T|m> = \begin{cases} n + \frac{1}{2}, & \text{if } n = m \\ \frac{1}{2}\sqrt{(n+1)(n+2)}, & \text{if } n = m + 2 \\ 0, & \text{otherwise} \end{cases}$$ (17.55)

V_{nm} can be written in terms of the matrix element

$$<n|e^{-ax}|m> = \pi^{\frac{1}{2}}e^{a^2/4}n!m!N_n N_m \sum_{p=|n-m|\ step\ 2}^{n+m}$$

$$\times \frac{(-a)^p}{[\frac{1}{2}(n+m-1)]![\frac{1}{2}(n+1-m)]![\frac{1}{2}(m+1-n)]!} \ .$$

a. Verify the above analytical results for the matrix elements. Suggestion: use the relation

$$e^{-s^2+2sx} = \sum_{n=0}^{\infty} \frac{H_n(x)}{n!}s^n$$

to calculate the matrix elements of V.

b. Use the above results for the matrix elements to write a program which implements the same algorithm as used in **Program variation**. That is, vary c_n by a random amount between $[-\delta, \delta]$, compute ΔE, and accept the change only if $\Delta E < 0$. Choose the initial guess $c_0 = 1$ and $c_n = 0$ for $n \neq 0$ and retain the first five terms in (17.50). Do several runs and determine your best estimate for the ground state energy E_0. Compare your estimate to the exact result $E_0 \approx 0.582$. How do your results change if ten terms are retained? It is suggested that you choose $\delta = 0.1$ for your initial runs. How does your estimate for the ground state energy change if δ is reduced?

Think of other problems for which the combination of the variational approach and Monte Carlo methods will lead to useful results. Another possibility is to use a combination of variational Monte Carlo and random walk methods to find even better trial wave functions.

REFERENCES AND SUGGESTIONS FOR ADDITIONAL READING

E. E. Anderson, *Modern Physics and Quantum Mechanics*, W. B. Saunders (1971). An undergraduate text which includes examples of wave packet motion.

J. B. Anderson, "A random walk simulation of the Schrödinger equation: H_3^+," *J. Chem. Phys.* **63**, 1499 (1975); "Quantum chemistry by random walk. H ^{2}P, H_3^+ D$_{3h}$ $^1A'_1$, H_2 $^3\Sigma_u^+$, H_4 $^1\Sigma_g^+$, Be ^{1}S," *J. Chem. Phys.* **65**, 4121 (1976); "Quantum chemistry by random walk: Higher accuracy," *J. Chem. Phys.* **73**, 3897 (1980). These three papers describe the basic procedure for the random walk method, extensions for improved accuracy, and applications to simple molecules.

G. Baym, *Lectures on Quantum Mechanics*, W. A. Benjamin (1973). A good discussion of the Schrödinger equation in imaginary time is given in Chapter 3.

H. A. Bethe, *Intermediate Quantum Mechanics*, W. A. Benjamin (1964). Applications of quantum mechanics to atomic systems are discussed.

Jay S. Bolemon, "Computer solutions to a realistic 'one-dimensional' Schrödinger equation," *Am. J. Phys.* **40**, 1511 (1972).

Siegmund Brandt and Hans Dieter Dahmen, *The Picture Book of Quantum Mechanics*, John Wiley & Sons (1985). Many computer generated pictures of quantum wave functions in different contexts are shown.

David M. Ceperley and Berni J. Alder, "Quantum Monte Carlo," *Science* **231**, 555 (1986). A survey of some of the applications of quantum Monte Carlo methods to physics and chemistry.

D. F. Coker and R. O. Watts, "Quantum simulation of systems with nodal surfaces," *Mol. Phys.* **58**, 1112 (1986).

Robert M. Eisberg, *Applied Mathematical Physics with Programmable Pocket Calculators*, Mc-Graw-Hill (1976). Chapter 8 discusses a direct numerical solution of the one-dimensional Schrödinger equation.

Robert M. Eisberg and Robert Resnick, *Quantum Physics*, John Wiley & Sons (1974). See Appendix F for a discussion of the numerical solution of Schrödinger's equation.

R. P. Feynman, "Simulating Physics with Computers," *Int. J. Theor. Phys.* **21**, 467 (1982). A provocative discussion of the intrinsic difficulties of simulating quantum systems.

J. P. Killingbeck, *Microcomputer Quantum Mechanics*, Adam Hilger (1983). A book on numerical methods as well as quantum mechanics.

Steven E. Koonin, *Computational Physics*, Benjamin/Cummings (1986). Solutions of the time-dependent Schrödinger equation are discussed in the context of parabolic partial differential equations in Chapter 7. Chapter 8 discusses Green's function Monte Carlo methods.

P. K. MacKeown, "Evaluation of Feynman path integrals by Monte Carlo methods," *Am. J. Phys.* **53**, 880 (1985). The author dicusses projects suitable for an advanced undergraduate course.

J. R. Merrill, *Using Computers in Physics*, Houghton Mifflin Co. (1976). Our approach to the time-dependent Schrödinger equation is based on Merrill's discussion.

William H. Press, Brian P. Flannery, Saul A. Teukolsky, and William T. Vetterling, *Numerical Recipes*, Cambridge University Press (1986). The numerical solution of the time-dependent Schrödinger equation is discussed in Sec. 17.2.

Peter J. Reynolds, David M. Ceperley, Berni J. Alder, and William A. Lester Jr., "Fixed-node quantum Monte Carlo for molecules," *J. Chem. Phys.* **77**, 5593 (1982). This paper describes a random walk algorithm for use in molecular applications including importance sampling and the treatment of Fermi statistics.

D. Saxon, *Elementary Quantum Mechanics*, Holden-Day (1968). Numerical solutions of Schrödinger's equation are discussed in Chapter VI.

L. I. Schiff, *Quantum Mechanics*, 3rd. ed., McGraw Hill (1968). A discussion of approximation methods for bound states is given in Chapter 8.

EPILOGUE:
THE SAME PROGRAMS
HAVE
THE SAME SOLUTIONS

18

We emphasize that the same methods which have been discussed in the context of classical mechanics and statistical physics can be applied to a wide variety of natural phenomena.

18.1 THE UNITY OF PHYSICS

Although we have discussed many topics and applications, we have covered only a small fraction of the possible computer simulations of the physical world. However we know that the same principles and algorithms apply to many kinds of phenomena, and as Feynman has cogently expressed, *"The same equations have the same solutions."* Hence the same Monte Carlo methods that we have applied to the diffusion of particles in a gas and to the analysis of quantum mechanical wave functions can also be applied to the diffusion of neutrons in graphite. Less obvious perhaps is that similar Monte Carlo methods can be used to analyze problems in quark confinement and chemical kinetics. Indeed the increasing role of the computer in research is strengthening the interconnections of the various subfields of physics and the relation of physics to other areas.

Not only has the computer made us more aware of the unity of physics, it has helped us think of phenomena in new ways which complement the more traditional methods. Since we have discussed many examples in the context of physics, we give an example from theoretical ecology. Consider a simple predator-prey model of sharks and fish. Assume that the birth rate of the fish is independent of the number of sharks and that each shark kills a number of fish proportional to the number of the fish. The latter asssumption would be correct if each shark searched a constant area, the areas searched by different sharks did not overlap, and each shark found a constant proportion of fish in that area. If we assume that $F(t)$, the number of fish at time t, changes continuously, we can write

$$\frac{dF(t)}{dt} = [b_1 - d_1 S(t)]F(t) \qquad (18.1)$$

where $S(t)$ is the number of sharks at time t and b_1 and d_1 are constants independent of F and S. We now need an equation for the rate of change of the sharks. A plausible assumption is that the number of offspring produced by each shark is proportional to the number of fish eaten by the shark. If we also assume that the death rate is constant, we have

$$\frac{dS(t)}{dt} = [b_2 F(t) - d_2]S(t) \qquad . \qquad (18.2)$$

Equations (18.1) and (18.2) are known as the Lotka-Volterra equations. Note that the assumption that the growth rate in (18.2) is proportional to the product of the number of the two populations is similar to the principle of mass action in chemical kinetics, that is, the rates of reaction increase as the products of the concentration of the molecules. The two coupled equations can be analyzed by standard methods and solved numerically using the Euler-Cromer algorithm. Can you explain why the dynamical behavior of (18.1) and (18.2) is cyclic?

In the above predator-prey model the numbers of predator and prey were assumed to change continuously. We now summarize an alternative predator-prey model which can be most simply posed as a computer algorithm. The model we will describe is a two-dimensional cellular automaton known as Wa-Tor (see references).

i. For a desired concentration of fish and sharks, place fish and sharks at random on the sites of a rectangular grid. The fish and sharks are assigned random ages.

ii. At time step t_n consider each fish sequentially. Determine the number of nearest neighbor sites which are unoccupied at time t_{n-1} and move the fish at random to one of the unoccupied sites. If all four nearest neighbor sites are occupied, the fish does not move.

iii. If a fish has survived for a multiple of *fbreed* time steps, the fish has a single offspring. The new fish is placed at the old position of the parent fish.

iv. At time step t_n consider each shark sequentially. If all the nearest neighbor sites of the shark at time t_{n-1} are unoccupied, the shark moves at random to one of the four unoccupied sites. If one or more of the adjacent sites is occupied by a fish, the shark moves at random to one of the occupied sites and eats the fish.

v. If a shark moves *nstarve* times without eating, the shark dies. If a shark survives for a multiple of *sbreed* time steps, the shark has a single offspring. The new shark is placed at the previous position of the parent shark.

What is the dynamical behavior of Wa-Tor? Do Wa-Tor and the Lotka-Volterra equations exhibit similar behavior? Is the Wa-Tor model realistic? What are the advantages and disadvantages of each approach? See the references for suggestions for the numerical values of the parameters. Can you imagine how the Wa-Tor model might be modified to simulate a chemical reaction?

18.2 PERCOLATION AND GALAXIES

In addition to allowing us to consider more complex nonlinear problems, the computer has reinforced a contemporary theme in physics, the unifying role of collective behavior. That is, systems composed of many individual constituents will exhibit common properties under certain conditions, even though there might be differences in the nature of the constituents and in their mutual interaction. In the following we give two examples of collective behavior in the context of epidemology and the structure of spiral galaxies. Our discussion follows closely the article by Schulman and Seiden (see references).

Consider an imaginary disease called *percolitis*. The disease conveys no immunity and its incubation and duration periods are each 24 hours. Suppose the disease is so benign that its sufferers are able to come into contract with every member of the community. At $t = 0$ one person contacts the disease from a source outside the community. Let N be the total population, t the time measured in days, p the transmission probability, and $n(t)$ the expected number of diseased individuals at time t. Convince yourself that for $N = 1000$ and $p = 0.0005$, the chance that there will be anyone suffering from the disease one week later is vanishingly small. On the other hand suppose that $p = 0.002$. Then $n(t = 1) = 2$, $n(t = 2) \approx 4$, and the odds are overwhelming that after some time there will be an average number of approximately 800 victims. Can you determine the critical probability p_c such that for $p < p_c$ the average number of victims is zero, and for $p \geq p_c$ the average number of victims is non-zero?

Note that no assumptions were made as to which individuals will become infected. The percolitis model is an example of a simple type of percolation for which an analytical solution is possible. What modifications of the model might make it more realistic? Will these modifications change the qualitative behavior of the model? Are complete analytical solutions possible in general?

We will now summarize the percolation-based model of Schulman and Seiden, list **Program galaxy**, a True BASIC implementation of the model, and encourage you to explore its properties. The basic fact that allows the use of a percolation model in galaxies is propagating star formation. A region of the galaxy might have the necessary ingredients for star formation—molecular gas, proper temperatures, and densities—but, if left alone, nothing happens. However, if a shock wave from a supernova passes through the gas, there is a good chance that a star will be formed. The supernova is itself the result of an earlier nearby star formation. Hence we can think of a given region of the galaxy as being like a percolitis-susceptible individual—without a source there is no percolitis. Rather than determining which regions have the necessary conditions for star formation, we summarize all the uncertainity and variability in a single parameter p, the probability that a supernova explosion in one region gives rise to star formation in a neighboring region.

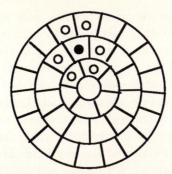

Fig. 18.1 The nature of the polar grid used in **Program galaxy**. Each cell has the same area and has on the average six nearest neighbors. The filled circle denotes an active region of star formation. At the next time step it can induce star formation in cells containing open circles. Note that as time passes, the neighbors in adjacent rings will change because of differential rotation.

Fig. 18.2 Galactic structure generated by **Program galaxy**. The parameters are the number of rings $Nr = 49$, the initial number of active cells $Nc = 500$, circular velocity $v = 1.0$ (200 km/sec), the probability of induced star formation $p = 0.18$, the time step $dt = 10$ (10^7 years), and the duration of the run $tmax = 50$. (Test your program for $Nr = 10$ and $Nc = 75$.)

The other important observation we need to make about spiral galaxies is that galaxies do not rotate rigidly (with a constant angular velocity), but to a good approximation rotate with a constant circular velocity. The properties of random self-propagating star formation and constant circular velocity are incorporated into **Program galaxy** as follows. Imagine a galaxy to be divided into concentric rings, which in turn are divided into cells of equal size (see Fig. 18.1). Each cell corresponds to a region of space the size of a giant molecular cloud and moves with the same circular velocity v. The angular velocity is given by $\omega = v/r$, where r is the distance of the ring from the center of the galaxy. At time t_n each cell is either occupied (active or inactive) or unoccupied. An occupied cell remains active for only one time step. At time t_{n+1} the neighbors of each active cell are activated with a probability p. More details of the simulation are shown in Fig. 18.1 and in **Program galaxy**. A typical galaxy simulation is shown in Fig. 18.2.

```
PROGRAM galaxy
! model proposed by Schulman and Seiden
DIM L(0 to 50,300)
DIM Lnew(0 to 50,300)
CALL parameter(Nr,Nc,v,dt,tmax,p)
CALL initial(Nr,Nc,L,Lnew)
DO
    CALL rotate(Nr,v,dt,L)
    CALL growth(Nr,p,L,Lnew)
    CALL spiral(Nr,L)
    LET t = t + dt
LOOP UNTIL t > tmax
END

SUB parameter(Nr,Nc,v,dt,tmax,p)
  INPUT prompt "number of rings = " : Nr
  INPUT prompt "number of initial star clusters = ": Nc
  INPUT prompt "circular velocity = ": v
  INPUT prompt "growth probability = ": p
  INPUT prompt "time step = ": dt
  INPUT prompt "maximum time = ": tmax
END SUB
```

```
SUB initial(Nr,Nc,L(,),Lnew(,))
  RANDOMIZE
  ! calculate initial location of each cell
  FOR ir = 1 to Nr
    LET da = 2*pi/(6*ir)
    FOR ia = 1 to 6*ir
      LET L(ir,ia) = ia*da
    NEXT ia
  NEXT ir
  ! occupy cells at random
  FOR ic = 1 to Nc
    LET ix = int(Nr*rnd + 1)
    LET iy = int(Nr*rnd + 1)
    LET ir = sqr(ix*ix + iy*iy)
    IF ir <= Nr then
      LET ia = int(1 + 6*ir*rnd)
      LET L(ir,ia) = -L(ir,ia)          ! occupied cells are negative
      LET Lnew(ir,ia) = 1               ! active cells
    END IF
  NEXT ic
END SUB

SUB rotate(Nr,v,dt,L(,))
  FOR ir = 1 to Nr
    ! v is constant and angular velocity w changes
    LET w = v/ir
    FOR ia = 1 to 6*ir
      LET anew = abs(L(ir,ia)) + w*dt
      LET anew = mod(anew,2*pi)         ! new angle
      LET L(ir,ia) = sgn(L(ir,ia))*anew
    NEXT ia
  NEXT ir
END SUB
```

```
SUB growth(Nr,p,L(,),Lnew(,))
   ! Lnew is new occupancy
   FOR ir = 1 to Nr
      ! maximum acute angle between nearest neighbor cells
      LET acute = 2*pi/(5.95*ir)
      ! minimum reflex angle between nearest neighbor cells
      LET reflex = 2*pi - acute
      FOR ia = 1 to 6*ir                    ! ia labels cells
         IF Lnew(ir,ia) = 1 then
            LET Lnew(ir,ia) = 0             ! cell active for only one time step
            FOR jr = ir - 1 to ir + 1
               IF (jr > 0) and (jr <= Nr) then
                  FOR ja = 1 to 6*jr
                     IF L(jr,ja) > 0 then
                        LET dis = abs(abs(L(ir,ia)) - abs(L(jr,ja)))
                        IF (dis < acute) or (dis > reflex) then
                           IF rnd < p then
                              LET L(jr,ja) = -abs(L(jr,ja))   ! new occupied cell
                              LET Lnew(jr,ia) = 1             ! new active cell
                           END IF
                        END IF
                     END IF
                  NEXT ja
               END IF
            NEXT jr
         END IF
      NEXT ia
   NEXT ir
END SUB
```

```
SUB spiral(Nr,L(,))
  ! plot results
  CLEAR
  SET window -85,85,-55,55
  FOR ir = 1 to Nr
    FOR ia = 1 to 6*ir
      IF L(ir,ia) < 0 then
        LET a = abs(L(ir,ia))
        LET x = ir*cos(a)
        LET y = ir*sin(a)
        FOR i = 1 to 30                    ! plot occupied cells
          LET xp = x + 0.5 - rnd
          LET yp = y + 0.5 - rnd
          PLOT POINTS: xp,yp
        NEXT i
      END IF
    NEXT ia
  NEXT ir
END SUB
```

Of course our brief discussion of galaxies is not meant to convince you that the mechanism proposed by Schulman and Seiden is correct. Rather our purpose is to show how an alternative point of view can suggest new approaches in different fields.

18.3 WHAT ARE COMPUTERS DOING TO PHYSICS?

There is probably no need to convince you that computers are changing the way we think of the physical world. The question "How can I formulate this problem on a computer?" has lead to new insights into old problems and is allowing us to consider new ones.

What will be the effect of computers in physics education? The most common use of computers has been to assist students to understand topics that have been in the curriculum for many years. So far the computer has not qualitatively changed the way we learn nor the topics we study. What will happen when computers become as common as calculators? Will computer simulation and numerical analysis make analytical methods less important? Will tables of integrals become as obsolete as slide rules? Should calculus retain its traditional importance in the curriculum? Do we "understand" a natural phenomenon if we are able to construct a computer model which allows us to make predictions that agree with experiment? Is it necessary to obtain at least some analytical results? What do you think should be the role of computers in education?

REFERENCES AND SUGGESTIONS FOR ADDITIONAL READING

We have not discussed many areas of physics and related fields where computer simulations are becoming increasingly important. In addition to the references given at the end of each chapter, some additional general references are given below.

R. M. Anderson, "Population ecology of infectious disease agents," pp. 318–355 in R. M. May, ed. *Theoretical Ecology: Principles and Applications*, Blackwell (1981).

John W. Clark, Johann Rafelski, and Jeffrey V. Winston, "Brain without mind: Computer simulation of neural networks with modifiable neuronal interactions," *Phys. Repts.* **123**, 215 (1985).

Michael Creutz, Laurence Jacobs, and Claudio Rebbi, "Monte Carlo computations in lattice gauge theory," *Phys. Repts.*, **95**, 201 (1983).

Norman Cusack, *The Physics of Structurally Disordered Matter*, Taylor & Francis (1987).

A. K. Dewdney, "Computer Recreations," *Sci. Amer.* **251**, 14 (December 1984). A discussion of the Wa-Tor model.

Zvonko Fazarinc, "A viewpoint on calculus," *Hewlett-Packard Journal* **38**, 38 (March, 1987).

Richard P. Feynman, Robert B. Leighton, and Matthew Sands, *Lectures on Physics, Vol. II*, Addison-Wesley (1964). Our chapter title has been adapted from the subtitle of Sec. 12.1, "The same equations have the same solutions."

A. A. Harms and O. E. Hileman, "Chemical clocks, feedback, and nonlinear behavior," *Am. J. Phys.* **53**, 578 (1985). See also Irving R. Epstein, "Patterns in Time and Space," *Chem. & Eng. News* **65**, 24 (1987).

Carlo Jacoboni and Lino Reggiani, "The Monte Carlo method for the solution of charge transport in semiconductors with applications to covalent materials," *Rev. Mod. Phys.* **55**, 645 (1983).

Roger Peyret and Thomas D. Taylor, *Computational Methods for Fluid Flow*, Springer-Verlag (1983).

David E. Rumelhart and James L. McClelland, *Parallel Distributed Processing: Explorations in the Microstructure of Cognition*, Vol. 1: *Foundations*, MIT Press (1986). See also Vol. 2 on applications.

Lawrence S. Schulman and Philip E. Seiden, "Percolation and Galaxies," *Science* **233**, 425 (1986). A discussion of percolitis is also given. The authors note that for finite N the disease always dies out eventually, but the expected time for the eradication of the disease grows exponentially with N.

James D. Spain, *BASIC Microcomputer Models in Biology*, Addison-Wesley (1982).

W. Williamson Jr. and G. C. Duncan, "Monte Carlo simulation of nonrelativistic electron scattering," *Am. J. Phys.* **54**, 262 (1986).

APPENDICES

Appendix F   INDEX OF TRUE BASIC PROGRAMS—PART II

We list the page numbers of the True BASIC programs given in Part II of this text.

Index of True BASIC Simulation Programs

Appendix G LISTING OF FORTRAN PROGRAMS

In the following we list our FORTRAN 77 translations of eight of the True BA-SIC programs given in Part II of the text. The programs were run on a VAX 11/750. Since the development of FORTRAN preceded the widespread availability of graphics displays, standard FORTRAN includes no graphics statements or subroutines. As an example of the use of a graphics package with FORTRAN, our programs illustrate the use of PLOT 10 (Tektronix), a common graphics package available on the VAX and other computers. On most computers PLOT 10 can also be called from Pascal. A brief description of the PLOT 10 graphics subroutines used in the programs is given in Table D1.

CHAPTER 10

```
        PROGRAM integ
*       compute integral of f(x) from x = a to x = b
        CALL initial(a,b,h,n)
        CALL rectangle(a,b,h,n,area)
        CALL output(area)
        STOP
        END

        SUBROUTINE initial(a,b,h,n)
*       a = lower limit of integration, b = upper limit
        a = 0.0
        b = 0.5*3.14159
        WRITE(6,*) 'number of intervals = '
        READ(5,*) n
        h = (b - a)/n
        RETURN
        END
```

```
        SUBROUTINE rectangle(a,b,h,n,area)
        x = a
        sum = 0
        DO 100 i = 0,n - 1
            sum = sum + f(x)
            x = x + h
100     CONTINUE
        area = sum*h
        RETURN
        END

        SUBROUTINE output(area)
        WRITE(6,13) area
13      FORMAT(2x, 'area = ',F12.7)
        RETURN
        END

        FUNCTION f(x)
        f = cos(x)
        RETURN
        END
```

CHAPTER 11

```
        PROGRAM rwalk
*       Monte Carlo simulation of random walk in d = 1
        DIMENSION prob(-64:64)
        CALL start(p,N,ntrial,iseed)
        DO 100 itrial = 1,ntrial
            CALL walk(ix,p,N,iseed)
*           collect data after N steps
            CALL data(ix,xcum,x2cum,prob)
100     CONTINUE
        CALL aver(N,ntrial,xcum,x2cum,prob)
        STOP
        END
```

```
        SUBROUTINE start(p,N,ntrial,iseed)
        WRITE(6,*) 'random number seed (positive integer)  = '
        READ(5,*) iseed
*       number of trials
        ntrial = 100
*       probability of step to the right
        p = 0.5
        WRITE(6,*) 'maximum number of steps = '
        READ(5,*) N
        RETURN
        END

        SUBROUTINE walk(ix,p,N,iseed)
*       walk N steps
*       initial position for each trial
        ix = 0
        DO 100 istep = 1,N
           IF (ran(iseed).le.p) then
              ix = ix + 1
           ELSE
              ix = ix - 1
           ENDIF
100     CONTINUE
        RETURN
        END

        SUBROUTINE data(ix,xcum,x2cum,prob)
        DIMENSION prob(-64:64)
        xcum = xcum + ix
        x2cum = x2cum + ix*ix
        prob(ix) = prob(ix) + 1
        RETURN
        END
```

```fortran
      SUBROUTINE aver(N,ntrial,xcum,x2cum,prob)
*     average values for N-step walk
      DIMENSION prob(-64:64)
      znorm = 1.0/ntrial
      xbar = xcum*znorm
      x2bar = x2cum*znorm
      DO 10 i = -N,N
          prob(i) = prob(i)*znorm
          WRITE(6,13) i,prob(i)
13        FORMAT(2x,i6,f10.5)
10    CONTINUE
      var = x2bar - xbar*xbar
      sigma = sqrt(var)
      WRITE(6,*) 'mean displacement = ', xbar
      WRITE(6,*) 'sigma = ', sigma
      RETURN
      END
```

CHAPTER 12

```
        PROGRAM percl
        DIMENSION lat(100,100),r(100,100),icl(100,100),np(5000)
        DIMENSION mass(5000)
        CALL start(L,p,ntrial,iseed)
        DO 100 itrial = 1,ntrial
35          CALL assign(L,r)
            CALL occupy(L,p,lat,r)
            CALL cluster(L,lat,icl,np)
*           test vertical spanning
            CALL span(L,icl,np,1,ivert)
*           test horizontal spanning
            CALL span(L,icl,np,2,ihori)
            IF ((ivert + ihori).eq.0) then
*               does not span in either direction
                ispan = 0
            ELSEIF ((ivert*ihori).eq.0) then
*               spans in only one direction
                ispan = ivert + ihori
                IF (ivert.ne.0) spvert = spvert + 1
                IF (ihori.ne.0) sphori = sphori + 1
            ELSE
*               spans in both directions
                IF (ivert.eq.ihori) then
                    ispan = ivert
                    spvert = spvert + 1
                    sphori = sphori + 1
                ELSE
*                   two different spanning clusters -> skip this trial
                    GO TO 35
                ENDIF
            ENDIF
*           compute mass of each cluster
            CALL size(L,icl,np,mass,labmax)
*           compute mean cluster size of non-spanning clusters
            CALL mean(labmax,mass,ispan,clsize,sum)
            cltot = cltot + clsize
*           compute probability that site belongs to spanning cluster
```

```
        CALL Pinf(mass,ispan,sum,zPinf)
        zPtot = zPtot + zPinf
*       compute radius of gyration of largest non-spanning cluster
        CALL radius(L,icl,np,mass,labmax,ispan,radgyr)
        radtot = radtot + radgyr
100     CONTINUE
      CALL output(ntrial,spvert,sphori,cltot,zPtot,radtot)
      STOP
      END

      SUBROUTINE start(L,p,ntrial,iseed)
      WRITE(6,*) 'enter linear dimension of lattice'
      READ(5,*) L
      WRITE(6,*) 'enter site occupation probability'
      READ(5,*) p
      WRITE(6,*) 'enter seed, positive integer'
      READ(5,*) iseed
      WRITE(6,*) 'enter number of trials'
      READ(5,*) ntrial
      RETURN
      END

      SUBROUTINE assign(L,r)
*     assign random number to each site of lattice
      DIMENSION R(100,100)
      DO 10 i = 1,L
         DO 10 j = 1,L
            r(i,j) = ran(iseed)
10       CONTINUE
      RETURN
      END
```

```
        SUBROUTINE occupy(L,p,lat,r)
*       occupy lattice sites
        DIMENSION lat(100,100),r(100,100)
        DO 10 i = 1,L
           DO 10 j = 1,L
              IF (r(i,j).le.p) then
                 lat(i,j) = -1
              ELSE
                 lat(i,j) = 0
              ENDIF
10      CONTINUE
        RETURN
        END


        SUBROUTINE cluster(L,lat,icl,np)
*       determine labels of sites
*       labels stored in icl, proper label array is np
        DIMENSION lat(100,100),icl(100,100),np(5000)
        DO 10 k = 1,1000
           np(k) = 0
10      CONTINUE
        DO 15 i = 1,L
           DO 15 j = 1,L
              icl(i,j) = 0
15      CONTINUE
        nclust = 0
        IF (lat(1,1).lt.0) CALL newcl(nclust,icl,np,1,1)
        DO 20 i = 2,L
           IF (lat(i,1).lt.0) then
              ileft = i - 1
              IF (lat(ileft,1).lt.0) then
                 icl(i,1) = icl(ileft,1)
              ELSE
                 CALL newcl(nclust,icl,np,i,1)
              ENDIF
           ENDIF
20      CONTINUE
```

```
      DO 30 j = 2,L
        IF (lat(1,j).lt.0) then
          jdown = j - 1
          IF (lat(1,jdown).lt.0) then
            icl(1,j) = icl(1,jdown)
          ELSE
            CALL newcl(nclust,icl,np,1,j)
          ENDIF
        ENDIF
        DO 40 i = 2,L
          IF (lat(i,j).lt.0) then
            jdown = j - 1
            ileft = i - 1
            IF (icl(i,jdown) + icl(ileft,j).eq.0) then
              CALL newcl(nclust,icl,np,i,j)
            ELSE
              CALL neigh(lat,icl,np,i,j)
            ENDIF
          ENDIF
40      CONTINUE
30    CONTINUE
      RETURN
      END


      SUBROUTINE newcl(nclust,icl,np,i,j)
*     start new cluster, called by subroutine cluster
      DIMENSION icl(100,100),np(5000)
      nclust = nclust + 1
      icl(i,j) = nclust
      np(nclust) = 0
      RETURN
      END
```

```
      SUBROUTINE neigh(lat,icl,np,i,j)
*     assign cluster labels from neighbors
      DIMENSION lat(100,100),icl(100,100),np(5000)
      jdown = j - 1
      ileft = i - 1
      IF (lat(i,jdown)*lat(ileft,j).gt.0) then
         CALL choice(icl,np,i,j,ileft,jdown)
         RETURN
      ENDIF
      IF (icl(i,jdown).gt.0) then
         icl(i,j) = icl(i,jdown)
         RETURN
      ENDIF
      icl(i,j) = icl(ileft,j)
      RETURN
      END


      SUBROUTINE choice(icl,np,i,j,ileft,jdown)
*     assign cluster labels if there is a choice of neighbors
      DIMENSION icl(100,100),np(5000)
      IF (icl(ileft,j).eq.icl(i,jdown)) then
         icl(i,j) = icl(ileft,j)
      ELSE
*        neighbors have different labels
         nleft = icl(ileft,j)
         ndown = icl(i,jdown)
         CALL proper(np,nleft)
         CALL proper(np,ndown)
         kmax = max0(nleft,ndown)
         kmin = min0(nleft,ndown)
         icl(i,j) = kmin
         IF (kmax.ne.kmin)np(kmax) = kmin
      ENDIF
      RETURN
      END
```

```
        SUBROUTINE proper(np,label)
*       define proper label array, np
        DIMENSION np(5000)
10      IF (np(label).eq.0) RETURN
        label = np(label)
        GO TO 10
        END


        SUBROUTINE span(L,icl,np,idir,ispan)
*       determine existence of spanning cluster by checking whether
*       there are sites with same proper label on top and
*       bottom (vertical) or left and right (horizontal) edges of lattice
*       idir specifies direction, idir = 1 is vertical, otherwise
*       horizontal test, ispan = label of spanning cluster
        DIMENSION icl(100,100),np(5000)
        DO 100 i1 = 1,L
           IF (idir.eq.1) then
              iarg = i1
              jarg = 1
           ELSE
              iarg = 1
              jarg = i1
           ENDIF
           IF (icl(iarg,jarg).gt.0) then
              n1 = icl(iarg,jarg)
              CALL proper(np,n1)
              DO 20 i2 = 1,L
                 IF (idir.eq.1) then
                    iarg = i2
                    jarg = L
                 ELSE
                    iarg = L
                    jarg = i2
                 ENDIF
```

```
            IF (icl(iarg,jarg).gt.0) then
                n2 = icl(iarg,jarg)
                CALL proper(np,n2)
                IF (n1.eq.n2) then
                    ispan = n1
                    RETURN
                ENDIF
            ENDIF
20          CONTINUE
        ENDIF
100  CONTINUE
     ispan = 0
     RETURN
     END

     SUBROUTINE size(L,icl,np,mass,labmax)
     DIMENSION icl(100,100),np(5000), mass (5000)
     DO 10 k = 1,1000
         mass(k) = 0
10   CONTINUE
     labmax = 0
     DO 100 i = 1,L
        DO 100 j = 1,L
            IF (icl(i,j).gt.0) then
                label = icl(i,j)
                CALL proper(np,label)
                IF (label.gt.labmax) labmax = label
                mass(label) = mass(label) + 1
            ENDIF
100  CONTINUE
     RETURN
     END
```

```
       SUBROUTINE mean(labmax,mass,ispan,clsize,sum)
 *     compute mean cluster size of non-spanning clusters
       DIMENSION mass(5000)
       sum = 0
       sum2 = 0
       DO 10 n = 1,labmax
          IF (n.ne.ispan) then
             sum = sum + mass(n)
             sum2 = sum2 + mass(n)**2
          ENDIF
 10    CONTINUE
       clsize = sum2/sum
       RETURN
       END


       SUBROUTINE Pinf(mass,ispan,sum,zPinf)
 *     compute probability of belonging to spanning cluster
       DIMENSION mass(5000)
       IF (ispan.eq.0) then
 *        no spanning cluster
          zPinf = 0.0
          RETURN
       ENDIF
       zPinf = mass(ispan)/(sum + mass(ispan))
       RETURN
       END


       SUBROUTINE radius(L,icl,np,mass,labmax,ispan,radgyr)
 *     compute radius of gyration of largest non spanning cluster
 *     first find largest non-spanning cluster
       DIMENSION icl(100,100),np(5000),mass(5000)
       maxcl = 0
       xcm = 0.0
       ycm = 0.0
       r2 = 0.0
```

```
        DO 50 k = 1,labmax
          IF ((mass(k).ne.0).and.(k.ne.ispan)) then
            IF (mass(k).gt.maxcl) then
              maxcl = mass(k)
              maxk = k
            ENDIF
          ENDIF
50      CONTINUE
*       compute r**2 and center of mass
        DO 100 i = 1,L
          DO 100 j = 1,L
            IF (icl(i,j).gt.0) then
              label = icl(i,j)
              CALL proper(np,label)
              IF (label.eq.maxk) then
                xcm = xcm + i
                ycm = ycm + j
                r2 = r2 + i*i + j*j
              ENDIF
            ENDIF
100     CONTINUE
*       compute radius of gyration (subtract center of mass)
        r2cm = (xcm*xcm + ycm*ycm)/(maxcl*maxcl)
        radgyr = sqrt(r2/maxcl - r2cm)
        RETURN
        END

        SUBROUTINE output(ntrial,spvert,sphori,cltot,zPtot,radtot)
        spvert = spvert/ntrial
        sphori = sphori/ntrial
        cltot = cltot/ntrial
        zPtot = zPtot/ntrial
        radtot = radtot/ntrial
        WRITE(6,*) 'fraction vertically spanning = ',spvert
        WRITE(6,*) 'fraction horizontally spanning = ',sphori
        WRITE(6,*) 'mean cluster size(non-spanning) = ',cltot
        WRITE(6,*) 'prob.of being in spanning cluster = ',zPtot
        WRITE(6,*) 'rad.of gyration of largest cluster = ',radtot
        RETURN
        END
```

CHAPTER 13

```
      PROGRAM invasion
*     compute invasion percolation cluster, plot cluster,
*     print fraction occupied and P(r)
      DIMENSION r(100,50),perx(2000),pery(2000)
      CALL setup(Lx,Ly,iseed)
      CALL assign(Lx,Ly,r,perx,pery,iseed)
      CALL invade(perx,pery,r,Lx,Ly)
      CALL aver(Lx,Ly,r)
      STOP
      END


      SUBROUTINE setup(Lx,Ly,iseed)
      WRITE(6,*) 'Lattice size in y direction = '
      READ(5,*) Ly
      WRITE(6,*) 'random number seed = '
      READ(5,*) iseed
      Lx = 2*Ly
*     initiate graphics and define window coordinates
      CALL initt(1200)
      CALL dwindo(0.0,float(Lx+1),0.0,float(Ly+2))
      RETURN
      END


      SUBROUTINE assign(Lx,Ly,r,perx,pery,iseed)
*     assign random numbers to each site
*     occupy first column
*     assign second column as perimeter sites
      DIMENSION r(100,50),perx(2000),pery(2000)
      DO 200 j = 1,Ly
*          occupy first column
           r(1,j) = 1
           CALL box(1,j)
*          assign random numbers to the rest of the jth row
           DO 100 i = 2,Lx
               r(i,j) = ran(iseed)
100        CONTINUE
```

```
*            r(i,j) set greater than 2 for perimeter sites
             r(2,j) = 2 + r(2,j)
*            sort perimeter sites
             CALL sort(perx,pery,r,2,j,j)
200   CONTINUE
      RETURN
      END


      SUBROUTINE sort(perx,pery,r,i0,j0,nper)
*     binary sort, divide list in half, determine in which half new number
*     belongs, divide this half in half again and determine in which half
*     the new number belongs. Continue this process until the precise
*     position for the new number is determined
      DIMENSION r(100,20),perx(2000),pery(2000)
*     if only one perimeter site
      IF (nper.eq.1) then
             perx(nper) = i0
             pery(nper) = j0
             RETURN
      ENDIF
*     if new site is less than all previous perimeter sites
      i = perx(nper-1)
      j = pery(nper-1)
      IF (r(i0,j0).lt.r(i,j)) then
             perx(nper) = i0
             pery(nper) = j0
             RETURN
      ENDIF
*     begin shell sort, k2 = middle of list, k1,k3 = ends of list
      k1 = 1
      k3 = nper - 1
      k2 = (k1 + k3)/2
100   CONTINUE
*     loop until find precise position
      i = perx(k2)
      j = pery(k2)
*     determine which half of list new site is in
```

```
        IF (r(i0,j0).gt.r(i,j)) then
            k3 = k2
        ELSE
            k1 = k2
        ENDIF
*       new middle
        k2 = (k1 + k3)/2
        IF ((k1.eq.k2).or.(k2.eq.k3)) then
*           precise location found and it equals k3
*           move sites above k3 up one position each
            DO 10 kk = nper,k3+1,-1
                perx(kk) = perx(kk-1)
                pery(kk) = pery(kk-1)
10          CONTINUE
            perx(k3) = i0
            pery(k3) = j0
            RETURN
        ENDIF
        GO TO 100
        RETURN
        END


        SUBROUTINE sort2(perx,pery,r,i0,j0,nper)
*       standard insertion sort method, largest argument of perx
*       and pery contain smallest value
        DIMENSION r(100,20),perx(2000),pery(2000)
        DO  200 k = 1,nper-1
            i = perx(k)
            j = pery(k)
            IF (r(i0,j0) .gt. r(i,j)) then
*               insert new site
                DO 100 kk = nper,k+1,-1
                    perx(kk) = perx(kk-1)
                    pery(kk) = pery(kk-1)
100             CONTINUE
```

```
               perx(k) = i0
               pery(k) = j0
               RETURN
            ENDIF
200      CONTINUE
*        new site smaller than all previous perimeter sites
         perx(k) = i0
         pery(k) = j0
         RETURN
         END


         SUBROUTINE invade(perx,pery,r,Lx,Ly)
*        nnx and nny are arrays designating positions of nearest
*        neighbors relative to a site
         DIMENSION r(100,20),perx(2000),pery(2000)
         DIMENSION nnx(4),nny(4)
         DATA nnx/1,-1,0,0/
         DATA nny/0,0,1,-1/
         nper = Ly
         DO 1000 idummy = 1,5000
            i = perx(nper)
            j = pery(nper)
            nper = nper - 1
*           occupied sites have values between 1 and 2
            r(i,j) = r(i,j) - 1
            CALL box(i,j)
            DO 100 nn = 1,4
*              find new perimeter sites
               nx = i + nnx(nn)
               ny = j + nny(nn)
*              periodic boundary conditions in y
               IF (ny .gt. Ly) then
                  ny = 1
               ELSEIF (ny.lt.1) then
                  ny = Ly
               ENDIF
```

```
*          new perimeter site
           IF (r(nx,ny).lt.1) then
               r(nx,ny) = r(nx,ny) + 2
               nper = nper + 1
               CALL sort(perx,pery,r,nx,ny,nper)
           ENDIF
100     CONTINUE
*          stop when cluster reaches right edge
           IF (i.gt.Lx) RETURN
1000  CONTINUE
       RETURN
       END


       SUBROUTINE aver(Lx,Ly,r)
*      find fraction occupied and probability of being occupied
*      for middle half of lattice
       DIMENSION r(100,20)
       DIMENSION p(0:20),ns(0:20)
       Lmin = Lx/3
       Lmax = 2*Lmin
*      number of sites in middle half
       n = (Lmax - Lmin + 1)*Ly

       DO 200 i = Lmin,Lmax
          DO 100 j = 1,Ly
             iarg = 20*(amod(r(i,j),1.0))
             ns(iarg) = ns(iarg) + 1
             IF ((r(i,j) .gt. 1).and.(r(i,j) .lt. 2) ) then
                occupied = occupied + 1
*               probability function P(r)
                p(iarg) = p(iarg) + 1
             ENDIF
100     CONTINUE
200   CONTINUE
```

```
*        wait until input to print results to file on unit 9
         fraction = occupied/n
         CALL finitt(1,1)
         WRITE(9,*) 'fraction = ',fraction
         DO 300 i = 0,20
             rr = i/20.0
             IF (ns(i) .gt. 0) WRITE(9,*) rr, p(i)/ns(i)
300      CONTINUE
         RETURN
         END


         SUBROUTINE box(i,j)
*        draw filled box with 11 line segments
         x0 = i - 0.5
         y0 = j - 0.5
         DO 10 k = 0,10
             y = y0 + k*0.1
             CALL movea(x0,y)
*            draw line relative to x0,y
             CALL drawr(1.0,0.0)
10       CONTINUE
*        dump output buffer
         CALL tsend
         RETURN
         END
```

CHAPTER 14

```
         PROGRAM entropy
*        compute entropy using Ma's coincidence counting method
         DIMENSION mleft(10),mright(10),micro(0:2000)
         CALL start(nl,nr,mleft,mright,micro,nexch,iseed)
*        exchange particles
         CALL exch(nl,nr,nexch,mleft,mright,micro,iseed)
*        compute coincidence rate and entropy
         CALL output(nexch,micro)
         STOP
         END
```

```
      SUBROUTINE start(nl,nr,mleft,mright,micro,nexch,iseed)
*     input parameters and choose initial configuration of particles
      DIMENSION mleft(10),mright(10),micro(0:2000)
      INTEGER*4 iseed
      WRITE(6,*) 'total number of particles = '
      READ(5,*) N
      WRITE(6,*) 'number of particles on the left = '
      READ(5,*) nl
      WRITE(6,*) ' random number seed, positive integer = '
      READ(5,*) iseed
*     number of particles on the right
      nr = N - nl
      micro(0) = 0
      DO 100 il = 1,nl
*        list of particle numbers on left side
         mleft(il) = il
*        initial microstate
         micro(0) = micro(0)*2 + 2
100   CONTINUE
      DO 200 ir = 1,nr
*        list of particle numbers on right side
         mright(ir) = ir + nl
200   CONTINUE
      WRITE(6,*) 'number of exchanges = '
      READ(5,*) nexch
      RETURN
      END


      SUBROUTINE exch(nl,nr,nexch,mleft,mright,micro,iseed)
*     exchange particle number on left corresponding to ileft
*     with particle on right corresponding to iright
      DIMENSION mleft(10),mright(10),micro(0:2000)
      INTEGER*4 iseed
      DO 100 iexch = 1,nexch
*        randomly choose array indexes
         ileft = int(ran(iseed)*nl + 1)
         iright = int(ran(iseed)*nr + 1)
         jleft = mleft(ileft)
         jright= mright(iright)
```

```
*          new particle number in left array
           mleft(ileft) = jright
*          new particle number in right array
           mright(iright) = jleft
*          determine new microstate
           micro(iexch) = micro(iexch - 1) + 2**jright
           micro(iexch) = micro(iexch) - 2**jleft
100   CONTINUE
      RETURN
      END


      SUBROUTINE output(nexch,micro)
*     compute coincidence rate and entropy
*     total number of comparisons
      DIMENSION micro(0:2000)
      ncoin = 0
      ncomp = nexch*(nexch - 1)/2
*     compare microstates
      DO 200 iexch = 1,nexch - 1
          DO 100 jexch = iexch + 1,nexch
              IF (micro(iexch).eq.micro(jexch)) ncoin = ncoin + 1
100       CONTINUE
200   CONTINUE
*     coincidence rate
      rate = float(ncoin)/float(ncomp)
      IF (rate.gt.0) S = alog(1.0/rate)
      WRITE(6,*) 'estimate for entropy = ', S
      RETURN
      END
```

CHAPTER 15

```
      PROGRAM conduct
*     demon algorithm for one-dimensional Ising model
*     allows heating and cooling at end sites
      DIMENSION s(1000),edemon(1000),edcum(1000),zmgcum(1000)
      CALL start(n,nmcs,s,zJ,iseed,nheat)
      DO 100 imcs = 1,nmcs
         DO 50 i = 1,n-2
            istep = (imcs - 1)*(n-2) + i
            IF (mod(istep,nheat).eq.0) CALL heat(n,zJ,s,edemon)
            CALL change(n,edemon,s,zJ,accept,iseed)
50       CONTINUE
         CALL data(n,s,edemon,zmgcum,edcum)
100   CONTINUE
      CALL averg(n,nmcs,zmgcum,edcum,accept)
      STOP
      END


      SUBROUTINE start(n,nmcs,s,zJ,iseed,nheat)
*     read parameters from screen, write to unit 9
      DIMENSION s(1000)
      WRITE(6,*) 'number of spins = '
      READ(5,*) n
      WRITE(9,*) 'number of spins = ',n
      WRITE(6,*) 'number of Monte Carlo steps per spin = '
      READ(5,*) nmcs
      WRITE(9,*) 'number of Monte Carlo steps per spin = ',nmcs
      WRITE(6,*) 'coupling constant = '
      READ(5,*) zJ
      WRITE(9,*) 'coupling constant = ',zJ
      WRITE(6,*) 'random number seed = '
      READ(5,*) iseed
      WRITE(9,*) 'random number seed = ',iseed
      WRITE(6,*) 'time between end updates = '
      READ(5,*) nheat
      WRITE(9,*) 'time between end updates = ',nheat
```

```fortran
      DO 100 i = 1,n
*         put initial configuration in random state
          IF (ran(iseed).gt.0.5) then
              s(i) = 1
          ELSE
              s(i) = -1
          ENDIF
100   CONTINUE
      RETURN
      END


      SUBROUTINE change(n,edemon,s,zJ,accept,iseed)
      DIMENSION s(1000),edemon(1000)
*     compute random spin from 2 to n-1
      ispin = int(ran(iseed)*(n-2) + 2)
*     spin flip dynamics, trial energy change = de
      de = 2*zJ*s(ispin)*(s(ispin-1) + s(ispin+1))
      IF (de.le.edemon(ispin)) then
          s(ispin) = -s(ispin)
          accept = accept + 1
          edemon(ispin) = edemon(ispin) - de
      ENDIF
      RETURN
      END


      SUBROUTINE data(n,s,edemon,zmgcum,edcum)
*     accumulate data
      DIMENSION s(1000),edemon(1000),edcum(1000),zmgcum(1000)
      DO 10 i = 1,n
          edcum(i) = edcum(i) + edemon(i)
          zmgcum(i) = zmgcum(i) + s(i)
10    CONTINUE
      edemon(1) = 0
      edemon(n) = 0
      RETURN
      END
```

```
          SUBROUTINE averg(n,nmcs,zmgcum,edcum,accept)
*         normalize accumulated data and print results
          DIMENSION zmgcum(1000),edcum(1000)
          znorm = 1.0/nmcs
          accept = accept*znorm/(n-2)
          WRITE(6,*) 'acceptance ratio = ',accept
          WRITE(9,*) 'acceptance ratio = ',accept
*         edcum for spin 1 (or n) equals the heat rate added(taken out)
          WRITE(6,*) 'rate of heat added = ',edcum(1)*znorm
          WRITE(6,*) 'rate of heat taken out = ',edcum(n)*znorm
          DO 10 i = 2,n-1
             edave = edcum(i)*znorm
             IF (edave.ne.0.0) temp = 4.0/alog(1.0 + 4.0/edave)
             zmag = zmgcum(i)*znorm
             WRITE(6,13) i,edave,temp,zmag
             WRITE(9,13) i,edave,temp,zmag
13           FORMAT(1x,i4,3(2x,f13.5))
10        CONTINUE
          RETURN
          END


          SUBROUTINE heat(n,zJ,s,edemon)
*         attempt to add heat at spin 1 and take it out at spin n
          DIMENSION s(1000),edemon(1000)
          IF ((s(1)*s(2).gt.0).and.(s(n)*s(n-1).lt.0)) then
             edemon(1) = edemon(1) + 2*zJ
             s(1) = -s(1)
             edemon(n) = edemon(n) - 2*zJ
             s(n) = -s(n)
          ENDIF
          RETURN
          END
```

CHAPTER 16

```
      PROGRAM Ising2
*     Metropolis algorithm for the two-dimensional Ising model
      DIMENSION spin(32,32),w(-4:4)
      CALL start(N,L,T,nmcs,spin,E,M,w,iseed)
      DO 100 imcs = 1,nmcs
         CALL Metrop(N,L,spin,E,M,w,ratio,iseed)
         CALL data(E,M,ecum,e2cum,xmcum,xm2cum)
100   CONTINUE
      CALL output(N,nmcs,ecum,e2cum,xmcum,xm2cum,ratio)
      STOP
      END

      SUBROUTINE start(N,L,T,nmcs,spin,E,M,w,iseed)
      DIMENSION spin(32,32),w(-4 :4)
      WRITE(6,*) 'linear dimension of lattice = '
      READ(5,*) L
*     number of spins
      N = L*L
      WRITE(6,*) 'number of Monte Carlo steps per spin = '
      READ(5,*) nmcs
      WRITE(6,*) 'reduced temperature = '
      READ(5,*) T
      WRITE(5,*) 'random number seed = '
      READ(5,*) iseed
*     random initial configuration
      DO 200 j = 1,L
         DO 100 i = 1,L
            IF( ran(iseed) .lt. 0.5 ) then
               spin(i,j) = 1
            ELSE
               spin(i,j) = -1
            ENDIF
*           net magnetization
            M = M + spin(i,j)
100      CONTINUE
200   CONTINUE
```

```
*        compute initial energy E
         DO 300 j = 1,L
            IF ( j .eq. L ) then
               iup = 1
            ELSE
               iup = j + 1
            ENDIF
            DO 400 i = 1,L
               IF ( i .eq. L )then
                  iright = 1
               ELSE
                  iright = i + 1
               ENDIF
               sum = spin(i,iup) + spin(iright,j)
*              total energy
               E = E - spin(i,j)*sum
400      CONTINUE
300      CONTINUE
*        compute Boltzmann probability ratios
*        argument of w = sum of four neighbors
         e4 = exp(-4.0/T)
         e8 = e4*e4
*        argument of exp = change in energy
         w(4) = e8
         w(-4) = e8
         w(2) = e4
         w(-2) = e4
         RETURN
         END


         SUBROUTINE Metrop(N,L,spin,E,M,w,ratio,iseed)
         DIMENSION spin(32,32),w(-4 :4)
         DO 100  ispin = 1,N
*           randomly select location of spin
            i = int(L*ran(iseed) + 1)
            j = int(L*ran(iseed) + 1)
*           determine neighbor spin values
*           periodic boundary conditions
            CALL periodic(i,j,L,spin,isum)
```

```
          IF (spin(i,j)*isum .le. 0 ) then
              CALL accept(i,j,M,E,isum,spin,ratio)
          ELSEIF ( ran(iseed) .lt. w(isum) ) then
              CALL accept(i,j,M,E,isum,spin,ratio)
          ENDIF
100   CONTINUE
      RETURN
      END

      SUBROUTINE periodic(i,j,L,spin,isum)
*     determine sum of neighbor values using periodic
*     boundary conditions
      DIMENSION spin(32,32)
      IF ( i .eq. 1 ) then
          left = spin(L,j)
      ELSE
          left = spin(i - 1,j)
      ENDIF
      IF ( i .eq. L ) then
          iright = spin(1,j)
      ELSE
          iright = spin(i + 1,j)
      ENDIF
      IF ( j .eq. 1 ) then
          idown = spin(i,L)
      ELSE
          idown = spin(i,j - 1)
      ENDIF
      IF ( j .eq. L ) then
          iup = spin(i,1)
      ELSE
          iup = spin(i,j + 1)
      ENDIF
      isum = left + iright + iup + idown
      RETURN
      END
```

```
SUBROUTINE accept(i,j,M,E,isum,spin,ratio)
DIMENSION spin(32,32)
spin(i,j) = -spin(i,j)
ratio = ratio + 1
M = M + 2*spin(i,j)
E = E - 2*spin(i,j)*isum
RETURN
END


SUBROUTINE data(E,M,ecum,e2cum,xmcum,xm2cum)
*     accumulate data after every Monte Carlo step per spin
ecum = ecum + E
e2cum = e2cum + E*E
xmcum = xmcum + M
xm2cum = xm2cum + M*M
RETURN
END


SUBROUTINE output(N,nmcs,ecum,e2cum,xmcum,xm2cum,ratio)
znorm = 1/float(nmcs*N)
*     averages per spin
ratio = ratio*znorm
eave = ecum*znorm
e2ave = e2cum*znorm
save = xmcum*znorm
s2ave = xm2cum*znorm
WRITE(6,*) 'acceptance ratio = ',ratio
WRITE(6,*) 'mean energy per spin = ',eave
WRITE(6,*) 'mean square energy per spin = ',e2ave
WRITE(6,*) 'mean magnetization = ', save
WRITE(6,*) 'mean square magnetization = ',s2ave
RETURN
END
```

CHAPTER 17

```
      PROGRAM wp
*     plot propagation of a quantum mechanical wavepacket
      DIMENSION ar(-100:100),ai(-100:100),prob(-100:100)
      DIMENSION prl(-100:100,-100:100),pim(-100:100,-100:100)
      CALL param(zk0,width,x0,xmin,h,dk,dt,tmax,m,N)
      CALL packet(width,x0,m,dk,ar,ai)
*     CALL free(m,N,zk0,dk,h,ar,ai,prl,pim)
      CALL barrie(m,N,zk0,dk,h,ar,ai,prl,pim)
      ntime = tmax/dt
      DO 10 itime = 0,ntime
         t = itime*dt
         CALL move(t,m,N,zk0,dk,h,prl,pim,prob)
         CALL plot(prob,xmin,xmax,N,h)
10    CONTINUE
*     end plot, move cursor to position 1,1
      CALL finitt(1,1)
      STOP
      END


      SUBROUTINE param(zk0,width,x0,xmin,h,dk,dt,tmax,m,N)
      WRITE(6,*) 'maximum value of x = '
      READ(5,*) xmax
      WRITE(6,*)'minimum value of x = '
      READ(5,*) xmin
      WRITE(6,*) 'step length = '
      READ(5,*) h
*     N = number of positions calculated
      N = (xmax - xmin)/h
      WRITE(6,*) 'central wavevector = '
      READ(5,*) zk0
      WRITE(6,*) 'number of wavevectors = '
      READ(5,*) m
      WRITE(6,*) 'width of wavepacket in x space = '
      READ(5,*) width
      WRITE(6,*) 'initial position of packet = '
      READ(5,*) x0
```

```
        dk = 2.0/(width*m)
        m = m/2
        N = N/2
        WRITE(6,*) 'time interval = '
        READ(5,*) dt
        WRITE(6,*) 'total time = '
        READ(5,*) tmax
        WRITE(6,*) 'maximum value of psi squared = '
        READ(5,*) ymax
        CALL initt(120)
        CALL dwindo(xmin,xmax,-0.1,ymax)
        RETURN
        END


        SUBROUTINE packet(width,x0,m,dk,ar,ai)
*       compute Fourier coeficients
        DIMENSION ar(-100:100),ai(-100:100)
        sum2 = 0.0
        DO 100 ik = -m,m
            dzk = ik*dk
            a = exp(-dzk*dzk*width*width/4.0)
            ar(ik) = a*cos(-dzk*x0)
            ai(ik) = a*sin(-dzk*x0)
            sum2 = sum2 + ar(ik)*ar(ik) + ai(ik)*ai(ik)
100     CONTINUE
        znorm = dk*sqrt(1.0/(sum2))
        DO 200 ik = -m,m
            ar(ik) = ar(ik)*znorm
            ai(ik) = ai(ik)*znorm
200     CONTINUE
        RETURN
        END
```

```fortran
      SUBROUTINE free(m,N,zk0,dk,h,ar,ai,prl,pim)
      DIMENSION prl(-100:100,-100:100),pim(-100:100,-100:100)
      DIMENSION ar(-100:100),ai(-100:100)
      DO 100 ik = -m,m
         zk = zk0 + ik*dk
         DO 50 ix = -N,N
            arg = zk*ix*dx
            fr = cos(arg)
            fi = sin(arg)
            prl(ik,ix) = fr*ar(ik) - fi*ai(ik)
            pim(ik,ix) = fr*ai(ik) + fi*ar(ik)
50       CONTINUE
100   CONTINUE
      RETURN
      END


      SUBROUTINE move(t,m,N,zk0,dk,h,prl,pim,prob)
      DIMENSION prl(-100:100,-100:100),pim(-100:100,-100:100)
      DIMENSION prob(-100:100)
      DO 100 ix = -N,N
         psir = 0.0
         psii = 0.0
         DO 10 ik = -m,m
            zk = zk0 + ik*dk
            arg = -0.5*zk*zk*t
            fr = cos(arg)
            fi = sin(arg)
*           real and imaginary parts of psi
            psir = psir + fr*prl(ik,ix) - fi*pim(ik,ix)
            psii = psii + fi*prl(ik,ix) + fr*pim(ik,ix)
10       CONTINUE
         prob(ix) = psir*psir + psii*psii
100   CONTINUE
      RETURN
      END
```

```
      SUBROUTINE barrie(m,N,zk0,dk,h,ar,ai,prl,pim)
      DIMENSION ar(-100:100),ai(-100:100)
      DIMENSION prl(-100:100,-100:100), pim(-100:100,-100:100)
*     compute a(k)(exp(ik1x) + b exp(-ik1x)) for x > 0
*     and a(k)*c*exp(ik2x) for x > 0
      WRITE(6,*) 'barrier height = '
      READ(5,*) V0
      DO 100 ik = -m,m
         zk1 = zk0 + ik*dk
         E = 0.5*zk1*zk1
         IF (E.gt.V0) then
            zk2 = sqrt(2.0*(E - V0))
            br = (zk1 - zk2)/(zk1 + zk2)
            bi = 0.0
            cr = 2.0*zk1/(zk1 + zk2)
            ci = 0.0
         ELSE
            zk2 = sqrt(2.0*(V0 - E))
            denom = zk1*zk1 + zk2*zk2
            br = (zk1*zk1 - zk2*zk2)/denom
            bi = 2.0*zk1*zk2/denom
            cr = 2.0*zk1*zk1/denom
            ci = -2.0*zk1*zk2/denom
         ENDIF
         DO 40 ix = -Nx,0
            arg = zk1*ix*h
            cs = cos(arg)
            si = sin(arg)
*           next 2 lines use sin(-kx) = -sin(kx) and cos(-kx) = cos(kx)
            fr = cs + br*cs + bi*si
            fi = si + bi*cs - br*si
            prl(ik,ix) = fr*ar(ik) - fi*ai(ik)
            pim(ik,ix) = fr*ai(ik) + fi*ar(ik)
40       CONTINUE
```

```
        DO 60 ix = 1,N
            arg = zk2*ix*h
            IF (E.gt.V0) then
                cs = cos(arg)
                si = sin(arg)
            ELSE
                cs = exp(-arg)
                si = 0.0
            ENDIF
            fr = cr*cs - ci*si
            fi = ci*cs + cr*si
            prl(ik,ix) = fr*ar(ik) - fi*ai(ik)
            pim(ik,ix) = fr*ai(ik) + fi*ar(ik)
60      CONTINUE
100     CONTINUE
        RETURN
        END


        SUBROUTINE plot(prob,xmin,N,h)
        DIMENSION prob(-100:100)
*       erase screen
        CALL newpag
*       draw tick marks
        DO 10 i = -N,N
            x = i*h
            CALL movea(x,0.0)
            CALL drawa(x,0.01*h)
10      CONTINUE
*       plot horizontal line, x = xmax after above loop
        CALL movea(xmin,0.0)
        CALL drawa(x,0.0)
*       plot wavefunction squared
        CALL movea(-N*h,prob(-N))
        DO 20 i = -N,N
            x = i*h
            CALL drawa(x,prob(i))
20      CONTINUE
        RETURN
        END
```

Appendix H   LISTING OF PASCAL PROGRAMS

In the following we list our Pascal translations of eight of the True BASIC programs given in Part II of the text. The programs were run using Macintosh Pascal. Relatively minor changes are needed for other versions of Pascal. The graphics procedures used in the Pascal programs are from the Macintosh toolbox and can be called from other programming languages on the Macintosh. A brief summary of the Macintosh graphics procedures is given in Table E1.

CHAPTER 10

```
program integ (input, output);
(* compute integeral of f(x) from x = a to x = b *)
var
   a, b, h, area : real;
   n : integer;

procedure initial (var a, b, h : real;
                   var n : integer);
begin
   a := 0.0;                        (* lower limit *)
   b := 0.5 * 3.14159;             (* upper limit *)
   write('number of intervals = ');
   readln(n);
   h := (b - a) / n                 (* mesh size *)
end;

function f (x : real) : real;
begin
   f := cos(x)
end;

procedure rectangle (a, b, h : real;
                     n : integer;
                     var area : real);
var
   x, sum : real;
   i : integer;
```

```
      begin
        x := a;
        sum := 0.0;
        for i := 0 to n - 1 do
            begin
                sum := sum + f(x);
                x := x + h
            end;
        area := sum * h
    end;

    procedure outdat (area : real);
    begin
        writeln('area = ', area : 12 : 7)
    end;

  begin                                   (* main *)
    initial(a, b, h, n);
    rectangle(a, b, h, n, area);
    outdat(area)
  end.
```

CHAPTER 11

```
    program random_walk (input, output);
    (* Monte Carlo simulation of a random walk in d = 1 *)
    const
        xmax = 64;
    type
        list = array[-64..64] of real;
    var
        prob : list;
        p : real;                         (* probability of step to the right *)
        x, xcum, x2cum, itrial, ntrial, nstep : integer;
```

```
procedure initial (var p : real;
                   var nstep, ntrial, xcum, x2cum : integer;
                   var prob : list);
var
   i : integer;
begin
   ntrial := 100;                  (* number of trials *)
   p := 0.5;                       (* probability of step to the right *)
   write('maximum number of steps = ');
   readln(nstep);
   write('random number seed (negative integer) = ');
   readln(iseed);
   (* initialize data to 0 *)
   xcum := 0;
   x2cum := 0;
   for i := -nstep to nstep do
       prob[i] := 0
end;

function rnd : real;
(* return random number between 0 and 1 using the Macintosh toolbox *)
(* function random returns a random number between -32768 and 32767 *)
(* better random number generators can be found in Numerical Recipes *)
begin
   rnd := (random + 32768.0) / (32768.0 + 32767.0)
end;

procedure walk (var x : integer;
                p : real;
                nstep : integer);
var
   istep : integer;
begin
   x := 0;                         (* initial positiion for each trial *)
   for istep := 1 to nstep do
      if rnd <= p then
         x := x + 1
      else
         x := x - 1
end;
```

```pascal
procedure data (var x, xcum, x2cum : integer;
                var prob : list);
begin
   xcum := xcum + x;
   x2cum := x2cum + x * x;
   prob[x] := prob[x] + 1
end;

procedure average (nstep, ntrial, xcum, x2cum : integer;
                   var prob : list);
(* average values for nstep walk *)
var
   norm, xbar, x2bar, sigma, variance, probability : real;
   x : integer;
begin
   norm := 1.0 / ntrial;
   xbar := xcum * norm;
   x2bar := x2cum * norm;
   for x := -nstep to nstep do
      begin
         probability := prob[x] * norm;
         writeln(x : 6, probability : 10 : 5)
      end;
   variance := x2bar - xbar * xbar;
   sigma := sqrt(variance);
   writeln('mean displacement = ', xbar : 10 : 5);
   writeln('sigma  = ', sigma : 10 : 5)
end;

begin                             (* main *)
   initial(p, nstep, ntrial, xcum, x2cum, prob);
   for itrial := 1 to ntrial do
      begin
         walk(x, p, nstep);
         data(x, xcum, x2cum, prob)      (* collect data after nstep walk *)
      end;
   average(nstep, ntrial, xcum, x2cum, prob)
end.
```

CHAPTER 12

```
program site_perc (input, output);
(* draw site percolation configurations *)
const
    boxlength = 250;
    margin = 10;
type
    list = array[1..50, 1..50] of real;
var
    L : integer;
    r : list;

    procedure initial (var L : integer);
    begin
        write('linear dimension of lattice = ');
        readln(L);
        (* draw cell sides *)
        framerect(margin, margin, boxlength + margin, boxlength + margin)
    end;

    function rnd : real;
    (* return random number between 0 and 1 using the function *)
    (* random which returns a random number between -32768 and 32767 *)
    (* better random number generators can be found in Numerical Recipes *)
    begin
        rnd := (random + 32768.0) / (32768.0 + 32767.0)
    end;

    procedure lattice (L : integer;
                        var r : list);
    (* assign random number to each site and draw lattice sites *)
    var
        col, row, x, y : integer;
        scale : real;
    begin
        scale := boxlength / L;
        for row := 1 to L do              (* draw lattice sites *)
```

```
            begin
                y := round((row - 0.5) * scale) + margin;
                (* associate box of linear dimension unity with each site *)
                for col := 1 to L do
                    begin
                        x := round(scale * (col - 0.5)) + margin;
                        (* assign random number to each lattice site *)
                        r[col, row] := rnd;
                        (* plot point at each site *)
                        moveto(x, y);
                        lineto(x, y)
                    end
            end
end;

procedure configuration (L : integer;
                                var r : list);
(* occupy sites for given p *)
var
    s : list;
    p, scale : real;
    row, col, x, y, size : integer;
begin
    for row := 1 to L do
        for col := 1 to L do
            s{col, row] := 0;
    scale := boxlength / L;
    while p <= 1.0 do
        begin
            write('probability p = ');
            readln(p);
            (* half length of box for occupied sites *)
            size := round(0.5 * scale);
            for row := 1 to L do
                begin
                    y := round(scale * (row - 0.5)) + margin;
                    for col := 1 to L do
                        if (r[col, row] < p) and (s[col, row] <> 1.0) then
```

```
                      begin                    (* newly occupied sites *)
                         x := round(scale * (col - 0.5)) + margin;
                         paintrect(y - size, x - size, y + size, x + size);
                         s[col, row] := 1.0            (* occupied site *)
                      end
              end
        end
   end;

   begin                                    (* main *)
      initial(L);
      (* assign random number to each site and draw  lattice sites *)
      lattice(L, r);
      configuration(L, r)  (* occupy sites for given p *)
   end.
```

CHAPTER 13

```
   program single_cluster (input, output);
   (* compute fractal dimension of percolation cluster *)
   (* use Hammersely, Leath, Alexandrowicz algorithm *)
   type
      list = array[1..200] of integer;
   var
      L : integer;
      p : real;
      s : list;

   procedure parameter (var L : integer;
                             var p : real);
   begin
      write('maximum radius of cluster = ');
      readln(L);
      write('site occupation probability = ');
      readln(p)
   end;
```

```pascal
function rnd : real;
(* compute random number between 0 and 1 *)
begin
    rnd := (random + 32768.0) * (1.5259e-5)
end;

procedure grow (L : integer;
                p : real;
                var s : list);
(* compute percolation cluster *)
var
    i, k, x, y, xn, yn, nper, nn, r : integer;
    r2 : real;
    px, py : array[1..5000] of integer;
    lat : array[-50..50, -50..50] of integer;
    nx, ny : array[1..4] of integer;
(* nx and ny are arrays designated positions of nearest *)
(* neighbors relative to a site *)
begin
    for r := 1 to 2 * L do
        s[r] := 0;
    for x := -L to L do
        for y := -L to L do
            lat[x, y] := 0;
    lat[0, 0] := 1;
    nx[1] := 1;
    nx[2] := -1;
    nx[3] := 0;
    nx[4] := 0;
    ny[1] := 0;
    ny[2] := 0;
    ny[3] := 1;
    ny[4] := -1;
    for i := 1 to 4 do
        begin
            px[i] := nx[i];
            py[i] := ny[i]
        end;
```

```
nper := 4;                        (* initial number of perimeter sites *)
repeat
    k := 1 + trunc(rnd * nper);       (* select one perimeter site at random *)
    x := px[k];
    y := py[k];
    if (rnd < p) then
        begin
            (* site tested and occupied *)
            lat[x, y] := 1;
            r2 := x * x + y * y;
            r := round(sqrt(r2));           (* distance from origin *)
            s[r] := s[r] + 1;               (* number at distance r *)
            (* in arrays px and py replace newly occupied site *)
            (* by last site in the list of perimeter sites *)
            px[k] := px[nper];
            py[k] := py[nper];
            nper := nper - 1;
            for nn := 1 to 4 do            (* find new perimeter sites *)
                begin
                    xn := x + nx[nn];
                    yn := y + ny[nn];
                    if ((lat[xn, yn] = 0) and (abs(xn) <= L) and (abs(yn) <= L)) then
                        begin
                            nper := nper + 1;
                            px[nper] := xn;
                            py[nper] := yn
                        end
                end
        end
    else
        begin
            (* site tested but not occupied *)
            lat[x, y] := -1;
            px[k] := px[nper];
            py[k] := py[nper];
            nper := nper - 1
        end;
    until (nper < 1)        (* until all perimeter sites in box tested *)
end;
```

```
procedure plot (L : integer;
              s : list);
const                              (* minimum screen coordinates used *)
   y0 = 250;
   x0 = 50;
var
   xmax, ymax, scalex, scaley, hashx, hashy : integer;
   x, y, r, xcoor, ycoor, mass : integer;
begin
   mass := s[1];
   xmax := trunc(ln(L) + 1);
   ymax := trunc(ln(4 * L * L) + 1);
   scalex := 400 div xmax
   scaley := 200 div ymax;
   hashy := 10;                    (* hash mark sizes *)
   hashx := 15;
   (* plot axes *)
   moveto(x0, y0 - ymax * scaley);
   lineto(x0, y0);
   lineto(x0 + xmax * scalex, y0);
   (* label axes *)
   moveto(250, 270);
   drawstring('ln(r)');
   moveto(3, 80);
   drawstring('ln(M)');
   (* draw hash marks on axes *)
   for x := 1 to xmax do
      begin
         xcoor := x * scalex + x0;
         moveto(xcoor, y0);
         lineto(xcoor, y0 - hashy)
      end;
   for y := 1 to ymax do
      begin
         ycoor := y0 - scaley * y;
         moveto(x0, ycoor);
         lineto(x0 + hashx, ycoor)
      end
```

```
            (* plot ln(mass enclosed) vs ln(r) *)
            for r := 2 to L do
                begin
                    mass := mass + s[r];
                    x := x0 + trunc(scalex * ln(r));
                    y := trunc(y0 - scaley * ln(mass));
                    paintrect(y - 1, x - 1, y + 1, x + 1)
                end
        end;

begin                           (* main *)
    parameter(L, p);
    grow(L, p, s);
    plot(L, s)
end.
```

CHAPTER 14

```
program entropy (input, output);
(* compute entropy using Ma's coincidence counting method *)
type
    list = array[1..10] of integer;
    state = array[0..2000] of integer;
var
    micro : state;
    right, left : list;
    nl, nr, nexch : integer;
```

```pascal
procedure start (var nl, nr, nexch : integer;
                 var left, right : list;
                 var micro : state);
(* input parameters and choose initial configuration of particles *)
var
    ir, il, N : integer;
begin
    write('total number of particles = ');
    readln(N);
    write('number of particles on the left = ');
    readln(nl);
    nr := N - nl;                    (* number of particles on the right *)
    micro[0] := 0;
    for il := 1 to nl do
       begin
          left[il] := il;        (* list of particle numbers on left side *)
          micro[0] := micro[0] * 2 + 2        (* initial microstate *)
       end;
    for ir := 1 to nr do
       right[ir] := ir + nl;     (* list of particle numbers on right side *)
    write('number of exchanges = ');
    readln(nexch)
end;

function rnd : real;
(* generate random number between 0 and 1 *)
begin
    rnd := (random + 32768.0) / (32768.0 + 32767.0)
end;

function power (n : integer) : integer;
(* returns 2 to the power n *)
var
    i, p : integer;
begin
    p := 1;
    for i := 1 to n do
       p := p * 2;
    power := p
end;
```

```
procedure exch (var nl, nr, nexch : integer;
                    var left, right : list;
                    var micro : state);
(* exchange particle number on left corresponding to ileft *)
(* with particle on right corresponding to iright *)
var
    iexch, ileft, iright, jleft, jright : integer;
begin
    for iexch := 1 to nexch do
        begin
            (* randomly choose array indexes *)
            ileft := trunc(rnd * nl + 1);
            iright := trunc(rnd * nr + 1);
            jleft := left[ileft];
            jright := right[iright];
            left[ileft] := jright;      (* new particle number in left array *)
            right[iright] := jleft;     (* new particle number in right array *)
            (* determine new microstate *)
            micro[iexch] := micro[iexch - 1] + power(jright);
            micro[iexch] := micro[iexch] - power(jleft)
        end
end;
```

```pascal
procedure outdat (nexch : integer;
                       var micro : state);
(* compute coincidence rate and entropy*)
(* total number of comparisons *)
var
    iexch, jexch, ncomp, ncoin : integer;
    rate, S : real;
begin
    ncomp := nexch * (nexch - 1) div 2;
    ncoin := 0;
    (* compare microstates *)
    for iexch := 1 to nexch - 1 do
        for jexch := iexch + 1 to nexch do
            if (micro[iexch] = micro[jexch]) then
                ncoin := ncoin + 1;
    rate := ncoin / ncomp;  (* coincidence rate *)
    if (rate > 0) then
        S := ln(1.0 / rate);
    writeln('estimate for entropy = ', S)
end;

begin                              (* main *)
    start(nl, nr, nexch, left, right, micro);
    exch(nl, nr, nexch, left, right, micro);         (* exchange particles *)
    outdat(nexch, micro)                  (* compute coincidence rate and entropy *)
end.
```

CHAPTER 15

```pascal
program ideal_demon (input, output);
(* demon algorithm for the one-dimensional ideal classical gas *)
type
    list = array[1..100] of real;
var
    vel : list;
    N, nmcs, imcs, i : integer;
    esystem, edemon, vtot, dvmax, escum, vcum, edcum, accept : real;
```

```
procedure initial (var N, nmcs : integer;
                   var esystem, edemon, vtot, dvmax : real;
                   var vel : list);
var
   i : integer;
   vinitial : real;
begin
   write('number of particles = ');
   readln(N);
   write('number of Monte Carlo steps = ');
   readln(nmcs);
   write('initial energy of system = ');
   readln(esystem);
   edemon := 0;                          (* demon energy *)
   write('maximum change in velocity = ');
   readln(dvmax);
   vinitial := sqrt(2 * esystem / N);
   vtot := 0;
   (* all particles same initial velocities *)
   for i := 1 to N do
      begin
         vel[i] := vinitial;
         vtot := vtot + vinitial        (* total velocity of system *)
      end
end;

function rnd : real;
begin
   rnd := (random + 32768.0) / (32768.0 + 32767.0)
end;
```

```pascal
procedure changes (N : integer;
                   var esystem, edemon, vtot, dvmax, accept : real;
                   var vel : list);
var
   dv, vtrial, de : real;
   ip : integer;
begin
   dv := (2 * rnd - 1) * dvmax;        (* trial change in velocity *)
   ip := trunc(rnd * N + 1);           (* select random particle *)
   vtrial := vel[ip] + dv;             (* trial velocity *)
   de := 0.5 * (vtrial * vtrial - vel[ip] * vel[ip]);    (* trial energy change *)
   if (de <= edemon) or (de <= 0) then
      begin
         vel[ip] := vtrial;
         vtot := vtot + dv;            (* total velocity of system *)
         accept := accept + 1;
         edemon := edemon - de;
         esystem := esystem + de
      end
end;

procedure data (var esystem, edemon, vtot, escum, vcum, edcum : real);
begin
   edcum := edcum + edemon;
   escum := escum + esystem;
   vcum := vcum + vtot
end;
```

```
procedure averages (N, nmcs : integer;
                         escum, vcum, edcum, accept : real);
var
    norm, edave, vave, esave : real;
begin
    norm := 1 / (nmcs * N);
    edave := edcum * norm;          (* average demon energy *)
    accept := accept * norm;        (* ratio of acceptances *)
    (* system averages per particle *)
    norm := norm / N;
    esave := escum * norm;          (* mean energy per system particle *)
    vave := vcum * norm;            (* mean velocity per system particle *)
    writeln('mean demon energy = ', edave : 10 : 5);
    writeln('mean system energy per particle = ', esave : 10 : 5);
    writeln('mean velocity per particle = ', vave : 10 : 5);
    writeln('acceptance ratio = ', accept : 10 : 5)
end;

begin                              (* main *)
    initial(N, nmcs, esystem, edemon, vtot, dvmax, vel);
    accept := 0.0;
    escum := 0.0;
    edcum := 0.0;
    vcum := 0.0;
    for imcs := 1 to nmcs do
        for i := 1 to N do
            begin
                changes(N, esystem, edemon, vtot, dvmax, accept, vel);
                (* accumulate data after each trial change *)
                data(esystem, edemon, vtot, escum, vcum, edcum)
            end;
    averages(N, nmcs, escum, vcum, edcum, accept)
end.
```

CHAPTER 16

```
program Ising2 (input, output);
(* Metropolis algorithm for the two-dimensional Ising Model *)
type
    lattice = array[1..32, 1..32] of integer;
    list = array[-4..4] of real;
var
    spin : lattice;
    w : list;
    N, L, imcs, nmcs : integer;
    T, E, M, ratio, ecum, e2cum, mcum, m2cum : real;

function rnd : real;
(* generate random number between 0 and 1 *)
begin
    rnd := (random + 32768.0) / (32768.0 + 32767.0)
end;

procedure initial (var N, L, nmcs : integer;
                        var spin : lattice;
                        var T, E, M : real;
                        var w : list);
var
    i, j, up, right, sum : integer;
    e4, e8 : real;
begin
    write('linear dimension of lattice = ');
    readln(L);
    N := L * L;                    (* number of spins *)
    write('number of Monte Carlo steps per spin = ');
    readln(nmcs);
    write('reduced temperature = ');
    readln(T);
    (* random initial configuration *)
    for j := 1 to L do
        for i := 1 to L do
```

```
        begin
            if (rnd < 0.5) then
                spin[i, j] := 1
            else
                spin[i, j] := -1;
            M := M + spin[i, j]              (* net magnetization *)
        end;
    (* compute initial energy E *)
    for j := 1 to L do
        begin
            if (j = L) then
                up := 1
            else
                up := j + 1;
            for i := 1 to L do
                begin
                    if (i = L) then
                        right := 1
                    else
                        right := i + 1;
                    sum := spin[i, up] + spin[right, j];
                    E := E - spin[i, j] * sum            (* total energy *)
                end
        end;
    (* compute Boltzmann probability ratios *)
    (* argument of w := sum of four neighbors *)
    e4 := exp(-4.0 / T);
    e8 := e4 * e4;
    w[4] := e8;
    w[-4] := e8;
    w[2] := e4;
    w[-2] := e4
end;
```

```pascal
procedure pbc (var i, j, L, sum : integer;
               var spin : lattice);
(* determines sum of neighbor values using periodic *)
(* boundary conditions *)
var
    left, right, up, down : integer;
begin
    if (i = 1) then
        left := spin[L, j]
    else
        left := spin[i - 1, j];
    if (i = L) then
        right := spin[1, j]
    else
        right := spin[i + 1, j];
    if (j = 1) then
        down := spin[i, L]
    else
        down := spin[i, j - 1];
    if (j = L) then
        up := spin[i, 1]
    else
        up := spin[i, j + 1];
    sum := left + right + up + down
end;

procedure accept (i, j, sum : integer;
                  var spin : lattice;
                  var ratio, M, E : real);
begin
    spin[i, j] := -spin[i, j];
    ratio := ratio + 1;
    M := M + 2 * spin[i, j];
    E := E - 2 * spin[i, j] * sum
end;
```

```
procedure Metropolis (N, L : integer;
                          var spin : lattice;
                          var E, M, ratio : real;
                          var w : list);
var
    ispin, i, j, sum : integer;
begin
    for ispin := 1 to N do
        begin
            (* randomly select location of spin *)
            i := trunc(L * rnd + 1);
            j := trunc(L * rnd + 1);
            (* determine nearest neighbor spin values *)
            (* periodic boundary conditions *)
            pbc(i, j, L, sum, spin);
            if (spin[i, j] * sum <= 0) then
                accept(i, j, sum, spin, ratio, M, E)
            else if (rnd < w[sum]) then
                accept(i, j, sum, spin, ratio, M, E)
        end
end;

procedure data (var E, M, ecum, e2cum, mcum, m2cum : real);
(* accumulate data after every Monte Carlo step per spin *)
begin
    ecum := ecum + E;
    e2cum := e2cum + E * E;
    mcum := mcum + M;
    m2cum := m2cum + M * M
end

procedure outdat (N, nmcs : integer;
                      ecum, e2cum, mcum, m2cum, ratio : real);
var
    norm, eave, e2ave, save, s2ave : real;
begin
    norm := 1.0 / (nmcs * N);
```

```
          (* averages per spin *)
          ratio := ratio * norm;
          eave := ecum * norm;
          e2ave := e2cum * norm;
          save := mcum * norm;
          s2ave := m2cum * norm;
          writeln('acceptance ratio = ', ratio);
          writeln('mean energy per spin = ', eave);
          writeln('mean square energy per spin = ', e2ave);
          writeln('mean magnetization = ', save);
          writeln('mean square magnetization = ', s2ave)
       end;

  begin                              (* main *)
       initial(N, L, nmcs, spin, T, E, M, w);
       for imcs := 1 to nmcs do
          begin
             Metropolis(N, L, spin, E, M, ratio, w);
             data(E, M, ecum, e2cum, mcum, m2cum)
          end;
       outdat(N, nmcs, ecum, e2cum, mcum, m2cum, ratio)
  end.
```

CHAPTER 17

```
  program eigen (input, output);
  var
       V0, a, xmax, dx, x0, y0, xscale, yscale : real;

       procedure parameter (var V0, a, xmax, dx : real);
       begin
          write('well depth = ');
          readln(V0);
          write('half width of well = ');
          readln(a);
          write('maximum value of x to be plotted = ');
          readln(xmax);
          write('step size dx = ');
          readln(dx)
       end;
```

```
procedure plot_potential (V0, a, xmax : real;
                          var xscale, yscale, x0, y0 : real);
(* set up graphics scaling parameters and draw potential *)
begin
    xscale := 512 / (2.0 * xmax);
    yscale := 300 / (2.0 * 10.0);
    x0 := xscale * xmax;
    y0 := yscale * 10.0;
    moveto(trunc(x0 - xmax * xscale), trunc(y0 + 6 * yscale));
    lineto(trunc(x0 - a * xscale), trunc(y0 + 6 * yscale));
    lineto(trunc(x0 - a * xscale), trunc(y0 + 9 * yscale));
    lineto(trunc(x0 + a * xscale), trunc(y0 + 9 * yscale));
    lineto(trunc(x0 + a * xscale), trunc(y0 + 6 * yscale));
    lineto(trunc(x0 + xmax * xscale), trunc(y0 + 6 * yscale))
end;

function V (x, V0, a : real) : real;
(* compute potential function V(x) *)
begin
    if x > a then
        V := V0
    else
        V := 0.0
end;

procedure Euler (V0, a, dx, xmax, xscale, yscale, x0, y0 : real);
var
    i, j, parity : integer;
    x, phi, dphi, d2phi, E : real;
begin
    write('even or odd parity (1 or -1) ');
    readln(parity);
    repeat
        write('E = ');
        readln(E);
        (* set up initial values at x = 0 *)
```

```
                    if parity = -1 then
                        begin
                            phi := 0.0;
                            dphi := 0.0
                        end;
                    else
                        begin
                            phi := 1.0;
                            dphi := 0.0
                        end;
                    x := 0.0;
                    repeat                          (* compute wave function *)
                        x := x + dx;
                        d2phi := 2.0 * phi * (V(x, V0, a) - E);
                        dphi := dphi + d2phi * dx;
                        phi := phi + dphi * dx;
                        (* plot wave function *)
                        i := trunc(x0 + xscale * x);
                        j := trunc(y0 + yscale * phi);
                        moveto(i, j);
                        lineto(i, j);
                        i := trunc(x0 - xscale * x);
                        j := trunc(y0 + yscale * phi * parity);
                        moveto(i, j);
                        lineto(i, j)
                    until (x > xmax) or (abs(phi) > 10)
                until E = 0                    (* to stop program enter E = 0 *)
        end;

begin                                  (* main *)
    parameter(V0, a, xmax, dx);
    plot_potential(V0, a, xmax, xscale, yscale, x0, y0);
    Euler(V0, a, dx, xmax, xscale, yscale, x0, y0)
end.
```

SUBJECT INDEX: PARTS I AND II